Essays on Ethics and Method is a selection of the shorter writings of the great nineteenth-century moral philosopher Henry Sidgwick. Sidgwick's monumental work *The Methods of Ethics* is a classic of philosophy; this new volume is a fascinating complement to it. These essays develop further Sidgwick's ethical ideas, respond to criticism of the *Methods*, and discuss rival theories. Other aspects of Sidgwick's thought are also illuminated, in particular his interests in method, verification, and proof. The essays show Sidgwick to be a forerunner of twentieth-century analytical philosophy: they illustrate his emphasis on common sense and ordinary language, and exemplify not only his care, clarity, and precision, but also the wit and humour that are not prominent in his longer works. Marcus Singer provides a substantial editorial introduction to Sidgwick and his intellectual context. The volume will be a rich resource for anyone interested in moral philosophy or the development of modern analytical philosophy.

Henry Sidgwick *c.*1856
aged 18

Henry Sidgwick *c.*1877

ESSAYS ON ETHICS AND METHOD

Henry Sidgwick

Edited, with an Introduction, by
Marcus G. Singer

CLARENDON PRESS · OXFORD

2000

OXFORD
UNIVERSITY PRESS

Great Clarendon Street, Oxford OX2 6DP

Oxford University Press is a department of the University of Oxford.
It furthers the University's objective of excellence in research, scholarship,
and education by publishing worldwide in

Oxford New York

Athens Auckland Bangkok Bogotá Buenos Aires Calcutta
Cape Town Chennai Dar es Salaam Delhi Florence Hong Kong Istanbul
Karachi Kuala Lumpur Madrid Melbourne Mexico City Mumbai
Nairobi Paris São Paulo Shanghai Singapore Taipei Tokyo Toronto Warsaw

with associated companies in Berlin Ibadan

Oxford is a registered trade mark of Oxford University Press
in the UK and in certain other countries

Published in the United States
by Oxford University Press Inc., New York

© in this volume Oxford University Press, 2000
Editorial material © Marcus Singer, 2000

British Library Cataloguing in Publication Data

Data available

Library of Congress Cataloging in Publication Data

Data available

ISBN 0-19-825022-3
ISBN 0-19-825023-1 (pbk.)

1 3 5 7 9 10 8 6 4 2

Typeset by Graphicraft Limited, Hong Kong
Printed in Great Britain
on acid-free paper by
TJ International Ltd.,
Padstow, Cornwall

To the Memory of

Brand Blanshard
(1892–1987)

William K. Frankena
(1908–1994)

Richard B. Brandt
(1910–1997)

and

Alan Donagan
(1925–1991)

Contents

PART I. ETHICS

PART II. VALUE THEORY AND MORAL PSYCHOLOGY

PART III. METHOD: TRUTH, EVIDENCE, AND BELIEF

PART IV. COMMENTS AND CRITIQUES

PREFACE

I first heard of Henry Sidgwick when, as an undergraduate at the University of Illinois right after World War II, in Fred Will's course on Theory of Knowledge I read some portions of William Pepperell Montague's *Ways of Knowing* and came across his glowing reference to Sidgwick's *Methods of Ethics*. A year or so later, when I was a graduate student at Cornell, Stuart Brown suggested that I read Sidgwick's *History of Ethics* and Broad's *Five Types of Ethical Theory*. This was good advice, and I have ever since recommended these books to students beginning the study of ethics. The next year I signed up for Brown's ethics seminar, on Hobbes, Butler, Sidgwick, and Bradley. This was a fascinating seminar; the counterpoint involved was marvelous. A paper I wrote for that seminar was entitled 'Generalization in Sidgwick's Ethics'. As I later came to see, it was not really a good paper—even though Brown thought well of it—, but it was the beginning of a life-long interest in both Sidgwick and generalization.

I first contemplated compiling a selection of Sidgwick's papers in 1961 or 1962, and broached the subject to my editors at both Knopf and Scribner's. The response was the same in both cases: there was not enough interest in Sidgwick to warrant such a venture. After (the late) Eugene Freeman, editor of *The Monist*, arranged a special issue for 1974 to celebrate the centennial of the publication of *The Methods*, he approached me with the idea of editing for the Open Court Publishing Company a collection of Sidgwick's essays in collaboration with Jerry Schneewind. Schneewind and I exchanged some ideas on contents, but then Professor Freeman decided that, given the relative lack of interest (at the time) in the Sidgwick *Monist* issue, there would not be enough interest to warrant Open Court in publishing a selection of Sidgwick's essays. A while later Bill Hackett, of Hackett Publishing Company, was in touch with Schneewind and me about editing a selection of Sidgwick's essays, but he decided that such a project would have to wait until Hackett reprinted *The Methods of Ethics* (1981), and then Bill Hackett died, and, independently of that, Schneewind lost interest in the project. And that was that, for quite a while. Meanwhile, I continued teaching Sidgwick in seminars and tutorials, included some Sidgwick material in my *Morals and Values* (Scribner's 1977), and in a National Endowment for the Humanities Seminar for College Teachers that I directed in the summer of 1983 made available and assigned a number of Sidgwick's epistemological as well as some of his ethical essays.

Bart Schultz, shortly after the publication of his *Essays on Henry Sidgwick*—which in turn developed out of a conference on 'Henry Sidgwick as Philosopher and Historian' that he had arranged at the University of Chicago in 1990, almost certainly the first such conference ever held—suggested that we collaborate on a selection of Sidgwick's essays. With my capacity for learning from the past not wholly obliterated, I at first demurred, but after a while, as Bart is very persuasive, I finally agreed. We started drawing up tentative tables of contents for discussion (and eventually discovered that we had some deep-seated disagreements about some of the items to be included—and God knows how they would have been resolved), and while we were in the discussion stage, Peter Momtchiloff of Oxford University Press told me that he had heard that I was preparing a selection of Sidgwick's essays, and that he would like to consider it for publication. By this time, obviously, interest in Sidgwick had increased somewhat. So I sent Mr Momtchiloff a prospectus and tentative table of contents, and he eventually sent me a contract, with the result that you are now perusing. Sometime in the middle of this process, however, Bart Schultz decided to withdraw from the project, and so I was again alone with it. The end result, curiously enough, is very close to what I had first been planning in the early 1960s. So here it is, at last, Sidgwick's *Essays on Ethics and Method*.

In 1983 or so I organized a Sidgwick Society. Its goals were summed up in its original prospectus:

The Society has been founded out of admiration for the character of Henry Sidgwick and the way he practiced philosophical inquiry: careful, cautious contemplation, considering all points and every possibility, along with his resolute aim at truth and clarity and clarified understanding, his widespread interest in nearly every area of philosophy and in so many other areas of inquiry and life, and his resolute good sense, good judgment, and good will. Thus the Society has as its object the pursuit and support and emulation of such ideals.

A somewhat later statement read this way:

The Society does not do anything—it holds no meetings, publishes no journals, papers, or newsletters, collects no dues. It engages in no activities of any sort whatever. It just *is*, and it exists as a tribute to Henry Sidgwick and the example he set in his intellectual work and life. It does not consist of a group of disciples, nor does it set forth any ideology. The very ideas of discipleship and of ideology are altogether inconsistent with the ideals and practices of its namesake. Its members, rather, seek to honor and to emulate the disinterested and impartial search for truth and illumination that animated and stimulated Henry Sidgwick, and which serves for them as a model of disinterested search for understanding.

The interest generated in this Society, and the number of requests received from people who wanted to be invited to be members, was amazing. There was, starting in the 1980s at least, much greater interest in Sidgwick than we had previously known about, and we can be pretty sure the interest was not generated by there being no dues, no meetings, and no duties. A number of distinguished philosophers told me that they were honored to be on the Board of Directors, or the Executive Committee, although a number of them have, unfortunately, since left us, possibly for a realm where they can carry on uninterrupted discussions with Henry Sidgwick. These include Brand Blanshard (the first president of the Sidgwick Society), Dick Brandt, Bill Frankena, and Alan Donagan (the chief member of the Whewell Wing of the Sidgwick Society). With the publication of this book, the Directorship will devolve elsewhere—and there is a rumor that the Sidgwick Society will then have a web page, a sure sign, in the age of the Internet, of having arrived.

I have, over the years, accumulated a number of debts in connection with Sidgwick, which it is here a pleasure to acknowledge. I have learned more about Sidgwick than I can readily specify from the four unhappily departed persons listed in the dedication, and also from Jack Rawls, Jerry Schneewind, Bart Schultz, Janice Daurio, A. Phillips Griffiths, Jim Griffin, and Jack Smart, as well as from a number of the writers listed in the bibliography. This does not relieve these personages from all responsibility for what is here included and what I have said herein about Sidgwick, though it may relieve them from some. (A list of those from whom I have not learned anything of significance about Sidgwick would be, to be sure, much longer, too long to be included here. But even if the list were shorter it would almost certainly be inadvisable to publish it.)

Over the years in which I have been teaching Sidgwick's ethics I received valuable stimulation from a number of outstanding students. These include William Langenfus and Michael F. McFall (both of whom served at different times as my research assistants and located Sidgwick and Sidgwick-related materials for me, making me aware of important papers and discussions I had not known of before), Storm Bailey, Robert F. Card, Margaret (Peggy) Carter, Norman Gillespie, Jennifer Hoepner, Abel Pablo Iannone, Bryce Jones, Lenore Gutenstein Kuo, Stephen Luebke, Maria Christina Lugones, Hans Oberdiek, Michael A. Reiter, Walter Schaller, John R. Schmidt, and the late Hardy Jones. Kenneth Cooley provided special stimulation in several seminars. And these are just the people whose names I remember, at the moment; there must be at least as many whose names have eluded me. Despite the reputation Sidgwick's *Methods* has acquired over the years for being 'dull' or 'boring', these seminars were always very lively; none of the people who stayed the course thought the book dull.

Bart Schultz supplied me with copies of papers that I did not already have, in particular Chapter 1, the unpublished paper on Utilitarianism, and I am of course grateful as well for his advice and counsel. He should be regarded as the unlisted second editor, as the voice behind the scenes. Terry Penner supplied me with the Latin transliterations of some Greek terms, for which I am duly grateful. Nancy LeDuc faithfully transcribed on to computer disk some of the essays that could not be adequately photocopied for publication and was also a ready and steady hand with the photocopier. And Tom Maloney, of the Interlibrary Loan

Department of the University of Wisconsin Memorial Library, rendered service above and beyond the call of duty on an occasion when time was of the essence. The photographs of Sidgwick, one taken (probably) in 1856 when he was an undergraduate of 18, the other taken *circa* 1877 were sent to me some time ago by Ann Baer, a great-niece of Sidgwick and honorary member of the Sidgwick Society, taken from her 'grandfather Arthur Sidgwick's album'. She gave me freedom to use these items as I thought best. I am sure she would be happy at their reproduction here. My wife, Blanche Ladenson Singer, as she has often done in the past, scrutinized a good deal of what I have written, and with her talent for spotting redundancies, obscurities, and infelicities of style enabled me to eliminate a number I otherwise might not have seen. And I am pleased to express my appreciation for the excellent copy editing of Virginia Williams of Oxford University Press, whose sharp eyes saved me from a number of blunders and who made a number of very helpful suggestions for improvement of wording. Finally, my gratitude, and that of all Sidgwick scholars, to Charlotte Jenkins, philosophy editor at Oxford University Press, for her invaluable help and assistance.

It should be acknowledged that there has been some silent editing of Sidgwick's text: an occasional deletion of an excess word, supplying of a word inadvertently omitted in the original, or some refinement of punctuation. Often when a word judged inadvertently omitted in the original has been inserted, the insertion is enclosed in square brackets. But there has been no extensive modification. The quintessentially Sidgwickian style remains. In 1885 Sidgwick said about J. S. Mill, for whom of course he had great admiration in general: 'What I really envy him is his style; whenever I have by accident tried to say something that he has said before, without knowing, his way of saying it always seems indefinitely better' (*Memoir*, 420–1). I think Sidgwick was right on this. None the less, Sidgwick was able to write certain things that Mill did not and could not. This book is evidence of that, along with *The Methods of Ethics* and his other works.

Derek Parfit wrote to me some time ago (I hope he does not mind my quoting him here): 'I firmly believe that if there is any single book which it would be for the best that everyone doing moral philosophy could assume that everyone thoroughly knew, it would be *The Methods*', a thought with which I have some tendency to agree, and which I have tried to apply in my teaching of moral philosophy. It is to be hoped that the present assemblage of Sidgwick's lesser-known writings will stimulate the interest, and the consequent knowledge, that Parfit hoped for.

MGS

Madison, Wisconsin
September 1999 and March 2000

Abbreviations

The titles of Sidgwick's books, and of three journals in which his writings appeared with some frequency, are abbreviated as follows. Full bibliographical details on the books are provided in Section I of the Bibliography at the end of the book.

DEP	*The Development of European Polity* (1903)
EP	*The Elements of Politics* (1891)
GSM	*Lectures on the Ethics of Green, Spencer, and Martineau* (1902)
HE	*Outlines of the History of Ethics* (1886)
IJE	*International Journal of Ethics*
JSPR	*Journal of the Society for Psychical Research*
LPK	*Lectures on the Philosophy of Kant and other Philosophical Lectures and Essays* (1905)
ME	*The Methods of Ethics* (1874)
MEA	*Miscellaneous Essays and Addresses* (1904)
Mem.	*Henry Sidgwick: A Memoir* (1906)
PE	*Practical Ethics* (1898)
Phil.	*Philosophy, Its Scope and Relations* (1902)
PPE	*Principles of Political Economy* (1883)
PSPR	*Proceedings of the Society for Psychical Research*

Introduction:
The Philosophy of Henry Sidgwick

'Pure white light!' exclaimed a British philosopher in my hearing some fifty years ago when the conversation turned to Henry Sidgwick. That sums up pretty well what his contemporaries thought of him. He stood in their view as the exemplar of objectivity in thought, of clear and passionless under-standing. The light he threw on his subject was uniquely uncolored by feeling, prejudice, or desire.

Brand Blanshard[1]

Even as philosophers go, Henry Sidgwick is not very well known. Most reasonably well-educated people will have heard of Plato, of Aristotle, of Kant, Hegel, and Marx, of Emerson, Mill, Dewey, Russell, Santayana, and Nietzsche—but not of Sidgwick. The reason is not far to seek. Sidgwick was, and is, a philosopher's philosopher. Even though he was well known amongst cultivated readers of his own time, and had articles and reviews in much of the literate periodical litera-ture of the time, he did not, in his treatises at any rate, write to or for a general audience. He wrote long, complicated, technical treatises, in a rather forbidding style, for an interested and professional audience, in ethics, political theory, and political economy, and even today, although most professional philosophers will have heard of him, very few know his work well and even fewer know the extent and range and depth of his work.

I. Who Sidgwick Was

Henry Sidgwick was born 31 May 1838, at Skipton in Yorkshire, the third son and fourth child of William Sidgwick and Mary Crofts Sidgwick, who had married in 1833. His father, an ordained clergyman and headmaster of a school, died in 1841. His mother then settled near Bristol with her four surviving children. She was a woman of considerable determination, intelligence, and culture, and taught him Latin until he went to school at the age of 10. In 1852 Henry became a student at Rugby School and in 1855 he entered Trinity College, Cambridge, where he stayed

---

[1] Brand Blanshard, *Four Reasonable Men*, 181. Full references to works cited in this introduction are contained in the bibliography at the end of the book.

the rest of his life. He was a brilliant student with a wide range of interests. After winning numerous prizes, he graduated with honors in 1859 and was immediately elected a Fellow of Trinity. In 1883 he was elected Knightbridge Professor of Moral Philosophy.

In the 1860s he was confronted by a crisis of conscience resulting from his realization that he could no longer believe the Thirty-nine Articles of the Church of England, subscription to which was at the time a condition of holding a Fellowship. After long and difficult deliberation, in 1869 he resigned his Fellowship. (He was not the first to do this: Leslie Stephen had resigned his Tutorship for similar reasons in 1862.) Almost immediately thereafter he was appointed to a Lectureship in Moral Science at the College, a post not requiring such subscription. Owing in part to Sidgwick's example and reputation, in 1871 the requirement for academic posts of subscription to the Articles was rescinded by Act of Parliament, and Sidgwick was later on reappointed a Fellow of Trinity. Sidgwick wrote a pamphlet, *The Ethics of Conformity and Subscription* (1870), reflecting this profound experience of his life.[2] Some later writers, reviewing the problems and paradoxes of the Victorian Age, were given to poking fun at Sidgwick for what they regarded as excessive conscientiousness. This experience of Sidgwick's is evidence of the strength of his own conscience and moral sense, not an out-of-the-way attribute for a philosopher—especially a moral philosopher —to possess. There were a number of other Fellows of Oxford and Cambridge colleges with similar religious doubts who managed to overcome these scruples in order to hold on to their positions. Sidgwick later referred to this period in his life as his 'years of "storm and stress" as regards religious convictions and ecclesiastical relations'[3] (*Mem.*, 33), and in an autobiographical fragment dictated about a fortnight before his death he said:

---

[2] Reading this work today, more than one hundred years later, and in a cultural setting so vastly different from that reflected in it, it strikes this reader as having little if any relevance to the problems of ethical philosophy. Later on Sidgwick wrote a shorter version of it, 'The Ethics of Religious Conformity', given as an address in November 1895 to the West London Ethical Society, *International Journal of Ethics* (1896); this has somewhat greater relevance.

[3] *Henry Sidgwick, A Memoir*, by Arthur Sidgwick (his brother) and Eleanor Mildred Sidgwick (his widow), is a prime source for information on Sidgwick's life and essential for all who would study Sidgwick's work in depth. It is cited here simply as *Mem.*, with page number. Apart from the narrative, it contains extensive selections from Sidgwick's voluminous correspondence with numerous friends as well as from a journal Sidgwick kept from 1884 onward. Maynard Keynes's comment on it is amusing: 'I have never found so dull a book so absorbing' (R. F. Harrod, *Life of Keynes*, 117.) It is absorbing; to say it is 'dull'—which is, manifestly, a highly emotive term—says something about the sayer. But Keynes was, at that time, a member of the Bloomsbury Group, and Keynes and his friends were entranced, almost hypnotized, by G. E. Moore and Moore's *Principia Ethica*; this apparently made it *de rigueur* to debunk Sidgwick. There is an interesting account of the Bloomsbury Circle in Noel Annan's *Leslie Stephen*, 123–6; there is another in Harrod, *Life of Keynes*, ch. 5. Keynes's further remark about Sidgwick, in 1906 when Keynes was 22, is also choice: 'He never did anything but wonder whether Christianity was true and prove that it wasn't and hope that it was.' A sympathetic account of Bloomsbury is provided by Tom Regan in *Bloomsbury's Prophet*.

I had been led back to philosophy . . . by the question that seemed to me continually to press with more urgency for a definite answer—whether I had a right to keep my Fellowship. I did my very best to decide the question methodically on general principles, but I found it very difficult, and . . . it was while struggling with the difficulty thence arising that I went through a good deal of the thought that was ultimately systematised in the *Methods of Ethics*. (*Mem.*, 38)

It can be seen from this that Sidgwick's crisis of conscience had important philosophical consequences. As he had said some years before (1863) 'It is a horrid nuisance to have to put one's principles into practice' (*Mem.*, 97).

The predicament he felt himself to be in is described in a letter of 1880:

'What criterion have you of the truth of any of the fundamental beliefs of science, except that they are consistent, harmonious with other beliefs that we find ourselves naturally impelled to hold?' . . . this is precisely the relation that I find to exist between Theism and the whole system of my moral beliefs. Duty is to me as real a thing as the physical world, though it is not apprehended in the same way; but all my apparent knowledge of duty falls into chaos if my belief in the moral government of the world is conceived to be withdrawn.

Well, I cannot resign myself to disbelief in duty; in fact, if I did, I should feel that the last barrier between me and complete philosophical scepticism, or disbelief in truth altogether, was broken down. Therefore I sometimes say to myself 'I believe in God'; while sometimes again I can say no more than 'I *hope* this belief is true, and I must and will act as if it was.' (*Mem.*, 347–8)

We have here an echo of Kant's moral argument for belief in God and also a sort of pre-echo of James's pragmatic justification for religious belief. Although Sidgwick did not actually move in either of these directions, we can get a realization from this letter of how much this predicament bothered him.

When he first went to Cambridge, Sidgwick originally concentrated on both classics and mathematics, but his interests soon broadened to include philosophy in all its branches. In addition, he had a great interest in languages; besides mastering Latin and Greek, he studied and mastered German, Arabic, and Hebrew. His initial incentive for studying these last two was his interest in the scientific study of the Bible, but his linguistic studies worked incidentally to broaden his base in philosophy. He was also exceptionally well read in literature, and had a special interest in poetry and drama, as is shown by his writings in literary criticism and on Shakespeare (some of which are reprinted in *Miscellaneous Essays and Addresses*).

In 1876 Henry married Eleanor Mildred (Nora) Balfour, sister of Sidgwick's former pupil Arthur Balfour, later prime minister of England. In part because of the influence on him of the works of John Stuart Mill, in particular *The Subjection of Women*, Sidgwick developed a great interest in improving the education of women. He was instrumental in founding Newnham College (opened in October 1875), the first college for women (after Girton, which opened in 1869 but two miles outside Cambridge), and eventually expanding the university curriculum, against considerable opposition, so as to include women as candidates for examination and later, much later, as degree candidates. In 1880 Nora became the second principal of Newnham, and Henry and Nora moved into one of the buildings of Newnham College. Although at first he was not in favor of female suffrage—early in his life he regarded the idea as 'violently radical'—his position on this matter soon changed. In a letter to the *Spectator* of May 1884 he said:

So long as the responsibility is thrown on women, unmarried or widows, of earning their own livelihood in any way that industrial competition allows, their claim to have the ordinary constitutional protection against any encroachments on the part of other sections of the community is *prima facie* undeniable. And surely . . . this broad and obvious consideration ought to prevail against any ingenious arguments that may be constructed for concluding that the interests of women are not, as a matter of fact, likely to be encroached upon. (*Mem.*, 73)

Sidgwick was greatly interested in Psychical Research, another interest he shared with his wife. He was one of the founders and the first president, starting in February 1882, of the Society for Psychical Research, with the object of 'making an organised and systematic attempt to investigate that large group of debatable phenomena designated by such terms as mesmeric, psychical, and spiritualistic' (*Mem.*, 358). Sidgwick was eager to determine whether the validity of such phenomena could be established by scientific modes of proof, and was by no means a gullible victim of the numerous charlatans then promoting their wares. In part this interest was stimulated by the religious questions that had been bothering him for so many years. For even though Sidgwick came to doubt the truth of most of the prescribed tenets of Christianity—such as the doctrines of the divinity and the resurrection of Christ—he was still inclined, indeed anxious, to hold on to some version of theism, and he had hopes, albeit skeptical hopes, that these theistic beliefs could receive some measure of confirmation through psychical research. He was looking for proofs, though he never succeeded in finding any. He believed that 'the possibility of direct proof of continued individual existence after death could not be neglected either from a theological or an ethical point of view' (*Mem.*, 43). His main hope was that such proof would help resolve what he came to call the Dualism of the Practical Reason, by showing that it is ultimately and in the long run in everyone's own individual interest to pursue and promote the general happiness. But this method of proof failed him, as did all others he considered.

Over the course of his life Sidgwick belonged to a number of discussion societies, which had a profound influence on his thinking and on his reactions to the opinions of others. One of these groups was the Apostles, a small group of intellectually oriented men at Cambridge who met every Saturday evening to discuss essays presented by members. Sidgwick said that the Apostles had 'more effect on his intellectual life than any one thing that happened to him afterwards' (*Mem.*, 32), and he characterized its spirit, which 'absorbed and dominated' him as

the spirit of the pursuit of truth with absolute devotion and unreserve by a group of intimate friends, who were perfectly frank with each other, and indulged in any amount of humorous sarcasm and playful banter, and yet each respects the other, and when he discourses tries to learn from him and see what he sees. Absolute candour was the only duty that the tradition of the society enforced. No consistency was demanded with opinions previously held—truth as we saw it then and there was what we had to embrace and maintain, and there were no propositions so well established that an Apostle had not the right to deny or question, if he did so sincerely and not from mere love of paradox . . . (*Mem.*, 34–5)

Another such group was the Grote Club, presided over in a loose sense by John Grote, then Knightbridge Professor of Moral Philosophy, which met once or twice a term at Grote's home (*Mem.*, 133–8). (See 'A Note on Grote'.) Still another was the Metaphysical Society (1869–80), which met in London at the Grosvenor Hotel about once a month (*Mem.*, 220 ff.), and which in turn was succeeded, some years later, by the Synthetic Society (*Mem.*, 556).

In addition, Sidgwick offered a great number of courses of lectures, on a variety of subjects, as can be seen from the titles of his posthumous works. (And the variety can be seen from the various topics covered in his essays as well as from these posthumous collections of lectures.) He lectured on metaphysics, epistemology, ethics, history of ethics, political theory, political economy, political history, Kant's philosophy, and so on. One may well wonder how Sidgwick managed to combine all this activity, his teaching and lecturing, his reading, necessarily voluminous, his work on behalf of the education of women, his extra lecturing to the women at Newnham Hall, his activities in connection with the Society for Psychical Research, his active participation in college and university affairs and in these various discussion societies, and his later role in establishing the Mind Association, with his philosophical work. How did he manage to get all this work done? Yet he did. And he also managed to attend plays, occasionally to play tennis and golf, to cultivate an interest in art, and continue to read novels and poetry. And he had a fabulous memory for poetry. The only art in which he had no interest was music—perhaps because he was tone deaf.

II. *The Methods of Ethics*

The Methods of Ethics, Sidgwick's greatest work, is a dominant work of ethical theory, regarded by many of those best qualified to judge as the ethical treatise par excellence. Apart from the *Outlines of the History of Ethics*, it is the one work by Sidgwick that has remained almost continually in print through its seven editions extending from 1874 through 1901 to the present. Through most of the twentieth century, even though interest in it waxed and waned along with serious interest in ethical theory, it has continued to be read and studied by those—at one time relatively few—with a genuine interest in the subject. And interest in it has sharply increased in recent years, stemming largely from the work of John Rawls and J. B. Schneewind.

Sidgwick wrote other treatises besides *The Methods of Ethics*—*The Principles of Political Economy* (1883) and *The Elements of Politics* (1891)—and both these works also went through several editions. But, though they are still to some extent studied and discussed, none of his other works has achieved the fame and the status of *The Methods* or has been discussed and referred to as much. Although there was a short period in the 1950s when *The Methods* was out of print and not easy to obtain, in 1962 two publishers independently of each other brought out reprints of the seventh edition of 1907, and, considering that it went through seven editions up until 1907, five of them in Sidgwick's lifetime, the work has remained almost continually in print since its first publication.

Yet, despite its fame and renown, *The Methods* is often regarded as a difficult work, hard to read, and hard to understand. There is some justice to this claim; since Sidgwick was writing a treatise, he was trying to avoid controversy as much as possible, though not always with great success, and he was trying to keep his own personality out of the work as far as he could—with the odd result that in the process he managed, despite himself, to inject it.

III. The Argument of *The Methods*

Sidgwick characterized his work as 'essentially an attempt to introduce precision of thought into a subject usually treated in a too loose and popular way' (*Mem.*, 295). He says in the preface: 'I have thought that the predominance in the minds of moralists of a desire to edify has impeded the real progress of ethical science; and that this would be benefited by an application to it of the same disinterested curiosity to which we chiefly owe the great discoveries of physics',

and with this view I have desired to concentrate the reader's attention, from first to last, not on the practical results to which our methods lead, but on the methods themselves. I have wished to put aside temporarily the urgent need which we all feel of finding and adopting the true method of determining what we ought to do; and to consider simply what conclusions will be rationally reached if we start with certain ethical premises, and with what degree of certainty and precision. (*ME*, p. vi)

Although the main outline of the *Methods* is actually pretty well known by this time, it does not follow that it is well understood. Sidgwick tells us, in his essay 'Some Fundamental Ethical Controversies' (Ch. 6, this vol.), that the book mainly deals with 'methods' rather than 'principles'. In *The Methods* Sidgwick says:

My object . . . is to expound . . . the different methods of ethics that I find implicit in our common moral reasoning; to point out their mutual relations; and where they seem to conflict, to define the issue as much as possible. In the course of this endeavour I am led to discuss the considerations which should, in my opinion, be decisive in determining the adoption of ethical first principles; but it is not my primary aim to establish such principles. (*ME*, 14)

(Sidgwick's view on 'the establishment of ethical first principles' is presented in his paper of that title (Ch. 5, this vol.).) By a 'method of ethics' Sidgwick means 'any rational procedure by which we determine what individual human beings "ought"—or what it is "right" for them—to do' (*ME*, 1). And by a 'rational procedure' he appears to mean a procedure of reasoning to a conclusion, presumably from premises, though it is possible that the concept is meant to include any procedure that is not irrational. (On this matter he is silent.)

For a long time Sidgwick was regarded as the last of the outstanding utilitarians of the nineteenth century and *The Methods* as 'the last authoritative utterance of traditional utilitarianism'.[4] This assessment is not absolutely wrong, but it is not altogether right either, and it is considerably misleading in that it fails to bring out the main aims and accomplishments of *The Methods*. Sidgwick's main aim in *The Methods*, on his own testimony, was not to establish utilitarianism, although it may appear that way on a cursory reading. His aim—that is, one main aim—was to explore impartially the methods of ethics, the procedures used in common life to determine what ought to be done. He finds and distinguishes three: egoism (or egoistic hedonism), intuitionism, and utilitarianism (or universalistic hedonism). In Book I of *The Methods* he makes a number of distinctions important for the subject, including the crucial distinction between a *method* and a *principle*—thus emphasizing that his primary concern is with the *methods*, not the principles, of ethics.[5] Book II is devoted to a dispassionate examination of egoism as a method of ethics, that is to say, as a method of determining what one ought to do by taking one's own ultimate good as the ultimate aim of action. In the process he brings out the difficulties in applying hedonism—the idea that pleasure is what is ultimately good—in a way that has not been matched since. Book III is devoted to exploring intuitionism, or the morality of common sense, as Sidgwick conceived of it, since he believed that implicit acceptance of some form of intuitionism is characteristic of common-sense morality. Sidgwick distinguishes three forms of intuitionism, on the basis of the 'difference in generality in the intuitive beliefs recognised as ultimately valid'. Three levels of generality are distinguished:

---

[4] Ernest Albee, *A History of English Utilitarianism*, 359. 'Traditional' utilitarianism may be understood to mean individualistic and hedonistic. Albee's discussion of Sidgwick is still worth reading; among other things it traces out the changes in some of the more important doctrines and chapters from one edition to another.

[5] Janice Daurio, 'Sidgwick on Moral Theories and Common Sense Morality', has some fascinating and original ideas on the crucial matter of Sidgwick's distinction between method and principle.

'moral judgements on single acts' with no regard for their consequences; 'general rules prescribing particular kinds of acts'; and 'more universal and fundamental principles', which have no immediate or obvious application to conduct (*ME*, 103). These three forms of Intuitionism are called respectively Perceptual (particular case intuitionism), Dogmatic (general rule intuitionism), and Philosophical (abstract principle intuitionism), and when Sidgwick speaks of Intuitionism he usually means the second, Dogmatic or general rule Intuitionism.

Dogmatic Intuitionism corresponds to the morality of common sense, and Sidgwick's detailed and comprehensive examination of common-sense morality (the morality, he says, that is his own as much as anyone's) is almost universally regarded as the greatest achievement of its kind since the work of Aristotle. Sidgwick concludes that despite the pervasive character of common-sense morality, its rules are vague and indefinite and can come into conflict, and in cases of perplexity it is inadequate to provide practical guidance and therefore inadequate by itself as a method of ethics. He concludes also that common-sense morality is 'unconsciously utilitarian', in the sense that when such practical difficulties arise, common sense unconsciously resorts to the utilitarian method to resolve them.

The utilitarian method, which is the method of determining what ought to be done by taking the general good, or the greatest happiness on the whole, as the ultimate end of action, is examined in Book IV, and does not itself come off unscathed. Along with other problems, Sidgwick raises questions about the differences that obtain in applying the utilitarian method in a society of utilitarians and in a society not made up of utilitarians, a distinction not heretofore thought of. He concludes that, despite the problems connected with the use of the intuitionist method, utilitarians must recognize that they themselves are imbued with common-sense morality, and that the latter, despite its defects, cannot be changed rapidly or by decree or by the mere application of a theory. So the Utilitarianism he ends up with is Utilitarianism on an Intuitionistic basis, and Utilitarianism, by parity of reasoning, can be said to be unconsciously intuitionistic.

The fundamental principles of Philosophical Intuitionism are the intuitively self-evident axioms of prudence or egoism, justice, and rational benevolence. The principle of egoism is that one ought to aim at maximizing one's own good. The principle of justice is that 'it cannot be right for A to treat B in a manner in which it would be wrong for B to treat A, merely on the ground that they are two different individuals, and without there being any difference between the natures or circumstances of the two which can be stated as a reasonable ground for difference of treatment' (*ME*, 380), which can also be stated as whatever is right for one person must be right for any similar person similarly situated. And the principle of rational benevolence is that 'each one is morally bound to regard the good of any other individual as much as his own', which together with the principle of justice is the basis for the 'fundamental principle of Utilitarianism' (*ME*, 387), that everyone ought to aim at maximizing good, or at bringing about the greatest happiness on the whole. (There is some dispute about the exact number of self-evident principles Sidgwick comes up with; for more on this matter, see Lacey, 'Sidgwick's Ethical Maxims' and Schneewind, *Sidgwick's Ethics*.)

Sidgwick is not content merely to state these 'axioms' and have them regarded without argument as intuitively certain or self-evident. He actually provides four tests for self-evidence: (1) 'the terms of the proposition must be clear and precise'; (2) 'the self-evidence of the proposition must be ascertained by careful reflection'; (3) 'the propositions accepted as self-evident must be mutually consistent'; and (4) there must be at least approximate consensus on the part of competent judges on the self-evidence, or at least the manifest truth, of the proposition in question, 'for the denial by another of a proposition that I have affirmed has a tendency to impair my confidence in its validity' (*ME*, 338–42). And Sidgwick concludes that the abstract principles or axioms of prudence, justice, and benevolence satisfy these tests, whereas the rules of Dogmatic Intuitionism, or Common-Sense morality, do not. So Sidgwick's doctrine is not truly one of intuitionism, as it has been historically understood, even though he himself picked up this term from Reid and Price and, in his own century, Whewell. A pure intuitionist would have either quite different tests of self-evidence, or, more likely, none at all that is not contained within the privileged intuition itself.

However, Sidgwick is troubled by the conflict he perceives between the 'self-evident' axioms of egoism (or rational prudence) and of benevolence (or utilitarianism). How can the principle of rational egoism—that one ought rationally to aim at a maximum of good to oneself—be reconciled with the apparently self-evident principle of rational benevolence—that one ought rationally to aim at the maximum of good for everyone? This problem, that of the Dualism of the Practical Reason, in which practical reason by valid reasoning seems irrevocably at odds with itself, is one that plagued Sidgwick all his life; though he never gave up hope of finding a solution for it, he had not found one at the time of his death. In somewhat different terminology, the problem is one of reconciling self-interest and duty, and is one that has existed in ethics from its inception. In Sidgwick's *Methods* it takes on a technical form in which the problem is even more pronounced.[6]

---

[6] W. R. Sorley, in *A History of English Philosophy*—a valuable work of marvelously compressed information and insight—has an analysis of Sidgwick's dualism that is worth some consideration: 'It would appear . . . that this dualism was not adequately tested by [Sidgwick] and that it really arises from the ambiguity of the term prudence. Prudence may mean either "regard for one's own good on the whole" or (what is not the same thing) the principle that "hereafter as such is neither less nor more valuable than now." Both forms of statement are used by Sidgwick; but only the latter has a claim to express an absolute ethical principle; and it is not inconsistent with the axiom of benevolence' (pp. 280–1). There is a considerable literature on Sidgwick's Dualism of the Practical Reason; see Schneewind, *Sidgwick's Ethics*, ch. 13 and p. 418; other interesting discussions as well as further references may be found in *The Monist*, Sidgwick issue (1974) and in Schultz's *Essays on Sidgwick*; in the former, see especially the essay by Frankena, in the latter see the introduction by Schultz, esp. pp. 33–7, and the essays by Mackie, Frankena, and Brink.

In the nineteenth century value theory was not sharply distinguished from ethical theory, but with the advent of different conceptions of 'the good', or of 'utility', early in the twentieth century, the distinction was made. Sidgwick's value theory is provided by hedonism, the theory that pleasure, or a balance of pleasure over pain, is the only thing that is good in itself, everything else that is good being good only as a means to this ultimate end. This is the hedonistic conception of happiness, and Sidgwick ends up defining 'ultimate good' as a state of consciousness felt as desirable, so that, he says, 'Ultimate Good can only be conceived as Desirable Consciousness', identified with 'Happiness or Pleasure' (*ME*, 398). On this criterion, then, rational egoism is identified with egoistic hedonism: what is ultimately good for any agent is that agent's greatest happiness on the whole; and utilitarianism is universalistic hedonism, so that Utilitarianism is 'the ethical theory that the conduct which, under any given circumstances, is objectively right, is that which will produce the greatest amount of happiness on the whole; that is, taking into account all whose happiness is affected by the conduct' (*ME*, 411). But the utilitarian principle, that the right act is the one, among all the available alternatives, that produces the best consequences, can be held without accepting the hedonistic value theory,[7] and the sort of ethical theory set forth by Sidgwick has come to be called hedonistic utilitarianism. Nothing more need be said about this distinction here. The classical utilitarians, making no such distinction, judged the value of the consequences by the happiness or unhappiness produced.

A problem that Sidgwick appears not to have noticed is that, given his criteria of self-evidence, if there really is a conflict between the principle of egoism and the principle of rational benevolence (which provides the basis for utilitarianism), then not both of these principles can be self-evident, for 'the propositions accepted as self-evident must be mutually consistent'. This is a standing problem, which I only mention here.[8]

IV. The Aims of *The Methods*

Sidgwick says at the outset that his 'immediate object . . . is not Practice but Knowledge':

I have desired to concentrate the reader's attention, from first to last, not on the practical results to which our methods lead, but on the methods themselves. I have wished . . . to consider simply what conclusions will be rationally reached if we start with certain ethical premises, and with what degree of certainty and precision. (*ME*, p. vi)

[7] This move was made, not long after Sidgwick's death, by G. E. Moore, *Principia Ethica*, and Hastings Rashdall, *The Theory of Good and Evil*. Rashdall called this view 'Ideal Utilitarianism'.

[8] This problem was first noticed by James Seth, 'The Ethical System of Henry Sidgwick', 180, though Seth only notices the point, he does not pursue it.

This theoretical aim of the *Ethics* may be contrasted with the announced aim of the *Politics*, which is said to be practical, not theoretical:

The primary aim of this book is to set forth in a systematic manner the general notions and principles which we use in ordinary political reasonings. Now, ordinary political reasonings have some practical aim in view: to determine whether the *constitution* or the *action* of government ought to be modified in a certain proposed manner. Hence, the primary aim of our study must be similarly practical: we must endeavour to determine what *ought* to be, so far as the constitution and action of government are concerned, as distinct from what is or has been . . . (*EP*, 3rd edn., 1908: 6–7).

Why this difference in aim? One reason is that in the *Politics* Sidgwick is not dealing with methods and principles of politics, but with institutions and agencies. But the main one, it seems certain, is that in the *Politics* Sidgwick is already using the utilitarian doctrine and method, which he thinks he has established in *The Methods*:

We have thus arrived at the utilitarian doctrine that the ultimate criterion of the goodness of law, and of the actions of government generally, is their tendency to increase the general happiness . . . The happiness then of the governed community will be assumed as the ultimate end of legislation . . . [We] have agreed to take general happiness as our ultimate end . . . (*EP*, 39–40)[9]

We have now noticed a number of aims of *The Methods*, as stated by its author. But, in addition, Schneewind has argued, very plausibly, that 'The main line of argument . . . is an attempt to show how the apparently self-evident axioms are involved in the systematization of our moral knowledge'.

The central thought . . . is that morality is the embodiment of the demands reason makes on practice under the conditions of human life, and that the problems of philosophical ethics are the problems of showing how practical reason is articulated into these demands.[10]

This assessment certainly contains a large measure of truth, but it does not displace the statements set down above, some of them by Sidgwick himself, as to his main aims in *The Methods*. It supplements them, in a particularly insightful way. And this enables us to see that *The Methods of Ethics*, always regarded as an

---

[9] William Havard has some acute things to say about Sidgwick's works on politics and economics, e.g., 'If not the first, [*The Elements of Politics*] was among the earliest works on the "principles of modern politics," and therefore may be listed among the innovations leading to the current division of political science into several specialized branches. But its claim to recognition does not rest entirely on its originality of approach, for even today it is a valuable index to the institutional problems of the modern state' (*Sidgwick and Later Political Philosophy*, 148). Also (pp. 150–1): 'It is doubtful whether a work like *Elements of Politics* could have been written before the end of the nineteenth century . . . that era was the time in which the modern liberal state was completely rationalized . . . the institutional problems of the present rational liberal state are virtually the same as those with which Sidgwick dealt in 1891.'

[10] Schneewind, *Sidgwick's Ethics*, 61, 303–4.

especially complex work, is more complex and rich than had heretofore been imagined. For it is also true, as Rawls (among others) has said, that *The Methods* 'is the clearest and most accessible formulation of . . . "the classical utilitarian doctrine" . . . What makes *The Methods of Ethics* so important is that Sidgwick is more aware than other classical authors of the many difficulties this doctrine faces, and he attempts to deal with them in a consistent and thorough way . . . Sidgwick's book . . . is the most philosophically profound of the strictly classical works . . .'. And Rawls has also claimed that *The Methods of Ethics* is 'the first truly academic work in moral theory, modern in both method and spirit. Treating ethics as a discipline to be studied like any other branch of knowledge, it defines and carries out in exemplary fashion . . . some of the comprehensive comparisons that constitute moral theory'.[11] But not only is *The Methods of Ethics* complex in an especially intriguing way, so is Sidgwick's philosophy as a whole.

V. The Reception of *The Methods*

The Methods was regarded as important on first publication, as is shown by the vast amount of discussion, criticism, and commentary it engendered. The first volume of *Mind*, in 1876, contained two reviews, one by A. Bain, 'Mr. Sidgwick's Methods of Ethics', the other by H. Calderwood, 'Mr. Sidgwick on Intuitionalism'. In 1877 F. H. Bradley published a pamphlet entitled *Mr. Sidgwick's Hedonism: An Examination of the Main Argument of the Methods of Ethics*. But Bradley, who was understandably disturbed by Sidgwick's hedonism, did not come near to grasping 'the main argument of *The Methods*'. Bradley's was the first extended discussion. The second was by F. Y. Edgeworth, *New and Old Methods of Ethics, or 'Physical Ethics' and 'Methods of Ethics'* (1877). In a note in *Mind*, 1877, the editor said that 'The interest that continues to be excited by *The Methods of Ethics*, shown also in the recent appearance of Mr. Bradley's pamphlet . . . is a notable fact in English philosophy at the present day, and there should remain due record of it in the pages of this Journal' (p. 167).

The second edition of *The Methods* came out in 1877, and Sidgwick, eager to avoid controversy in his treatise, said:

In revising my work, I have endeavoured to profit as much as possible by all the criticisms on it that have been brought to my notice, whether public or private. I have frequently deferred to objections, even where they appeared to me unsound, if I thought I could avoid controversy by alterations to which I was myself indifferent . . . The book is already more controversial than I could wish; and I have therefore avoided encumbering it with any polemics of purely personal interest . . . (*ME*, p. ix).

[11] John Rawls, foreword to the Hackett edn. of *The Methods of Ethics* (1982); *The Journal of Philosophy*, 77 (1980), 555–7.

Sidgwick's characteristic concern for his readers led him to publish the 'numerous alterations and additions . . . in a separate form, for the use of purchasers of my first edition'. The supplement to the first edition ran to over 120 pages, that to the second edition to 184 pages. (No supplement was printed with any of the later editions.)

In the preface to the fourth edition, 1890, Sidgwick says that he has expanded the argument in one or two places 'to meet objections ably urged by Mr. Rashdall in *Mind* (April 1885)'. Rashdall's assessment of *The Methods of Ethics*, contained in that article, is very high indeed:

The Methods of Ethics has long been recognized as a philosophical classic. It is one of those books of which it is safe to prophesy that no advance in philosophic doctrine will ever render them obsolete. It is not merely a piece of acute and subtle philosophical criticism but a work of art with a unity and beauty of its own as much as a dialogue of Plato or of Berkeley. And nothing is so well calculated to increase the reader's admiration for Prof. Sidgwick's literary skill as a comparison of the successive revisions to which he has subjected it. Every edition represents a nearer approach to artistic perfection. By far the greater number of changes in the present edition affect only the exposition of the author's views. Redundances of every kind, discussions or parentheses which might seem a little unnecessary or not obviously relevant to the main line of thought . . . have been pruned away; while the portions of the work in which the author's fundamental doctrines are unfolded, have undergone amplification and expansion. With each successive revision the main issues stand out more sharply and unmistakably, and the arguments become clearer and more telling.[12]

This statement by a contemporary, exuberant as it is, would not seem worthy of notice now, if it did not appear to manifest something like prescience, and if it were not for the fact that it is only the first of a number of similar estimates. C. D. Broad's is now famous:

Sidgwick's *Methods of Ethics* seems to me to be on the whole the best treatise on moral theory that has ever been written, and to be one of the English philosophical classics . . . He combined deep moral earnestness with complete coolness and absence of moral fanaticism. His capacity for seeing all sides of a question and estimating their relative importance was unrivalled; his power of analysis was very great; and he never allowed the natural desire to make up one's mind on important questions to hurry him into a decision where the evidence seemed inadequate or conflicting.

Broad's judgment was seconded thirty years later by Brand Blanshard:

C. D. Broad startled some readers by his judgment that Sidgwick's *Methods of Ethics* is 'on the whole the best treatise on moral theory that has ever been written', but it is a judgment with which . . . I should concur . . . For combined subtleness, thoroughness, lucidity, and fairness, I know of no equal to it in ethical literature . . . Sidgwick's acuteness

---

[12] Hastings Rashdall, 'Professor Sidgwick's Utilitarianism', 200.

was equalled by his sanity and moral seriousness; and for judicial detachment—the somewhat bleak, but clear, full light in which he sees things—he stands quite alone . . . in philosophical history . . . To most types of reader, Sidgwick is irredeemably dull, while writers
with far feebler intellectual powers who speak in terms of prophecy, like Nietzsche and
Kierkegaard, are listened to with a respect they ill deserve. But for those who want to
know simply what ethical theories make sense and what do not, and who are bored with
attempts to make the subject interesting, Sidgwick's book is supreme.[13]

Such opinions are apt to seem extravagant, and of course they are not universally accepted. If they were, they would not be so striking. But Broad and
Blanshard have not been alone in this estimate, and it is interesting that such judgments have been made by philosophers who agreed neither with Sidgwick's
Hedonism nor with his Utilitarianism. Consider the appraisal of W. P. Montague,
which antedates that of both Broad and Blanshard:

Since the time when, as a student of Professor Palmer at Harvard, I read Sidgwick's
Methods of Ethics, I have had the ambition to follow in a small way the plan of that great
work, and to set forth as best I could the methods of logic and epistemology disentangled
from the more exciting problems of metaphysics.

Sidgwick's book still seems to me one of the greatest of philosophic essays . . . In the
general plan of treatment as well as in the subtitle of my book I have registered my obligation to Sidgwick.[14]

But (with the possible exception of Rashdall, and his opinion on this matter
is difficult to fathom) many of those who agree on the philosophical merits of
The Methods agree that it is afflicted with grave literary defects. As Broad goes on
to say:

Yet he has grave defects as a writer which have certainly detracted from his fame. His style
is heavy and involved, and he seldom allowed that strong sense of humor, which is said
to have made him a delightful conversationalist, to relieve the uniform dull dignity of his
writing. He incessantly refines, qualifies, raises objections, answers them, and then finds
further objections to the answers. Each of these objections, rebuttals, rejoinders, and sur-
rejoinders is in itself admirable, and does infinite credit to the acuteness and candour of
the author. But the reader is apt to become impatient; to lose the thread of the argument;
and to rise from his desk finding that he has read a great deal with admiration and now
remembers little or nothing.

A complaint akin to this had actually been voiced forty years earlier by L. A.
Selby-Bigge, a contemporary, so Sidgwick surely was aware of the problem:

Of the Methods of Ethics it is especially hard to be critical; its very virtues have made it peculiarly difficult to grasp, or, at least, to judge; there are so many candid admissions, so many

---

[13] C. D. Broad, Five Types of Ethical Theory, 143; Brand Blanshard, Reason and Goodness, 90–1.
[14] William Pepperell Montague, The Ways of Knowing, or The Methods of Philosophy, 5.

able and eloquent statements of the other side, so little suppression of material facts, that many readers have professed respectful failure to entirely understand the author's views sooner than commit themselves to a treatment of it which they feel would be very possibly unfair and very probably incomplete. Few who have read the book have not learnt much from it; but I think, there are also few who are quite certain what it all comes to.[15]

There are of course those who would agree on the literary defects without agreeing on the philosophical merits. Thus Alfred North Whitehead once said that he had 'read *The Methods of Ethics* as a young man and found it so stodgy that he had been deterred from ever reading any book on ethics since'.[16] I note this as an interesting example of inference, curious from a great logician. The question of the philosophical merits of *The Methods*, however, I take as settled, despite the claims of some distinguished dissenters; in my view the only question worth taking seriously is what it all comes to, and to what extent it accomplishes its aims. But its defects as a piece of writing are surely evident to anyone who has taken the trouble to peruse it. Sidgwick's writing is overloaded with qualifications, distinctions, and hedges, and the book has a solemnity about it, and a tediousness of tone, almost altogether unrelieved by humor. And these problems do tend to make the work neither as clear nor as precise as Sidgwick had set out to make it.[17]

Sidgwick himself said of *The Methods* that it would never have popular appeal, would interest specialists only. 'It is a book [he said shortly before its publication] too technical to give me any general reputation; indeed it can scarcely be said to belong to literature' (*Mem.*, 291; 11 July 1874). Other remarks in the *Memoir* along these lines include: 'I think the contribution to the *formal* clearness and coherence of our ethical thought which I have to offer is just worth giving: for a few speculatively minded persons—very few' (*Mem.*, 277; Feb. 1873). Again (p. 292):

---

[15] Broad, *Five Types*, 144; L. A. Selby-Bigge, 'Some Fundamental Ethical Controversies', 93. Another view, that of Noel Annan, is worth recording here: 'Sidgwick's *Methods of Ethics* was prolix, over-subtle, badly-organised and lacked the literary charm of Bradley's *Ethical Studies*; yet it is the finest treatise on moral philosophy of the age, because Sidgwick by his analysis of logical terms, and of epistemological and psychological questions shows the reader what he means and how he infers. Stephen failed to recognise its importance because he fell into the error of the amateur in thinking that pre-occupation with problems of logical inference is an exercise in academic logomachy and that these problems could be swept away by a bold approach from another flank' (*Leslie Stephen*, 215–16). It is curious that Annan speaks of Sidgwick's 'analysis of logical terms', for Sidgwick was not analyzing 'logical' terms—perhaps this was a misprint for 'ethical'. Or perhaps this indicates something of Annan's understanding of the matter.

[16] Reported in Harrod, *Life of Keynes*, 76–7.

[17] In his *Autobiography* (1883), Anthony Trollope said (ch. 19), 'Of all the needs a book has the chief need is that it be readable'. But Trollope was writing of novels and travel books, in particular his own, and in general of books written with the intention of making money, not of philosophical treatises, very few of which are written with the aim of making money. Of course, it does not follow that a philosophical work should aim at being unreadable. And Trollope would no doubt have been unable to fathom the publication, some forty or fifty years later, of such novels as *Ulysses* and *Finnegans Wake*.

'The book is written in a rather obscure and technical style, intended primarily for students . . .' (1874). And (p. 295): 'It is addressed . . . to . . . [a] very limited public . . .' (Jan. 1875). One of the most illuminating remarks Sidgwick made on the *Methods* is also from January 1875: '. . . it is essentially an attempt to introduce precision of thought into a subject usually treated in a too loose and popular way, and therefore I feel cannot fail to be somewhat dry and repellent' (p. 295). Little did he realize the number of professional thinkers who would be repelled by it, even some who themselves had a cultivated capacity for writing in an obscure and repellent manner.

Sidgwick, however, was capable of writing with verve, directness, and humor, just as he was capable of brilliant conversation. The evidence on this last point is considerable. J. J. Thomson, who knew him, says of him: 'He was one of the most brilliant talkers of his time . . . in the opinion of most people, the most brilliant in Cambridge.' Thomson goes on to say:

He often took part in discussions at meetings of the Fellows when suggested changes came under consideration. His speeches were a very enjoyable intellectual treat, but they did not, I think, have much effect on the division. He was sometimes accused of sitting on the fence, but it was rather that he kept vaulting over it from one side to the other, giving arguments at one time in favour of the proposal, and following them with arguments against. Thus, whatever a man's opinion might be, he got new arguments in its favour and voted as he had intended.[18]

This last point is certainly reminiscent of Sidgwick's style in *The Methods of Ethics*. But Sidgwick did say that his piece on 'Bentham and Benthamism' (Ch. 24 this vol.) 'is the first thing that I have written for years in which I have aimed at all at literary effect' (*Mem.*, 327). Readers may judge for themselves how well he succeeded in his aim. What is especially significant about this remark is its implication that in most of his writing he was not 'aiming at literary effect'. (He had said earlier, in 1871, 'I have found that I write slowly and with great labour', *Mem.*, 252.)

And Sidgwick was aware of the problem, as is indicated by this passage from a letter to Maitland written 5 January 1900: 'I for many years committed the error of imagining an *ideal* reader for my book and writing for him. Since I took to writing for the probably actual reader, I think my philosophic style has exhibited a slight modicum of improvement' (*Mem.*, 578–9).

But no matter how much he tried to work on improving his philosophic style, Sidgwick was not a stylist, writing limpid, elegant, rhythmic prose, in the manner of, say, Russell, or Santayana, or even Bradley. And perhaps his way of thinking

---

[18] J. J. Thomson, *Recollections and Reflections*, 294–5. Curiously apropos here, though it was not said about Sidgwick, is the following observation by Lytton Strachey: 'The most lasting utterances of a man are his studied writings; the least are his conversations. His letters hover midway between these two extremes; and the fate which is reserved for them is capable of infinite gradations, from instant annihilation up to immortality' (*Characters and Commentaries*, 3).

and writing philosophy prohibited his being a stylist, in that manner. If so, we are all the gainers.[19]

Sidgwick's sense of humor, moreover, was not always absent from his writing. His concept of 'highly profound nonsense' is an example of this. It appears in a letter of July 1870:

> Day after day I sit down to my books with a firm determination to master the German Heraclitus, and as regularly I depart to my Mittagsessen with a sense of hopeless defeat. No difficulty of any other writer can convey the least conception even of the sort of difficulty I find in Hegel. My only consolation is . . . that every other philosophical work I take up seems easy. But no amount of difficulty alone would distress my spirit if there was not added the paralysing doubt whether, after all, I am not breaking my head over highly profound nonsense. (*Mem.*, 230)

And there is a story, which I presume true, that when he was reading McTaggart's dissertation submitted for a fellowship he remarked to his fellow examiners, 'I can see that this is nonsense, but is it the right kind of nonsense?' (Blanshard, *Four Reasonable Men*, 221). This is not only philosophical penetration operating, it is also a sense of humor.

Sidgwick's concern to avoid controversy, though manifest in his treatise, is not a noteworthy feature in the numerous journal articles he wrote, even those replying to criticisms. Nor was irritation, sarcasm, or combativeness always absent from his writing. This comes out in his philosophic exchanges and polemical writing, perhaps most prominently in his exchange with F. H. Bradley. The careful, cautious, difficult style of *The Methods* is certainly not evident in this exchange, which admittedly could be something of an exception, since it gives evidence of some deep personal antagonism—something not altogether absent from the exchanges other philosophers had with Mr Bradley.

Thus we seem to have something like two sides to Sidgwick, one of them, the one most widely known today, open, impartial, careful, cautious, judicious, attempting to see all sides of a controversy, to understand sympathetically the point of view of those who differ with him, and to arrive at a solution satisfactory all around. This is the Sidgwick of the treatises. And this is the Sidgwick of whom it was said, by various competent contemporaries, that 'no more truthful man . . . ever lived', 'he cultivated a disposition of fairness towards opponents', and 'he never argued for victory'.[20] Even allowing for the exaggeration characteristic of

---

[19] Blanshard's contrary view on Sidgwick's style should be noted: 'Sidgwick had what many philosophers seem to lack altogether, a writer's ear. If one reads him aloud (an excellent test of any writer . . .), one finds that the rhetorical emphasis corresponds very well with the emphasis required by the sense. His English is standard English; he prefers the simple word; he detests pedantry . . .' (*Four Reasonable Men*, 221).

[20] These statements are by, respectively, F. W. Maitland, John Neville Keynes, and A. J. Balfour, in *Mem.*, 306, 307, and 311.

obituaries and funeral orations, a definite picture emerges. On the other hand, there appears another Sidgwick: quick-tongued, humorous, ready-witted, always ready for controversy. No doubt this other picture is also something of an exaggeration. None the less there was this side to Sidgwick. This comes out in some of his letters, as for instance, this statement from a letter of 1864: 'Oxford presents a striking contrast to Cambridge in respect of the much greater stir and activity of the intellectual life that is kept up there. It is partly due to the hot controversies that are always raging there, which keep people's minds always thinking . . .' (*Mem.*, 106). Again, a month later: 'I am sorry you are in so nightmarish a state. Have you been reading Carlyle or any such poison?' (*Mem.*, 107). In 1862, 'I wish I was at Oxford, where they are always having exciting controversies which keep them alive. Nothing is so fertile in jokes and happy sayings as a good semi-theological row' (*Mem.*, 74). Then, reflecting perhaps the other side of his nature, from 1863: 'This is a disagreeable age to live in; there are so many opinions held about everything, and the advocates of each abuse their opponents so violently that it quite frightens a modest man' (*Mem.*, 100).

What we have, then, is a situation in which a philosopher, renowned for the brilliance and wit of his conversation and his excellence and lucidity as a teacher, reverts to a dull, difficult, and forbidding style in his formal writings, in which he is attempting to set forth a system of philosophy, and, in particular, to establish something about the right and proper method of philosophical inquiry. And this is, actually, what Sidgwick was trying to do—in addition to, and perhaps on top of, the other things mentioned.

VI. Ethics and Method in Sidgwick

We have now noticed several accounts of Sidgwick's aims in *The Methods of Ethics*, each of them with something to be said for it, and each of them in its own way meritorious—as long as it is not taken as exclusive, incompatible with the others. There is an especially important aim, however, just mentioned, which now needs some exposition. I have said that in his formal writings, especially in *The Methods*, Sidgwick was attempting to set forth a system of philosophy, and, in particular, to establish something about the right and proper method of philosophical inquiry, something important about philosophic method. This aim is not really explicit in *The Methods*, where he is explicitly discussing the methods of *ethics*, but it is there in latent form, and it becomes more noticeable in his later works, especially those on method and evidence. This concern becomes explicit in the following passage, from 1898:

It is the primary aim of philosophy to unify completely, bring into clear coherence, all departments of rational thought; and this aim cannot be realized by any philosophy that leaves out of its view the important body of judgments and reasonings which form the subject matter of Ethics.[21]

Now this concern, and the coordinate concern with being true to and account-ing for common sense, by 'systematizing' it, is implicit all through *The Methods of Ethics*. Sidgwick also says that no 'philosophical theory can ever be established, if we are not to accept as evidence of its truth that it introduces unity, harmony, systematic coherence into our thought, and removes the conflict and contradic-tion which would otherwise exist in the whole or some department of it' (*Mem.*, 605).

From these statements it would appear that the standard interpretation of Sidgwick as an empiricist is far from adequate, and that he had more in common with his idealistic rivals—Green and Bradley—than has hitherto been recognized. His placing such emphasis on coherence is evidence for this.[22] His essay on the 'Incoherence of Empirical Philosophy' is further evidence of it, as are the fol-lowing passages:

... I cannot admit ... that verification by experiences and cogent demonstrations from incontrovertible premises are the only modes of attaining the kind and degree of certitude which we require for a 'working philosophy ...' This contention appears to me itself con-trary to experience: that is, to experience of the manner in which conviction has actually been reached in the progress of human knowledge. ... Consider examples of the intel-lectual process by which new convictions have actually been substituted for old ones in the progress of empirical sciences: it seems to me that such changes repeatedly take place not because new experiences, really crucial, have *proved* the new opinion right and the old one wrong: it is rather that the new opinion is seen to harmonise better with previously known facts, and with men's whole conception of the course of nature ...

In short, the more we examine the process of change in what is commonly accepted as knowledge, the more we find that the notion of 'verification by experience'—in the sense of 'verification by particular sense-perceptions'—is inadequate to explain or justify it. The criterion that we find really decisive, in case after case, is not any particular new sense-perception, or group of new sense-perceptions, but consistency with an elaborate and complex system of beliefs, in which the results of an indefinite number of perceptions and inferences are combined ... (*Mem.*, 606, 607; emphasis in original)

Now this systematizing and harmonizing role is just the role that Sidgwick conceives Utilitarianism to play with regard to our moral thought—our common moral judgments and reasonings that Sidgwick regards as the morality of com-

---

[21] 'On the Nature of the Evidence for Theism' (1898), in *Mem.*, 604.

[22] The very last sentence of *The Methods of Ethics* bears on this point: 'If ... we find that in our supposed knowledge of the world of nature propositions are commonly taken to be universally true, which yet seem to rest on no other grounds than that we have a strong disposition to accept them, and that they are *indispensable to the systematic coherence of our beliefs*,—it will be more difficult to reject a similarly supported assumption in ethics, without opening the door to universal scepti-cism' (7th edn., 509; emphasis added).

mon sense—and the main way in which he attempts to establish utilitarianism as an ethical theory, both in *The Methods of Ethics* and elsewhere. But *The Methods of Ethics*, though it is certainly a treatise in ethics, is not just about *ethics*. It is also about *method*, and hence about philosophy itself. This aspect of it has been neglected.

That this is the direction in which Sidgwick's thought was aiming is brought out in *Philosophy, its Scope and Relations*, a very readable work (and one obviously unread by those who regard Sidgwick's writing as stodgy). The book is based on a course of lectures Sidgwick gave starting in 1892; in it he says that his 'metaphysical standpoint' is

speaking broadly that of what has been called since Reid the Philosophy of Common Sense . . . there is this advantage in putting questions from the point of view of Common Sense: that it is, in some degree, in the minds of us all, even of the metaphysicians whose conclusions are most opposed to it . . . It is the view with which we all start when we begin to philosophize . . .

. . . [I]n speaking of Common Sense I do not mean entirely unscientific Common Sense, but the Common Sense of educated persons rectified by a general acquaintance with the results and methods of physical science. (*Phil.*, 42, 43)

On Sidgwick's view, the ultimate aim of philosophy is to coordinate theoretical and practical philosophy and to connect 'fact and ideal in some rational and satisfactory manner'. Accordingly, his aim is to systematize, coordinate, make consistent and coherent, clarify and make precise, the main data of the subject and bring it into line with a theory that would explain this data and in turn be supported and clarified by this process. This is the procedure he followed in his ethical theory and in his treatment of philosophy itself. In his view, philosophy 'uses primarily . . . the dialectical method, *i.e.*, the method of reflection on the thought which we all share, by the aid of the symbolism which we all share, language' (*Phil.*, 30, 49). This is the method of *The Methods of Ethics*, and is the method Sidgwick thinks is the most sensible and appropriate method of philosophy. Thus the *critical* appeal to, and defense of, common sense, through the *critical* medium of considering and analyzing ordinary language, with the emphasis here on 'critical'.

In his *Hundred Years of Philosophy*, John Passmore says that 'Sidgwick, an influential thinker, is best known for his work in moral and political philosophy'. There can be no argument with this. It is manifestly true. But in the one brief paragraph he devotes to Sidgwick, Passmore goes on to say: 'He wrote little on pure philosophy—and that little, included in the posthumous *Philosophy, Its Scope and Relations* . . . and *Lectures on the Philosophy of Kant and other Philosophical . . . Essays* . . . is not of the first importance.' Here I think Passmore is mistaken, though it may be that our different assessments are based on different criteria of importance. Passmore continues:

But two general features of his work are interesting: his lively criticism of 'historicism' and his defence of commonsense, which led him to stand out firmly against nineteenth-century Idealism. . . . The appeal to 'commonsense', indeed, came to be as noteworthy a feature of the Cambridge, as it had been of the Scottish, philosophers. (p. 197)

This last statement is also true. Passmore had stated in his preface that he was restricting himself to 'epistemology, logic and metaphysics'—which is what he takes to be 'pure philosophy'—and therefore he would deal not at all with ethics or social philosophy. Furthermore, his criterion for inclusion is: 'to what extent have the ideas of this writer entered into the public domain of philosophical discussion in England?' (p. 7). He adds that the space he has 'allocated to writers by no means corresponds to [his] own judgment of their individual merits', a rather disarming disclaimer. So there is no point in arguing with Passmore's assessment of the importance of Sidgwick's ideas on what Passmore calls 'pure philosophy'. Argument on this score, if appropriate at all, is best reserved for another context. It is true that Sidgwick's ideas on method, on truth, evidence, and belief did not 'enter into the public domain of philosophical discussion in England'. They affected it none the less, through his appeal to common sense and the attempt to both rely on and to analyze ordinary language, as is best seen in the influence of G. E. Moore. For the two works by Sidgwick that Passmore mentions make plain how Sidgwick was the forerunner if not the founder of twentieth-century analytical philosophy, and manifest in a pronounced way his attempt to analyze, comprehend, and clarify ordinary language—the language that all of us use in ordinary everyday life—as well as his reliance on critical common sense. Thus they illustrate and illuminate, along with *The Methods of Ethics*, his characteristic method of philosophical inquiry: his aim of attaining truth by working through opposing views, an aim that is explicit in the following passage from Sidgwick's *Lectures on the Ethics of Green, Spencer, and Martineau*:

. . . error in philosophy, or at least error that is or has been widely accepted, is never error pure and simple, but contains an element of the truth exaggerated and distorted by neglect of other elements; so that an examination of these one-sided and partial views is a fitting preparation for the completer and more balanced view which sums up the elements of truth contained in errors that are or have been current. (p. 316)

VII. A Negative Note

Does Sidgwick's work have defects? Well, every philosopher's work has. But one decidedly negative assessment should be got out of the way first. In his provocative *Short History of Ethics*, Alasdaire MacIntyre devotes no more space to Sidgwick than did Passmore, even though MacIntyre's book is not restricted to 'pure philosophy'. He describes Sidgwick as a touching figure whose defects are usually the defects of his age. . . . And in his moral philosophy he mirrors his age also. . . . Sidgwick's account of the methods of ethics misses questions beyond those which he explicitly discusses [which sounds suspiciously like a tautology—MGS]. The background to his account is the moral consciousness of his day, taken as given. Philosophy appears as essentially a clarifying rather than a critical activity. In this respect Sidgwick's is a ghost that haunts much recent writing.[23]

This last statement sounds portentous, the trumpet call of a would-be revolutionary. But the whole paragraph is an attempt to debunk on the part of someone with a radically different point of view. It is true that Sidgwick's moral and political outlook was on a number of matters conservative—certainly as compared with Bentham and Mill, for he was certainly no radical reformer[24]—and that in his philosophy, especially his philosophy as presented in *The Methods*, he was more concerned with clarification than with criticism of the moral standards of his society. But this account mysteriously ignores Sidgwick's pioneering work in helping found Newnham College and in advancing the education of women, and later in advocating female suffrage—hardly conservative opinions at the time. It also overlooks Sidgwick's key role in developing a philosophical school at Cambridge against conservative opposition. His resigning his fellowship on conscientious grounds was also not conservative, even though one looking back over a century later can fail to appreciate—and therefore feel free to poke fun at— the problem then facing him. Finally, as a philosophical assessment of Sidgwick's work this account has been pretty well itself refuted by the work of, among others, Rawls and Schneewind.

As an assessment of Sidgwick's overall moral acuity, however, it may in a way—a rather perverse way—have hit a target, even if only a glancing blow. For Sidgwick does express some curious views, some of them with the weight of theory behind them, some of them not.

Once Sidgwick had come to accept hedonistic utilitarianism, albeit on an intuitionistic basis, as the best and most satisfactory method and principle of ethics,

[23] Alasdaire MacIntyre, *A Short History of Ethics*, 243–4. In his preface MacIntyre says: 'No one could write in English on the history of moral philosophy and not feel awed by the example of Henry Sidgwick's *Outlines of the History of Ethics* . . . The perspective of my book is necessarily very different from that of Sidgwick, but the experience has increased my admiration for him' (p. vii). This is curious. For it should have been evident that Sidgwick's *History* could only have been written by a philosopher of exceptional insight as well as great historical knowledge. Perhaps MacIntyre overlooked Sidgwick's statement in a letter of 1866: 'I hate the history of philosophy even more than any other history; it is so hard to know what any particular man thought, and so worthless when you do know it' (*Mem.*, 140). But when this was written Sidgwick was only 27, and several years away from writing the *Methods* and his *History* (1878 for the *Encyclopedia Britannica* article, revised and published as the book in 1886). It is manifest from any reading of the *History* that in it Sidgwick was not merely doing history, but was writing philosophy—as was MacIntyre in his *History*.

[24] Notice Sidgwick's rather acid comment on Bentham's view of the morality of common sense in Ch. 1, p. 8: '. . . the Utilitarianism of Bentham is too purely destructive, and treats the morality of Common Sense with needless acrimony and contempt.'

he went along, I think uncritically, with the maximizing propensity embedded by it. There is, for instance, the matter of population. Sidgwick holds that, 'supposing the average happiness enjoyed remains undiminished . . . utilitarianism directs us to make the number of people enjoying it as great as possible . . .'. However, 'if we foresee . . . that an increase in numbers will be accompanied by a decrease in average happiness or *vice versa*', a problem arises that Sidgwick was acute enough to see. His solution is that:

. . . strictly conceived, the point up to which, on Utilitarian principles, population ought to be encouraged to increase, is not that at which average happiness is the greatest possible —as appears often to be assumed by political economists of the school of Malthus—but that at which the product formed by multiplying the number of persons living into the amount of average happiness reaches its maximum. (*ME*, 415–16)[25]

Now Sidgwick is aware of what he calls the 'grotesque . . . show of exactness' exhibited by such reasoning. That is not the main problem. The main problem is that Sidgwick rejects out of hand, without argument, the average happiness criterion in favor of the total happiness criterion, and never even questions the appropriateness of either criterion. And Sidgwick is not simply reporting on what the utilitarian view is, he is actually supporting this view, and never asks whether the point made is a point in its favor or against it. But this implication of the 'strictly conceived' utilitarian principle is surely paradoxical, even on Sidgwick's own conception of paradox. On Sidgwick's conception, moral paradox is whatever is contrary to common-sense morality. Thus: 'Attempts at . . . confutation . . . can only take one of two forms: (1) demonstration of inconsistency in the system assailed, and (2) demonstration of paradox—i.e., of conflict with the common sense of mankind.'[26] And if this conflict does not prove the principle so understood wrong, it surely indicates the need for some re-examination, some defense of the adoption of the 'greatest total' criterion. Otherwise the adoption is arbitrary, and this in turn is contrary to reason. But Sidgwick never provides this defense.

For reasons similar to those on which he commits himself to population increase in pursuit of a statistic, Sidgwick maintains that 'a universal refusal to propagate the human species would be the greatest of conceivable crimes from a Utilitarian point of view' (*ME*, 487). But this immediately raises a question about the reasonableness of the 'Utilitarian point of view', a question Sidgwick neglects to deal with. Again, Sidgwick maintained that it is the 'legitimate business on utilitarian principles' of civilized nations 'to civilize the world', even where this requires them to 'commit acts which cannot but be regarded as aggressive by the

---

[25] Cf. *inf.*, Ch. 1, p. 7, where Sidgwick makes the same point in only slightly different words.
[26] 'Some Fundamental Ethical Controversies' (1889), 473; in this vol., Ch. 6: 35 ff.

savage nations whom *it is their business to educate and absorb'*.[27] Even though the hindsight of a hundred years later, after two world wars, worldwide revolutions against exploitation and imperialism, mass starvation, terrorism, torture, and brutal slaughter on an unprecedented scale, can enable us to see the unwisdom of these ideas to a greater extent than was available to Sidgwick in his period of history, it is not outrageously contrary to common sense to suggest that even in his time the objectives he proclaimed were not sustained by common sense (though they might have been sustained by public opinion), but were rather the conclusions drawn from his utilitarianism, with its maximizing ideology. And it seems evident that, for all his caution and circumspection, Sidgwick, normally so close to common sense, on such occasions and on such matters permitted his common sense to be overcome by his maximizing philosophy.

And he did know better, as is brought out by this passage from *Philosophy, its Scope and Relations*:

I think no study of historical morality can leave unimpaired the influence of mere custom and opinion on the unreflective individual, or of the blind emotional impulse normally connected with custom and tradition. That anything is right, *because* an overwhelming majority of human beings think so and act accordingly, becomes a manifestly untenable inference, when we contemplate the monstrous beliefs as to right and wrong which this overwhelming majority has entertained and acted on in previous ages. (*Phil.*, 167–8; emphasis in original)

And to complete the equation, we must contemplate the same thing—'the monstrous beliefs as to right and wrong which the overwhelming majority has entertained and acted on'—in our own age, as well as in Sidgwick's.

To be sure, what is contrary to common sense at one period may not be contrary to common sense at another. And there is certainly danger in evaluating the standards of an earlier time on the basis of the standards of one's own. Many institutions and kinds of actions now approved of may come to be disapproved of in a later age, when there is more information and, perhaps, also a change of view. But many of the monstrosities of colonialism—such as exploitation, oppression, racism, and slavery—are wrong in themselves, and this assessment is not subject to the shifting winds of doctrine.

VIII. Finale

In what turned out to be his last public appearance, Sidgwick went to Oxford to deliver a paper on the philosophy of T. H. Green, the burden of which was that

[27] *Ethics of Green, Spencer, and Martineau*, 236, emphasis added. Cf. a letter of 1861: 'I believe in "Be fruitful and multiply." I think the most crying need right now is a better organised colonisation. To think of the latent world-civilization in our swarm of fertile Anglo-Saxon pauperism' (*Mem.*, 66). Of course he was very young then. But he wasn't later.

there was a fundamental inconsistency in Green's thinking. Sidgwick's paper opens this way:

It is said that an undergraduate once, being asked in examination to describe the economic conditions of the inhabitants of the Hebrides, stated that they 'earn a precarious livelihood by washing one another's clothes.' It has often seemed to me that . . . the phrase would aptly describe a considerable part of the industry of modern metaphysicians . . .[28]

This is pretty good, and might even still apply. At the end of the discussion

. . . a prominent Hegelian made the . . . suggestion that such fundamental incoherence merely indicated that the region of the ultimate difficulties of thought had been reached, and inferred that both sides of the contradiction should be sustained . . . After replying to the other criticisms, [Sidgwick] went on to say that 'as for the remarks of the last speaker, he had never been able to make out from the school to which he evidently belonged how they managed to distinguish the contradictions which they took to be evidence of error from those which they regarded as intimations of higher truth' (*Mem.*, 586 n.)

This is even better, and it has some interesting philosophical implications. Are there inconsistencies that are evidence of some higher truth? Certainly there have been some that have led to strikingly new and important ideas.[29]

---

[28] 'The Philosophy of T. H. Green', *Mind*, 10 (1901), 18.

[29] In preparing this introduction I have drawn freely from the following previously published writings: 'The Many Methods of Sidgwick's Ethics' (1974); 'Schneewind's Sidgwick' (1982); 'Common Sense and Paradox in Sidgwick's Ethics', 1986; and the article 'Henry Sidgwick' (1992). For it soon became apparent that trying to say something other than what I had said before, or to say what I had said before in different words, was too strained and artificial. And, although some learned disquisition to the contrary could undoubtedly be mounted, it is really not possible to plagiarize from oneself.

A Note on the Contents

Sidgwick's *Methods of Ethics* is, as works of Sidgwick's go, comparatively well known. Certainly it is Sidgwick's most widely read and most frequently commented-on work. But his occasional essays are for the most part not known to those who would be interested in them, and a number of them are important for bringing out the background of *The Methods of Ethics* and the ideas that went into its making. Hence the object of this volume: to make available to students, teachers, scholars, and other interested readers essays of Sidgwick's not easily available, to supplement *The Methods of Ethics*, and to bring out how Sidgwick thought about related and distinctly relevant matters not covered in *The Methods of Ethics*. The book has been organized on the theory that interested readers of Sidgwick's *Methods of Ethics* would profit from having available Sidgwick's essays on other subjects, some not directly connected with ethics, which illuminate other aspects of his philosophy. Thus there are papers included here in which Sidgwick responds to criticisms of *The Methods*, others in which he criticizes the works of others. And there are others that illuminate other aspects of his philosophy, his epistemological views, his interest in philosophical method, in verification and proof, and in the idea of method itself.

Part I contains Sidgwick's essays on some fundamental questions of ethical theory. 'Utilitarianism', from 1873, previously unpublished, contains a brief account of Sidgwick's understanding of Utilitarianism: his utilitarian theory in outline, shorn of the complications in which it is embedded in *The Methods*. 'The Theory of Evolution in its Application to Practice' is Sidgwick's attempt to deal with the ethical implications of the theory of evolution. Darwin's *Origin of Species* had been published in 1859 and Sidgwick was certainly aware of it, but he had been criticized for not having taken explicit account of it. This essay is Sidgwick's response to such criticisms. (It was responded to in a succeeding issue of *Mind* by Frederick Pollock, who later acquired fame as the co-author, with Frederic Maitland, of the great *History of English Law* and for his massive and fascinating correspondence with Justice Oliver Wendell Holmes.)[1] In the preface to the second edition of *The Methods* Sidgwick says that he had 'been led, through study of the theory of evolution . . . to attach somewhat more importance to this theory than [he] had previously done'. 'Calderwood on Intuitionism in Morals' and 'Barratt on "The Suppression of Egoism" ' are responses to specific criticisms. Sidgwick said:

---

[1] *The History of English Law*, by Pollock and Maitland; *Holmes–Pollock Letters*; ed. Howe. Pollock, who was a man of parts, also wrote a well-regarded study of Spinoza: *Spinoza: His Life and Philosophy*.

I find that more than one critic has overlooked or disregarded the account of the plan of my treatise, given in the original preface and in sec. 5 of the introductory chapter: and has consequently supposed me to be writing as an assailant of two of the methods which I chiefly examine, and a defender of the third. Thus one of my reviewers seems to regard Book iii (on Intuitionism) as containing mere hostile criticism from the outside: another has constructed an article on the supposition that my principal object is the 'suppression of Egoism' . . . (*ME*, p. x)

Apart from the piece on evolution, two of the most substantial essays in Part I are 'The Establishment of Ethical First Principles'—a topic on which he had said relatively little in the *Methods*—and 'Some Fundamental Ethical Controversies', from 1889. This is actually Sidgwick's own commentary on the *Methods of Ethics*, and as such it is of fundamental importance. In it Sidgwick attempted to meet some objections and clarify some points on which there had been some misunderstanding. It appeared in the period in which revisions for the fourth edition were going forward and elicited two responses in the next number of *Mind*, by T. Fowler and L. A. Selby-Bigge. The essay on the relation of ethics to sociology gives us Sidgwick's view, in more compressed and specific form, on how ethical theory, a normative study, differs from sociological studies, which are meant to be descriptive. In this period sociology had not yet established itself as a separate study, was then considered part of philosophy, and Sidgwick himself had previously written on it. And it nicely supplements the view, expressed in Chapter 8, on the distinction between 'is' and 'ought' that Sidgwick had been maintaining for some considerable time. 'Law and Morality' is a chapter from *The Elements of Politics*, in which Sidgwick explains his conception of positive morality—the accepted morality of society—and how it relates to positive law; even though he had discussed positive morality in *The Methods*, he had not there defined it in this way or in this context.

As mentioned in the Introduction, Sidgwick did not himself distinguish between moral theory and value theory, and one could easily regard Part II of this book as Section 2 of Part I, for the two parts are closely connected. 'Pleasure and Desire', 1872, had been largely incorporated by Sidgwick in the first edition of *The Methods* (as ch. iv of Book I), and as Sidgwick explains in the preface to the second edition, in the light of criticism was considerably revised for its appearance in later editions. Here is the original article, pre-*Methods* and pre-criticism. Chapters 11 and 12 are further discussions of the value and psychological questions Sidgwick felt obliged to deal with, given his adherence to hedonism and the importance of desire in his moral theory, and which also very much interested him. Sidgwick was stimulated to write the latter essay, 'The Feeling-Tone of Desire and Aversion', by a paper by H. R. Marshall in a previous issue of *Mind*, and it is a rather acute piece of psychological analysis. The essay on 'Unreasonable Action' was reprinted by Sidgwick in his *Practical Ethics*; it is, however, such a penetrating analysis of what is involved in unreasonable action, in acting contrary to reason, that it was judged essential to include it herein, for it is a prime example of Sidgwick's great skill in analysis. It is a classic philosophical paper, relates as much to theoretical as to practical ethics, and is on a topic of perennial importance.

Sidgwick's *Practical Ethics*, recently reprinted and currently available again, brings out Sidgwick's great interest, now little known, in issues of practical ethics and casuistry—unusual for a utilitarian, especially one of the nineteenth century. It also brings out the distinctive Sidgwickian way of dealing with questions of practical or applied ethics, not determinable from the *Methods*. Sidgwick was early on involved in the Ethical Culture Movement, founded by Felix Adler, was a 'Leader' of an ethical culture group in Cambridge, and this interest is manifested in his *Practical Ethics*. Because the book is now available again the only essay from it used here is 'Unreasonable Action'. (For some discussions of Sidgwick's *Practical Ethics*, see the Pritchard entry in the Bibliographical Notes at the end of the book.)

Part III, on method—in particular, on evidence, truth, and belief—contains five of Sidgwick's essays on epistemological questions: his theory of knowledge in brief form. 'Verification of Beliefs' is another pre-*Methods* essay, which provides insight into how Sidgwick dealt with the general question of how to verify beliefs, both factual and normative. (The previous year, 1870, Sidgwick had presented a very similar paper, entitled 'The Verification of Beliefs', to the Metaphysical Society; privately printed, this was never published, and although there is considerable overlap between the two papers, there are some different points made. After some deliberation on the matter, it was decided to reprint here the previously published paper, Chapter 14 herein, on the ground that it contains Sidgwick's more developed view on the subject, resulting from, no doubt, the previous year's discussion at the Metaphysical Society.) Chapter 15, 'Incoherence of Empirical Philosophy', brings out further how Sidgwick was not an empiricist in the sense in which he understood 'empirical philosophy', that is, as the basic philosophical presupposition running through the philosophies of Locke, Berkeley, Hume, and Mill, the four great British empiricists, and which was dominant in British philosophy at the time (and also much later). Sidgwick, although he 'admits the force of the general presumption in favour of Empiricism', none the less raises questions about 'the cardinal doctrine of Empiricism—that all trustworthy cognitions are either mediately or immediately empirical'. Therefore this paper also is about method. And, given Sidgwick's pointed criticism of empiricism, the claim—often made—that he was a disciple of John Stuart Mill would seem to be in need of some more specific defense. 'The Philosophy of Common Sense', although explicitly about Thomas Reid, also presents Sidgwick's own philosophy of common sense, and is consequently not primarily a commentary on someone else's ideas. And this paper, or the ideas expressed in it, though rarely if ever explicitly noticed in later discussions, none the less had a profound influence on what in the early twentieth century came to be referred to as 'the Cambridge School of Philosophy'. The papers on the 'Criteria of Truth and Error' belong together, the second being originally an appendix to the first, since Sidgwick did not live to write the paper succeeding Chapter 17 that he had planned to write. They also illustrate Sidgwick's moderate and carefully reasoned approach to problems of truth and falsehood, and link to the pre-*Methods* paper on the 'Verification of Beliefs'.

Part IV contains discussions Sidgwick wrote of other works on ethical theory and some extended comments on other theories, especially those of T. H. Green, Herbert Spencer, and James Martineau—the main alternatives to utilitarianism at the time, as Sidgwick saw the matter, apart from Whewellian Intuitionism. (Although Sidgwick wrote a number of essays on Kant's Critical Philosophy, Kant's metaphysics and epistemology, and even his philosophy of mathematics, he wrote hardly anything—and nothing specifically—on Kant's ethics, and his failure to come to terms adequately with Kant's ethics may be the most difficult thing to understand about his approach to ethics and the most serious deficiency in it.)[2] This Part also contains three pre-*Methods* pieces. John Grote, an earlier holder of the Knightbridge Chair and one of Sidgwick's teachers at Cambridge, wrote mainly to clarify his own mind, was not interested in publication. Hence his most significant works were unfinished, and were finished and brought to publication by J. B. Mayor, one of several who thought them too important to allow them to remain dormant. Both of Sidgwick's reviews of John Grote's posthumous *Examination of the Utilitarian Philosophy* are included herein. That both are included calls for some explanation: there is, admittedly, some repetition, but the amount is slight, and Sidgwick managed to say different things in each; this may illustrate, among other things, Sidgwick's capacity to write differently for different audiences. Another point of interest is that they contain some of Sidgwick's most pointed criticisms of John Stuart Mill's Utilitarian theory. James Fitzjames Stephen, older brother of Leslie Stephen, attempted to demolish John Stuart Mill's Essay *On Liberty*; in *Liberty, Equality, Fraternity* he made it manifest that he was opposed to all three. Sidgwick's review was not one that Fitzjames Stephen thought worthy of notice in the second edition of his book, though that should not stop us from noticing it. But it is of interest for what it shows us of Sidgwick's acute though respectful controversial style, and also for what it tells us about Sidgwick's views on Mill's arguments on liberty.

Perhaps the most intriguing controversy of Sidgwick's philosophical life was generated by his review of F. H. Bradley's *Ethical Studies* of 1876. The ensuing exchange between Bradley and Sidgwick is certainly worth reviving. Bradley was a keen controversialist and dialectician, and an unrivalled stylist, and he

---

[2] Sidgwick published the following essays on Kant's philosophy: 'The So-Called Idealism of Kant', 1879; 'Kant's Refutation of Idealism', 1880; 'A Criticism on the Critical Philosophy', parts I and II, 1883; 'Kant's View of Mathematical Premises and Reasonings', parts I and II, 1883. Note: nothing on Kant's ethics, except for what is in the *History* (pp. 271–7) and *The Methods*.

and Sidgwick had almost totally opposite views on just about every question of philosophy, actual and imaginable. The reader who wants to learn more is invited to learn about Bradley's *Ethical Studies* at first hand (the best way is by reading it) and also to examine Bradley's pamphlet of 1877, 'Mr. Sidgwick's Hedonism'. Sidgwick took notice of this pamphlet in the preface to the second edition of *The Methods*: 'a third [critic] has gone to the length of a pamphlet under the impression (apparently) that the "main argument" of my treatise is a demonstration of Universalistic Hedonism. I am concerned to have caused such misdirection of criticism: and I have carefully altered in this edition the passages which I perceive to have contributed to it.' The passages that Bradley took such vehement exception to do not appear in the second or later editions. Although no longer strictly applicable, Bradley's critique is still of interest. In the meantime Chapters 22 and 23 are here to whet the reader's interest. In his short (posthumous) book on Sidgwick (1970) Gwilym James said 'Bradley trained on Sidgwick's book in a footnote to an essay in *Ethical Studies* a brilliant burst of machine gun fire; and then, in a brochure he put out in 1877 on the subject of *The Methods of Ethics* he brought up his full armoury and blew Sidgwick's position, as I venture to think, to pieces' (p. 33). I quote this with no further comment here. (My comment on it, though not especially reserved, is none the less reserved for the Bibliographical Notes, Sect. IV.)

Sidgwick's long article on Bentham and Benthamism gives us Sidgwick's considered opinion of the founder of classical utilitarianism, and is an essay in which he took special pains with his style. The remaining pieces in Part IV are all reviews, critical notices, or extended discussions of books and theories that excited interest at the time. Herbert Spencer—one of the most renowned thinkers of the period, a great advocate of evolution, who had immense influence on, for example, American industrialists of the Gilded Age, though he is hardly read or even noticed today—developed an influential ethical theory over a long stretch of time, with some changes in the interval. Consequently the reader is here treated to two of Sidgwick's discussions of Spencer. And Thomas Fowler's *Progressive Morality*, though practically unknown today, has some features that are worth knowing. Leslie Stephen, a prolific writer on English philosophy and English Utilitarianism,[3] also believed strongly in the importance of evolution for ethics, which he details in his nicely written but rather loosely reasoned *Science of Ethics*. James Martineau is another writer of the time who is hardly known today, and is even less read, but Sidgwick thought it important to lecture on Martineau's *Types of Ethical Theory* (in the posthumously published *Lectures on the Ethics of Green, Spencer, and Martineau*) and to discuss it in *The Methods*. Of the several pieces

---

[3] Author, among other works, of *History of English Thought in the Eighteenth Century*, and *The English Utilitarians*. Stephen was the founding editor of the *Dictionary of National Biography* (DNB); after Sidgwick's death he wrote the *DNB* article on Sidgwick. For more on Stephen, see Annan's *Leslie Stephen* and other works listed below.

Sidgwick wrote on Martineau's book—they had some interchanges on the matter—'Idiopsychological Ethics' best represents Sidgwick's view of it.

In her preface to Sidgwick's *Lectures on the Ethics of Green, Spencer, and Martineau*, E. E. Constance Jones said:

Readers of *The Methods of Ethics* have sometimes complained that it does not contain a more detailed consideration of Green's ethical theory. Green's *Prolegomena to Ethics* did not appear until after the publication of the early editions of Professor Sidgwick's book. The same is true of Mr. Herbert Spencer's *Principles of Ethics*, and of Dr. Martineau's *Types of Ethical Theory*, which latter is probably the most influential recent work on Ethics from an entirely 'intuitional' standpoint. The following lectures are thus to some extent supplementary to *The Methods of Ethics*. (p. vi)

And Sidgwick himself provided, later on in the book, further explanation along the same lines when he said:

. . . one understands more thoroughly what a man thinks and why he thinks it, when one understands clearly why he rejects the various opposed views which other minds have found acceptable . . . [My] present course of Lectures is framed on substantially the same principle: it appeared to me that having expounded my own system in my book, what I could further do in the way of making it clear would be best done in the form of criticism on the views of others. (*GSM*, 315)[4]

Sidgwick had close connections with the editor of *Mind*—indeed, he was one of the main guarantors of the Mind Association—and may very well have had first choice in reviewing books in the areas of his interest. The ones reviewed here are some of the ones he chose to notice, and constitute the main rivals to Sidgwick's own Intuitionistic and Hedonistic Utilitarianism and his view of how ethics should be studied. As such, the essays in Part IV help provide anyone interested in Sidgwick's major work with a rounded view of the whole of his moral philosophy.

These considerations should make it plain why this collection constitutes a valuable adjunct to Sidgwick's monumental *Methods of Ethics*, and the essays contained herein should also be of interest on their own account. My own understanding of *The Methods*, as well as of ethics, over the years was considerably enhanced by reading these essays. And I also acquired a much greater appreciation of Sidgwick as a person, a thinker, and, yes, a writer.

On 3 March 1901, William James wrote from Rome to his friend James Sully: 'Yes! H. Sidgwick is a sad loss, with all his remaining philosophic wisdom unwritten.'[5] This work contains some of Sidgwick's previously written philosophic wisdom with which William James might not have been familiar.

---

[4] I have argued elsewhere that Sidgwick, all things considered, failed to appreciate the force of Bradley's and Green's criticisms of 'greatest happiness' as 'ultimate end' and of the very conception of 'a greatest possible sum of pleasure' (*Nous*, 1982: 347–9). (Geoffrey Thomas, in *The Moral Philosophy of T. H. Green*, expresses a concurring view.)

[5] *The Letters of William James*, ii: 141.

A Note on Grote

The extent of the influence of John Grote on Sidgwick is something on which we can only speculate. Grote is a figure much ignored today. W. R. Sorley says of him:

Grote thought and wrote simply to get at the truth of things and without any view of impressing the public. A 'belief in thought' upheld him: 'a feeling that things were worth thinking about, that thought was worth effort.' He did not seek reputation as a philosophical writer, and he has not gained it. His direct influence has been restricted to a limited number of other thinkers, through whom it has passed to wider circles without any definite trace of its origin. (*History of English Philosophy*, 264)

And Passmore says:

Grote's philosophy is in manner an early, perhaps the first, example of that Cambridge spirit . . . which was to reach its culmination in the work of G. E. Moore. His conversational, informal, italicised style, his acute, particularised, but not scholarly criticisms, his preference for 'the language of ordinary men' as distinct from 'the language of philosophers', are all prophetic of Moore. (*A Hundred Years of Philosophy*, 52–3 n).

It is interesting—perhaps quite in character—that Passmore goes directly from Grote to Moore, ignores Sidgwick entirely, even though it is apparent that Sidgwick is the intermediate figure—student of Grote, teacher of Moore.

Moore said (in his *Autobiography* in the Moore Schilpp volume, p. 16), that of the five people he studied philosophy with he

gained least from personal contact with Sidgwick. His personality did not attract me, and I found his lectures rather dull. [These were the lectures on the ethics of Green, Spencer, and Martineau; it is interesting, though not altogether surprising, that in her preface to GSM Constance Jones reports that 'Professor Sidgwick's students listened to (these lectures) with delight' (p. vii). Obviously, there was at least one exception to this claim.] From his published works, especially, of course, his *Methods of Ethics*, I have gained a great deal, and his clarity and his belief in Common Sense were very sympathetic to me . . .

Schneewind informs us that

We do not know much about what Sidgwick thought of Moore, but in a letter of 1900 he comments on a report that Moore has brought out a book: 'Moore! I did not know he had published any *Elements of Ethics*. I have no doubt they will be acute. So far as I have seen his work, his *acumen*—which is remarkable in degree—is in excess of his *insight*.' (*Sidgwick's Ethics*, 16–17)[1]

---

[1] Moore did not himself publish 'any *Elements of Ethics*', a book based on a series of lectures Moore gave in 1898 at the London School of Ethics and Political Philosophy, even though in 1902 the work

There is further information on Grote in Schneewind's article on Grote in the Edwards *Encyclopedia* (1967); in Schneewind's *Sidgwick's Ethics* (esp. pp. 117–21, 181–6); and in his 'Sidgwick and the Cambridge Moralists', in Schultz's *Essays on Sidgwick* (pp. 93–121).[2] Also of interest is John R. Gibbins, 'John Grote and Modern Cambridge Philosophy' (*Philosophy* (1998), 453–77); unfortunately not very well-written, it is none the less informative on a little-known yet influential figure, who is of interest in his own right, and on the background of analytical philosophy at Cambridge, and therefore on the background of analytical philosophy in the twentieth century.

was accepted for publication by the Cambridge University Press. Sidgwick was reacting to a rumor then going around that 'they had *already* been published' (Regan, cited *inf.*, p. xxv). However, they have since been edited and published by Tom Regan, who has an illuminating introduction (pp. xiii–xxxviii) on the history of the lectures and the work: G. E. Moore, *Elements of Ethics* (1991). Professor Regan has also edited and brought to publication a useful companion work, G. E. Moore, *The Early Essays* (1986), which brings out that 'the early Moore', as Regan so aptly refers to him, was a speculative metaphysician, a philosophical idealist, and follower of Bradley and Kant. The early Moore was the only Moore Sidgwick knew. And Sidgwick's 'clarity and belief in Common Sense were [only] sympathetic' to the later Moore.

[2] In the bibliography to his *Sidgwick's Ethics*, on pp. 451 and 456, Schneewind lists two works on Grote, a book by Lauchlin D. MacDonald (1966) and an article by Charles E. Whitmore (*Philosophical Review*, 1927). I have not examined these.

Part I

�֎

Ethics

1. Utilitarianism

In writing the present paper, it has been my object to avoid all but incontrovertible propositions. I have, therefore, left on one side many interesting questions; and have been careful not to dogmatise upon any point where scientific certainty did not appear to be attainable. If it be thought strange to offer to a society that exists for purposes of debate, a series of incontrovertible propositions, I would urge, first, that in most discussions on Utilitarianism I find one or more of these propositions, at important points of the argument, implicitly ignored; and secondly, that a wide experience shows that an ethical or metaphysical proposition is not the less likely to provoke controversy because it is put forth as incontrovertible.

By Utilitarianism I mean the ethical theory that the externally or objectively right conduct, under any circumstances, is such conduct as tends to produce the greatest possible happiness, to the greatest possible number of all whose interests are affected.

The statement is not yet quite definite, but whatever vagueness attaches to it will (I hope) be removed in the course of my observations.

And first, let us distinguish this doctrine from others of a quite different nature to which the term 'Utilitarian' has been applied, but with which Utilitarianism, as above defined, has no necessary connection, though with some of them it has a certain natural affinity.

I. Utilitarianism, according to the definition, is an ethical, and not a psychological doctrine: a theory not of what is, but of what ought to be. Therefore, more particularly, it does not include the following psychological theories:—(1) the proposition that in human action, universally or normally, each agent seeks his own individual happiness or pleasure. This is obviously compatible with any theory of ethics, *i.e.*, of right and wrong in outward conduct. For, as Aristotle says, our idea of a virtuous man includes the characteristic that he takes pleasure in doing what he thinks he ought to do; and the question whether we are to say that he does his duty because he recognises it as duty, or because he finds a moral pleasure in doing it, whatever importance it may have from some points of view, has at least no necessary connection with the question what conduct he ought to

[This paper, not previously published, was privately printed for discussion at a meeting of the Metaphysical Society held on Tuesday, 16 December 1873, at the Grosvenor Hotel, at 8.30 p.m. This was one year prior to the publication of *The Methods of Ethics*, and is the first account Sidgwick gave of the views and strategy to be presented in book iv of that work. Ed.]

pursue. It may be said that from the psychological generalisation that all men do seek pleasure there is a natural transition to the ethical principle that pleasure is what they ought to seek. But, in the first place, this transition is at best only natural, and not logical or necessary; and secondly, the ethical conclusion to which we thus pass is primarily that of Egoism or Egoistic Hedonism (which states the agent's *own* happiness as the ultimate end of his actions), and not of Utilitarianism, as I have defined it. Clearly, from the fact that every one actually does seek his own happiness, we cannot conclude, as an immediate and obvious inference, that he ought to seek the happiness of other people.

Nor (2) is Utilitarianism, as a theory of ethics proper, connected with the doctrine (belonging to what may be called ethical psychology), that the moral sentiments are derived from experiences of non-moral pleasures and pains.

For (a) these moral sentiments are now (considered as facts of our present consciousness), independent impulses, often conflicting with the more primary impulses from which they are thought to be derived, and having each its own proper pleasure and pain consequent on its being followed or resisted. And it seems quite arbitrary (and indeed opposed to our general notions of progress and development) to assume that impulses earlier in the growth of the individual or of the race ought always, in case of conflict, to prevail over those that have emerged at a later period; especially as the former* are commonly thought to be lower and coarser. In a similar way, the pleasures of the Fine Arts seem to be derivative from, and a kind of complex reflection of, more primitive sensations and emotions; but that is not thought a reason why a cultivated person should now prefer the latter to the former.

And (b) it must be observed, on the other side, that however true this account of our moral sentiments may be, the conduct to which they impel us is none the less liable to conflict with the dictates of Rational Utilitarianism. For these sentiments will have been derived, on this theory, from a very partial experience of the effects of conduct, apprehended and interpreted by very imperfect sympathy and intelligence.

Indeed (3), even if we hold with Hume that our present moral likings always attach to conduct that gives non-moral pleasure, directly or indirectly, to ourselves or to others, and our moral aversions to the reverse, the question still remains undetermined whether we ought simply to yield to these sentiments, or to replace or control them by Bentham's calculus of consequences. Nay, further, the mere recognition and explanation of these sentiments, as facts of consciousness, does not necessarily affirm the ultimate and supreme authority either of the sentiments themselves or of Rational Utilitarianism (as above defined). For it may be held that these, along with other impulses, are properly under the dominion

---

* [The original text has 'the latter', clearly an error; 'the former' is almost certainly what is meant. Ed.]

of Rational Self-love; and that it is really only reasonable to gratify them, in so far as we expect to find our own private happiness in such gratification.

II. It may seem superfluous to state that Utilitarianism (in my sense) or Universalistic Hedonism, as it might be called, is not to be confounded with the Egoistic Hedonism to which I have just referred. In fact the two principles are *primâ facie* incompatible, as a regard for the interests of society at large frequently imposes on the individual the (at least apparent) sacrifice of his own interests.

III. I understand Utilitarianism to supply a principle and method for determining the objective or material rightness of conduct. The distinction and occasional separation between this and subjective or formal rightness, rightness of intention; and the question which of the two is intrinsically better and more valuable; need not be taken as decided by Utilitarianism. The two kinds of rightness cannot present themselves to anyone as competing alternatives, in the case of his own future conduct. No doubt they may so present themselves in our dealings with others; for the question may then arise whether and how far we ought to induce others, by non-moral motives such as the fear of punishment, to do what we think right contrary to their consciences. But this question seems to present equal difficulties, whatever theory of ethics we adopt.

Let us now examine the principle itself somewhat closer. It propounds as ultimate end and standard of right conduct 'the greatest happiness of all concerned', or (as the interests of some of the persons concerned must sometimes be sacrificed to the interests of the remainder) 'the greatest possible happiness' of 'the greatest possible number'. Now each of these notions requires somewhat more determination and explanation to make it quite clear. In the first place, 'happiness' must be understood as equivalent to 'pleasure'. It has, I think, been always so understood in recent times, both by Utilitarians and their opponents; though in the ethical controversies of Greece very different views were held as to the relation of the corresponding notions *eudaimonia* and *hēdonē*. And even at the present day, many persons declare that 'happiness' is something quite different from 'pleasure'. But such persons seem to use the term 'pleasure' in a narrower sense than Utilitarians, who include under it all satisfactions and enjoyments, from the highest to the lowest, all kinds of feeling or consciousness which move the will to maintain them when present, and to produce them when absent. So understood, Pleasure cannot be distinguished from Happiness, except that Happiness is rather used to denote a sum or series of those transitory feelings each of which we call a Pleasure. The Utilitarian, then, aims at making the sum of preferable or desirable feelings in the world, so far as it depends on his actions, as great as possible. But here another qualification is required. For much of our conduct inevitably produces pain as well as pleasure to ourselves or to others; and a recognition of the undesirability of pain, seems an inseparable concomitant and counterpart of that recognition of the desirability of pleasure on which Utilitarianism is based. And in fact, Utilitarians have always treated pain as the negative quantity of pleasure. So that, strictly speaking, Utilitarian right conduct is that which produces not the greatest amount of pleasure on the whole, but the greatest surplus of pleasure over pain, the pain being conceived as balanced against an equal amount of pleasure, so that the two mutually annihilate each other for purpose of ethical calculation.

There is therefore an assumption involved in the very notion of Maximum Happiness, the magnitude and importance of which have somewhat escaped notice. It is assumed that all pleasures are capable of being compared quantitatively with each other and with all pains,—that every kind of feeling has a certain intensive quantity, positive or negative (or perhaps zero), in respect of preferableness or desirableness, and that this quantity can be known; so that each can be weighed in ideal scales against every other. Unless this be assumed, the notion of Maximum Happiness is logically impossible; the attempt to make 'as great as possible' a sum of elements not quantitatively commensurable, is as much a mathematical absurdity as an attempt to subtract three ounces of cheese from four pounds of butter. It does not come within my plan to discuss whether this assumption be justifiable or not, but I wish to point out that it is at any rate not verifiable by experience, and that very plausible objections may be brought against it on empirical grounds. For though, no doubt, we all of us are continually comparing pleasures and pronouncing one preferable to another, we are all aware that in different moods we perform the same comparison with different results; sometimes we are more susceptible of enjoyment from one source, and sometimes from another; and similarly, in respect of our sensitiveness to pains. How, then, can we be sure that we are ever in a perfectly neutral mood, in which all pleasures are represented according to their true hedonistic value? How can we tell that such a mood is actually possible, and not a philosophical chimaera? And the difficulty is increased when we take into account the different preferences of different persons. How, e.g., can we decide scientifically the old controversy between intellectual and sensual pleasures? When Plato and Mill tell us that we must trust the decision of the intellectual man, because he has tried both, the argument is obviously inadequate, for we can never tell that he is capable of experiencing sensual pleasures equal in degree to those of the sensualist; and in fact, it often appears on various grounds probable that he is not so capable. Therefore just as, for comparing the pleasures of a single individual, we have to assume a neutral or standard mood, in which he is free from any of those tendencies to over-estimate or under-estimate particular pleasures or pains, to which he continually finds himself liable in other moods; so for the Utilitarian comparison we require to assume a standard man, who can represent to himself the pleasures of all men as they actually are, free from any bias for or against any kind of pleasure or pain. I repeat that I am not arguing against these assumptions; but since Hedonism is often regarded as 'Relativism' applied to morals, it seems important to show that, on the contrary, the hedonistic comparison necessarily assumes an absolute standard of preferableness in feeling which cannot be empirically exhibited: and that the 'principle of Relativity', if rigorously applied, would render Utilitarianism a logical impossibility.

So much for 'Greatest Happiness'; let us now consider the notion of 'Greatest Number'. The first question is, Number of what? Sentient beings generally, or any particular kind of them? Any selection is *primâ facie* arbitrary and unreasonable; and in fact, Utilitarians have generally adopted the former alternative. I notice this chiefly because the scientific difficulties of the hedonistic comparison just discussed seem thus considerably increased. Practically, Utilitarians have confined themselves almost entirely to human pleasures; adding, I suppose, to the assumptions above mentioned a further special assumption (also incapable of empirical proof) as to the comparative inferiority of the pleasures of the inferior animals. But even if we confine our attention to human beings, the notion of 'greatest number' is not yet quite determinate. For we can to some extent influence the number of future human beings, and the question arises, how, on Utilitarian principles, this number ought to be determined. Now, of course, the more the better, supposing average happiness to remain the same. But supposing we foresee that an increase in numbers will be accompanied with a decrease in average happiness, or *vice-versâ*, how then shall we decide? It seems clear that, on the Utilitarian method, we have to weigh the amount of happiness enjoyed by the extra number against the happiness lost by the remainder. I notice this, because the Malthusian economists often seem to assume that *no* increase of numbers can be right which involves *any* decrease in average happiness. But this is clearly inconsistent with the Utilitarian principles which these economists commonly avow; on these principles, the point up to which population ought to increase is not that at which average happiness is a maximum, but at which the product formed by multiplying the number of men into the amount of average happiness is the greatest possible.

If now the principle of Utilitarianism may be considered as sufficiently determined, as far as the limits of the present paper admit, I should like to say a few words about its proof. It may be said that it is impossible to 'prove' a first principle; and this is of course true, if by proof we mean a process which exhibits the principle in question as an inference from premises upon which it remains dependent for its certainty: for these premises, and not the inference drawn from them, would then be the real first principles. Nay, if Utilitarianism is to be *proved* to a man who already holds some other moral principles, say to an Intuitional or Common-Sense moralist, who regards as final the principles of Truth, Justice, Obedience to authority, Purity, &c.; or to an Egoist who regards his own interest as the ultimately reasonable end of his conduct: the process must be one which establishes a conclusion actually *superior* in validity to the premises from which it starts. For the Utilitarian prescriptions of duty are *primâ facie* in conflict, at certain points and under certain circumstances, both with Intuitional rules, and with the dictates of Rational Egoism: so that Utilitarianism, if accepted at all, must be accepted as overruling Intuitionism and Egoism. At the same time, if the other principles are not throughout taken as valid, the so-called proof does not seem to be addressed to the Intuitionist or Egoist at all. How shall we deal with this dilemma? and how is such a process (certainly very different from ordinary proof) possible or conceivable? It seems that what is needed is a line of argument which, on the one hand, allows the validity, to a certain extent, of the principles already accepted, and on the other hand, shows them to be imperfect—not absolutely and independently valid, but needing qualification and completion. It may be worth while to investigate briefly such a line of argument in the two cases of Intuitionism and Egoism respectively. To the Intuitionist the Utilitarian endeavours to show that the principles of Truth, Justice, &c., have only a dependent and subordinate validity: arguing either that the principle is really only affirmed by Common Sense as a general rule admitting of exceptions, as in the case of Truth; or that the fundamental notion is vague, and needs further determination, as in the case of Justice; and further, that the different rules are liable to conflict with each other, and that we require some higher principle to decide the issue just raised; and again, that the rules are differently formulated by different persons, and that these differences admit of no intuitional solution, while they show the vagueness and ambiguity of the common moral notions, to which the Intuitionist appeals; and that in all these cases Common Sense naturally turns to the Utilitarian principle for the further determinations and decisions required. Thus the relation between Utilitarianism and Intuitionism seems to have both a positive and a negative aspect. Positively Utilitarianism supports and sustains the general validity of the current moral rules, by showing a further justification of them, besides the intuitive recognition of their stringency, and also a principle of synthesis and method of binding them into a complete and harmonious system. Negatively, in order to show them dependent and subordinate to its own principle, it has to exhibit their imperfections, as above. I may observe that each of these two aspects has been too exclusively prominent in different periods of English ethical thought. Utilitarianism, as introduced by Cumberland, is too purely conservative; it dwells entirely on the general conduciveness of moral rules to the general good, and ignores the imperfections of these rules as commonly conceived. On the other hand, the Utilitarianism of Bentham is too purely destructive, and treats the morality of Common Sense with needless acrimony and contempt.

The relation between Utilitarianism and Egoism is much more simple, though it seems hard to state it with perfect exactness, and in fact, it is formulated very differently by different writers who appear to be substantially agreed, as Clarke, Kant, and Mill. If the Egoist strictly confines himself to stating his conviction that he ought to take his own happiness or pleasure as his ultimate end, there seems no opening for an argument to lead him to Utilitarianism (as a first principle). But if he offers either as a reason for this conviction, or as another form of stating it, the proposition that his happiness or pleasure is objectively 'desirable' or 'a good', he gives the requisite opening. For the Utilitarian can then point out that *his* happiness cannot be more objectively desirable or more a good than the happiness of any one else; the mere fact (if I may so put it) that *he is he* can have nothing to do with its objective desirability or goodness. Hence starting with his own principle, he must accept the wider notion of universal happiness or pleasure as representing the real end of Reason, the absolutely Good or Desirable: as the end, therefore, to which the action of a reasonable agent ought to be directed.

It is to be observed that the *proof* of Utilitarianism, thus addressed to the Egoist, is quite different from an exposition of the *sanctions* of Utilitarian rules; *i.e.*, the pleasures and pains that will follow respectively on their observance and violation. Obviously such an exposition cannot lead us to accept Utilitarianism as a first principle, but only as a conclusion deduced from or a special application of Egoism. At the same time, the two, proof and sanction, the reason for accepting the greatest happiness of the greatest number as (in Bentham's language) the 'right and proper' end of action, and the individual's motives for making it his end, are very frequently confused in discussion.

This is the last point that it seemed to me necessary to clear up, in order to obtain a distinct idea of that theory of right conduct which I believe to be generally meant by the term Utilitarian, and of its relation to other theories of the right or reasonable in human action. Whether my statements are incontrovertible or not, I think that when the issues raised by them are definitely settled, it will perhaps be more profitable than at present to discuss the question whether one is or is not a Utilitarian.

2. The Theory of Evolution in its Application to Practice

Current philosophical notions, characteristic of the most recently accepted system or manner of thought in any age and country, are apt to exercise over men's minds an influence which is often in inverse ratio to the clearness with which the notions themselves are conceived, and the evidence for the philosophical doctrines implied in their acceptance is examined and estimated. For any such notion may easily have different shades of meaning, and according to the relations in which it is used may imply many distinct propositions, which have no necessary connection with each other, and for which the evidence is very various, both in kind and degree: while yet, with whatever portion of this implication it may be employed, it is apt to carry with it the impressiveness and *prestige* which it naturally possesses as the last outcome of philosophical reflection. The fallacy of which we thus run a risk cannot be exactly classed among Bacon's 'Idola Fori', or his 'Idola Theatri', as it is neither due to the defects of popular language, nor to the defects of philosophical method: we must rather call it a hybrid between the two species, resulting from the communication between the Theatrum and the Forum, now much more fully established than it was in the time of Bacon. There would seem to be a peculiar danger of this fallacy in the practical conclusions deduced from the Theory of Evolution: as such deductions are various, complicated, and widely interesting, while they have not yet been systematically treated by any of the accepted expositors of Evolutionism. It is my object in the present paper to guard against this danger by distinguishing different propositions enforced or implied in the doctrine of Evolution as commonly accepted; and considering them severally in their bearing on Ethics, that is, on the Theory of Right or Rational Conduct. With this object, it will not be necessary to enter upon the fundamental question, whether the doctrine of Evolution is merely historical or properly philosophical: whether it merely gives us a probable explanation of the past, or such a justification of it as reason demands. In so far as I myself accept the doctrine, it is entirely on the former view: but adequately to justify this position would require a separate essay. Nor, again shall I have occasion to pursue the notion of Evolution beyond the limits of organic life: as the influence on practice which any speculations as to the past and future

[Published in *Mind*, OS, 1/1 (1876), 52–67. There is an interesting response by Frederick Pollock in *Mind*, 1876.]

motions of inorganic matter may have is obviously so slight and indirect that we need not take it into consideration.

I. The widest sense in which the term Evolution is used appears to be merely exclusive of Special Creation. Thus, Mr. Spencer says that in forming 'a conception of the mode in which living bodies in general have originated . . . we have to choose between two hypotheses,—the hypothesis of Special Creation and the hypothesis of Evolution'. This latter hypothesis, as he immediately explains, is that 'the multitudinous kinds of organisms that now exist, or have existed during past geological eras, . . . have arisen by insensible steps, through actions such as we see habitually going on'. Similarly, when Mr. Darwin speaks of 'Evolution *in any form*', he seems to mean the general hypothesis just stated, in contradistinction to his own special hypothesis of Evolution by Natural Selection. It should be observed that in the above statement the production of living organisms out of inorganic matter is implicitly excluded from the hypothesis; for it is not held generally, nor by the writers to whom I have referred, that this is among the actions which we see habitually going on. What we do see is that living things change slightly in the course of their life, and also produce other living things somewhat different from themselves; the hypothesis, then, is that all the differences among living organisms, which we must conceive as having begun to exist at some point in the history of the organic world, have been produced by the accumulation of these slight differences. And without examining minutely the possibility of living things being brought to our planet from without, we may take it for granted that most of the living things that have existed on this earth have also begun to exist there.

Now in the controversial *mêlée* which has been kept up for half a generation about the 'Darwinian Theory', it is sometimes forgotten that the hypothesis of Evolution, *in this wider and more general signification*, is sustained by an immense force of scientific presumption, independent of all special evidence. We cannot suppose, without contradicting the fundamental assumption on which all our physical reasoning proceeds, that an organism or any other material thing that has begun to exist, was not formed out of pre-existent matter by the operation of pre-existent forces according to universal laws; so that if we do not suppose each new organism to be developed out of some pre-existing organism, we are forced to regard it as causally connected in some totally unknown way with inorganic matter; and this is an alternative which few will embrace. And, again, it is manifestly illegitimate to assume that any new organic form was produced suddenly, *per saltum*, and so in a manner of which experience affords us no example; until it is proved that it could not have been produced by the gradual accumulation of such slight variations as experience shows us continually occurring.

On this point I need not perhaps dwell long. It is more necessary to argue that the theory of Evolution, thus widely understood, has little or no bearing upon ethics. It is commonly supposed that it is of great importance in ethical controversy to prove that the Moral Faculty is derivative and not original: and there can be little doubt that this conclusion follows from the theory which we are now considering. For when we trace back in thought the series of organisms of which man is the final result, we must—at some point or other, it matters not where—come to a living being (whether called Man or not) devoid of moral consciousness; and between this point and that at which the moral faculty clearly presents itself, we must suppose a transition-period in which the distinctly moral consciousness is gradually being derived and developed out of more primitive feelings and cognitions. All this seems necessarily involved in the acceptance of Evolution in any form; but when it is all admitted, I cannot see that any argument is gained for or against any particular ethical doctrine. For all the competing and conflicting moral principles that men have anywhere assumed must be equally derivative: and the mere recognition of their derivativeness, apart from any particular theory as to the *modus derivandi*, cannot supply us with any criterion for distinguishing true moral principles from false. It is perhaps more natural to think that this recognition must influence the mind in the direction of general moral scepticism. But surely there can be no reason why we should single out for distrust the enunciations of the moral faculty, merely because it is the outcome of a long process of development. Such a line of argument would leave us no faculty stable and trustworthy: and would therefore end by destroying its own premises. It is obviously absurd to make the validity or invalidity of any judgments depend on the particular stage in the process of development at which this class of judgments first made their appearance; especially since it is an essential point of the Evolution-theory to conceive this process as fundamentally similar in all its parts. And it may be further observed that some of our most secure intellectual possessions are truths (such as those of the higher mathematics) of which the apprehension was not attained until long after the moral faculty was in full play.

All this is so evident, that what seems to need explanation is rather the fact that so much importance is commonly attached to the question as to the 'origin of the moral faculty'. I am disposed to connect it with that change in the common mode of regarding moral questions, which, in the history of English ethical thought, was effected by the influence of Butler. So long as the moral faculty was regarded[1] as really a faculty of 'intuition' or rational apprehension of objective right and wrong, the history of these intuitions could seem of no more importance to the moralist as such than the history of our perception of space is to the geometer as such. But when the cognitive element of the moral consciousness fell into the background, and it came to be considered chiefly on its impulsive side, as a spring of action claiming a peculiar kind of authority, the validity of the authority seemed to depend on the assumption of an original legitimate constitution of human nature, and the proof that the moral impulse was derived seemed to

---

[1] As (*e.g.*) by Cudworth, Clarke, and the earlier orthodox moralists generally.

afford at least presumptive evidence that its authority was usurped. For the old conception of Nature, used as supplying a practical standard (whether in Ethics, Politics or Theoretical Jurisprudence) always suggested a fixed and unchangeable type, created once for all, and therefore both original and in a certain sense universal notwithstanding numerous actual divergences. This latter notion has now entirely vanished from the regions of political and jural speculation, under the influence of the Historical method: in Ethics it still lingers: but the Theory of Evolution (which may be regarded as the final extension of the Historical method) is likely soon to expel it altogether from practical Philosophy.

II. Still reflection shows that the conception really essential to Butler's system, of a definite type or ideal of human existence by conformity to which conduct is made 'right' or 'good', is in no way irreconcilable with the doctrine which we are examining. In fact the term 'Evolution' naturally suggests not merely a process of continual change, but one that brings into continually greater actuality or prominence a certain form or type, a certain complex of characteristics, which is conceived as having had a latent existence at the outset of the process. If, then, this type be regarded as in itself right or good, its place in a moral system will correspond to that of the 'Nature' of prae-evolutional writers. Either notion professes to meet the largest demands of the moralist, by establishing a clear and definite relation between 'what is' and 'what ought to be'; though the demands are met in a different way in each case. On the older view we have to ascertain the ideal of humanity, partly by tracing history backwards to the cradle of the individual or of the race, and partly by discerning and abstracting the permanent type amid the variations and imperfections of actual men and societies. On the newer view we see it gradually realised more and more as the process which constitutes the life of the universe goes on. In either case the duty of realising this ideal furnishes the supreme rule of conduct; though on the latter view we have the satisfaction of knowing that the normal operation of the Power manifested in the universe is continually producing, to an ever greater extent, the result which we rationally desire.

Here, then, in our analysis of the notion of Evolution, we have at length come upon an element of fundamental practical importance; though it is an element of which the presence is somewhat latent and obscure. Probably all who speak of Evolution mean by it not merely a process from old to new, but also a progress from less to more of certain qualities or characteristics. But that these characteristics are intrinsically good or desirable is more often implied than explicitly stated: otherwise it would be more clearly seen that this ethical proposition cannot be proved by any of the physical reasonings commonly used to establish the doctrine of Evolution. The truth is that the writers who have most occupied themselves in tracing the course of man's development have often not been practised in that systematic reflection on the play of their own moral faculty which is essential to clearness of thought in the discussion of ethical principles. In Comte's system, for example—and to Comte, perhaps, more than to any other single man, the triumph of the Historical Method in Politics is due—no clear reason seems to be given why the Progress, which is the end of the statesman and the philanthropist, should coincide with the Progress that the Sociologist has ascertained to be a fundamental fact of human history. It is certainly not from any blind confidence in the natural order of the Universe that Comte takes as a first principle of practice that we are to help mankind forward in the direction in which, speaking broadly, it tends to go. Yet this does seem to be his fundamental precept; for though he takes pains to show that an increase of Happiness attends on Progress, he never uses the production of Happiness as the end and criterion of proper moral and intellectual culture. It is rather the 'bringing into ever greater prominence the faculties characteristic of humanity' to which he bids us direct our efforts; while, again, the development which we find in human history is defined as 'le simple essor spontané . . . des facultés fondamentales toujours pré-existantes, qui constituent l'ensemble de notre nature'. Such phrases remind us that we cannot take Comte as a representative of Evolutionism: and that his notion of development is transitional between the old doctrine of fixed types of human nature, and the new doctrine of a perpetual process of life, in which humanity, as we commonly conceive it, is but a stage accidentally marked off by the fact of our living now. A disciple of Mr. Darwin knows nothing of 'always pre-existent fundamental faculties characteristic of humanity'. In his view, as our ancestors were other and less than man, so our posterity may be other and more. If he includes in his conception of Evolution the notion of perpetual Progress in certain definite characteristics, these must evidently be characteristics which belong to all living things as such, though they appear with ever greater prominence as the evolution of life proceeds. Shall we then say that Progress consists in increasing complexity of organisation, or (to use Mr. Spencer's more precise phrase) in more and more 'definite coherent heterogeneity' of changes in the living being correspondent to changes in its environment? But Progress thus interpreted seems no longer adapted to give us the ultimate end or first principle of Practice. For, though we sometimes use the terms 'higher' and 'lower organisms' in a way which might seem to imply that mere complexity of organisation is *intrinsically* preferable or desirable; still, perhaps, no one would deliberately maintain this, but only that it is desirable as a means to some further end. And this end would be commonly taken to be increase of Happiness; which most Evolutionists believe to be at least a concomitant of Progress. 'Slowly but surely,' writes Mr. Spencer, 'Evolution brings about an increasing amount of happiness,' so that we are warranted in believing that 'Evolution can only end in the establishment of the most complete happiness.' On this view, the Theory of Evolution in its practical aspects would appear to resolve itself into Utilitarianism, with the suggestion of a peculiar method for pursuing the utilitarian end. For, if nature is continually increasing Happiness, or the excess of pleasure over pain in the whole sum of sentient existence, by continually perfecting the 'correspondence between life and its environment', this latter should perhaps be taken by us as the general means to the former end and the immediate object of our efforts.

III. A different view, however, is sometimes taken of the fundamental character of Evolutional ethics, which may be conveniently introduced by considering an ambiguity in the phrase I have just quoted. For the term 'correspondence', or the nearly equivalent terms 'adjustment' and 'adaptation', as employed by Mr. Spencer and his disciples, appear to blend two different meanings; or, perhaps, to imply the necessary connexion of two distinct characteristics. They imply, namely, that the more exactly and discriminatively the changes in an organism represent or respond to the different changes in its environment, the more will the organism be 'fitted to its conditions of existence' in the sense of being qualified to preserve itself under these conditions. But it seems that we cannot assume that this connexion will hold universally; for the responsiveness (*e.g.*) of an invalid's organism to surrounding changes is often more discriminating than that of a man in strong health, though less effective for self-preservation. Indeed, the common notion of 'delicacy of organisation' blends the attribute of subtle responsiveness to external changes with the very opposite of strong and stable vitality. Having then to choose between discriminating responsiveness and tendency to self-preservation, an Evolutionist may take the latter as the essential characteristic of the well-being of an organism. And rising to a universal point of view, and considering the whole series of living things of which any individual organism forms a link, he may define 'general good' or 'welfare'—as Mr. Darwin does—to consist in 'the rearing of the greatest number of individuals in full health and vigour [and with all their faculties perfect][2] under the conditions to which they are subject'. Here we have a very different notion from Happiness offered us as representing the ultimate end and standard of right conduct. Mr. Darwin, indeed, contrasts the two, explicitly rejecting 'general happiness' as the standard, and thus distinguishes his ethics from Utilitarianism as commonly understood.

But can we really declare that when we apply the terms 'good' or 'bad' to the manner of existence of an organised being, we mean simply to attribute to it more or less of the tendency to self-preservation, or to the preservation of its kind? Certainly such a reduction of the notion of 'well-being' to 'being' (actual and potential) would be a most important contribution from the doctrine of Evolution to ethical science. But it at least conflicts in a very startling manner with those ordinary notions of Progress and Development, which I have already noticed as combining ethical and physical import. For, in our use of these notions, it is always implied that certain forms of life are qualitatively superior to others,

---

[2] I have put this clause in brackets, because the term 'perfect' implies some standard of 'good' or 'well-being'; and if this standard were different from that which the definition gives, the definition would be palpably faulty; while if it be the same, the clause seems superfluous.

independently of the number of individuals, present or future, in which each form is realised. Whereas the doctrine above stated, if pressed to its logical results, would present to us all equally numerous species as *primâ facie* on a par in respect of goodness, except, indeed, that the older (and so generally the 'lower', as we commonly estimate) would seem the better, in so far as we have more evidence of their capacity to exist under the physical conditions of our globe. A closer investigation would, of course, disclose many differences in the prospects of future existence enjoyed respectively by the different forms, but these would but rarely and accidentally correspond to the commonly recognised differences of lower and higher. And if we confine ourselves to human beings, to whom alone the practical side of the doctrine applies, is it not too paradoxical to assert that 'rising in the scale of existence' means no more than 'developing further the capacity to exist'? A greater degree of fertility would thus become an excellence outweighing the finest moral and intellectual endowments; and some semi-barbarous races must be held to have attained the end of human existence more than some of the pioneers and patterns of civilisation. In short, when fairly contemplated, the doctrine that resolves all virtues and excellences into the comprehensive virtue

'of going on, and still to be'

can hardly find acceptance. At the same time, we must admit that ζῆν (in Aristotelian phrase) is a necessary condition of εὖ ζῆν; and, since living at all has been a somewhat difficult task to human communities, until a very recent period in the history of our race, the most important part of the function of the moral sense has consisted in the enforcement of those habits of life which were indispensable to the mere permanent existence of any society of human beings. This seems to me the element of truth in Mr. Darwin's view, and in that hypothetical construction of the origin and growth of the moral sense with which he has connected it. We may admit further that any defect in the capacity for continued existence would be a fault in a social system which no excellences of a different kind can counterbalance; but this is a very different thing from saying that all possible improvement may be resolved into some increase of this capacity.

IV. If, then, the Well-being of living things is somewhat different from their mere Being, however secured and extended in space or time, what is the content of this notion 'well' or 'good'? I have elsewhere tried to show that the only satisfactory answer to this question is that of the old-fashioned Utilitarianism which Mr. Darwin and his disciples are trying to transcend. The only rational ultimate ground, in my opinion, for pronouncing any sentient being in a 'good' condition, is that its condition is calculated to produce as great an amount as is under the circumstances possible of Happiness, that is, pleasant or desirable feeling or consciousness: taking into consideration not its own happiness only—for we have no rational ground for preferring this to any other happiness—but that of all sentient beings, present or future, on whose manner of existence it exercises any influence. If this be so, it only remains to ask how far the notion of Progress or Elevation in the scale of life, as understood by Evolutionists, supplies us with clear guidance to the right means for attaining this ultimate end. Now, no doubt, in comparing the happiness of man with that of the lower animals, or the happiness of civilised man with that of savages, we commonly assume that amount of happiness varies according to degree in scale of organisation. We do this because what we really mean by 'higher life' seems, when we look closely at the notion, to be convertible with *more* life. As Mr. Spencer says, 'we regard as the highest life that which shows great complexity in the correspondences, great rapidity in the succession of them, and great length in the series of them'; the two former characteristics supplying a measure of the intensive quantity of life lived in a given time, and the latter adding its extensive quantity. And the experience of mankind, as a whole—though there are not wanting individual dissentients—seems to support the belief that Conscious or Sentient Life is, speaking broadly and on the average, desirable; that some degree of pleasure is the normal state of sentient beings as such and pain abnormal. Thus it follows that the 'higher' such a being stands in the scale of organisation, the happier it is, generally speaking. In accordance with this general principle we regard the exercise of more varied and complicated activities, the extension of sympathy with the pleasures and pains of others, the development of scientific and historical interests, of aesthetic sensibilities, &c.—which might all be brought under the general notion of 'progress in the correspondence between the organism and its environment'—as involving generally an increase of happiness. Still, in so far as we pursue any of these elements of culture for their own sakes, our pursuit is closely guided and checked by experience of the pleasure derived from them; and it would seem that this ought to be so. For, in the first place, the connexion above stated is not universal, as the more intense life may be intensely painful; and, independently of this, the notions of Culture, Elevation of Life, or Perfection of Organisation are not sufficiently definite to be substituted for that of Happiness as the immediate object of rational pursuit; indeed, the pleasure actually experienced seems often a better test of true development in any direction, than the latter (as otherwise estimated) can be of the pleasure that will ultimately accrue.

But the fact is that in the ordering of an individual man's life, Development or Perfection of Organisation scarcely comes into competition with Happiness as an end of action. For in this case we cannot alter the structure of the organism much or directly, but only to a slight extent by altering its functions; and the functions of each civilised man are, in most cases, determined for him by a combination of imperious bodily necessities and fixed social relations, and are exercised not for their own sakes but in order to provide adequately some more indispensable means of happiness. It is rather when we pass from the individual human being to consider the far more modifiable social organism of which he forms a part, that it becomes of fundamental importance to know whether the doctrine of Evolution can guide us to the form of organisation most productive of happiness. For, if this be so, the efforts of the statesman and the philanthropist should be primarily directed to the realisation of this form, and empirical utilitarianism would be, to a great extent, superseded in the political art. The right social order would, no doubt, approve itself as such by the general experience of happiness resulting from it; but it would become unscientific to refer to this experience as determining the settlement of great political questions.

Before, however, we consider if our knowledge of sociology is sufficiently advanced to enable us to define the political ideal, we must notice one fundamental difficulty in constructing it, which arises inevitably from the relation of the individual man to society. For the most prominent characteristic of the advanced development of any organism is the specialisation—or, as Mr. Spencer calls it, 'differentiation'—of the functions of its different parts. Obviously the more this is effected, the more 'definite coherent heterogeneity' will be realised in the organism and in its relations to its environment. But obviously too, this involves *pro tanto* a proportionally less degree of variety and complexity in the life of each individual member of the society whose functions are thus specialised; and their life becoming narrow and monotonous must become, according to our present hypothesis, less happy. This result has often been noticed by observers of the minute sub-division of labour which is a feature of our industrial progress: but the same sort of *primâ facie* conflict between individual and social development occurs in considering most of the great problems of modern politics; such as the relations between rich and poor generally, the relations between governors and governed, and the relations of the sexes. Now, as it is the individual, after all, who feels pleasure and pain, it is clear that his development (or happiness) must not be sacrificed to attain a higher form of social organisation; the latter end can only be sought within the limits fixed by the former; the point then is to determine what these are. It may be thought, perhaps, that the history of past stages in the evolution of society will indicate the reconciliation or compromise between individual and social development to which the human race has gradually been working up. It would seem, however, that history rather shows us the problem than its solution. For, while a continually greater specialisation of functions is undoubtedly an ever-present feature of social development, we have to notice as proceeding side by side with this a continually fuller recognition of the rights and claims of the individual as such. And this, giving a point of view from which the elements of the community are regarded as equal and similar, considerably qualifies, and, to some extent, counterbalances the tendency to 'heterogeneity' above noticed; it is obvious, *e.g.*, that an ancient society with a fully developed caste-system, where the existence of the individual was absorbed in and identified with his social function, was, in some respects, more heterogeneous than our own, in spite of the greater differentiation of functions in the latter. Hence we have on the one hand an ever increasing social inequality, and, on the other hand, an ever profounder protest against this inequality; and, whatever the right compromise between these conflicting tendencies may be, it does not seem possible to determine it by any deduction from the doctrine of Evolution.

For when we turn to examine the principles of social construction propounded by eminent sociologists, we see very plainly that any attempt to determine the political ideal by a scientific formula of Social Evolution must at least fail in obtaining that 'consensus of experts', which is, to common men, the most satisfactory guarantee of scientific method. Those thinkers who are most confident of having discovered the law of progress seem hopelessly disagreed as to the next term in the series. For example, Comte teaches us that the 'influence dispersive du principe de la spécialisation', tending in its extreme form to a 'sorte d'automatisme humain', must be met by a corresponding development of that 'réaction nécessaire de l'ensemble sur les parties', which constitutes the proper function of government. 'L'intensité', he says, 'do cetto fonction régulatrice, bien loin de devoir decroître à mesure que l'évolution humaine s' accomplit, doit, au contraire, devenir de plus en plus indispensable'; and actually, he holds, we find the two tendencies to specialisation and to central regulation developing, as progress goes on, so as to balance each other by a continually proportionate increase. And certainly the amount of regulation contemplated in Comte's Utopia would seem sufficient to counteract any conceivable development of centrifugal impulses. While Mr. Spencer is no less confirmed by sociological study in his opposite doctrine that the proper function of government is what he calls 'negatively-regulative control', viz.: the prevention of mutual interference and the enforcement of free contracts among the members of a community. Mr. Spencer supports his ideal of organisation by a reference to biological analogies; but, here again, his view is diametrically opposed to that of our most eminent living morphologist.[3] In this diversity of opinion, it is perhaps premature to consider the practical results that would follow from our attaining really scientific prevision of the social relations of the future. But I must observe that it would still remain to be proved that the mere advance to a higher stage in social organisation is necessarily accompanied with a proportionate increase of happiness. Past history shows us the greatest differences in the prosperity of different nations on approximately the same level of social development; and it seems most reasonable to suppose that such prevision of social changes as we are likely to attain will rather define the limits within which the political art has to operate than furnish the principles of the art itself.

V. Hitherto, in considering the bearing of Evolutionism on the theory of right conduct, we have assumed that such conduct is to be not only objectively rational, or the best means of realising what is ultimately good; but also subjectively

[3] Cf. Professor Huxley's essay on 'Administrative Nihilism'.

rational, consciously chosen by the agent as a means to this end. This, however, though in the view of most moralists it seems to be the ideal form of human action, is manifestly not the universal or even the most common form. Men are prompted to action by other appetites and desires far more frequently than by the desire to do what is reasonable or right: so that some ethical writers even ignore the very existence of this latter motive, and regard human action as always stimulated by one or other of the more special impulses; including what are called 'moral sentiments', or immediate unreflective likings and aversions for particular kinds of conduct, contemplated without reference to any ulterior end. Indeed the operation of such unreflective impulses appears to be the most prominent element in the common notion of 'conscience': so that the denomination by the Utilitarian school of the common morality which they wish to supersede as 'instinctive' or 'sentimental' is not infrequently accepted by other than Utilitarian Moralists. Now, if the doctrine of Evolution, in its application to the origin and growth of such instinctive impulses generally, and in particular of moral sentiments, is able to exhibit these as Nature's means of attaining that general happiness which is the conscious end of Utilitarian calculation; a reconciliation between 'instinctive' and Utilitarian morality seems to be effected, which composes the long conflict between the two schools. This is, at any rate, the claim put forward by Mr. Spencer and other expositors of evolutionism.

In proceeding to examine the claim, we must first consider how this part of the Evolution doctrine is supposed to be proved. Two methods of proof have been put forward, fundamentally distinct, but yet not incompatible: in fact, so far from incompatible that one of them almost needs to be supplemented by the other. One method consists in the application to sociology of that hypothetical-deductive use of the theory of Natural Selection which has of late years been common among biologists of the Darwinian school. Moral sentiments, it is said, are impulses that tend to the maintenance of society: hence a tribe in which they were accidentally developed would tend to be victorious over other tribes in the struggle for existence: and thus moral sentiments would come to be a part of the essential characteristics of humanity: hence we may conclude that it was in this way that they were actually generated. It will be seen that this view of the moral sentiments is in immediate connection with that account of the Well-being of an organism which, distinguishing it from Happiness, reduces it (as I have already noticed) to Being actual and potential. In order therefore to harmonise it with Utilitarianism we require a further application of the same deductive method: as thus—Men are stimulated to actions and abstinences in proportion as they find these in the long run pleasurable and their opposites painful: therefore tribes, whose members derive the greatest balance of pleasure over pain from actions and modes of existence conducive to the preservation of the tribe will have a distinct advantage in the struggle for existence: therefore the societies that in the long run survive will be so constituted that the maximum happiness of their members will be attained by conduct tending to the preservation of society. But even the most roseate optimism must admit that this double harmony between pleasant and preservative conduct, and between individual and universal well-being, is ideal and future: that it does not represent accurately the present, and still less the past experience of the human race. And hence (as Mr. Darwin himself has not failed to observe), the theory of natural selection has less explanatory efficacy here than it has in its usual biological applications. For in those the variations naturally selected are taken as accidental, or at least no explanation of them is necessary for the justification of the theory: we have only to assume generally a slight indefinite tendency to vary from the parental type in the propagation of life, and then the action of the environment will do the rest. But in the case of the sociological changes above-mentioned, this simple account of the matter is hardly admissible. For as the interest of the community continually involves more or less sacrifice of the individual, especially in the early stages of human history which the theory contemplates, any individual varying in the direction of morality would be liable to be cut off, and would fail to propagate his peculiar type.[4] We require therefore some further explanation of the tendency of human character to take this particular line of change. For it will hardly do to reply that a *tribe* which manifested this tendency would necessarily flourish: the chances are so very much against the production of a tribe of which the individuals accidentally combine to maintain an individually unprofitable variation in one special direction. This further explanation is found in the second method to which I referred, which is the one employed by Mr. Herbert Spencer. His theory, briefly given, is this: that experienced pleasures and pains produce secondary likings and aversions for pleasure-causing and pain-causing conduct, which from being habitual become organic and so capable of being transmitted to posterity: and that through the interdependence of interests that results from gregariousness and the interchange of emotions that results from sympathy, it is the common experience of *all* that practically operates in producing these derivative sentiments and habits; so that they ultimately appear as instincts tending to promote the interests of the community.

It appears to me that these two methods, taken together, furnish a highly plausible explanation of the development of morality in a race of animals gregarious, sympathetic, and semi-rational—such as we may conceive man to have been in

[4] 'It is extremely doubtful whether the offspring of the more sympathetic and benevolent parents, or of those who were the most faithful to their comrades, would be reared in greater numbers than the children of selfish and treacherous parents belonging to the same tribe. He who was ready to sacrifice his life, as many a savage has been, rather than betray his comrades, would often leave no offspring to inherit his noble nature. The bravest men, who were always willing to come to the front in war, and who freely risked their lives for others, would on an average perish in larger numbers than other men. Therefore it hardly seems probable that the number of men gifted with such virtues, or that the standard of their excellence, could be increased through natural selection, that is, by the survival of the fittest.'—Darwin, *Descent of Man*, ch. v., p. 130 (2nd. ed.).

the prae-moral stage of his development. But I fail to see how we are thus helped to a solution of the conflict between the Utilitarian and Intuitional schools of Ethics: in so far, that is, as either school professes to supply not merely a psychological explanation of human emotions, but an ethical theory of right conduct. For, putting aside the discrepancy before noticed between General Happiness and the Preservation of Race, we are still left asking the question: what ought we to do when Moral Sentiment comes into conflict with the conclusions of Rational Utilitarianism? Granting that both are really akin and spring from the same root, which ought we to obey, Reason or Instinct? As far as I can see, the 'reconciliation' proposed by Evolutionists results in a practical surrender on one side or the other; though it is not always clear on which side, and a plausible case may be made out for either. On the one hand it may be said that Moral Sentiments (or other derivative likings and aversions) constitute Nature's guidance to Happiness; and that our power of calculating pleasures and pains is so imperfect as to make it really rational in the pursuit of happiness, to disregard the results of conscious calculation when they are clearly in conflict with any of these embodiments of unconscious reasoning and outgrowths of ages of experience. On the other hand it may equally be urged that the symbolical representation and comparison of experienced pleasures and pains which we call the exercise of practical reason, is only the final phase of that adaptation of the organism to its circumstances which in its earlier phases took place by the development of these secondary instincts: that, in short, if Instinct is really implicit (utilitarian) reason, it is better to perform the calculation explicitly. Certainly we can balance any statement of the sources of fallibility in utilitarian calculation by an equally impressive demonstration of the imperfections and misguidance of instinct.

It may perhaps be said that an Evolutionist theory does not profess to prove that Utilitarian and Intuitional Ethics coincide in detail, but only to afford them a broad general ground of reconciliation. But in this case it seems to me ethically superfluous, whatever historical interest it may have. For this general result may be much more easily and satisfactorily attained by a survey of men's actual moral sentiments, and a comparison of them with the conclusions of utilitarian calculation. The practical disagreements between different schools of moralists, though their magnitude and importance are perhaps commonly underrated—certainly bear a small proportion to their agreements: but a theory of the origin of morality which merely explains the latter can hardly be said to effect a settlement of ethical controversy.

3. Professor Calderwood on Intuitionism in Morals

In Mind II. Prof. Calderwood published a criticism on the first chapter of Book III of my *Methods of Ethics*. This criticism involved important misapprehensions of my meaning and drift, which, as they are naturally though not necessarily connected with the fundamental differences between my point of view and my critic's, it may be useful briefly to point out.

(1.) Prof. Calderwood has somewhat misunderstood the general aim of the part of my treatise which deals with Intuitionism. He supposes me to be criticising from the outside a particular school or sect of moral philosophers. My endeavour was rather to unfold a method of reaching practical decisions which I find (more or less implicit) in the ordinary thought of the society of which I am a part, and to some extent in the natural processes of my own mind; and after tracing its different phases, to estimate carefully their scientific value. The doctrine which is called by the name Intuitionism is only one of those phases. Its scientific claims appear to me incomparably the most important, and it therefore chiefly occupies my attention during the remainder of the Book: but in the first four sections of the chapter criticised I have not yet come to speak of it specially. Thus the vagueness in my language (in these sections) of which Prof. Calderwood complains is a necessary incident of my plan of discussion. I begin by taking the notions which I have to use as I find them in common thought as expressed in common language; and I let them become gradually more definite, as my discussion brings into view distinctions in the general objects which they represent. What does the 'plain man' (to whose consciousness Butler and other moralists have so pointedly referred) mean by Moral Intuition? Merely, I think, the immediate cognition of the rightness or wrongness of actions. His usage of the term does not exclude either universal abstract intuitions or particular concrete intuitions: but of the two, I think, he more often means the latter. As I have said (*M. of E.* p. 85) 'we most commonly think of the dictates of conscience as relating to particular actions: and when a man is bidden, in any particular case, to "trust to his conscience" it commonly seems to be meant that he should exercise a faculty of judging morally this particular case without reference to general rules, and even in opposition to conclusions obtained by systematic deductions from such rules'. The case is stated much more strongly in the following passage from a

[From *Mind*, 1/4 (1876), 563–6.]

work which has recently appeared, Mr. Bradley's *Ethical Studies* (p. 176):—'On the head that moral judgments are not discursive, no one, I think, will wish me to stay long . . . in practical morality no doubt we may reflect on our principles, but I think it is not too much to say that we *never* do so, except where we have come upon a difficulty of particular application. If any one thinks that a man's *ordinary* judgment 'this is right or wrong' comes from the having a rule *before* the mind and bringing the particular case under it, he may be right; and I cannot try to show that he is wrong. I can only leave it to the reader to judge for himself. We say we "see" and we "feel" in these cases, not we "conclude." We prize the advice of persons who can give no reasons for what they say, etc., etc.'

This statement seems to me far too sweeping: but it may help to convince Prof. Calderwood and those who think with him, that I was right in giving at the outset of my Book III an account of Intuitionism which did not exclude the manner of thought here described as typical. In respect of the comparative value of this kind of intuition I altogether disagree with Mr. Bradley. I have no doubt that reflective persons, in proportion to their reflectiveness, come to rely rather on abstract universal intuitions relating to classes of cases conceived under general notions; and I prefer the moral thought of the reflective few to that of the unreflective many. Accordingly, these are the intuitions which I am chiefly occupied with examining in the subsequent chapters of the book. Prof. Calderwood may perhaps think that I ought to have confined myself to the consideration of Intuitionism in its most philosophical form. But this would have led me at once to Utilitarianism: because I hold that the only moral intuitions which sound philosophy can accept as ultimately valid are those which at the same time provide the only possible philosophical basis of the Utilitarian creed. I thus necessarily regard Prof. Calderwood's Intuitionism as a phase in the development of the Intuitional method, which comes naturally between the crude thought of Butler's 'plain man' and the Rational Utilitarianism to which I ultimately endeavour to lead my reader.

(2.) This view made it difficult for me to give a definition of Intuitionism which should be at once clear, fair and useful. I could not give as its fundamental doctrine 'that moral principles are intuitively known': because, in my opinion, this would not distinguish it from Utilitarianism, or indeed from any other method of reasoning to moral conclusions. In all such reasonings there must be some ultimate premises: which, as they are not known as inferences from other truths, must be known directly—that is, by Intuition. In order to raise a substantial issue, it seemed necessary in defining Intuitionism to exclude expressly the Utilitarian view, that the rightness of actions is to be ascertained by inference from an estimate of their consequences. But it was evident, again, that to exclude this without qualification would have been an absurd exaggeration of the antithesis which I had to define. No Intuitionist ever maintained that *all* our conduct can be ordered rightly without any calculation of its effects on human happiness. On the contrary, this calculation, for ourselves and for others, is expressly inculcated by the maxims of Prudence and Benevolence, as commonly understood. It is only from certain special portions of the whole region of conduct that Utilitarian foresight is shut out: and all thoughtful Intuitionists admit the importance of defining carefully these domains of special jurisdiction. For example, they are careful to tell us that the maxim of Veracity does not relieve as from the obliga-tion of considering whether what we say is likely to give happiness or to cause pain to others: it only excludes all such considerations in so far as they may appear to justify falsehoods. Hence in stating as the fundamental assumption of Intui-tionism 'that we have the power of seeing clearly what actions are right and reasonable in themselves, apart from their consequences', I thought it needful to add 'to some extent'. These words Prof. Calderwood has unfortunately mis-understood as qualifying the *clearness* of the moral vision assumed; whereas they were only intended to limit its range.

(3.) If then the practical issue between the Intuitional and Utilitarian methods be thus precisely raised: if the question be put, whether in respect of certain kinds of conduct our moral faculty furnishes us with self-evident imperatives, which ought to be obeyed without regard to consequences, we have next to consider how this question is to be decided. Here, if I could trust my own moral faculty alone, as it acts at present, I should say that no further test is needed than the Cartesian, if rigorously applied. If I ask myself whether I see clearly and distinctly the self-evidence of any particular maxims of duty, as I see that of the formal prin-ciples 'that what is right for me must be right for all persons in precisely similar circumstances' and 'that I ought to prefer the greater good of another to my own lesser good': I have no doubt whatever that I do not. I am conscious of a strong impression, an opinion on which I habitually act without hesitation, that I ought to speak truth, to perform promises, to requite benefits, &c., and also of power-ful moral sentiments prompting me to the observance of these rules; but on reflection I can now clearly distinguish such opinions and sentiments from the apparently immediate and certain cognition that I have of the formal principles above mentioned. But I could not always have made this distinction; and I believe that the majority of moral persons do not make it: most 'plain men' would probably say, at any rate on the first consideration of the matter, that they saw the obligations of Veracity and Good Faith as clearly and immediately as they saw those of Equity and Rational Benevolence. How then am I to argue with such persons? It will not settle the matter to tell them that they have observed their own mental processes wrongly, and that more careful introspection will show them the non-intuitive character of what they took for intuitions; especially as in many cases I do not believe that the error is one of mis-observation. Still less am I inclined to dispute the 'primitiveness' or 'spontaneousness' or 'originality' of these apparent intuitions. On the contrary, I hold that here, as in other depart-ments of thought, the primitive spontaneous processes of the mind are mixed with error, which is only to be removed gradually by comprehensive reflection upon the results of these processes. Through such a course of reflection I have endeavoured to lead my readers in chaps. 2–10 of Book III of my treatise: in the hope that after they have gone through it they may find their original apprehension of the self-evidence of moral maxims importantly modified. This whole view of mine seems so new to Prof. Calderwood, that he can only reply that 'correction of intuitions or of spontaneous utterances of conscience is impossible, and the proposal of it absurd'—a forcible statement, but hardly an effective argument.

4. Mr. Barratt on 'The Suppression of Egoism'

Mr. Barratt's article on the 'Suppression of Egoism' is based upon a fundamental misapprehension of the drift of my treatise. He appears to have overlooked the statement in my preface that 'all the different methods developed in it were expounded and criticised from a neutral position, and as impartially as possible'; and also § 5 of my introductory chapter, in which my position and mode of treating the subject are further explained. For the reasons given in this latter passage, I avoided stating explicitly my own ethical view, or even suggesting it with any completeness: but I thought it would be pretty clear to the reader that it is not what Mr. Barratt controverts as the 'Suppression of Egoism', but rather what, in No. V. of *Mind*, I attributed to Butler, describing it as 'the Dualism of the Practical Reason'. This view is stated most succinctly (in Butler's terminology, which is not exactly mine) in the following passage at the end of the Third Sermon on Human Nature: 'Reasonable self-love and conscience are the two chief or superior principles in the nature of man: because an action may be suitable to this nature, though all other principles are violated; but becomes unsuitable if either of those are.' I do not (I believe) differ substantially from Butler in my view of reasonable self-love, nor (theology apart) in my view of its relation to conscience, nor again do I differ from him in regarding conscience as essentially a function of the practical reason ('moral precepts' he says in the *Analogy*, p. ii. c. 8, 'are precepts the reason of which we see'). My difference begins when we come to consider what among the precepts of conscience we really do see to be reasonable. Here my view may be briefly given by saying, that I identify a modification of Kantism with the missing rational basis of the ethical utilitarianism of Bentham, as expounded by J. S. Mill. I consider the fundamental formula of conscience to be that one ought not to prefer one's own good to the greater good of another: this (like Kant's Categorical Imperative) is a purely formal principle, and is evolved immediately out of the notion of 'good' or 'desirable', if this notion is used absolutely; as it then must mean 'desirable from a universal point of view', or 'what all rational beings, as such, ought to aim at realising'. The substantial difference between me and Mr. Barratt is that he rejects this notion, at least as applied to concrete results. On this point I confidently appeal to the common moral consciousness of mankind: (*e.g.*) it is certainly the common belief that the design of

[From *Mind*, 2 (1877), 411–12.]

the Creator of the world is to realise Good: and in this belief the notion 'good' must be used absolutely. But I should admit Mr. Barratt's objection to the reasoning by which (see p. 360), I endeavour to exhibit the self-evidence of this formula, if that reasoning were intended—as Mr. Barratt has taken it—as a confutation of the principle of Rational Egoism. Since, however, it is manifest, at the close of the treatise, that I do not consider the principle of Rational Egoism to have been confuted, but only contradicted; and since I carefully explain, on p. 392, how in my view this confutation is avoided, I confess that I can hardly understand my critic's misunderstanding.

As regards the 'Physical Method' of ethics, it is enough to say that there cannot possibly be any such 'method' in the sense in which I use the term, *i.e.*, rational procedure for determining what ought to be done here and now. Ethical conclusions can only be logically reached by starting with ethical premises: how the latter are got, it was no part of my plan to consider. I presume that even Mr. Barratt hardly means to maintain that practical principles can be in any sense proved by physical methods.

[The paper Sidgwick refers to on page 27, line 10, as in 'No. V. of *Mind*' is 'Hedonism and Ultimate Good' (1877), Ch. 12 in this volume. Ed.]

5. The Establishment of Ethical
First Principles

I cannot but think that the readers of ethical treatises—the remark applies to Utilitarian and Intuitional moralists alike—must often be perplexed by the manner in which their authors deal with the propositions which they present as first principles. They begin by declaring that first principles are, as such, incapable of proof, and then immediately proceed to make what at least an untutored mind can hardly distinguish from an attempt to prove them. The apparent inconsistency is indeed easy to explain; for all, or almost all, *soi-disant* ethical first principles are denied to be such by at least respectable minorities; hence we naturally expect our moralist not merely to propound his first principles, but also somehow to provide us with rational inducements for accepting them. Still, the dilemma in which he is placed is a somewhat serious one, and seems to me to deserve more systematic examination than it has yet received. On the one hand, it seems undeniable that first principles cannot stand in need of what is strictly to be called proof: they would obviously cease to be first principles if they were exhibited as dependent for their certainty on the acceptance by the mind of certain other truths. Yet, on the other hand, when we are dealing with any subject where there is a conflict of opinion as to first principles, we can hardly refuse to give reasons for taking our side in the conflict: as rational beings conversing with other rationals it seems absurd that we should not be able to explain to each other why we accept one first principle rather than another. And how can these reasons be valid if they do not prove the first principle which they (to use Mill's phrase) 'determine the mind' to accept?

To find a way out of this difficulty we require, I think, to take Aristotle's distinction between logical or natural priority in cognition and priority in the knowledge of any particular mind. We are thus enabled to see that a proposition may be self-evident, *i.e.*, may be properly cognisable without being viewed in connexion with any other propositions; though in order that its truth may be apparent to some particular mind, there is still required some rational process connecting it with propositions previously accepted by that mind.

For instance, I may begin by regarding some limited and qualified statement as self-evident, without seeing the truth of the simpler and wider proposition of which the former affirms a part; and yet, when I have been led to accept the

[From *Mind*, 4 (1879), 106–11.]

latter, I may reasonably regard this as the real first principle, and not the former, of which the limitations and qualifications may then appear accidental and arbitrary. Thus, to take an illustration from the subject of Ethics, with which I am here primarily concerned, I may begin by laying down as a principle that 'all pain of human or rational beings is to be avoided'; and then afterwards may be led to enunciate the wider rule that 'all pain is to be avoided'; it being made evident to me that the difference of rationality between two species of sentient beings is no ground for establishing a fundamental ethical distinction between their respective pains. In this case I shall ultimately regard the wider rule as the principle, and the narrower as a deduction from it; in spite of my having been led by a process of reasoning from the latter to the former. Or again (as I have elsewhere argued)[1] I may start with the egoistic maxim that 'it is reasonable for me to take my own greatest happiness as the ultimate end of my conduct'; and then may yield to the argument that the happiness of any other individual, equally capable and deserving of happiness, must be no less worth aiming at than my own; and thus may come to accept the utilitarian maxim that 'happiness generally is to be sought' as the real first principle; considering the egoistic maxim to be only true in so far as it is a partial and subordinate expression of this latter.

This then is one species of the rational process that we are considering; by which we are logically led to a conclusion which yet when reached we regard as a first principle. We start with a proposition which appears self-evident; we reflect on it and analyse it into a more general proposition with a limitation; concentrating our attention on the limitation, we see that it is arbitrary and without foundation in reason; we deny its validity and substitute for our original principle the wider statement of which that affirmed a part.

There is another quite different process by which a similar result may possibly be reached. We may be able to establish some general criteria for distinguishing true first principles (whether ethical or non-ethical) from false ones; and may then construct a strictly logical deduction by which, applying their general criteria to the special case of ethics, we establish the true first principles of this latter subject. How far such a methodological deduction is actually in our power, I will presently consider. At any rate, I should maintain that there is no third way of establishing ethical principles. The premisses of our reasoning, when strictly stated, must, if not methodological, be purely ethical: that is, they must contain, implicitly or explicitly, the elementary notion signified by the term 'ought'; otherwise, there is no rational transition possible to a proposition that does affirm 'what ought to be'. It may be true that in the development of human minds judgments of the former kind are found among the antecedents of the latter; e.g., a man may be actually led by contemplating purely physical facts to enunciate a moral law; but

---

[1] Cf. Methods of Ethics, III. c. 13 and IV. c. 2.

I know no way of exhibiting this process as logically cogent, and consequently valid for all minds.

This point will, I think, be easily admitted when it is considered in this abstract way; but I find it frequently ignored in current ethical arguments. *E.g.*, many writers seem to hold with Mill[2] that the psychological generalisation that all men desire pleasure can be used to establish the ethical proposition that pleasure is what we ought to aim at. In Mill's argument the paralogism is partly concealed by the ambiguity of the word 'desirable'; for if by 'desirable' we merely mean what *can* be desired, the inference that pleasure is desirable because it is actually desired is obviously both irresistible and insignificant. But if we are seeking (as Mill is) for an ethical principle, from which practical rules may be deduced and which therefore must contain implicitly the notion 'ought', I cannot see how we are logically to reach such a principle through the most extensive observation of what men actually desire. And the same may be said of all attempts to construct an ethical system on a basis of physical fact; or on the basis of any other kind of psychical facts except ethical beliefs. We may affirm *à priori* that there must be a gap in all such reasonings—where the notion 'ought' is introduced—which does not admit of being logically bridged over.

Let us now examine the question above-reserved; *viz.*, whether it is possible to state any general characteristics by which true first principles may be distinguished from false ones; besides, that is, the characteristic of being self-evident to the mind that contemplates them. Such criteria would certainly be useful, if they can be found: since the history of thought makes it only too clear that the human mind, philosophic and unphilosophic, is liable to affirm as self-evidently true what is afterwards agreed to be false. No doubt the Cartesian condition of 'clearly and distinctly conceiving' whatever we affirm to be self-evident affords a partial protection against such errors; by carefully conforming to it we may often avoid mistaking mere habitual assumptions, or beliefs inadvertently accepted on authority, for intuitive truths. But though this precaution is a valuable one, it is certainly not adequate: as an inspection of the first principles of Cartesian physics will sufficiently show. It is therefore important to examine what Reid and others have to offer in the way of further criteria. Of these there seem to be chiefly two which have obtained a wide currency and on which considerable stress has been laid by thinkers of more than one school; *viz.*, (1) Universality (or approximate universality) of acceptance,—'consent of learned and unlearned', and (2) Originality, as inferred from the early date at which certain beliefs make their appearance in any particular mind. I propose to consider each of these separately.

First, however, I would observe that it makes a fundamental difference whether these or any similar criteria are used as supplementary to the characteristic of

---

[2] *Cf. Utilitarianism*, c. 4.

apparent self-evidence, or as substitutes for it. It seems to me a cardinal defect of Reid's philosophy that he leaves this difference in the back-ground, and does not always make it clear from which of the two points of view he is arguing. Regarded in the former light, I should quite admit the importance of the criterion of 'consent', the logical value to any individual mind of the agreement with other minds in any given intuition. It may be thought, perhaps, that so long as any proposition presents itself as self-evident, we can feel no need of anything more, though we may afterwards come to regard it as false: since self-evidence, *ex vi termini*, leaves no room for any doubt that a supplementary criterion could remove. But this view does not sufficiently allow for the complexity of our intellectual processes. If we have once learnt, either from personal experience or from the history of human thought, that we are liable to be mistaken in the affirmation of apparently self-evident propositions, we may surely retain this general conviction of our fallibility along with the special impression of the self-evidence of any proposition which we may be contemplating; and thus, however strong this latter impression may be, we shall still admit our need of some further protection against the possible failure of our faculty of intuition. Such a further guarantee we may reasonably find in 'general consent'; for though the protection thus given is not perfect—since there are historical examples of untrue propositions generally accepted as self-evident—it at least excludes all such error as arises from the special weaknesses and biases of individual minds, or of particular sections of the human race. A proposition which presents itself to my mind as self-evident, and is in harmony with all the rest of my intuitions relating to the same subject, and is also ascertained to be accepted by all other minds that have been led to contemplate it, may after all turn out to be false: but it seems to have as high a degree of certainty as I can hope to attain under the existing conditions of human thought.

The case is very different when the argument from 'consent' is used not to confirm but to override my individual judgment as to the self-evidence of any proposition. Even so it may afford a sufficient ground for a practical decision: certainly if I found myself alone *contra mundum*, I should think it more probable that I was wrong than that the world was, and such a balance of probability is enough to act on: but I could not treat the proposition in question as sufficiently known for purposes of scientific reasoning. For the argument establishing it would equally establish the defective condition of the individual intellect that failed to see its truth: and would therefore afford a general probability of error in any exercise of that intellect on the subject to which the proposition related.

Let us pass to consider the second of the above-mentioned criteria, Originality. It seems to me that the stress laid on this by Reid and other writers is chiefly due to a psychological assumption now almost exploded; *viz.*, that the human mind exists at birth in a condition which, though imperfect, in so far as undeveloped, is at least free from positive faults: in which, therefore, the exercise of its cognitive faculties, so far as it is capable of exercising them, must result in truth. It is hardly necessary at the present day to point out how entirely this assumption lacks scientific foundation: since not only is this original uncorrupted state of the human intellect nowhere given in experience, but we do not find any approximation to it as we trace back the history of any individual man, or of the human race generally, to its sources. Indeed there probably remain but few thinkers who conceive themselves in a position to urge the ascertained originality of any belief as positive evidence of its truth. There seem, however, to be still some who would apply the criterion negatively; holding that if we can explain the derivation of an apparently self-evident belief, we thereby show its apparent self-evidence to be illusory. This view I propose briefly to consider.

The supposed explanation must consist in stating either (1) the physical or (2) the psychical conditions of the mental phenomenon which is said to be derived. Now on the physiological question I speak with all diffidence: but I believe that physiologists have no such knowledge of the bodily conditions under which true and false beliefs respectively are produced, as could possibly justify us in invalidating an apparently self-evident proposition on physiological grounds; except in the case of mental derangement revealed by physical symptoms, or of beliefs that are normally received through the operation of the organs of sense. A clairvoyant may have reason to distrust his visions because they come with his eyes closed; but I am aware of no similar grounds for discrediting ethical intuitions.

It will seem then that the explanation that is to invalidate the self-evidence of an apparent intuition must be psychological. Now it is universally held, by English psychologists at least, that we know Mind only as a series of transient phenomena—except so far as we are allowed to know the permanence, identity, and free causality of the subject of these phenomena; a point which does not now concern us. At any rate the psychological 'derivation' of any belief or other mental phenomenon can be at most an account of the transient psychical facts— whether beliefs or merely feelings—which experience shows to be invariable antecedents of the phenomenon explained. We have no ground for supposing these antecedents really to persist in their consequent under a changed form, when they have apparently passed away. It is necessary to lay stress on this, because several writers of the Associational school assume the right of transferring chemical conceptions to psychical change; and regard mental phenomena as 'compounded' of their antecedents just as a piece of matter is conceived to be composed of its chemical elements. I have never seen any justification for this procedure. Certainly the analogy of material chemistry fails to justify it. When the coexistence of the two antecedents oxygen and hydrogen is followed by the appearance of the heterogeneous matter called water, we have two distinct reasons for conceiving the oxygen and hydrogen to have a latent existence in the water; first that the weight of the water exactly corresponds to the weight of the oxygen and the hydrogen, and secondly that we can reverse the process of change and exhibit the water as the immediate antecedent of the oxygen and hydrogen.

But neither of these reasons exists—nor any other that I am aware of—for attributing more compositeness to any mental phenomenon than we can discern in it by direct introspective analysis.

If then it be admitted that the so-called 'explanation' of an apparent intuition can only consist in a statement of its antecedents, not its elements, we have to ask in what way such a statement can affect the question of its truth or falsehood. Some writers really seem to think that the mere fact of a belief having been caused is a ground for distrusting it, unless we can show that its causes have been such as to make it true. But this doctrine lands us at once in universal scepticism; since the premisses of any such demonstration must be beliefs, which having been caused will themselves require to be proved true. Unless indeed it is held that the ultimate premisses of all reasoning are uncaused!—a paradox which I have no ground for attributing to the writers in question. Otherwise if all beliefs are equally in the position of having had invariable antecedents, it is obvious that this characteristic alone cannot serve to invalidate any of them.

If therefore an apparently self-evident proposition is to be discredited on account of its derivation, it must be not merely because, as a psychical phenomenon, it is the consequent of certain antecedents, but because it can be shown from experience that these particular antecedents are more likely to produce a false belief than a true one. I am far from denying that such a demonstration is possible in the case of some propositions that have been put forward as self-evident ethical principles: but I do not remember to have ever seen it systematically attempted.

6. Some Fundamental Ethical Controversies

The discussion that follows seems to require a few words of excuse and explanation, on account of the triteness of the topics discussed, and the difficulty of saying anything substantially new upon them. So long as ethical thought is alive and disagreement continues on fundamental points, controversy must continue; at the same time I have no sure hope that the present profound disagreements are likely to be terminated, as similar disputes have been terminated in the progress of the exact sciences, by the rational confutation of all divergent opinions except one. Attempts at such confutation can only take one of two forms: (1) demonstration of inconsistency in the system assailed, and (2) demonstration of paradox —i.e., of conflict with the common sense of mankind. The former method is often recognised as completely effective against certain parts of a system as expounded; but it is always difficult to feel sure that these parts are really vital, and that the substance of the doctrine assailed may not be so remodelled as to avoid the demonstrated inconsistency: nor may we even say that only one internally consistent system is possible to a reasonable man;—rather we seem able to conceive an indefinite number of internally consistent systems, and though, doubtless, all or most of these if fully worked out would involve paradoxical elements, we can rarely be sure that the paradoxes will be completely deterrent. For (2) demonstration of paradox cannot be formally cogent, unless the moralist convicted of paradox has expressly accepted Common Sense as a decisive authority; and even in this case it often cannot be made completely cogent, owing to the amount of vagueness and ambiguity, of division and disagreement, which we find in the moral common sense of any one social group in any one age, and the amount of change that we find as we pass from age to age and from group to group. For myself, I feel bound to say that though I have always been anxious to ascertain and disposed to respect the verdict of Common Sense in any ethical dispute, I cannot profess to regard it as final and indisputable: I cannot profess to hold that it is impossible for me ever to be right on an ethical point on which an overwhelming majority is clearly opposed to me. And as I cannot admit this myself, I cannot expect any similar admission from opponents. Accordingly I should like it to be understood that in what follows confutation of opponents is not aimed at; in fact, it is by the definite exclusion of this aim that I hope to impart a certain novelty of treatment to my familiar matter. What is aimed at is merely

[From *Mind*, 14 (Oct. 1889), 473–87. It was responded to by T. Fowler and L. A. Selby-Bigge in *Mind*, 15 (1890), 89–93 and 93–9.]

a diminution of the amount of misunderstanding which philosophical controversy —especially on fundamental points—has always involved. Probably, complete mutual understanding will never be reached until we have reached complete confutation of fundamental errors; but it seems easier to approximate to the former result, since we have all experienced the interest and satisfaction of comprehending an intellectual position with which we are yet obliged altogether to disagree.

I desire, therefore, to promote mutual understanding on some fundamental points of ethical controversy: by further explaining my own view where my original exposition of it (in my *Methods of Ethics*) appears from criticism to have been incomplete; and by pointing out where and why some further explanation of my critics' views is needed to enable me to understand them.

I. I may begin by saying that no other aim but this of removing misunderstandings could have induced me to recur to the ancient problem of the Freedom of the Will. I have no pretension of providing a theoretical solution of this problem; and, indeed, the first misunderstanding which I wish to remove is one which attributes to me such a pretension. A very courteous criticism of what I have previously written on this subject (in bk. i., ch. 5, of my *Methods of Ethics*) which I find in Mr. Fowler's *Principles of Morals*, pt. ii.,[1] concludes with this sentence: 'I venture to suggest that the difficulty raised by this antinomy is not really resolved in either direction by Professor Sidgwick's argument.' This is quite true; but my argument, as I conceived it, did not aim—as Mr. Fowler seems to suppose—at a *theoretical* solution of the difficulty caused by the conflict between what I called the 'formidable array of cumulative evidence offered for Determinism' and the Libertarian 'affirmation of consciousness in the moment of deliberate action': it aimed merely at a *practical* solution of the difficulty, by showing that for purposes of practical reasoning the two opposed arguments cannot really collide. I tried to show that, on the one hand, so far as we reason to any definite conclusions concerning the *future* actions of ourselves or other human beings, we inevitably consider them as determined by unvarying laws: if they are not completely so determined—and we cannot avoid concluding that they are not, if we accept the Libertarian proposition—then our reasoning is *pro tanto* liable to error; but the general recognition of this possibility of error can introduce no practical difference in the conclusions of such reasonings; since the most thorough-going belief in the freedom of human wills cannot be made the basis of any definite forecast as to the effects of the volitions assumed to be free. On the other hand, I tried to make clear that when we are ascertaining—according to any ethical principles and method—what choice it is reasonable to make between two alternatives of *present* conduct, it is as impossible for us to use Determinist conceptions as it is impossible to use Libertarian conceptions when we are endeavouring to

[1] Ch. ix., pp. 330–1.

forecast *future* conduct. Now, if both parts of this argument are accepted, I submit that a practical escape from the perplexities caused by the Free Will controversy —perplexities which many thoughtful persons have regarded as most gravely practical—has been completely provided: a theoretical solution has certainly not been provided, but neither has it been attempted.

I proceed to ask, then, if either part of my argument, as above summarised, is disputed. I do not find either in Mr. Fowler's, or in any other, recent discussion of the question, any reasoning directed against my contention as to the inapplicability of Libertarian conceptions in rational forecasts of the future conduct of human beings; nor do I find that Mr. Fowler at least definitely denies what I have said as to the irresistible affirmation of Freedom in the moment of deliberate action. But he seems to hold that this affirmation is effectively neutralised by the 'counter-argument' that 'we are not sufficiently acquainted with all the springs of action and their relative force', so that 'we may fairly argue that, if our experience were wider still, and we were fully acquainted with all the antecedent circumstances, every volition might be fully accounted for'. And this, or something like this, seems to be the answer that Determinists generally are disposed to give when Libertarians urge the 'immediate affirmation of consciousness'.

Now, I contend that the completest acceptance of the hypothetical conclusion of this counter-argument can have no practical effect, unless it leads men to abstain from the effort to act rationally, and consciously surrender themselves to the play of mere impulse; and I do not think that any Determinist will argue that his conclusion either ought to have, or does ordinarily have, this paralysing effect on the practical reason. If it does not have this effect on me, if I still attempt to act rationally, then inevitably—whatever may be the ethical principles on which I attempt to act—I cannot fail to experience the old eternal conflict between the judgment of reason and irrational impulse. And, whenever I experience this conflict, I cannot see how my actual consciousness of choosing between alternatives of conduct, one of which I conceive to be right or reasonable, can be affected by my admission of the hypothetical proposition that, 'if I were fully acquainted with all the antecedent circumstances of the volition that I am about to make, it might be fully accounted for'. It still remains impossible for me to regard the absence of adequate motive to do what I judge to be reasonable as a rational ground for not choosing to do it; and it remains impossible for me to think that I cannot now choose to do what I conceive to be reasonable,—supposing that there is no obstacle to my doing it except absence of adequate motive,—however strong may be my inclination to act unreasonably, and however uniformly I may have yielded to such inclinations in the past. I do not, of course, deny that the *difficulty* of resisting vicious inclination is made greater by previous surrenders to inclination; but I cannot conceive this difficulty becoming impossibility, so long as the consciousness of voluntary choice remains. I am quite willing to admit that this conviction *may* be illusory: that if I knew my own nature I *might* see it to be predetermined that, being so constituted and in such circumstances, I should act on the occasion in question contrary to my rational judgment. But I cannot conceive myself seeing this, without at the same time conceiving my whole conception of what I now call 'my' action fundamentally altered: I cannot conceive that if I contemplated the actions of my organism in this light I should refer them to my 'self'—i.e., to the conscious mind so contemplating—in the sense in which I now refer them. The admission, therefore, that my conviction of the possibility of my acting in accordance with reason *may* be illusory is an admission that can have no practical effect: I must use, in thinking about action, the only conception of human volition that is now possible to me; and this is strictly incompatible with the conception of my choice between rational judgment and irrational inclination as predetermined.

I do not quite know how far Determinists at the present day would deny the guarded statement that I have just given of the inevitableness of Libertarian conceptions. If they do not deny it, I think that most Determinists will probably admit that my *theoretical* suspension of judgment on the question of Free Will does not prevent me from attaining a complete *practical* solution of the difficulties of the question.

But it appears that Libertarians, if I may take Dr. Martineau as a specimen, are not willing to admit this; in fact, Dr. Martineau seems to regard the position that I take up as more untenable than that of a thorough-going Determinist.

'I can,' he says, 'understand and intellectually respect the thorough-going determinist intensely possessed by the conception of causality that rules through all the natural sciences, and never doubting that, as a "universal postulate," it must be driven perforce through the most refractory phenomena of human experience. I can understand the emphatic claim of the reflective moralist for the exemption of his territory from a law which admits of no alternative . . . But I cannot understand the intermediate mood which imagines the chasm of difference reducible to a step which, for all practical purposes, it is not worth while to bridge over or fill up.' Dr. Martineau can 'grant, indeed, that in drawing up an objective code of actions to be prohibited and required the two doctrines would not widely diverge in their results . . . but,' he thinks, it is inconceivable that the acceptance of Determinism should not make a fundamental 'difference of the dynamics of the moral life . . . On such a ground,' it seems to him 'you may build your mill of social ethics, with all its chambers neat and adequate, and its great wheel expecting to move; but you have turned aside the stream on which it all depends; the waters are elsewhere; and your structure stands dead and silent on the bank.'[2]

I understand the meaning of this eloquent passage to be that the conception of the Freedom of the Will supplies a moral motive to action which is necessarily withdrawn by the adoption of the Determinist conclusion: I do not, however, obtain from it any clear idea of the precise nature of the motive that is supposed

---

[2] *Types of Ethical Theory* (2nd ed.), vol. ii., p. 42.

to be supplied. As I have already said, I find the consciousness of freedom, in a certain sense, inseparable from the only conception of human volition that I am now able to form; and it is possible that Dr. Martineau may mean no more than this. But I find no practical difficulty in acting with the consciousness of free choice as above defined, while, at the same time, always reasoning on a purely Determinist basis in forecasting the future, or explaining the past actions of myself and others, and while also recognising that a reconciliation of these distinct intellectual attitudes is a speculative *desideratum*; and I do not see in what way a speculative conviction of the Freedom of the Will would either directly strengthen the motives to do what I judge to be, on the whole, reasonable, or weaken the force of the impulses that conflict with rational judgment;—unless it be through a certain process of theological reasoning which I do not regard as conclusive, and to which Dr. Martineau does not expressly refer.

I cannot see that the speculative belief on Free Will would alter my view of ultimate ends. If Happiness, whether private or general, be the ultimate end of action on a Libertarian view, it must be equally so on a Determinist view; and if Perfection is in itself admirable and desirable, it surely remains equally so whether any individual's approximation to it is entirely determined by inherited nature and external influences or not:—except so far as the notion of Perfection includes that of Free Will. Now Free Will is obviously not included in our common notions of physical and intellectual perfection; and it seems to me also not to be included in the common notions of the excellences of character which we call virtues: the manifestations of courage, temperance and justice do not become less admirable because we can trace their antecedents in a happy balance of inherited dispositions developed by a careful education.

Again, I do not see how the affirmation or negation of Free Will can reasonably affect our practical conclusions as to the fittest means for the attainment of any of these ultimate ends, so far as the connexion between means and end is believed to exist on empirical or other scientific grounds. I do not see how an act now deliberated on can be scientifically known to be less or more a means to any ulterior end, because it is predetermined; and, so far as in considering how we ought to act in any case we have to calculate the probable future actions of others and also of ourselves, I have already shown that our decision on the question of Free Will cannot practically affect such calculations. I admit, however, that the case is conceivably altered when we introduce theological considerations. According to the received view of the moral government of the world, the performance of Duty is the best means of attaining the agent's happiness largely through its expected consequences in another world in which virtue will be rewarded and vice punished by God: if, therefore, the belief in the existence of God and the immortality of the soul is held to depend on the assumption of Free Will, this latter becomes obviously of fundamental ethical importance. It is possible that this is what is really meant by Dr. Martineau in the passage before quoted; and if so, I cannot but admit that the denial of Free Will removes a rational motive to the performance of duty, so far as the reasonableness of duty is rested on the particular theological argument just mentioned. I must, however, point out that the assumption of Free Will cannot be said to be generally regarded as indispensable to the establishment of the belief in the moral government of the world, since an important section of theologians who have held this belief with most intense conviction have been Determinists.

I do not, however, wish to enter upon the theological argument at the threshold of which I have now arrived. If it is admitted (1) that the assumption of the Freedom of the Will is in a certain sense inevitable to anyone exercising rational choice, and (2) that the affirmation of Free Will as a point of speculative doctrine is only important ethically so far as it is implicated in a certain theological argument, then the misunderstandings which I am concerned to remove will have vanished.

II. In speaking of the notion of 'free' choice as inseparable from the only conception of conscious action that experience enables me to form, I have restricted my consideration to the choice between the alternatives of 'rational' and 'irrational' conduct. It is, I conceive, this alone that concerns us, from an ethical point of view; not the possibility of merely indeterminate choice,—of what Green calls an 'arbitrary freak of unmotived willing',—but the possibility of acting in accordance with our rational judgment when it conflicts with irrational impulses. The phrase just used affords a transition to a second fundamental misunderstanding, which I am anxious, if possible, to clear up;—all the more, because it is a misunderstanding among persons who are in general agreement as to the right method of dealing with particular ethical questions. According to my view, what I have just spoken of as a 'rational judgment' on a practical question is normally expressed in the form 'X is right' or 'X ought to be done'; and if the judgment be attained by deduction from a principle, such a principle is always capable of being expressed as a proposition in which the word 'right' or 'ought' occurs. The notion that these words have in common is, therefore, the same in different ethical systems: different systems give different answers to the fundamental question, 'what is right', but not, therefore, a different meaning to the question. The Utilitarian, in my view, affirms that 'what is right' in any particular case is what is most conducive to the general happiness; but he does not—or ought not to—mean by the word 'right' anything different from what an anti-utilitarian moralist would mean by it. Again, according to me, this fundamental notion is ultimate and unanalysable: in saying which I do not mean to affirm that it belongs to the 'original constitution of the mind', and is not the result of a process of development: that is a question of Psychology—or rather Psychogony—with which I am not concerned: I merely mean that as I now find it in my thought I cannot resolve it into, or explain it by, any more elementary notions. I regard it as co-ordinate with the notion expressed by the word 'is' or 'exists'. Possibly these and other fundamental notions may, in the progress of philosophy, prove capable of being arranged in some system of rational evolution; but I hold that no such system has as yet been constructed and that, therefore, the notions are now and for us ultimate.

I find, however, that these opinions do not seem to be shared by other writers who agree with me in adopting—with or without reserves and qualifications—the Utilitarian standard. But I find a great difficulty in making out exactly where the difference lies. Even in the case of Bentham, who uniformly aims at the most uncompromising clearness of exposition, I nevertheless find this difficulty. For instance, there is a passage in his *Principles of Morals and Legislation* (ch. i., § 10) in which he expressly controverts the opinion that I have just expressed as to the identity of the meaning of the terms 'right' and 'ought' in different ethical systems. He says:—

'Of an action that is conformable to the principle of utility'—*i.e.*, which has 'a tendency to augment the happiness of the community greater than any it has to diminish it'—'one may always say either that it is one that ought to be done, or at least that it is not one that ought not to be done. One may also say that it is right it should be done, or at least that it is not wrong it should be done; that it is a right action, at least that it is not a wrong action. When thus interpreted, the words *ought* and *right* and *wrong* and others of that stamp have a meaning; *when otherwise, they have none.*'[3]

This seems unmistakable; and we naturally infer that whenever Bentham is found using the words 'ought and right, and others of that stamp', he will mean by them 'what tends to augment the general happiness'. But how then are we to explain the proposition found in a note to the same chapter (§1, added July, 1822)—*viz.*, that his fundamental principle 'states the greatest happiness of all those whose interest is in question as being the right and proper, and only right and proper, end of human action'? We cannot surely suppose that he merely means to affirm that it is conducive to general happiness to take general happiness as the sole end of action. If not, what meaning can we give to the term in the proposition just quoted, except precisely the same meaning that it would have if used in a denial of this principle by an anti-utilitarian moralist?

Bentham unfortunately cannot answer; and I do not quite know who at the present day will answer for him. I therefore turn to Mr. Fowler, whose view—though it differs importantly from Bentham's—I have a somewhat similar difficulty in understanding. Mr. Fowler expressly states that he 'does not agree' with me 'in regarding as ultimate and unanalysable' the idea expressed by the word 'right' or 'ought'. His reasons for disagreeing are, as I gather, given in the following passage: 'We maintain (1) that the idea of right is relative to the circumstances in which man is placed; (2) that it is explicable by the idea of good; and (3) that it is possible to discover its origin and trace its growth in the history

---

[3] These last italics are mine.

both of the individual and of the race'.[4] Now of these reasons—which (I ought to say) are not expressly addressed to me—only the second appears to me *primâ facie* relevant to the particular point at issue between Mr. Fowler and myself. 'Relativity to the circumstances in which man is placed' seems to me a characteristic of the *application* of the idea of right, but I do not see that it affects the ultimateness and unanalysability of the idea itself; it affects the answer given to the question 'what is right', but not the meaning of the question. Again, as I have already said, the fullest knowledge of the origin and growth of the idea would not necessarily affect the question whether it is now capable of analysis; nor do I see that Mr. Fowler's account of its origin and growth contains anything that bears on this question—unless it be the second of the three statements above quoted, that the idea of right is 'explicable by the idea of good'.

What, then, does this 'explication' amount to? I thought at first that Mr. Fowler's meaning must be that 'rightness' is essentially an attribute of *means* not of *ends*, and really signifies that the object to which it is applied is thought to be the only fit means, or the means best fitted, to the realisation of some end, which we conceive as 'good' but not 'right',—although the notion of the end may not always be distinctly present in consciousness when we affirm 'rightness' of the means. This may hold, so long as we fix attention on actions as distinguished from their ulterior ends; but when we fix it on the *ends* of action, the question arises how the notion of 'good' is to be defined, and whether we do not conceive 'ultimate good' as the 'right and proper end of human action'—to use Bentham's phrase. It seems to me at any rate paradoxical to deny that we commonly think of certain ultimate ends—or the conscious adoption of these ends—as 'right': and other parts of Mr. Fowler's discussion would lead me to conclude that he does not mean to deny this. Thus he recognises (p. 227) that man has a 'reason capable of comparing the ends to which his feelings impel him', and that when this comparison is made we approve (p. 231) of the 'conscious choice of the greater good or lesser evil', even when it involves a sacrifice (p. 234) of 'the interests of ourselves to the interests of others': indeed he considers that it is in this conscious choice and the self-approval that supervenes thereon that 'morality first makes its appearance'. Again, he recognises as an element of 'the process of approbation' what he calls 'an act of judgment on the character' of the volition approved, besides and distinct from the mere 'feeling of satisfaction' which is sometimes denoted by the word 'approval'. I conclude, therefore, that the approval of the conscious choice of another's greater good in preference to the chooser's lesser good, is regarded by Mr. Fowler as a normal moral judgment: and I do not see how in this judgment the notion 'right' can fail to come in. For this judgment must be expressible in the proposition 'that conscious choice, &c., is right', and the word 'right' in this proposition cannot *mean* 'conducive to greatest good on

---

[4] The numbers are introduced by me for convenience of reference.

the whole', since that meaning would reduce the proposition to insignificance. In what way, then, can the idea of right, as used in the judgment of approval of the conscious choice of another's good in preference to one's own, be 'explicable by the idea of good'? And if no such explication is here admissible, may we not say that the idea of right, as here applied, is 'ultimate and unanalysable' in the sense in which, as above explained, I use the latter term?

III. I am the more concerned to get this point clear because the principle that another's greater good is to be preferred to one's own lesser good is, in my view, the fundamental principle of morality—the ultimate, irreducible basis to which reflection shows the commonly accepted rules of Veracity, Good Faith, &c., to be subordinate. And this leads me to a third point of fundamental importance on which it seems possible to clear away some misunderstanding: I mean what I have called the 'Dualism of the Practical Reason'. I am not particularly pleased with the phrase, which has a pretentious sound, and is perhaps liable to mislead by suggesting that I claim for my view a completeness of systematic construction which, on the contrary, I wish to avoid claiming; but it seemed the most convenient phrase to express the conclusion in which I was forced to acquiesce after a prolonged effort to effect a complete systematisation of our common ethical thought. Along with (a) a fundamental moral conviction that I ought to sacrifice my own happiness, if by so doing I can increase the happiness of others to a greater extent than I diminish my own, I find also (b) a conviction—which it would be paradoxical to call 'moral', but which is none the less fundamental—that it would be irrational to sacrifice any portion of my own happiness unless the sacrifice is to be somehow at some time compensated by an equivalent addition to my own happiness. I find both these fundamental convictions in my own thought with as much clearness and certainty as the process of introspective reflection can give: I find also a preponderant assent to them—at least implicit—in the common sense of mankind: and I find, on the whole, confirmation of my view in the history of ethical thought in England. I admit that it is only a minority of moralists who explicitly accept this dualism of rational or governing principles; but I think myself justified in inferring a wider implicit acceptance of the dualism from the importance attached by dogmatic moralists generally to the conception of a moral government of the world, and from the efforts of empirical utilitarians to prove—as in Bentham's posthumous treatise—that action conducive to greatest happiness generally is always also conducive to the agent's greatest happiness.

Well, I have to acknowledge that this dualism—at least, my statement of it—does not appear to be accepted by any of the writers who have criticised my book. This naturally shakes my confidence in the view; but it shakes it less than would otherwise be the case, because, while to some critics the sacrifice of self to others seems solely rational, others avow uncompromising egoism; and no one has seriously attempted to deny that the choice between one or other alternative

—according to any forecast of happiness based on mere mundane experience—is occasionally forced on us. I have not, therefore, seen cause to modify my view; but I admit that I put it forward without a sufficient rational justification, so far as Egoism is concerned. This objection was forcibly urged in a review of my book (2nd edition) by Prof. v. Giżycki in the *Vierteljahrsschrift für wissen-schaftliche Philosophie* (Jahrg. iv., Heft 1), where is was pointed out that I had made no attempt to show the irrationality of the sacrifice of self-interest to duty. I will not pause to explain how the plan of my book—concerned as it was with 'methods' rather than 'principles'—led to this omission: I quite agree with Prof. v. Giżycki that the missing argument, if demanded, ought to be supplied; and certainly the assumption upon which the rationality of Egoism is based has been denied by philosophers; though the denial seems to Common Sense so absurd that a serious demand for its explicit statement is rather paradoxical. The assumption is simply that the distinction between any one individual and any other is real and fundamental, and that consequently 'I' am concerned with the quality of my existence as an individual in a sense, fundamentally important, in which I am not concerned with the quality of the existence of other individuals. If this be admitted, the proposition that this distinction is to be taken as fundamental in determining the ultimate end of rational action for an individual cannot be disproved; and to me this proposition seems self-evident, although it *primâ facie* contradicts the equally self-evident proposition that my own good is no more to be regarded than the good of another.

If the question were put to me: 'But suppose that there is no practical solution of this contradiction, through any legitimately obtained conclusion or postulate as to the moral government of the world, or in any other way: what then? Do you abandon morality?' I should answer: 'Certainly not, but I abandon the idea of rationalising it completely. I should doubtless still, through sympathy and senti-ments protective of social well-being, imparted by education and sustained by communication with other men, feel a strong desire for the general observance of rules conducive to general happiness; and practical reason would still impel me to the performance of duty in the more ordinary cases in which what is recog-nised as duty is in harmony with self-interest properly understood. But, in the rare cases of a recognised conflict between self-interest and duty, practical reason, being divided against itself, would cease to be a motive on either side; the conflict would be decided by the comparative preponderance of one or other of two groups of non-rational impulses.' That is, I should lapse to the position which many utilitarians since Hume have avowedly held—that ultimate ends are deter-mined by feeling, not by reason. Here, as I understand, Prof. v. Giżycki would disagree: he holds that, while the demand for the reconciliation of Virtue and Happiness—which he recognises as normal to humanity—is merely an 'affectives Bedürfniss', the preference of Virtue or general happiness to private happiness is a dictate of reason, which remains no less clear and cogent, however ultimate and uncompensated may be the sacrifice of private happiness that it imposes. I do not deny this position to be tenable; since, even if the reality and essentiality of the distinction between one individual and another be granted, I do not see how to prove its fundamental practical importance to anyone who refuses to admit it; but I find such a refusal impossible to myself, and I think it paradoxical.

Suppose now that the reasonableness of the assumption required for the reconciliation of Duty and Self-interest—the assumption of the 'moral government' or 'moral order' of the world—is granted: suppose it granted that Virtue may be assumed to be always conducive to the virtuous agent's happiness on the whole, though the connexion between the two is not scientifically cognisable. The view of morality that I advocate—the systematisation of the morality of Common Sense on a utilitarian basis—does not then seem to involve any fundamental practical difficulty; though it is still liable to many doubts and disagreements as regards details, from the inevitable imperfections of the hedonistic method. It remains, however, open to a fundamental theoretical objection, urged by Mr. Rashdall in a penetrating criticism of my views which appeared in *Mind* No. 38. Mr. Rashdall considers that the 'central difficulty' of my position lies in the 'assignment of a different end to the individual and to the race'. He argues that if 'it is pronounced right and reasonable for A to make sacrifices of his own happiness to the good of B', as this must be equally right and reasonable for B, C and D, 'the admission that altruism is rational' compels us to conceive 'the happiness which we ought to seek for society', not as mere happiness but as 'moral happiness'. The ultimate end, for the race as well as for the individual, thus becomes composite: it consists of a higher good, Virtue, along with a lower good, Happiness, the two being so related that in case of conflict the higher is always to be preferred to the lower.

Here I admit, as in a sense true, the starting-point of Mr. Rashdall's argument; I admit substantially the contention that my view 'assigns a different end to the individual and to the race', though for a reason that I shall presently state, I regard this phraseology as misleading. But, granting to the full the alleged difference, I am unable to see why it constitutes a difficulty, since the individual is essentially and fundamentally different from the larger whole—the universe of sentient beings—of which he is conscious of being a part: just because he is conscious of his relation to similar parts of the same whole, while the whole itself has no such relation. I, therefore, do not see any inconsistency in holding that while it *would* be reasonable for the aggregate of sentient beings, if it could act collectively, to aim at its own happiness only as ultimate end—and *would* be reasonable for an individual to do the same if he were the only sentient being in the universe—it is yet *actually* reasonable for an individual to make an ultimate sacrifice of his happiness for the sake of the greater happiness of others, as well as reasonable for him to take his own happiness as ultimate end; owing, as before explained, to the double view which he necessarily takes of himself as at once an individual essentially separate from other individuals, and at the same time essentially a part among similar parts of a larger whole.

At the same time I am not prepared to deny that a consistent system might be worked out on the basis of such a composite End as Mr. Rashdall suggests, and I shall not attempt to prove, before seeing it in a fully developed form, that it would be more open to attack on the score of paradox than my own. But I can give a decisive reason for not accepting it myself: *viz.*, that when Virtue and Happiness are hypothetically presented as alternatives, from a universal point of view, I have no doubt that I morally prefer the latter; I should not think it right to aim at making my fellow-creatures more moral, if I distinctly foresaw that as a consequence of this they would become less happy. I should even make a similar choice as regards my own future virtue, supposing it presented as an alternative to results more conducive to the General Happiness; and for this reason, among others, while holding the fulfilment of Duty to be ultimately reasonable for the individual no less than the pursuit of self-interest, I think it misleading to say that Virtue is an ultimate good to the individual as well as Happiness. As I have explained in my *Methods of Ethics*, bk. iii., ch. ii, § 3, I distinguish the question 'whether the dictates of Reason are always to be obeyed' from the question 'whether the dictation of Reason is always to be promoted'; and, while I answer the former question unhesitatingly in the affirmative, I leave the latter to be determined by empirical and utilitarian considerations.

7. Law and Morality

§ 1. In an earlier chapter I incidentally noticed the distinction between Ideal Morality or the true moral code—by many conceived and spoken of as the 'Law of God'—and Positive Morality, or the rules of duty supported by the sanctions of public opinion in any given age and country. It does not fall within the plan of this treatise to discuss the principles of the true moral code—except so far as this relates to the conduct of Governments, or of private persons in their relations to Government. But the moral opinions and sentiments prevalent in any community form so important a consideration in practically determining how its government ought to act, that it is desirable to survey briefly the general relations of Positive Morality to Positive Law in a modern State.

I must begin by making more complete the general conception of 'legal' in contrast to 'moral' rules which was introduced in chap. ii. I there, following Bentham and Austin, regarded as 'legal' those rules of which the violation is repressed, directly or indirectly, by the action of Government or its subordinates; whereas the violation of a rule of positive morality is only punished by general disapprobation and its social consequences. This definition corresponds approximately to the usage of the term 'law' in a well-ordered society, and lays stress on a characteristic of fundamental importance. But this difference in the sanctions attached to legal and moral rules respectively is not the only general and important distinction that a comparison of the two systems of rules shows; there is a difference of another kind in the comparative definiteness and systematic coherence of the two codes, to which I wish now to draw attention.[1]

Let us first observe that it would not be quite exact to define a law as a rule actually enforced by governmental penalties; since judges and magistrates are admittedly liable to err, and when they err, it would be correct to say that they have 'mistaken the law', and applied a rule that is not really a part of the law of the land.[2] What, then, precisely is the intellectual process by which a right

---

[Ch. 13: 200–216 of *The Elements of Politics*, 2nd edn., 1897.]

[1] The comparison thus drawn between Positive Law and Positive Morality is of some importance, as we shall see, in respect of the practical relations between the two which it is the object of this chapter to discuss. But I have developed it at more length than I should otherwise have done in view of a subsequent discussion of International Law and Morality in chap. xvii., for which the comparison here made appears to me an indispensable preliminary.

[2] In England, indeed, a decision of the highest Court of Appeal can hardly be held to be inconsistent with law, since, by a professional custom that has now the force of law, all other judges are bound to decide subsequent cases in accordance with it; if, therefore, it is inconsistent with law as it has been, the Court must be held to have practically made new law in pronouncing it. But in

judicial decision may be reached? The answers to this question are somewhat different in different countries and at different times. In such a community as we have throughout contemplated, I have assumed the existence of some established organ of legislation, some body or combination of bodies, whose general commands relative to the social conduct of members of the community will be unquestioningly applied by judges and, generally speaking, obeyed by the bulk of private members of the community. As we saw, it does not follow that the rules which it is the practice of Courts to apply have been all derived from this source: but in some countries they have in the main been formally so derived; that is, codes have been framed intended to cover the whole or chief part of the field with which judicial decisions have to deal. So far, then, as this is the case the judge's function is merely to interpret the code; if it is clear and complete, the process is easy and straightforward: but if any of the terms used in it are vague, he has to give them a precise meaning; if they are distinctly ambiguous in ordinary use, he has to infer from the rest of the code which meanings are intended; if two rules in the same code are apparently inconsistent, he has to find out some means of reconciling them, or to decide which is to give way to the other. It will easily be understood that this function requires care and subtlety and trained skill, even in the simplest case of a code recently framed: but it becomes more complex and usually more difficult when some time has elapsed, in which the code has been importantly modified by fresh legislation; since this not only increases the aggregate of rules that have to be interpreted, but also still more the danger of inconsistency in them, from the new matter introduced at different times by legislatures differently composed.

And the complexity is greater still in such a case as our own, where, as we saw, a great part of the Law has had an origin independent of the action of the Legislature; being composed partly of old customary rules gradually made more definite by judicial interpretation, partly of rules introduced by judges at an earlier stage of our history, from Roman law or other foreign sources, or from their own moral consciousness. In this case Law presents itself as a system of rules, heterogeneous both in their intellectual origin and in the source of their obligation regarded from the judges' point of view,—some are binding because the Legislature has laid them down, others because previous judges have agreed in accepting them. But, whatever their origin, there are two conditions to which in their application as law they are universally subject: they must be interpreted so as to be mutually consistent, and cogent reasons for a decision in every case that presents itself must, if possible, be somehow extracted from them. It is in the fulfilment of these conditions that judicial skill is shown, and in the endeavour to

countries other than England and her dependencies and the United States, judges are not so definitely bound to decide according to precedents; so that the decision of one judge may be contradicted by the decision of another in a similar case, and then it will manifestly follow that one of the two decisions was not in accordance with law.

fulfil them under difficulties a certain amount of judicial law-making inevitably occurs from time to time; for if two rules as previously defined are found to collide, or if there are two competing analogies equally applicable to a case that is not clearly included under any pre-existing rule, the judge is forced to give a fresh determination to the law that it is his aim merely to interpret. It should be observed, however, that the limited legislative power thus placed in the hands of a judge in a modern civilised community, is not placed there because he is selected or qualified for the purpose of exercising it; rather, we may say that he is selected and qualified for the purpose of keeping it as much as possible unexercised. His primary duty is to apply the law as it is, not to make it what he thinks it ought to be; and the more conscientiously and skilfully he fulfils his primary duty, the more will his power of determining law be limited to cases that are really unprovided for or ambiguously provided for in the law as already determined. Sometimes, in such innovations the judge is doubtless influenced by considerations of abstract equity or utility, but only within the strict limits above explained; since, where the decision clearly most in harmony with the analogies of established law is plainly inexpedient, it would now be generally recognised as a case for the intervention of the Legislature. In any case, the result is that in one way or another, either by the authority of the judge or by that of the Legislature, divisions of opinion as to the right application of received legal rules—and also any marked divergences between such rules and what is generally regarded as expedient—tend to be continually removed. And as the development of Law goes on, the function of the judge is confined within ever narrowing limits; the main source of modifications in legal relations comes to be more and more exclusively the Legislature.

§ 2. I have examined with some minuteness the process of development of law in a modern community, because it is due to the special characteristics of this process that the differences in such a community between Law and Positive Morality, when compared merely as intelligible systems of rules without regard to the motive for obeying them, are as striking and instructive as the differences in the sanctions attached to the two systems. We can see how law naturally tends to be greatly superior to Positive Morality in definiteness and consistency; since in the case of moral rules there is no judicial process by which doubts as to what the accepted rule *is* on any question can be authoritatively settled, and no legislative process by which any divergence from what, in the opinion of thoughtful persons, *ought* to be established morality, can be at once and decisively removed.

And it may be observed that the differences between the two systems of rules, both in respect of sanction and in respect of systematic intelligibility, have tended to become more marked as modern civilisation has developed. In earlier stages of European civilisation, there has often been law in real operation, in the sense of a complicated system of precise rules applied to the guidance of men's conduct by experts whose authority is generally accepted, with little or no governmental force sustaining the acceptance of the rules.[3] Under these circumstances, Law approaches to Positive Morality in respect of its sanction; and, on the other side, in periods when casuistry has really flourished,—as in the period of the later Middle Ages,—Positive Morality has shown an approximation to Law in the elaborateness and precision of its rules. From the fourteenth century onward, the acumen and industry of ecclesiastical writers were largely occupied in working out in a quasi-legal manner a body of rules, to be applied in the confessional to the practical guidance of ordinary private members of the medieval community: while, before the Reformation, there was no disposition, at once strong, widespread, and unconcealed, to dispute the claim of these writers to authority in the matters with which they dealt.

If we ask why this quasi-legal treatment of morality fell into the disrepute in which it now lies, there is a twofold answer to be given,—apart from the general indignation caused by Jesuitry, the effect of which taken alone would doubtless only have been transient. Partly the belief came to be widely held that in matters of morality, speaking broadly, any one honest man is as much an expert as any other, and that it is his duty to exercise his own judgement and follow the light of his own conscience. Partly—so far as some further enlightenment of a plain man's conscience was felt to be a desideratum—experience was thought to have shown the danger of trying to obtain this enlightenment from the industry and ingenuity of systematic moralists, exercised in formulating precisely the generally accepted rules: since the quasi-legal process of scrutinising closely the cases of difficulty and apparent conflict among such rules, in order to draw the lines of duty clear, must tend to bring into demoralising prominence the uncertainty and disagreement among experts on moral questions: while the lack of an authority to decide controversies rendered it impossible to reduce the element of doubt and discussion in the manner in which it is continually reduced in the development of law. And thus, as I have said, the moral code of a modern country has come to be necessarily inferior as an intelligible system to its law, because in the case of the former every man is encouraged to think himself a judge, there is no final court of appeal, and no one can admit any external legislation.

The consequence of this is, not only that we find, in the generally accepted moral code of a modern society, an amount of conflict, vagueness, and uncertainty, that could not for a moment be tolerated in modern law: but also that, when we examine closely the aggregate of opinions and sentiments, the expression of which in word or act constitutes the effective sanction of positive morality,

---

[3] For instance, Maine, in his account of the ancient Irish Law developed by the Brehons (*Early History of Institutions*, chap. ii.), says that 'the process of the Irish Courts, even if it was compulsory, was at the utmost extremely weak'; and 'that it is at least a tenable view that the institutions which stood in the place of Courts of Justice only exercised jurisdiction through the voluntary submission of intending litigants'. Similarly—as I learn from Mr Bryce—in Iceland in the latter part of the tenth and the eleventh centuries the so-called Courts of Law had no coercive force at all.

we find, along with the generally accepted code, a number of special codes, more or less divergent from it on important points. What is called the code of honour—the rules of behaviour maintained by the *consensus* of gentlemen in modern Europe—is a well-known instance of this: but the same phenomenon is exhibited in some degree by various other divisions of society, based upon different grounds,—*e.g.*, by religious sects and parties, and the members of different trades and professions. And thus sometimes, owing to the predominance of particular religious sects or industrial classes, or of particular schools of thought or drifts of opinion, in different localities, we find noteworthy local variations in the prevalent judgment as to what is mischievous or the reverse in conduct.

§ 3. These differences become important when we proceed to consider the practical relations between the two systems of rules that we have been comparing. First, we have to recognise the possibility that Government, in legislating with a view to the general happiness of the governed, may come into conflict with the positive morality prevalent among them; may be led to enforce rights popularly regarded as wrongs, to compel men by legal penalties to do what they are commonly thought right in refusing to do, or to compel them to abstain from doing what is commonly thought innocent if not laudable. This is, indeed, less likely to happen in the case of legislators appointed by popular election, or even in the case of rulers, however appointed, whose education has tended to make them share the moral opinions and sentiments current in their community; since they are likely to share, among other current opinions, the belief that what is commonly thought right is conducive to the general happiness.* Still even in this case, owing to the divergences above noticed within the limits of the same community, such conflicts may occasionally arise: *e.g.*, the majority of a modern legislature may think it expedient to close theatres or public-houses on Sunday, when public opinion holds it allowable and desirable to keep them open, or to open museums and picture-galleries on the same day, when public opinion thinks it right to close them.[4] Any serious conflict of this kind is mischievous in two ways: by rendering it difficult to enforce the law in the particular case without an unusual exercise of force and consequent intense and diffused annoyance, and by its tendency to weaken the habit of obedience to law and government in the citizens generally. We cannot, indeed, therefore lay down that such a conflict is always to be avoided: the question must be decided in each particular case by a comparative forecast of the mischiefs just mentioned, and the good to be

---

* [Notice Sidgwick's assumption that everyone, including ordinary members of the common public, believes that 'what is commonly thought right is conducive to the general happiness'. Ed.]

[4] In the case of a community governed by foreigners the danger of this kind of conflict is, of course, much greater. Thus in several important legislative measures our Indian Government has acted contrary to the prevalent moral opinion of Hindoos: *e.g.*, in prohibiting infanticide and the burning of widows, in allowing the remarriage of widows, and in maintaining the rights of inheritance of converts to Christianity.

expected from the proposed legislation. But we may say generally that government ought to take all possible care to minimise the evil of this conflict, supposing it to be in some degree inevitable; thus, when any new governmental interference of a coercive kind is required to repress practices dangerous to social well-being, or otherwise to attain some important public end, it is expedient, if possible, that it should only take place after public attention has been strongly called to the need which the new regulations are designed to meet.[5]

Further, it is to be noted that even legislative measures that have the approval of the majority may come into collision with the moral beliefs and sentiments of important portions of the community: and the prospect even of this more limited conflict may be a weighty reason for deferring or modifying governmental interference that would be otherwise expedient. Even if the legislation in question is not exactly disapproved as immoral, it must always be a serious drawback to its expediency that it will have to contend with strong forces of desire, interest, and habit, without receiving effective support from Positive Morality.

Thus the actual condition of the positive morality of the community—including under the term all prevalent opinions as to the bad and good effects of actions—confines within rather narrow limits the power of an enlightened Government to act upon the community governed in conformity to the conclusions of the highest political wisdom of the time. On the other hand, it is no less important to note that the legislator has within limits a valuable power of modifying positive morality. Through the general habit of law-observance and the general recognition of the duty of obeying rules laid down by a legitimate authority—which we may expect to find in any well-ordered community—the legislator may obtain a general obedience to rules to which current morality is indifferent or even mildly averse; and then by the reaction of habitual conduct on opinion, a moral aversion to the opposite conduct may gradually grow up. In other cases, where Government interferes to prevent mischievous acts which are already vaguely regarded with some degree of moral disapprobation, the legislator or judge may produce a more sudden and impressive effect by giving sharpness and decision to this disapprobation. Especially we may say that the judicial organ of government is within certain limits accepted as a moral expert; if within these limits it classifies an act with crimes, public opinion is prepared so to regard it.

§ 4. But Positive Morality, in a well-ordered State, does not only support the action of Government: it has, of course, the further important function of regulating conduct in matters beyond the range of governmental coercion. To consider in detail how this function ought to be performed would be to write a

---

[5] In a state under popular government, it is of course impossible that any decided conflict between law and the moral opinion of a majority of the electorate should be more than very temporary.

treatise on ethics: but we may briefly note certain parts of social conduct where for special reasons the influence of moral opinion is indispensable or preferable, as a means of producing the kind of effects at which Law aims. In this survey it is convenient to distinguish between the *penalties* of Positive Morality and its *rewards*—between moral censure and moral approval or praise. It is to the operation of moral censure that our attention is naturally directed in studying the analogy between Law and Morality, and I shall accordingly begin by considering this: but, as we shall presently see, the respective functions of censure and praise cannot be sharply separated.

First, then, moral censure is the chief resource that remains available, when the means which the legislator employs fail to attain the end which he has in view, from accidental circumstances defeating their normal operation. For instance, granting that the conditions to which the legal validity of contracts is subjected are rightly imposed as generally suitable to the end in view, still particular cases may occur in which an engagement to do some lawful act was clearly made with full deliberation and without any coercion or misrepresentation or improper inducements, while at the same time the legal conditions have not been fulfilled. In such cases it is generally desirable that the violation of the engagement should be censured, though reparation cannot be legally exacted. So again, a testator may accidentally fail to make a valid will, though his intention may be expressed with sufficient clearness to make it the duty of his heir to conform to it if it is not in its nature improper: here, too, the moral opinion of persons acquainted with the circumstances may usefully take the place of the legal coercion that cannot be applied.

Secondly, there are cases in which the intervention of law is inapplicable as a remedy for undoubted mischief, owing to the general importance of leaving wide discretion to the private individuals who would have to be coerced. One chief case of this class is the treatment of children by parents: in order to maintain the parents' sense of responsibility on the one hand, and the child's habit of obedience and respect on the other, it does not seem generally expedient that Government should interfere with the domestic rule of the parent, unless there is evidence of gross neglect or cruelty; but there may easily be breaches of parental duty falling short of this, which may properly be visited with moral censure.

So again, we have before[6] seen that it is impossible to define the spheres of individual freedom for adults so that the observance of the limits may completely prevent all serious mutual annoyance; and, in particular, we have noted that the power which an individualistic system must necessarily secure to sane adults generally, of freely entering into and terminating economic relations with other individuals, may be used to injure and coerce those others. In such cases public

---

[6] See chap. iv. § 4.

opinion may importantly supplement law in repressing malevolent or intimidative exercise of legal freedom, and reducing mutual annoyance to a minimum; though it must be borne in mind that this very public opinion is itself a coercive force which, if misdirected, may do harm of this kind in the worst degree.

Again, there must always be cases, especially in the department of contract, in which the enforcement of strict legal rights would—owing to exceptional circumstances which a legislator or judge cannot safely take into account—be manifestly harsh in its effects, and would show a repulsive want of normal human sympathy.

Again, there are acts so highly detrimental to social wellbeing that it is desirable to supply a strong inducement to abstain from them, which are yet unsuitable objects of legal repression; because the temptations to do them being strong and concealment easy, it is impossible to prevent them altogether, while at the same time if they are driven into the greatest possible secrecy their mischief is liable to take a much more aggravated form. The leading case of this kind is intercourse of the sexes outside the conjugal relation: it has always been recognised that it is the special function of Positive Morality to keep this within the narrowest possible bounds, by affixing a strong stigma of discredit to such intercourse: but it has also been almost universally held that it would be unwise to make it legally punishable.

Finally, there is much mischief similar in kind to that which law aims at repressing, which it is expedient to leave to morality to deal with, merely because it is not sufficiently important in degree: such as insults and calumnies of minor gravity, deceptions and misrepresentations which have not caused any considerable amount of definite damage, though to leave them uncensured would tend to impair the pleasure and profit of social intercourse.

Let us turn to consider the matters in which the operation of morality by praise rather than censure is of special political importance. The chief case under this head is the expenditure of wealth for public ends, or for the mitigation of the most painful inequalities resulting from the present individualistic distribution of wealth. Expenditure of this kind, unless it shows marked unwisdom in the adaptation of means to ends, is almost universally praised; but abstinence from such expenditure is not commonly blamed in any particular case. Some censure, no doubt, is incurred by a rich man who spends his whole income in luxuries for himself and his family and in exchanging luxurious hospitalities with other rich men. But though he is censured in a broad way for this course of life, the censure is vague and general, and does not attach itself to abstinence from any particular act of philanthropy. It is—rightly, as I think—held that the struggle to get rich is socially useful, so far as it impels the struggler to render services to society deserving of high remuneration; and that any such restrictions on a rich man's freedom of expenditure, as would amount to graduated taxation enforced by moral censure, must tend to impair the stimulus to this useful effort. Still, undoubtedly, a powerful pressure—though rather in the form of praise than of censure—is exercised by public opinion on rich men in the direction of eleemo- synary and public-spirited expenditure, and is powerfully aided by all earnest teachers of the prevalent forms of religion; and under the influence of this moral pressure the amount of wealth and labour voluntarily devoted to the relief of dis- tress, and to the promotion of objects of public utility, is in any modern community so considerable, that it becomes an important factor in the practical determina- tion of the scope of governmental interference for similar purposes. Thus, for instance, political thinkers and statesmen, in advocating the English method of dealing with pauperism, have usually assumed not only that public poor-relief will be supplemented by private almsgiving, but that a fundamentally important part of the work may be left to the latter. As we saw, the distinctive principle of the English system is that Government is not to discriminate between the deserving and the undeserving poor, but to secure to all who are destitute a minimum of subsistence under conditions deterrent but not painful: and this principle would be rejected as too harsh by many who now accept it, were it not for the assump- tion that private almsgivers will be ready to undertake the task of discrimination which Government declines, and to accord more generous and tender treatment to those who have fallen into distress through undeserved calamities.

Similarly, as regards the building and maintenance of hospitals and asylums for persons physically and mentally afflicted, the provision for education in all grades, the promotion of culture by means of museums and libraries, the endow- ment of scientific research, and other ends of recognised public utility;—the ques- tion what Government should do cannot be answered unless we know what the liberality of private individuals may be expected to accomplish if Government does not interfere.

§ 5. Since, then, the force of opinion and sentiment in the community as to the social duties of individuals is so valuable to the government, both as support and as supplement, and so dangerous in antagonism, it remains to inquire how far it is a proper function of Government to take measures to stimulate and regulate this force.

The question, however, does not practically present itself in this simple form in the political societies of Europe and America; since in these societies the systematic teaching of morality to adults—and, to a great extent, the moral education of the young—are, by a firmly established custom, left in the hands of one or more of the different Christian churches: so that the problem of gov- ernmental interference for the moralisation of the citizens takes the form of a question as to the 'relations of Church and State'. Still, it seems desirable, in such a treatise as the present, to begin by considering the problem in a more general way.

Let us suppose, then, that we are dealing with a civilised community in which there is either no religion having general acceptance or important influence, or else only religions that have no important connexion with morality;—I mean religions in which the objects of worship are mainly conceived to be propitiated otherwise than by the performance of social duty:—and let us ask whether Government, under these circumstances, should undertake the business of teaching morality and stimulating moral sentiments. The answer to this question would seem to me to depend partly on the answer given to one of the most fundamental questions of moral philosophy: *viz.* whether the performance of social duty can be proved scientifically—with as strong a 'consensus of experts' as we find in established sciences generally—to be certainly or most probably the means best adapted to the attainment of the private happiness of the agent.

I. If we answer this question in the affirmative, it does not indeed follow that morality ought to be based on self-interest alone; but it would clearly be an important gain to social wellbeing to correct the erroneous and short-sighted views of self-interest, representing it as divergent from duty, which certainly appear to be widely prevalent in the most advanced societies, at least among irreligious persons. Hence there are at any rate strong reasons for regarding it as the duty of government, in the case supposed, to aim at removing this widespread ignorance and error by providing teachers of morality: and such a provision might be fairly regarded as indirectly individualistic in its aim, since to diffuse the conviction that it is every one's interest to do what is right would obviously be a valuable protection against mutual wrong. It does not, however, follow that it would be expedient to have morality taught—to adults at least—by salaried servants of government. For unless we assume the harmony between duty and self-interest to be demonstrable to an untrained intellect, such teaching would only be efficacious if the teachers inspired confidence: and the analogy of the sanitary instruction imparted by the medical profession suggests that confidence, in the degree required, would be more readily given to moralists freely chosen by those whom they advised. Further, in any cases of doubt or dispute, in which it might seem to be the interest of governing persons that the governed should act in the manner recommended by the moralists, the latter would be liable to the suspicion that they were biassed by the prospect of advancement or fear of dismissal: so that they would give but a feeble support to Government—just, perhaps, when their support was most needed. On the other hand, if this danger were partially met by securing the teachers from dismissal, the service would be liable to be encumbered with unfit persons.

II. But the objections against governmental provision of professional moralisers become much stronger, if we regard it as impossible to prove by ordinary mundane considerations that it is always the individual's interest in the present condition of human society to do his duty; or if, granting the evident coincidence of self-interest and duty, it is still held that self-regard should not be the normal motive to moral action. For in either of these cases the only teaching likely to be effective is such as will powerfully affect the emotions of the taught, no less than their intellects; we should, therefore, generally speaking, need teachers who themselves felt, and were believed to feel, sincerely and intensely, the moral and social emotions that it was their business to stimulate; and governmental appointment and payment would hardly seem to be an appropriate method of securing instructors of this type. If a spirit of devotion to a particular society or to humanity at large, and readiness to sacrifice self-interest to duty, are to be persuasively inculcated on adults, the task should, generally speaking, be undertaken by persons who set an example of self-devotion and self-sacrifice; and therefore by volunteers, rather than by paid officers. The case would be somewhat different with the more malleable natures of children: it would still be clearly expedient that schoolmasters as well as parents should seriously endeavour to promote the growth of moral habits and sentiments in the youthful minds committed to their charge. But it seems very doubtful how far, in the circumstances supposed, this growth would be most effectively promoted by formal instruction; and not rather partly by steady enforcement of received rules, with such incidental explanations of their *rationale* as can be effectively given,—as polite manners are now ordinarily taught; and partly by stimulating social sentiments through a well-selected study of literature and history, as patriotism and public spirit are now mainly promoted.

Let us now turn from the purely hypothetical problem that we have been discussing, to consider the form which the question of governmental interference to promote morality actually takes in modern European communities. For ordinary members of such communities, the connection of any individual's interest with his duty is established by the traditional Christian teaching as to the moral government of the world, and the survival of the individual after his corporeal death. Accordingly, this traditional teaching—though it by no means relies solely on appeals to self-interest—still always includes in its store of arguments appeals of this kind, having irresistible cogency for all hearers who believe the fundamental Christian doctrines. So far as the rules of duty thus taught are those commonly accepted by thoughtful persons, the value of the aid given to the work of government by this supply of extra-mundane motives to the performance of social duty can hardly be doubted. But the expediency of governmental action to secure this aid is importantly affected by the fact that the teachers who give it are actually organised in independent associations called churches, whose lines of division differ from—and to an important extent cut across—the lines of division of political societies; and which for the most part would resist strongly any attempt to bring them directly and completely under the control of the secular government. The practical question therefore is, whether government should leave these churches unfettered—treating them like any other voluntary associations based on free contract—or should endeavour to obtain a partial control over them in return for endowments or other advantages. I do not propose in this treatise to enter upon the historical or the theological aspects of this controverted question: but it is easy to show that the settlement of it is likely to be at once difficult and of great importance to political wellbeing. For, so far as the priest or religious teacher seeks not merely to provide a harmonious and satisfying expression for religious emotion, but also to regulate the behaviour of man to his fellows in domestic and civil relations,—using as motives the hope of reward and fear of punishment from an invisible source,—his function obviously tends to become *quasi-governmental*; accordingly, where religious belief is strong, the power given to the priesthood by its control of these extra-mundane motives renders it not only a valuable auxiliary to the ordinary or secular government in the business of maintaining the general performance of civic duty, but also a most formidable rival, in case of any conflict between the priesthood and the organs of secular government. A similar rivalry and conflict is of course possible between a non-religious association among the members of any political community and the government of that community: and history affords some striking examples of such rivalry, though none comparable in extent and importance to the conflict for power between 'Church and State' in Western Europe. I have accordingly thought it best to consider the question of governmental intervention in religious matters in a special chapter on the Relation of the State to Voluntary Associations[7] which will be more appropriately introduced after we have examined the organisation of secular government.

[7] Chap. xxviii.

8. The Distinction between 'Is' and 'Ought'

1. I shall assume at the outset of this necessarily short paper, that we are generally agreed as to the objects of thought to which the predicates 'is' and 'ought to be' are respectively appropriate; though I shall have occasion in the course of the paper to notice certain variations of opinion on both points. I shall also take 'what ought to be' to include what is commonly judged to be 'good', so far as attainable by human action, as well as what is commonly judged to be 'right', or 'the duty' of any human being. Of course 'good' and 'evil' as commonly used are wider and less stringent terms than 'right' and 'wrong'; since (1) the former are applicable to results out of the reach of human attainment—an abundant harvest next autumn or influenza in the winter—also (2) 'goods' may be incompatible, to attain a greater we may have to sacrifice a less. But even when unattainable, or not preferable in the circumstances, what is judged to be 'good' would appear to have the same quality as the term imports within the range of its practical application; 'good' is the kind of thing that we 'ought' to seek to produce or maintain *pro tanto* and so far as it is in our power.

For simplicity, I shall mean by 'good' in this discussion, 'ultimate good on the whole'; and to avoid complicating the discussion, I shall assume that what is good on the whole for any individual agent is also good on the whole for human society, the world of living things, or the cosmos, whichever we take to be the larger whole of which the individual is a part, and which is conceived to have an ultimate good capable of being increased or diminished, promoted or retarded, by human action. That is, I shall assume that 'what ought to be' is the same from the point of view of self-interest and from that of duty. The notion of 'right' or 'duty' is, however, more familiar in ethical discussion to the common moral consciousness of modern men—to which I shall refer as common sense—than the notion of 'ultimate good'. But I shall assume it to be admitted by common sense that, from the point of view of complete knowledge, the performance of a duty or a right act must be conceived to be either a part of ultimate good or a means to it.

Taking then the notion of Duty or Right act—I may assume it to be a continually recurrent element in the thought of an ordinary well-behaved person about his own life and that of others. In the thoughts of such men about duties, taken together and compared, there is doubtless more conflict and disagreement than in their thought about facts; but agreement much preponderates. Apart from

[From *Proceedings of the Aristotelian Society*, 2/1, part II (1891–2), 88–92.]

such conflict, there is a recognised variation of duties from man to man, but it is commonly assumed that this variation is on rational grounds, so that the duties of A, truly conceived, form one rationally coherent system with the duties of B. Such a system we may call a 'world of human duty', of which each man conceives the duties he assigns to himself and his immediate neighbours to be a part indefinitely better known to him than the rest; but he conceives the whole world of duty to be a subject of human knowledge, no less than the world of fact, though the former is lamentably divergent from the latter, in consequence of the general failure of men, in a greater or less degree, to do their duty. The divergence is equally palpable if we consider the 'good' results that might be brought about by the performance of duty, as compared with what actually takes place. From either point of view we judge that 'what ought to be' to a great extent 'is not', and we commonly conceive that its character as 'what ought to be' is entirely independent of whether it comes into actual being or not.

2. The question then is raised, whether this distinction between what is and what ought to be is ultimate and irreducible? I think it rash to affirm irreducibility, but I am certainly not satisfied with any proposed reduction proceeding on the lines of scientific thought on which such reduction is commonly attempted; i.e., I do not think the desired result can be attained by considering moral judgments from a psychological or sociological point of view, as elements in the conscious life of individuals or communities or races. No doubt moral judgments and their accompanying sentiments are a department of psychical fact, and we may analyse and classify them as such and investigate their causes, just as we should do in the case of any other psychical fact; but as long as they are regarded from this point of view, it seems impossible to explain or justify the fundamental assumption on which they all proceed, that some such judgments are true and others false, and that when any two such judgments conflict, one or both must be erroneous. One fact cannot be inconsistent with another fact; accordingly, regarded from a psychological or sociological point of view, A's judgment, e.g., that all gambling is wrong, does not conflict with B's judgment that some gambling is right; the question, which is true, does not arise and would have no meaning. The reduction, therefore, of duty to fact, on this line of thought if strictly pursued, eviscerates ethical thought of its essential import and interest.

It may be replied, perhaps, that in this argument I have not taken into account the notions of life and development, and their place in psychology and sociology, that possessing these notions, science in this department does not merely ascertain resemblances and general laws of coexistence and change, but in so doing brings out the notion of an end to which psychical and social changes are related as means, and in relation to which alone they are really intelligible; and that this end supplies the requisite reduction of 'what ought to be' to what is. For in this end—variously conceived as vital or social 'health' or 'equilibrium' or 'life measured in breadth as well as length',—we have (it is thought) a criterion of truth and error in moral judgments; if the acts they approve are conducive to this end, they may be counted true or normal, if not, false or abnormal.

To this I answer that End as a biological or sociological notion may, no doubt, be held convertible for practical purposes with ethical end; but that this can only be by an ethical judgment affirming the coincidence of the two: the two notions remain essentially distinct, though when affirmed to be coincident they are doubtless liable to be confused. From the mere knowledge that a certain result is what will be or preponderantly tends to be, it is impossible to infer that it ought to be; so far as it is inevitable, I obviously can have no duty with regard to it; so far as its coming may be promoted or retarded, it is my duty to promote it if I judge it good in comparison with that for which it would be substituted, and to retard it if I judge it to be comparatively bad. Perhaps I may suggest as a reason why this is often not clearly recognised, that in the terms such as 'social welfare' or 'social health', used to denote the sociological end, the ethical notion is surreptitiously introduced; they are states which have been implicitly judged to be good.

3. When I turn from the point of view of Science to that of Philosophy or Epistemology, before answering the question whether the difference between what is and what ought to be is irreducible, I require to know exactly what is meant by 'reduction'. Is the difference between two things reduced by merely discovering previously unknown resemblances between them? E.g., we may compare the circle and the parabola without knowing that they are both sections of the cone; should we say that the difference between them ascertained by this comparison is reduced by discovering their common relation to the cone? If so, I think it must be admitted that this kind of 'reduction' takes place when we contemplate the difference between 'what is' and 'what ought to be' from a philosophical or epistemological point of view. For from this point of view we regard the world of duty and the world of fact alike as objects of thought, and— real or supposed—knowledge, and discover similar relations of thought in both, relations of universal to particular and individual notions and judgments, of inductive to deductive method, &c.; whatever differences may appear between the two from this point of view are of a subordinate kind, and not greater than the differences between different departments of fact regarded as objects of thought and scientific method. True, if we adhere to common sense, the funda- mental difference remains that the distinction between 'truth' and 'error' in our thought about what is, is held to depend essentially on the correspondence, or want of correspondence, between Thought and Fact; whereas, in the case of 'what ought to be', truth and error cannot be conceived to depend on any similar relation except on a certain theological view of duty, which I will presently notice. Still, even this difference is at least reduced if we take the philosophical point of view; because, from this point of view, the supposed correspondence between Thought and what is not Thought is no longer so simple and intelligible as it

seems to common sense; it must be recognised as a difficult problem, whatever solution of it we may ultimately accept. It must be recognised that, even in the case of our thought about what is, though error may lie in want of correspondence between Thought and Fact, it can only be shown and ascertained by showing inconsistency between Thought and Thought, i.e., precisely as error is shown in the case of our thought about what ought to be.

Perhaps, too, the difference between 'what is' and 'what ought to be' may be reasonably held to be relatively reduced, when we contemplate, along with both, various forms of 'what might be' or 'might have been', as objects of more or less coherent thought for scientific or artistic purposes.

4. Finally, I must notice another method of 'reduction', at first sight plausible and more near to common sense than the philosophical. This proceeds on the theological assumption that the true rules of duty are Divine commands—whether made known by external revelation or through the conscience of the individual. Such commands, it is said, may be imperfectly known to any particular moral agent, either without his own fault—in which case their non-fulfilment will be pardoned—or through wilful neglect of known duty in the past, which has had the effect of impairing his moral insight; but in any case such commands have been uttered, and must be regarded as a part of universal fact. I think, however, that this reduction fails when we work it out. Firstly, we cannot define a Divine command—like a human command—as a wish combined with a threat—since we cannot attribute to God an ungratified wish. Shall we, then, conceive it simply as a threat? This would clearly offend common sense, which conceives God as not merely an 'Omnipotent Ruler', but also a Righteous Ruler, commanding in accordance with a rule of Right. But thus the difference we are considering emerges again in the form of a distinction between the Rule of Right in the Divine Mind and the Divine Power as manifested in the world of fact; and, emerging, it brings with it the formidable problem of the existence of evil, since we inevitably ask why God's power does not cause the complete realisation of ideal Right and Good. This question has received various answers, but it is hard to find an answer which does not maintain unreduced the difference between 'what is' and 'what ought to be'.

9. The Relation of Ethics to Sociology

In selecting the subject of my lecture this evening I was influenced by the title of the body to whose invitation I responded,—the London School of Ethics and Social Philosophy. For I take this title to imply that the studies of the school are not concerned only with ethics in the narrow sense:—*i.e.*, with the inquiry into the principles and method of determining what is right and wrong in human action, the content of the moral law, and the proper object of rational choice and avoidance. This is, indeed, a vast, comprehensive, and difficult subject, even if we pursue it, so far as possible, as a separate and independent inquiry; still, I take it to be the aim of your school not to confine the work of your students to the theory of what ought to be, of the ideal relations of human beings living in society; but rather to combine with this the scientific study of the actual relations of men regarded as members of societies, as they have been, are, and will be. For it is only by a combination of the two studies, that we can hope to attain that wider view which belongs to philosophy as distinguished from science; from which we endeavour to contemplate the whole of human thought—whether concerned with ideals or empirical facts—as one harmonious system. It is as a contribution to social philosophy thus understood that I offer the observations that follow on the relation of ethics to sociology.

But at the outset I find myself in some perplexity. In order to examine closely the relation between the two studies, we ought to be able to bring the general character and outline of each in turn clearly before our minds. Now, I may assume that my audience can do this in the case of ethics;—or, at least, as the range of the subject is somewhat vaguely and variously conceived—the brief description that I just now gave will suffice to indicate to you the body of systematic thought that I have in my mind when I use the term. But it is not so clear that I can assume this with regard to sociology; since, though the educated world has heard of sociology for about three-quarters of a century, it can hardly be said, in England at least, to have yet attained the rank of an established science,—at any rate, if academic recognition can be taken as a criterion of the establishment of a science. There is, so far as I know, no chair of sociology in any English university; it is not formally included in any academic curriculum; there is no elementary manual of English manufacture by which a student may learn to pass an examination in sociology with the least possible trouble. It is otherwise in the United

[A paper read before the London School of Ethics and Social Philosophy. Published in the *International Journal of Ethics*, 10/1 (Oct. 1899), 1–21.]

States, where sociology has already got both professorial chairs and hand-books. Perhaps in intellectual as well as industrial matters the Anglo-Saxons across the Atlantic are more apt than we are to seize and effectively apply new ideas. Still, the leading English philosophers of the latter half of the century, J. S. Mill and Herbert Spencer, have both devoted an important part of their energies to the exposition of the subject,—which, indeed, occupies three out of the ten volumes of Spencer's great system of synthetic philosophy. And, largely under their influence, in spite of the cold shade of official neglect in which it still lingers, the ideas of sociology have more and more tended to penetrate and pervade current ethical discussion. Take, as an instance of this, the following statement made some years ago by a writer of repute:

'A man's first and last duty is to see and do those things which the social organism of which he is a member calls upon him to do.'

'The social organism' is essentially a sociological conception; and if we admit this statement in its full breadth, we implicitly admit the claim—which the young science has in fact been making since its birth from the brain of Auguste Comte—to dominate the older subject of ethics and even to reduce it to a department of itself.

This claim I propose to examine in the present lecture; but, for the reasons I have just indicated, it seems best that before proceeding to examine it I should briefly sketch the aims and method of sociology as presented by the leading writers whom I have named.

Sociology, as conceived by Comte and Spencer, may be briefly described as an attempt to make the study of human history scientific by applying to it conceptions derived from biology, with such modifications as their new application requires. We have, however, for this purpose to include, along with history in the ordinary sense, a large part of what is commonly known as anthropology,—that is, the comparative study of the contemporary social conditions, and recent social changes so far as ascertainable, of those parts of the human race that have not arrived at a sufficiently advanced stage of civilization to have a history in the ordinary sense.

To begin, we may definitely conceive the objects which sociology studies as a number of groups of human beings, which at the outset I shall consider to be each an independent political or governed society, though this view must be taken subject to important modifications later on. Each such society may be to a great extent properly regarded—and I shall begin by regarding it—as having an organic life of its own, distinct from the lives of the individuals composing it. It is in this view that I call it an 'organism', meaning by the term first that such a group is not a mere aggregate of individuals, but an aggregate of which the members have definite relations that, though themselves subject to change, remain comparatively constant while the individuals change; and that these relations bind the individuals together into mutually dependent parts of a larger whole, performing mutually dependent functions. The society has thus a structure which so far resembles the structure of a living animal that its existence depends on its structure; it cannot cease to function and retain its structure, as a machine can. I further mean to imply that such a society goes through processes of growth and change which are at any rate largely caused—as the changes of a plant or animal —by interaction with its environment, physical and social; and especially changes by which it adapts or adjusts itself to its environment,—*i.e.*, tends to preserve itself amid changes in environing conditions even, if need be, by the occasional sacrifice of the lives of individual members. With this definite meaning, finding in such societies these characteristics, we may agree to call them organisms in spite of their unlikeness in other important respects to the organisms which biology studies.

Then, following Spencer and combining the results of history and archaeology with the study of less advanced societies now existing, somewhat as the biologist combines the results of geology with those of zoology and botany, we may note how the prevalent type of social organism, like the prevalent types of animals or plants, tends, as evolution goes on, to grow in mass both by multiplication of units within each group and by union of groups. We may note further how along with increase of mass goes development of social structure, by which the differentiation of its mutually dependent parts becomes continually more complex; until from the simplicity of a little tribe of hunters, with hardly any division of functions except what is connected with sex, we arrive ultimately at the complexity of a modern industrial society, with its vast diversity of occupations.

Spencer proceeds to draw an instructive parallel between the sociological and the biological differentiation of organs. He bids us observe in each case.

(1) A 'sustaining system', alimentary in the animal and industrial in the society,

(2) A 'distributing system', carrying about nutriment in the animal and commodities in the society, and

(3) A 'regulating and expending system'. By this last notion he represents analogy between the apparatus of nerves and muscles in an animal which carries on conflict with other animals and the governments and armies of political society; taking the governmental system as ultimately developed to correspond to the brain and nervous centres, the supreme deliberative assembly being analogous to the cerebrum.

So much for the resemblances between the social organism and the animal or plant. As we should expect, they belong primarily to the physical life of human societies; but when we turn to note the differences, we shall be led gradually to contemplate their intellectual life.

We may begin by observing that a political society has not, like an animal, a normal period of life and a normal series of vital changes from infancy to senility and death. Indeed, the political societies historically known to us do not ordinarily die unless they are assailed and structurally destroyed by other societies; and when death, in a certain sense, thus befalls any such society, it does not entail the death of the human beings composing it. Some of them, no doubt, perish in the collision, but the bulk of them are absorbed alive by the conquering society. Even in peace an important mingling of units from different societies goes on, as is most conspicuously illustrated at the present time by the comparatively new societies formed in America. They are largely made neither by 'multiplication of units' nor by 'union of groups', but by composition of units from a number of groups.

But it is still more important to observe that the social organism to which an individual is found to belong, through the social relations binding him to other men, becomes very different in its range as we pass from one set of relations to another. There is nothing corresponding to this in the case of an animal. Each animal has its own sustaining system, its own distributing system, and its own regulating and expending system, quite unconnected with the corresponding systems of other animals. The alimentary organs of one animal do not provide, nor its blood-vessels convey, nutriment to the organs of other societies, nor does its brain co-operate in directing their movements, except indirectly by producing external movements of its own organs. The case is quite otherwise with the organic life of societies. The channels of communication by which commodities are carried run, as we know, not only within states, but across states, almost ignoring their boundaries; and the same is true of the process of differentiation which localizes particular branches of industry in situations specially favourable to it, and thus tends to bind the inhabitants of the districts in question into one economic whole. We all know that England forms part of an economic system extending far beyond the limits of the British empire.

But again a very similar set of cross-divisions, lines of separation that cut across the boundaries of states, is found in what we cannot but regard as an important part of the regulative apparatus of social organisms: I mean the ecclesiastical systems. We all know how throughout the civilised world members from the same states are divided from another, and members of different states are united by communities formed for the purpose of religious instruction and worship. No fact is more striking in the history of regulating social agencies than the manner in which religions claiming to be world religions—Buddhism, Christianity, Mohammedanism—have arisen and spread and overleaped all the lines of separation of political societies; binding their converts through the most powerful ties of common beliefs and common worship into organisms quite different from states, though they come to have an elaborately differentiated quasi-political organisation. Now, in studying these ecclesiastical organisms from the outside, we might of course dwell on the social differences and relations between priests or monks and laymen, and the organisation of ecclesiastical government. But it would be a very shallow insight that did not penetrate further and recognise as the most essential social relation which binds human beings together on this side of their life community of thought and sentiment; a common stock of ideas and convictions about the universe, its ground and end, and human destiny. Hence, when the sociologist studies these ecclesiastical bodies, it is to the laws of change and growth of this intellectual and emotional context, this common body of ideas and sentiments, that his deepest attention should be directed.

And this is true also of the political regulation of social man. Mr. Spencer, as we saw, compares the brain of an animal with the supreme deliberative assembly of a nation. But surely the political brain of England is not limited to the six hundred and seventy respectable gentlemen who chiefly make our laws: it is to be found wherever political thought is going on which will take effect in determining the action of the English government. And if so, the history of political ideas shows that no modern nation has a brain strictly and entirely its own. If we insist on keeping the analogy, we have for the main movements of political thought to trace the operation and development of at least a West-European brain; whose range of influence in modern times has not only extended to European colonies in other parts of the globe, but has even included a people so alien in its origin and previous history as the Japanese.

And, finally, what I have said of religious and political ideas is equally true of moral ideas and sentiments. Indeed, throughout the history of European civilization morality has had an intimate connection both with religion and with polity. Still, the study of the development of morality and its conditions and laws of growth and change may be pursued, no less than the study of religious or political thought, as a partially independent branch of sociological inquiry; and when we so pursue it we soon find that the aggregate of human beings bound together spiritually by sharing a common moral life is not to be identified with any one of the political societies which we began by regarding as social organisms. And the same may be said in modern times of the possession of a common body of scientific knowledge; indeed, science is less modified by national differences than morality; and European science has united the educated portion of the Japanese people more completely with our educated world than European political ideas. Thus, in contemplating the continual enlargement of these spiritual bonds of social union we are irresistibly led—as the founder of sociology, Comte, was led—to an ideal future when the whole population of the globe will form, from an intellectual point of view, a single social organism. There is a striking passage, remarkable in a writer who claims to expound a purely positive method, in which Comte tells us that Sociology, reading the future into the past, 'represents the whole human race, past, present, and future, as constituting a vast and eternal social unit, where different organs, individual and national, concur in their various modes and degrees in the evolution of humanity'.

To sum up, as we pass from one aspect to another of the many-sided social life of man, we are led gradually from the conception of an indefinite number of social organisms, subject, like plants or animals, to the struggle for existence as a main factor in their development,—a conception which physical analogies and the contemplation of the earlier stages of human history combine to press on us,—to the idea of a single social organism, which a study of later civilised history, especially in its spiritual aspect, renders no less inevitable.

I turn now to examine the relation of sociology to ethics, and especially the claim of the former study to absorb the latter and reduce it to a subordinate department of itself. I may perhaps say that I come to the examination of this claim in an impartial spirit. Speaking as a professor of ethics, I do not consider myself as holding a brief for the independence of my subject. It is for the true good of any department of knowledge or inquiry to understand as thoroughly as may be its relation to other sciences and studies, to see clearly what elements of its reasonings it has to take from them, and what in its turn it may claim to give to them; and the value of this insight becomes greater in proportion as the steady growth of human knowledge, the steady extension of the range of human inquiry, brings with it a continually more urgent need for a clear and rational division of intellectual labour. If, therefore, the relation of ethics to sociology is truly one of subordination, it is important that students of ethics should fully recognise this truth and render due obedience to the superior authority.

Of course, in order that this authority, however ideally unquestionable, should be actually unquestioned, sociology must have become an established science, and be not merely struggling towards this position. And if I were speaking as an advocate of the claims of ethics to actual independence, I should have much to say on this topic. I should take the simple criteria of the real establishment of a science laid down by Auguste Comte, which we may briefly characterize as a Consensus of experts, Continuity and Prevision, and try the claims of sociology by the standards of its own founder. I should give you in Comte's own words his negative application of the test of continuity: 'When we find that recent works, instead of being the result and development of what has gone before, have a char-acter as personal as that of their authors and bring the most fundamental ideas into question',—then, says Comte, we may be sure we are not dealing with any doctrine deserving the name of positive science. And my brief would be stuffed with quotations from very recent treatises on sociology, whose authors—to quote a well-known epigram,—show themselves most emphatically 'conscious of one another's shortcomings'.

But this advocate's work is not now my affair. I wish to assume for the pur-poses of my present discussion that the struggle of sociology to become an estab-lished science, a struggle carried on now for three-quarters of a century, has been crowned with the success which I hope will ultimately crown it. I will assume that it has attained as much consensus as to principles, method, and conclusions, and as much continuity of development as the physical sciences dealing with organic life, and as much power of prevision as Comte hoped for it;—for he was not sanguine enough to suppose that sociology could ever predict with the exactness and minuteness of astronomy, and foretell the stages of a political revolution as astronomy foretells the stages of a solar eclipse.

Let us suppose this consummation attained and consider how far this scientific prevision of social effects will so far determine ethical reasonings as to reduce ethics to a subordinate department of sociology.

I think it must be admitted that this effect will be produced to a considerable extent, upon any view of ethics except the ultra-intuitional, in respect of the deduction of particular rules of morality from fundamental principles. For all schools, except that which takes the immediate judgments of conscience as infallible guides in all questions of conduct, admit that the application of moral principles to practice must be largely governed by foresight of consequences, and must therefore admit that rules of social behaviour will properly be determined in detail by the scientific prevision of social consequences so far as such prevision is available. We may compare, as a parallel case, the relation of the moral duty or virtue of temperance to human physiology, including pathology; the ethical maxim that the bodily appetites ought to be strictly obedient to the regulation of reason must receive its practical application from a forecast of consequences; and this, with the development of physiological knowledge, must change from a merely empirical to a more or less scientific forecast. We commonly recognise that the diet scientifically known to be promotive of health and efficiency is the truly temperate diet; and the most ascetic moralist has to admit that self-denial, no less than self-indulgence, must be limited and guided by medical prevision. Similarly we must admit that our social affections and sentiments will have to yield to the control and obey the guidance of sociological prevision when sociology has become a really established science.

Indeed, some effect of this kind has already been produced on current ethical notions and habits by the branch of sociology which has been separated from the general science of society, and received a development in advance of the rest under the name of political economy. For instance, under the influence of the economic forecast—deductively and inductively established—of the bad consequences of indiscriminate almsgiving, the old and eminent virtue of charity, in its narrower signification, has materially changed its practical content for the modern educated man, while retaining its principle and motive unchanged. Its application to conduct has become more complex and exacting; it is recognized as demanding thought and care, besides the mere altruistic preference of the satisfaction of others' desires to the satisfaction of our own, and as imposing restraints on sympathetic impulses as well as on self-regarding ones.

A similar effect of economic forecast on ethical conceptions and accompanying sentiments is traceable in the case of justice; but with the difference that in this case we have marked ethical divergences resulting from divergences in the economic or sociological prevision of consequences. Suppose we take the principle that desert ought to be requited as expressing the abstract essence of distributive justice. Its practical application cannot but be different, on the one hand, for the individualist who holds that any important relaxation in the competitive struggle for existence must result in the arrest and decline of human improvement, through the equalizing of the prospects of survival of the unfit along with the fit; and, on the other hand, for the socialist who forecasts a more rapid and effective improvement under the stimulus of altruistic affection, sympathy, and public spirit, when these nobler impulses are no longer starved and depressed by the egoistic habits and sentiments that necessarily result from the present competitive struggle. The former will tend to interpret the requital of desert to mean securing to each man the precise social value of his services; the latter will tend to interpret it to mean securing him what he requires for the most efficient performance of his social function.

Of course, as sociological prevision extends in range and increases in exactness, we must suppose fundamental divergences of this kind to diminish and a more decisive effect to be produced.

I have said enough to show the import of my admission as a representative of ethics that if we suppose sociology as an established science, we must suppose its forecast of social consequences to exercise a fundamentally important effect on the practical application of general ethical principles or maxims, and the deduction of subordinate rules of conduct from these.

I now turn to the more important and more disputable element of the claim of sociology to absorb and subordinate ethics,—*i.e.*, the claim not merely to modify the practical application of ethical principles, but to determine these very principles themselves.

Here, first, I quite admit that the connection of sociology, supposing it an established science, with the subject-matter of ethics must necessarily be so intimate and so comprehensive, that its claim to dominate and subordinate ethics is natural and almost inevitable; and we cannot be surprised that it should appear irresistible to students of sociology who have never made a systematic attempt to purge their moral notions of the confusions of popular thought. For, as we have seen, sociology undoubtedly comprehends in its subject-matter the study of morality as a social fact, and this study must include morality as a whole, the principles accepted in any age and country, no less than the accepted and current application of the principles to particular concrete problems of conduct. It is a part of the business of sociology—at least as important, from a purely sociological point of view, as any other part—to ascertain first the facts, and then, as far as possible, the laws of the development of moral opinions and sentiments, as one element in the development of human society as a whole; to show how it has influenced and been influenced by other elements in the whole social evolution; to trace it back, if possible, to its origin; and—always supposing sociology to have arrived at the stage of scientific prediction—to foretell its future conditions.

It is natural to infer that a sociology supposed able to accomplish all this—and I am willing, for the sake of argument, to make the supposition—would reduce ethics to a subordinate department of itself. I do not, however, think that this inference is logically sound. Indeed, I think that in most cases it arises from a confusion of thought that a little reflection ought to dispel.

To show this, let us suppose ethics and sociology as independent and established systems of thought, and then try to imagine a conflict between them, a conflict such as sometimes takes place between established sciences,—e.g., there was one some time ago between physicists and geologists as to the time of duration of the earth.

We shall find that we cannot really suppose such a conflict possible. No ethical proposition can possibly contradict a sociological proposition, since they cannot relate to the same subject-matter,—that is, so long as ethics is understood in the limited sense that I have defined and so long as sociology keeps strictly within the bounds of its domain as a positive science. Sociology thus conceived is strictly incapable of answering any ethical question, and ethics thus understood is strictly incapable of answering any sociological question,—for ethics is only concerned with what ought to be, and sociology, even when it deals with ethical judgments, is only concerned with what is, has been, and will be judged, and not at all with the question whether it is, has been, or will be truly judged. So far as any sociologist expresses any opinion on the latter point, he assumes a knowledge which the method of his science, regarded as a study of empirical fact, is quite incompetent to supply.

I do not think that this is likely to be disputed, so far as sociology is concerned with the mere ascertainment of particular facts, past and present; but it may be disputed in respect of the general truths which sociology as a science must be supposed to have established. And I admit that if we examine this dispute with care we shall find, not indeed a possible conflict between ethics and sociology, but a possible coincidence so close as, if actually accepted, to justify the view that sociology is destined to absorb ethics.

But here again I must point out that the dispute sometimes arises from mere confusion of thought. It is rightly seen that the aim of sociology is not merely to ascertain, but to explain, the variations and changes in social morality, and that this explanation must lie in reducing to general laws the diversity of moral opinions prevalent in different ages and countries; and it is vaguely thought that these general laws, at any rate when brought to a sufficiently high degree of generality, must coincide—if they do not clash—with ethical principles. But not only is there no *primâ facie* reason why they should coincide, but *primâ facie* every reason why they should not. For the sociological laws must explain and be manifested in the erroneous moral judgments that have been prevalent in human society no less than in true moral judgments; they must explain the prevalent opinion of certain groups of primitive men that successful thieving is honourable and virtuous, or that the revenge of a blood-relation is the holiest duty that man can perform, no less than the opposite moral opinions now prevalent in Europe.

There is, however, a subtler form of the same view which cannot be so decisively put on one side. It may be urged that the subject-matter of sociology, no less than the subject-matter of animal or vegetable biology, is a kind of organic life; and that as the varied structures and functions of animal or vegetable organisms can only be understood if we regard them as adapted or adjusted to the preservation either of the individual organism or its type, so sociology requires the same conception of adaptation to the end of social preservation in its explanation of social facts. Accordingly, morality, prevalent moral opinions and sentiments, being an important complex of relations among the members of a society, must be brought under the same general conception; so that the most comprehensive and fundamental sociological law, explaining the development of morality, will consist in just this statement of Preservation of the Social Organism as the end to which morality is normally and broadly a means,—though in any particular society at any particular time details of positive morality may not be perfectly adapted to this end. If this is so, it may be said the moralist must adopt this sociological end as his ultimate ethical end, since otherwise he would be setting up an ideal opposed to the irresistible drift of the whole process of life in the world, which would be obviously futile.[1]

Now, supposing a *consensus* of sociologists to declare that the preservation of the social organism is the one all-comprehensive end, by continual adjustment to which the actual evolution of morality may be simply and completely explained; and supposing a *consensus* of moralists to accept this sociological end as the ultimate good to the attainment of which all human action should be directed, then, I admit, it would be broadly true to say that ethics was absorbed by sociology. For on these hypotheses there would, firstly, be a complete coincidence between the sociological and the ethical end; and, secondly, as I have already explained, the working out of the rules conducive to the end must, so far as social morality is concerned, consist in an application of sociological knowledge. Ethics would not, indeed, even so, be exactly a branch of the science, but it would be an art based on the science and having as its fundamental principle the highest generalization of the science, modified so as to take on an ethical import.

It would still, I think, be *formally* important to insist that this fusion of studies can only be rationally effected by the judgment that identifies the sociological and the ethical ends; and that is not one to which the moralist can be cogently driven by any sociological arguments. For the argument that if he declines to

---

[1] Some writers would substitute 'welfare' or 'health' for 'preservation' in this reasoning. But unless 'welfare' or 'health' is interpreted to mean merely preservation in a condition favourable to future preservation, in which case simple preservation is still the ultimate end, the terms seem to me to introduce an ethical conception which cannot be arrived at by any strictly sociological method.

accept it he places himself in opposition to the process of nature is only forcible if we introduce a theological significance into our notion of nature, attributing to it design and authority; and this introduction of theology carries the sociologist beyond the limits of his special science. But, though it would be formally important to insist on this, the fusion would still be complete on the two hypotheses, sociological and ethical, above stated.

But neither of these hypotheses can be accepted as more than partially true.

Take the ethical question first,—can we regard the *mere preservation* of the life of a human being, or of any number of human beings combined in a society, as an ultimate and paramount end and standard of right action, apart from any consideration of the quality of the life preserved? I appeal confidently on this point—it is the only appeal possible—to the deliberate judgment of thoughtful persons, when the question is clearly set before it. Doubtless a fundamentally important part of the function of morality consists in maintaining habits and sentiments preservative of individual and social life; but this is because, as Aristotle said, in order to live well we must live. It does not follow that life is simply the ultimate end; since if all life were as little desirable as some portions of it have been in the experience of most of us we should judge anything tending to its preservation as unmitigatedly bad. It is not life simply, but good or desirable life, that is the ethical end; and though—as all students of your school will know —there is still much controversy as to the precise content of the notion 'good' in this application, it is a controversy which ethics has got to work through, and in settling which it cannot derive any material aid from sociology.

But, again, the sociological hypothesis seems to me equally unacceptable when put forward as a complete explanation of the facts to which it relates.

The view that morality has been developed under the influence of the struggle for existence among social organisms as a part of the complex adaptation of such organisms to the conditions of their struggling existence is, I think, a probable conjecture as regards the earlier stages of its development in prehistoric times. It is reasonable to suppose that the observance of duties to fellow-tribesmen within a primitive tribe tended to the survival of the tribe in the struggle for tribal existence, by increasing the internal coherence of the tribe and the effective co-operation of its members. But it is not reasonable to accept this as the main explanation of the evolution of morality even in primitive ages, because it is certainly not a cause that has had any great effect on the important changes in moral beliefs that have taken place in historic times. Take one of the greatest of such changes, that resulting in the conversion of the Greco-Roman civilised world to Christianity. Not only would it be obviously absurd to attribute this change to the struggle for existence among civilised societies; there is not even any adequate evidence that it had a preservative effect on the political society in which the conversion took place. I should conjecture that before Constantine its operation was the other way, considering the passive alienation of primitive

Christians from the secular society in which they lived, over which they believed a swift and sudden destruction to be impending. And, though this split between religion and the state was healed by Constantine, it is difficult, even after this, to see any tendency in Christianity to preserve the Roman empire, or even arrest its decline and fall. The Christian empire seems simply to continue the process tending towards surrender to the barbarians outside.

In short, the sociological hypothesis that I am now considering—so far as it is offered as a complete explanation of moral evolution—seems to me due to the one-sidedness of view which I before noted as a source of sociological error: the concentration of attention on the physical side of social life and its primitive conditions, unduly ignoring its spiritual side and the later stages of its development. And this is true, not of morality only, but of the development of knowledge, of art,—indeed of all the chief elements of that ideal good which we most deeply value in what we call the progress of civilization. We cannot say of the most signal contributions to this progress that they are always decisively preservative of the particular nation of which they are made; if we are to view them as adjustments of means to a social end, it can be no lesser or more limited end than the welfare of humanity at large.

I now turn to consider an objection that may be taken against the whole line of thought that I have adopted. I may be asked, 'Why insist on this artificial separation between the subjects of ethics and sociology? Why not allow the development of both to be influenced by the natural play of thought between the two? Why attempt the impossible task of keeping different portions of our thought on human relations in separate water-tight compartments?'

To objections of this kind my answer is,—First, that I fully recognize the propriety of the demand that our ethical and our sociological thought should be brought into clear and consistent relations: indeed, I regard the harmonizing of different sciences and studies as the special task of philosophy. I think, however, that the impulse to put together different lines of thought requires methodical restraint, because one of the most fruitful sources of error in philosophy has been over-hasty synthesis and combination without sufficient previous analysis of the elements combined. But, secondly, in order to avoid this error, I by no means wish to prevent altogether mutual influence, interpenetration of ideas, between the two studies I am now considering. I only urge that it should be carefully watched and criticised, in order that it may not be the source of confusion, which is especially dangerous in the condition of controversy and conflict of opinion on fundamental points from which neither sociology nor ethics has as yet successfully emerged. To illustrate this, let me consider first the current influence on ethics of sociological conceptions. I will take the fundamental conception of the social organism.

Although as a utilitarian I cannot regard mere preservation of the social organism as the ultimate end and supreme standard of right action, I recognise the value of the conception in making our general view of duty, whether framed on utilitarian or any other principles, fuller and truer. In any case it is important for an individual that he should not conceive himself merely as a member of an aggregate, capable of benefiting or injuring by his actions other individuals as such, but also as a member of a body formed of individual human beings bound into a whole by complex mutual relations; a whole of which the parts, whether individuals or groups, have functions diverse and mutually dependent. Adopting this conception, he will, whatever view he takes of the ultimate ethical end, judge actions largely by their effect in promoting or impeding the coherent and harmonious co-operation of different organs of society, and in strengthening or weakening habits and sentiments that tend to the efficient performance of social functions.

All this is highly important. But some writers seem drawn by the interest of the novel conception to regard it as supplying a complete determinant of duty. That is, it seems to be supposed that adequate guidance to particular duties is given in all cases by the facts of social relations. 'A man', it is said, 'finds himself as a member of a society in certain relations to other human beings. He is son, brother, husband and father, neighbour, citizen. These relations are all facts, and his duties lie in fulfilling the claims that are essential parts of these relations.' Now, no doubt the claims or conscious expectations connected with these relations, and the common recognition of these claims by other members of the society than those primarily concerned are important social facts. But it can hardly be maintained that it is an absolute duty to fulfil all such expectations, as they are to a certain extent vague, varying, liable to conflict with each other, sometimes unreasonable, sometimes sanctioned by custom but by custom 'more honoured in the breach than in the observance'. In short, so far as these claims are actual facts they are not indisputably valid and do not form a harmonious system, and the study of them as facts does not give a criterion of their validity and a means of eliminating conflict. In considering which of the demands made on us by our fellow-men have to be satisfied and which repudiated, and, when two conflict, which is to be postponed, we require a system of principles of right conduct which the study of social facts as such cannot alone give, but which it is the business of ethics to give.

On the other hand, just as this wide and quasi-architectonic use of sociological conception in ethics leads to a mistaken attempt to get the ideal out of the actual, so the converse influence of ethics on sociology leads to equally mistaken attempts to get the ideal into the actual,—*i.e.*, to predict a future state of society in harmony with ethical ideas without any adequate support in scientific induction from the known facts of past social evolution.

In criticising this 'evolutionary optimism', as we may call it, I ought to explain that I am not opposing optimism as a philosophical doctrine. I am not myself an optimist; but I have a great respect for the belief that, in spite of appearances to the contrary, the world now in process of evolution, is ultimately destined to reveal itself as perfectly free from evil and the best possible world. What I would urge is that, in the present state of our knowledge, this belief should be kept as a theological doctrine, or, if you like, a philosophical postulate, and that it should not be allowed to mix itself with the process of scientific inference to the future from the past.

The sociologist who brings his optimism into his sociological reasonings must, I think, find the tendency almost irresistible to give a one-sided prominence to those facts in the past history of society which make for a favourable view of its future progress and to ignore those facts which make for the opposite conclusion. It is only in this way that I can account for Mr. Spencer's belief, regarded by him as a strictly scientific inference from a survey of historical facts, that the evolution of human society will ultimately bring about a condition of social relations in which the voluntary actions of normal human beings will produce 'pleasure unalloyed by pain anywhere'. And, similarly, I think that his hypothetical conclusion that 'there needs but a continuance of absolute peace externally and a vigorous insistance on non-aggression internally to ensure the moulding of men into a form naturally characterized by all the virtues' has not really been reached by a strictly sociological method; but that the sociological reasoning which has led him to it has been influenced and modified throughout by an individualistic ideal formed prior to systematic sociological study.

I seem to find this confusing effect of 'evolutionary optimism' in an even more extreme though vaguer form in a good deal of popular discourse about progress. The believer in a good time coming often seems inclined to believe that what is coming is good because it is coming, no less than that what is good is coming because it is good. Now, granting the latter proposition to be well founded, it does not in any way imply the former; granting that man is destined to unalloyed bliss, still his road to this bright goal may be in parts very devious and distressful; and some of the most distressful turns that would otherwise be found in it may be avoidable evils, but only avoidable by vigorous resistance to present tendencies of change. This seems obvious enough: but it is an obvious truth which is liable to be missed because the opposite error is not explicitly propounded, but lurks in a vague acquiescence in the drift of events.

[It was only at the proof stage that I noticed, on page 68, line 6, an error on Sidgwick's part, in mixing up the words 'former' and 'latter', making the latter do the work of the former and vice-versa. I have interchanged the words to represent more accurately Sidgwick's meaning. Any reader who thinks the mistake is mine is of course free to change them back again. Ed.]

Part II

Value Theory and Moral Psychology

10. Pleasure and Desire

If anyone interested in observing contemporary opinion were asked what was the prevailing moral system in England at the present day, he would probably answer Utilitarianism. And if anyone interested in promoting practical morality had to state the most radical and morally important of the differences among human dispositions, he would probably take occasion to contrast the selfish and sympathetic man. It is, therefore, somewhat singular that the *former* answer should be ambiguous precisely in respect of the contrast pointed in the latter: that a 'Utilitarian', in common usage, should nearly as often mean one who acts from self-interest as one who aims at the general good; and that in the writings of professed assailants, as well as professed defenders of Utilitarianism; the Egoistic and Altruistic principles should frequently appear inextricably blended, or at least indissolubly connected.

At the same time it is not difficult to find reasons for this close union between principles and systems from one point of view so antagonistic. In the first place, both are equally opposed to the 'intuitional', or 'common-sense' morality: and the alliances of doctrines as of nations are as often due to common enmity as to natural affinity. But, further, the systems of Epicurus and Bentham are essentially similar in being both *dependent* systems; that is, in prescribing actions as means to an end distinct from, and lying outside the actions; and thus both consist of rules which are not absolute but relative, and only valid if they conduce to the end. Again, the ultimate end, or entity regarded as intrinsically good and desirable, is in both systems the same in quality, *i.e.*, pleasure, or, more strictly, the maximum of pleasure attainable, pains being subtracted. Besides, it is of course to a great extent true that the conduct recommended by Egoistic Hedonism coincides with that inculcated by Universalistic Hedonism (as for comparison's sake we may term Bentham's Utilitarianism). Though it is only in an ideal polity that 'self-interest well understood' leads to the perfect discharge of all social duties, still, in a tolerably well-ordered community it prompts to the fulfilment of most of them, unless under very exceptional circumstances. And, on the other hand, a sincere

[From *The Contemporary Review*, 19 (Apr. 1872), 662–72. The reader may wish to compare this essay with Bk. I, ch. 4 of *The Methods of Ethics*, also entitled 'Pleasure and Desire'. At the end of the Preface of the 1st edn. of *The Methods* Sidgwick says that 'chapter iv of Bk. i has been reprinted (with considerable modifications) from the *Contemporary Review*, in which it originally appeared as an article on "Pleasure and Desire" '. The modifications, however, are so considerable, and its interest is so considerable, that it was judged worthy of reprinting here, despite some occasional repetition. For, though similar in message, they differ considerably in style and form. Ed.]

Benthamite may fairly hold that his own happiness is that portion of the universal good which it is most in his power to promote, and which therefore is most especially entrusted to his charge. And the practical blending of the two systems is sure to go beyond their theoretical coincidence. It is much easier for a man to move in a sort of diagonal between egoistic and universalistic hedonism, than to be practically a consistent adherent of either. Few men are so completely selfish, whatever their theory of morals may be, as not occasionally to seek the general good of some smaller or larger community from natural sympathetic impulse unsupported by Epicurean calculation. And probably still fewer are so resolutely unselfish as never to find all men's good in their own with rather too ready conviction.

In spite of all this, the distinction between one's own happiness and that of people in general is so natural and obvious, and so continually forced upon our attention by the circumstances of life, that some other reason is required to explain the persistent confusion between the systems that respectively adopt either end as furnishing the right and reasonable standard for each individual's conduct. And such a reason is found in the theory of human action propounded by Bentham, and, generally speaking, maintained by his disciples. Though ethically Epicureanism and Benthamism may be viewed as standing in polar opposition, psychologically Bentham is in fundamental agreement with Epicureans. He holds that a man ought to aim at the maximum felicity of men in general; but he holds, also, that he always does aim at what appears to him his own maximum felicity—that he cannot help doing this—that this is the way his volition inevitably acts. Bentham takes every opportunity of putting these two propositions with characteristic sharpness and clearness. 'The greatest happiness of all those whose interest is in question is the only right and proper and universally desirable end of human action in every situation.' But 'in the general tenor of life, in every human breast, self-regard is predominant'; or, more explicitly, 'on the occasion of every act he exercises, every human being is led to pursue that line of conduct which, according to his view of the case, taken by him at the moment, will be in the highest degree contributory to his own greatest happiness, whatsoever be the effect of it in relation to the happiness of other similar beings, any or all of them taken together'. He goes on to refer those who doubt to the 'existence of the human species as being itself a proof, and a conclusive one'.

Hence if self-interest be not the 'right and proper end of action',[1] it is at any rate not wrong or improper, because it is inevitable. If Bentham is asked, 'Why then do you inveigh (as you certainly do with much bitterness and emphasis) against lawyers and statesmen who seek their own interest when it unfortunately happens

---

[1] As far as I am aware, this term is never applied to it in works written by Bentham himself. In the Deontology, and elsewhere where the composition is due to Dumont, we find a loose and vague syncretion of Egoistic and Universalistic Hedonism, which it is impossible to attribute to so exact and coherent a thinker.

to diverge from the public interest?' his answer is ready and clear: 'I do so with a view of removing the divergence; by my own disapprobation and the disapproba- tion of all I can persuade to sympathise with me, I would supply the force that is wanting to turn the wills of these public servants in the direction of public duty.' If he is asked again, 'But when you concern yourself about the public good, and call it the right and proper end of action, do not you recognise a principle of duty, obedience to which you prefer to your own pleasure?' he answers unhesitatingly, 'No I concern myself about the public good, *because in me selfishness has taken the form of public spirit*, and when I call it the proper end, I mean that I wish all other men to take it for such, with a view to its attainment, with which the attainment of my own greatest happiness is bound up'.

There is, therefore, in Bentham's mind no confusion and no logical connection between his psychological generalization and his ethical assumption. But it has been so common among moralists of all schools to identify the natural and the ideal, and to argue from what men universally or normally do to what they ought to do, that it is not surprising that a utilitarian of Bentham's school should be thought to approve of the egoism which he accepts as inevitable, and in some way to base upon it his universalistic hedonism. And we find that the latest expositor of utilitarianism, Mr. Mill, does try to establish a logical connection between the psychological and ethical principles, which he holds in common with Bentham, and to convince his readers that because each man naturally seeks his own hap- piness, therefore he ought to seek the happiness of other people.

Now, it is my object to prove that this psychological generalisation is in no important sense true. In so doing I do not wish to attack the utilitarianism of Bentham and Mr. Mill, with which I in the main agree, but to disentangle it from the egoistic hedonism with which their theory of human action continually causes it to be confounded.

It will be as well to quote the words in which Mr. Mill states the theory. 'It will hardly', he expects, 'be disputed that desiring a thing and finding it pleasant, aversion to it and thinking of it as painful, are phenomena entirely inseparable, or rather two parts of the same phenomenon': or, still more precisely, 'we desire a thing *in proportion* as the idea of it is pleasant'. It is important to notice the ital- icized words. For it must be admitted that if we leave them out, the experience of mankind would *primâ facie* confirm Mr. Mill's assertion. Most men would say that whatever they desired was always something which was pleasant in prospect. I shall presently argue that even this on closer examination seems to be an inexact account of consciousness. But few would assert that what they *most* desired was always that which they thought would give them most pleasure. It would be generally allowed that men not only desire, but are actually impelled to do what (even in the moment of yielding to the impulse) they know will cause them more pain than pleasure on the whole. 'Video meliora proboque, deteriora sequor' is as applicable to the Epicurean as to anyone else. If any evidence is needed of this, I cannot do better than quote Mr. Mill himself.[2] 'Men often, from infirmity of character, make their election for the nearer good, though they know it to be the less valuable; and this no less when the choice is between two bodily pleasures . . . They pursue sensual indulgences to the injury of health, though perfectly aware that health is the greater good.' I confess that I cannot reconcile this sentence with the one previously quoted from the same author. If we always desire more strongly what is in idea most pleasant, how can we choose what we know to be the less valuable pleasure?

It may be thought, however, that this is an exceptional case, offering an interesting psychological puzzle; but that it still remains true that the ordinary, normal phenomenon in the action of men is that each individual seeks his own greatest apparent pleasure; and that, in order to prove that the greatest pleasure is intrinsically desirable, we only require the proposition that the greatest pleasure is *ordinarily* desired, not that it is *always* so.

Before we examine this more qualified assertion, it will be as well to define our terms as clearly as possible. In the passage which I first quoted, Mr. Mill goes on to say that 'desiring a thing, and finding it pleasant, are, in strictness of language, two modes of naming the same psychological fact'. If this be the case, it is hard to see how the assertion we are discussing requires to be determined by 'practised self-consciousness and self-observation'; as the denial of it would involve a contradiction in terms. The truth is that there is an ambiguity in the word pleasure, which has always tended seriously to confuse the discussion of this question.[3] By pleasure we commonly mean an agreeable sensation not necessarily connected with desire or volition, as it may arise from external causes without having been foreseen or desired at all. But when we speak of a man doing something at his own 'pleasure', or as he 'pleases', we signify the mere fact of choice or preference; the mere determination of the will in a certain direction. Now, if by 'pleasant' we mean that which influences choice, exercises a certain attractive force on the will, it is not a psychological truth, but a tautological assertion, to say that we desire a thing in proportion as it appears 'pleasant'. But if we take 'pleasure' to mean 'agreeable sensation', it then becomes a really debatable question whether our active impulses are always consciously directed towards the attainment of agreeable (or the avoidance of disagreeable) sensations as their end. And this is what we must understand Mr. Mill to consider 'so obvious, that it will hardly be disputed'.

It is rather curious to find that the best-known of English moralists regards the exact opposite of what Mr. Mill thinks so obvious, as being not merely a universal fact of our conscious experience, but even a necessary truth. Butler distinguishes,

---

[2] 'Utilitarianism', C. 2, p. 14 (of 3rd edition).

[3] The confusion occurs in the most singular form in Hobbes, who actually identifies Pleasure and Appetite, 'this motion in which consisteth pleasure, is a solicitation to draw near to the thing that pleaseth'.

as is well known, 'self-love', or the impulse towards our own pleasure from 'particular movements towards particular external objects—honour, power, the harm or good of another'; the actions proceeding from which are 'no otherwise interested than as every action of every creature must from the nature of the case be; for no one can act but from a desire, or choice, or preference of his own'. Such particular passions or appetites are, he goes on to say, *necessarily presupposed by the very idea* of an interested pursuit; since the very idea of interest or happiness consists in this, that an appetite or affection enjoys its object'. We could not pursue pleasure at all, unless we had desires for something else than pleasure; for pleasure consists in the satisfaction of just these extra-regarding impulses.

Butler has clearly over-stated his case;[4] for many pleasures (as was just remarked) occur to us without any relation to previous desires, and it is quite *conceivable* that our appetitive consciousness should consist entirely of impulses towards such pleasures as these. But taken as a mere statement of actual fact, his doctrine faithfully represents a great, probably the greater part of our experience. Throughout the whole of our appetitive life we may distinguish (primary) *extra-regarding* impulses, desires of some end other than our own sensations, from secondary, reflexive, self-regarding impulses towards the pleasure which attends the fulfilment of the former.

I will begin with the appetites of hunger and thirst, because it is important to show that there is no difference between 'sensual' and 'intellectual' impulses as regards the point in question.

Hunger and thirst are impulses, due to bodily needs of food and drink representing themselves in consciousness. Their objects are respectively food and drink, not the pleasure that we shall feel while the food is being eaten and the water drunk.

It is, no doubt, true that appetite makes us regard food as pleasant, and is frequently and naturally accompanied with anticipation of the pleasure of eating; and further, that in proportion as the desire is strong, the anticipated pleasure appears great. These undeniable facts render the proposition which I am combating plausible, so that it requires careful introspective observation to convince us of its unsoundness. But I think such observation will show that conscious anticipation of pleasure is by no means an inseparable concomitant of appetite; and that, even when it exists, it is not its object. We may have a secondary desire of this pleasure along with the primary appetite, but the two are not to be identified. This statement I must again guard by admitting that the analysis which distinguishes the two is not applicable everywhere. Very often they are indistinguishably blended; and, as the evolution of consciousness is always from the vague to the definite, it is, perhaps, most exact to say that, in the earliest phase

---

[4] The same argument is put in a more guarded, and, I think, unexceptionable form by Hutcheson.

of any desire, the strictly extra-regarding impulse is not yet 'differentiated' (as Mr. Spencer would say) from the strictly self-regarding. Still this differentiation soon takes place, and there are many occasions when we can quite clearly distinguish the two elements by the different actions which they respectively prompt. For as the pleasure depends to a great extent, as Butler says (though not entirely), on the strength of the appetite: the desire of the pleasure prompts men not only to gratify, but to stimulate, the appetite. The gourmand, who takes a walk in order to enjoy his dinner, is impelled by one sensual impulse to aim at producing another: here, at least, we are in no danger of confounding the two.

Again, let us examine a class of pleasures which occupy a very important place —according to some judges, the most important—in our sensitive existence: the pleasures of *pursuit*. These illustrate peculiarly well the difference between the extra-regarding and self-regarding impulses, and also the dependence of pleasure on desire, instead of *vice-versâ*. Take, for example, the favourite amusement of rich Englishmen. What is the motive that impels a man to fox-hunting? It is not the pleasure of catching the fox. Nobody, before entering on the chase, represents to himself the killing of the fox as a source of gratification, apart from the eagerness produced by pursuit. It is upon this eagerness that the pleasure depends; the desire, stimulated to a strange intensity by vehement action, is the prior fact; and the pleasure arising when the desire is gratified is proportioned to the pre-existing desire. It will be said, however, that what the fox-hunter desires is, not to kill the fox, but to enjoy the pursuit. And, no doubt, this is his rational motive, that, in a tranquil state of his mind, initiates the whole series of actions. But the peculiarity of the case is that of these pleasures at which he rationally aims, the irrational desire to catch the fox is an essential condition. Before we can enjoy pursuing, we must temporarily want to catch—want it very vehemently and absorbingly. Hence the often-noted paradox which such activities present to the prudential reason: we cannot attain the prudentially rational end of maximum pleasure without exciting what are now[5] highly irrational impulses.

Another very important observation suggests itself in connection with these latter pleasures. In the case previously discussed, although we could distinguish appetite from the desire of the pleasures consisting in the satisfaction of appetite, there appeared no incompatibility between the two. The fact that the gourmand is dominated by the desire of the pleasures of eating in no way impedes the development in him of the appetite which is a necessary condition of these pleasures. But when we turn to the pleasures of the chase, we seem to perceive this incompatibility to a certain extent. In all forms of pursuit a certain enthusiasm is necessary to obtain full enjoyment. A man who enters on it in too epicurean a temper,

---

[5] I do not enter into the history of these impulses. In dealing with questions of which the decision depends, as Mr. Mill says, on 'practised self-consciousness and self-observation, assisted by observation of others', it seems to me important to put carefully aside the necessarily hypothetical method of historical psychology.

thinking too much of the pleasure, does not catch the full spirit of the chase; his eagerness never gets just the sharpness of edge which imparts to the pleasure its highest zest and flavour. Here comes into view what we might call the fundamental paradox of hedonism, that the self-regarding impulse, if too predominant, defeats its own end. This effect is not visible, or at any rate is scarcely visible in the case of purely sensual pleasures; and also where there is a very keen, natural susceptibility in any direction, the operation of the general law is counteracted. Hence we see, first, why epicureanism has always had, practically, in ordinary minds, a tendency to sensualism, which it certainly has not theoretically, because sensual pleasures are least of all diminished by directly pursuing them; and, secondly, why it has not had this tendency in philosophic minds, because in them the intellectual impulse is so strong originally as to resist the corrosive effect of the epicurean principle. But of a great part of our more refined enjoyments, intellectual and emotional, it seems true to say that in order to attain them, at any rate in their best form, the direction of our impulse must be objective, extra-regarding, not fixed upon our own sensations as its end. The activities upon which the pleasures attend seem to require a certain self-abandonment, incompatible with the conscious predominance of self-love. For example, the pleasures of thought and study (which the materialist Hobbes declares to be 'far exceeding all carnal delights') can only be enjoyed by those who have an ardour of curiosity which carries the mind temporarily away from self and its sensations. In all kinds of Art, again, the exercise of the creative faculty is attended by intense and exquisite pleasures; but in order to get them, one must forget them; the gaze of the artist is always said to be rapt and fixed upon his ideal of beauty. Still more clearly does the law appear when we contemplate the sympathetic activities and susceptibilities. Even Professor Bain admits that the desire to give pleasure to, and remove pain from, others constitutes an exception to his general theory that each individual's volition is determined by his own pleasures and pains, actual or ideal; and it is upon the existence of this strictly unselfish impulse that the much-commended pleasures of benevolence depend.

So far I have insisted on the felt incompatibility of the self-regarding and extra-regarding impulses only as a means of proving their essential distinctness. I do not wish to overstate it, as it has been not unfrequently overstated by the anti-hedonistic moralists who have been perfectly right in drawing attention to it. I believe that in the commonest state of our activity the incompatibility is only momentary, and does not prevent a real harmony from being attained by means of a sort of alternating rhythm of the two impulses in consciousness. Desire is, I think, not ordinarily a conscious impulse towards pleasure; but where there is strong desire in any direction, there is commonly keen susceptibility to the corresponding pleasures; and the most devoted enthusiast is sustained in his work by the recurrent consciousness of such pleasures. But it is important to point out that the familiar and obvious instances of real conflict between self-love and some extra-regarding impulses are not paradoxes and puzzles to be explained away, but occasional phenomena, which the analysis of our appetitive consciousness in the normal state, when there is no such conflict, would lead us to expect. Such conflict is generically the same, from a psychological point of view, whatever be the quality of the impulse which comes into collision with self-love; but the very important distinction introduced when we apply the ethical notions 'higher' and 'lower', and consider some impulses superior, others inferior in grade to self-love, has caused this resemblance to be overlooked. In the case of the appetites we consider (as Butler says) that self-love has a natural claim to rule; and if, yielding to a sensual impulse we take the course of action which is attended with less pleasure on the whole,[6] we condemn ourselves afterwards. But a similar result may occur in the case of a higher impulse, the subordination of which to self-love is not equally recognised by common sense; this involves us in a certain perplexity, which however is not due to any psychological anomaly but purely ethical, because the conduct appears to us in a certain sense irrational, and yet we do not condemn it. Let us represent to ourselves a case in detail. Suppose a man to have been for some time under the influence of a ruling passion of a noble kind: love of truth, love of beauty, or personal affection, or devotion to a cause, or desire to achieve any particular laudable end. For some time, perhaps, he has been borne along by a feeling in which the selfish and unselfish elements are not yet distinguished: he could not tell if asked whether he did what he was doing from a disinterested impulse or because he found his pleasure in it. But suddenly this passion or enthusiasm is thrown by circumstances into collision with other impulses and needs: the man is thus put into the attitude of prudential reflection, and finds, on estimation of probable resulting pleasures and pains, that the course of action to which his habitual impulse tends is distinctly opposed to the judgment of self-love. In fact, his enthusiasm demands a sacrifice; and he is at once able to distinguish clearly the proper external object of the impulse from the pleasure which normally attends its pursuit and attainment. He can ask the two distinct questions, 'Is the sacrifice intrinsically worth making?' and 'Will it repay me?' He is conscious that he can answer the second question in the negative, and yet the first in the affirmative. He can say, 'It will not repay me, but it is worth it, and it shall take place'.

I have been describing a phenomenon of by no means unfrequent occurrence even outside the sphere of properly moral impulses. But it is no doubt most common in the case of these latter; the sacrifice is generally demanded in the name of what is right, reasonable, virtuous. And here I would again appeal to Mr. Mill himself as a witness on my side; referring in this case to his Examination of Sir W.

---

[6] The victorious sensual impulse in this case is in general consciously directed towards pleasure; and the case is one of preference of a less pleasure to a greater, not of some external object to pleasure. Still it equally constitutes an exception to Mr. Mill's supposed universal law that desire is always proportioned to anticipated pleasure.

Hamilton's Philosophy. Readers may recall the passage in which he speaks of the supposed religious duty of worshipping as 'good' a Deity to whom the term is not applicable in any intelligible sense; rather than do so, he says, 'If such a Being can sentence me to hell for not so calling him, to hell I will go'. The case is of course purely hypothetical, being intended as a *reductio ad absurdum* of the belief in an incognizable God. But a hypothetical instance does just as well as a real one to test a principle; and this supplies me with just the hypothesis most perfectly adapted to illustrate my view. Mr. Mill avows, we may say, a hypothetical preference for hell.[7] Now he can hardly maintain that such preference would involve 'finding hell most pleasant', even in idea; as it is understood in the very notion of hell, that it is more painful to be there than to be anywhere else. He therefore recognizes the conceivability of a practical impulse tending in the direction of maximum infelicity; and even asserts that such an impulse could and would determine his volition.

To sum up, in contravention of the doctrine that our conscious active impulses are always directed towards the production of agreeable sensations in ourselves, I would maintain that we find everywhere in consciousness extra-regarding impulse, directed towards something that is not pleasure; that in many cases this impulse is so far incompatible with the self-regarding that the two do not easily coexist in the same moment of consciousness; and that more occasionally (but by no means rarely) the two come into irreconcilable conflict, and prompt to opposite courses of action. And this incompatibility (though it is important to notice it in other instances) is no doubt specially prominent in the case of the impulse towards the end which competes in ethical controversy with pleasure—the love of virtue for its own sake, or desire to do what is right as such, which in the view of stoicism is essential to right conduct.

It may be said that whatever be the case with our present adult consciousness, our original impulses were all directed towards pleasure, and that any impulses otherwise directed are derived from these by 'association of ideas'. I do not think this can be proved; and the results of observation, as far as we can carry it, seem to tend in the opposite way; as preponderant objectivity seems characteristic of the earlier stages of our consciousness, and the subjective attitude does not become habitual till later in life. But supposing the assertion were proved, it would have little bearing on the present question. The Hedonist says, 'I prove Pleasure to be intrinsically desirable by showing that all men actually do desire it'. It is answered that all men do not now desire pleasure, but rather other things: some in particular having impulses towards virtue, which may and do conflict with their desire for their own pleasure. It is no reply to this to say that all *once* desired pleasure, except on the assumption that our earlier impulses have a

---

[7] Mr. Mill, no doubt, draws a distinction between Desire and Will. But I think he means to imply, in the case supposed, a preference as well as a determination.

prerogative in validity over our later. But no one appeals from the artist's sense of beauty to the child's; nor are the truths of the higher mathematics thought to be less certainly true, because they can be only apprehended by a highly developed intellect. In fact, this disposition to attribute some strange importance and special authority to what was *first* felt or thought belongs to an antiquated point of view. In politics we have quite abandoned the idea that even if we could establish irrefragably the original condition of the human family, it would at all help to determine jural obligations in our existing societies. The corresponding opinion still lingers in psychology and ethics, but it may be expected not to linger very long; as the assumption that our earliest consciousness is most trustworthy is not only baseless, but opposed to the current theories of the Evolution and Progress.

11. Hedonism and Ultimate Good

It has often been observed that systematic enquiry into the nature of the Supreme End of human action, the *Bonum* or *Summum Bonum*, belongs almost exclusively to ancient ethical speculation; and that in modern ethics its place is supplied by an investigation of the fundamental Moral Laws, or Imperatives of the Practical Reason. While the ancients appear as chiefly endeavouring to determine the proper ultimate object of rational pursuit, the moderns are chiefly occupied in discussing the basis and validity of a received code of rules, for the most part restrictive rather than directive of human effort. But though this difference has frequently been noticed, I am not aware that any distinct explanation of it has ever been offered; while again there are many signs that ethical speculation in England has reached a point at which this old question as to the nature of Ultimate Good again presents itself as fundamental. If these signs are not misleading, it will be interesting to ascertain, from a comparison between ancient and modern thought, how far the speculative excursion which has ended in conveying us back to the old problem has brought us to face it from a new point of view, and under new conditions.

When we compare the Greek investigation of Ultimate Good with our own, we find an important difference in the very form of the fundamental question. What we, as moralists, are naturally led to seek, is the true account of *general* good; for most of us almost unhesitatingly assume that moral action, as such, must have relation to universal ends. But for the Greek moralist, the primary question as naturally and inevitably took an egoistic form.[1] The Good which he studied was 'good for himself', or for any other individual philosophic soul, enquiring after the true way of life. This difference is sufficiently obvious and has been noticed by more than one writer; but it has perhaps been somewhat obscured for modern readers by the antithetical fact, to which more attention has been drawn, that the political speculation of Greece differs from our own precisely in its non-individualistic character. There is really no contradiction between the assumption in ethics of the agent's private good as the ultimate determinant of rational action; and the assumption in politics of the good of the state—without regard to any 'natural rights' of its component parts—as the

[From *Mind*, OS, 2 (1877), 27–38.]
[1] This statement requires some qualification in so far as it concerns Plato, on account of his peculiar ontology. Still this does not so much affect the question Plato asked, as the answer he gave to it, and even that only to a limited extent; not (*e.g.*) in the *Philebus*, where the ἀγαθὸν investigated is just the ἀνθρώπινον ἀγαθὸν of Aristotle.

ultimate end and standard of right political organisation. Indeed it would not be difficult to show that the two assumptions naturally belong to the same stage in the development of practical philosophy. Still they have somewhat tended to confuse each other, through that blending of politics with ethics in philosophical discussion which characterises the period from Socrates to Aristotle; and the confusion has been further increased by the analogy between the Individual and the State, which forms the basis of Plato's most famous treatise. This very analogy, however, when carefully examined, brings out most strikingly the characteristic which it, at first, tends to obscure; for the individual man being considered as a polity of impulses, his good is made to consist essentially in the due ordering of the internal relations of this polity, and is only secondarily and indirectly realised in the relations of this complex individual to other men. And in Aristotle's detailed analysis of the moral ideal of his age, the fundamental egoism of the form in which it is conceived is continually illustrated, in striking contrast to the modern tendency to regard 'the scope and object of ethics as altogether social'.[2] The limits of Aristotle's Liberality are not determined by any consideration of its effect on the welfare of its recipients, but by an intuitive sense of the noble and graceful quality of expenditure that is free without being too lavish; and his Courageous warrior is not commended as devoting himself for his country, but as attaining for himself, even amid pains and death, the peculiar καλὸν of a courageous act.

No doubt we must bear in mind that this egoism is chiefly formal. The orthodox moralist, from Prodicus to Chrysippus, in recommending the preference of Virtue to Pleasure, is substantially recommending the sacrifice of individual inclinations to social claims; and the explicit 'communis utilitas nostrae anteponenda' of later Stoicism, (which in this respect forms a transition from the ancient point of view to the modern), is no doubt implicit in the practical teaching of earlier schools. Still the effect of the egoistic form is very clearly seen in the actual course of ethical discussion. It rendered it absolutely necessary for the orthodox moralist to settle the relation of the individual's virtue to his Pleasure and Pain. A modern moralist may leave this undetermined. He cannot of course overlook the paramount influence of pleasure and pain, in the actual determination of human actions; and he must be aware that the obtaining of future pleasure and the avoiding of future pain constitute at least the chief part of the common notion of 'happiness', 'interest', 'good on the whole', or whatever else we call the end which a prudent man, as such, has in view. But he may regard the discussion of this as bearing on the Sanctions of morality, not Morality itself; that is not on the theory of what duty is, but on the practical question how a man is to be made to do his duty. The Greek, however, who regarded the determination of the individual's good as supplying the fundamental principle on which the whole code of rules

---

[2] Cf. *Mind* III., p. 341.

for reasonable conduct must ultimately depend, was obliged at the outset to consider the popular view that this good was Pleasure. He either, with the Cyrenaics and Epicureans, accepted this view unreservedly, and held Virtue to be valuable merely as a means to the enjoyment of the virtuous agent; or, with Zeno, he rejected it altogether, and maintained that intrinsic valuelessness of pleasure; or with Socrates, Aristotle, and Plato in his soberer moods, he argued the inseparable connection of the best and really pleasantest pleasure with the exercise of virtue. The first position was offensive to the moral consciousness; the third imposed on it the necessity of proving what could never be really proved without either dialectical tricks or assumptions obviously transcending experience; and it was not surprising that the chief part of the moral earnestness of ancient society was ultimately enlisted on the side of the second alternative. Still the inhuman severity of the paradox that 'pleasure and pain are indifferent to the wise man', never failed to have a repellent effect; and the imaginary rack on which an imaginary sage had to be maintained in perfect happiness, was at any rate a dangerous instrument of dialectical torment for the actual philosopher.

Christianity extricated the moral consciousness from this dilemma between base subserviency and inhuman indifference to the feelings of the moral agent. It compromised the long conflict between Virtue and Pleasure, by transferring to another world the fullest realisation of both; thus enabling orthodox morality to assert itself, as reasonable and natural, without denying the concurrent reasonableness and naturalness of the individual's desire for bliss without alloy. Hence when independent ethical speculation recommences in England after the Middle Ages, we find that the dualism—if I may so say—of the Practical Reason, which Butler afterwards formulated, is really implicit in all the orthodox replies to Hobbes. It is not denied in these replies that man's 'natural good' is pleasure, or that the self-love which seeks the agent's greatest happiness is a rational principle of action; they are only concerned to maintain the independent reasonableness of Conscience, and the objective validity of moral rules derived from a quite other source than the calculations of self-interest. Thus, for example, though in Cumberland's view the ultimate end and rational basis of the moral code is 'commune bonum omnium rationalium', the obligation of the code on each individual 'rational' is imposed 'sub poena felicitatis amittendae aut propter spem ejusdem acquirendae'. And even Clarke, who is often thought to have carried his argument for the independence of morality up to the point of paradox, is yet after all found to make only the very moderate claim 'that Virtue deserves to be chosen for its own sake, and Vice to be avoided, though a man was sure of his own particular *neither to gain nor lose anything by the practice of either*'. But since in the actual world 'the practice of vice is accompanied with great temptations, and allurement of pleasure and profit, and the practice of virtue is often attended with great calamity, losses, and sometimes with death itself, this alters the question',— and, in fact, Clarke is of opinion, not only that men under these circumstances will not always prefer Virtue to Vice, but also that 'it is *not very reasonably to be expected* that they should'. Butler, however, was the first to give with perfect precision the *differentia* of what we may call broadly the modern view of Ethics, in stating 'reasonable self-love and conscience' as the '*two* chief or superior principles in the nature of man'; whereas it was a fundamental assumption of all the schools of philosophy that sprang from Socrates, that there is *one* naturally 'chief or superior principle' in every rational being which impels him to seek his own true good.

It is true that, when any attempt is made to relieve Ethics of its dependence on religion, the old difficulty as to the relation of Virtue to Happiness recurs; but it is no longer in the form of a dispute as to the true nature of the object of rational desire, but rather as the problem of reconciling the desire for one's own Good—good being more or less explicitly understood to be pleasure, enjoyment, satisfaction, agreeable feeling of some kind—with the performance of what reason dictates as Duty. This problem presents itself to most minds as of the very profoundest importance; and I cannot understand how any moralist can turn aside from it, or treat it with indifference. But I quite admit that its solution is not an essential pre-requisite of the construction of a moral code.

On what other principles, then, is this construction to be attempted? It appears to me that on this question there is far more substantial agreement among English moralists than is commonly supposed; and that the fundamental intuitions of conscience or the practical reason on which one school have always laid stress, are merely the expression in different aspects or relations of that ideal subordination of individual impulses to universal ends on which alone Utilitarianism, as a system of ethics, can rationally rest. Thus the essence of Justice or Equity, in so far as it is absolutely obligatory, is that different individuals are not to be treated differently, except on grounds of universal application: which grounds, again, are given in the principle of Rational Benevolence, that sets before each man the good of all others as an object of pursuit no less worthy than his own; while, again, other time-honoured virtues seem to be fitly explained as special manifestations of impartial benevolence under various normal circumstances of human life, or else as habits and dispositions indispensable to the maintenance of rational behaviour under the seductive force of various non-rational impulses. I admit that there are other rules which our common moral sense when first interrogated seems to enunciate as absolutely binding; but I contend that careful and systematic reflection on this very Common Sense, as expressed in the habitual moral judgments of ordinary men, results in exhibiting the real subordination of these rules to the fundamental principles above given. Then, further, this method of systematising particular virtues and duties receives very strong support from a comparative study of the history of morality; as the variations in the moral code of different societies at different stages correspond, at least generally, to differences in the actual or believed tendencies of certain kinds of conduct to promote the good of society. While, again, the account given by our evolutionists of the pre-historic condition of the moral faculty, which represents it as derived aboriginally from the social instincts, is entirely in harmony with this view. This convergence of several distinct arguments has had, I think, a considerable effect on contemporary thought; and probably a large majority of reflective persons are now prepared to accept 'Common Good' as the ultimate end for which moral rules exist, and the standard by which they are to be co-ordinated and their qualifications and mutual limitations determined.

There remains, no doubt, some difference of view between the converging lines of speculation, as to the whole or community of which the good is to be sought; since from one point of view we should state the end, in Cumberland's phrase, as the 'Common Good of Rational or Conscious Beings'; while from another it will be rather the good of the particular race of animals to which we belong. But this difference is easily reduced to latency in the idea of the Good of Humanity, and I do not propose at present to dwell upon it.

But neglecting this, and fixing our attention on the notion of Good, we have to ask whether this is less problematical in the case of humanity generally than Socrates found it to be in the case of the individual man. Have we not, after all, been simply brought round to the point from which ethical speculation started in Europe? If we try to define the Good, how shall we avoid revolving again through the old controversies?

A little reflection will show that we have, at any rate, got rid of one of the competing answers to the old question. We cannot now explain the general Good to consist in general Virtue; that is in the general fulfilment of the prohibitions and prescriptions of Common Sense morality. This would obviously involve us in a logical circle; as we have just settled that the ultimate standard for determining these prohibitions and prescriptions is just this general good.

Thus Pleasure, the other 'competitor for the Aristeia', as Plato says, is left without any rival of equally ancient prestige, and in a far better position relatively to ordinary morality. For (1) to regard Virtue merely as a means to the agent's private pleasure was undoubtedly offensive to the common moral consciousness of mankind. But no similar offence is given by the explanation of the Virtues as various forms and applications of Rational Benevolence, or auxiliary habits (as Courage, Temperance, &c.), necessary to the sustained and effective exercise of Rational Benevolence, amid the various temptations and dangers of human life; while the exercise of Benevolence has always been chiefly understood to mean giving pleasure to others and averting pain from them. And (2) we saw that when Self-love was once clearly distinguished from Conscience, it was naturally understood to mean desire for one's own pleasure; accordingly the interpretation of 'one's own good' which was peculiar in ancient thought to the Cyrenaic and Epicurean heresies, is adopted among the moderns, not only by opponents of independent and intuitive morality from Hobbes to Bentham, but also by the most prominent and approved writers of the Intuitional School. Indeed, to many of these latter it never seems to have occurred that this notion can have any other interpretation.[3] If, then, when any one hypothetically concentrates his attention on himself, good is naturally and almost inevitably conceived to be pleasure, it does not appear how the good of any number of human beings, however organised into a community, can be essentially different.

This, then, appears to me to be, in outline, the case for modern Utilitarianism or Universalistic Hedonism, as a study of the history of ethical thought presents it to us. I must now notice briefly the rival doctrines as to the nature of Good which seem to be chiefly maintained at the present time. It appears that Hedonism is attacked from two different points of view, which we may, perhaps, without offence, distinguish as Materialistic and Idealistic; each claiming to substitute an objective standard for the subjective criterion of 'amount of agreeable feeling'. I use 'Materialistic' to denote the view which considers individual men and human societies as Organisms, the condition and functioning of which can be ascertained by external observation, and pronounced good or bad without reference to the series of pleasurable or painful feelings which accompany such functioning. We thus seem to obtain a notion of Well-being or Welfare which may be substituted for Happiness as the ultimate end and standard of right action. Perhaps the notion may be more clearly explained by saying that it is obtained by extending to a race or a community of animals the idea of Health, as commonly attributed to an individual man. In an article in *Mind*, No. I., I mentioned that this view was incidentally adopted by Mr. Darwin in his chapter on the Moral Sense in his *Descent of Man*; and it seems to have been enthusiastically accepted and more fully developed by some of Mr. Darwin's disciples, among whom I may count Mr. Pollock, who replied to my article in No. III. of this journal. I have studied Mr. Pollock's courteous and carefully written answer, and am still unable to see exactly how he deals with the following dilemma. Either this notion of Well-being is entirely resolvable into 'conditions tending to preservation', or it includes something more. If the latter be admitted, we have to ask what is this something more which distinguishes well-being from mere being. In one place, Mr. Pollock seems to say that it is something at present undefinable: to which I can only answer, in Aristotle's words, that if we cannot get even a proximate definition of it, we shall be 'as archers without a mark, rather unlikely to attain the needful'. If, however, he falls back on the former alternative, as certainly other writers of his school seem disposed to do, and says that well-being is merely 'Being with the promise of future being', he surely comes into irreconcilable conflict with common sense. I do not wish to exaggerate this conflict. I admit that the most important part of the function of morality consists in maintaining habits and sentiments which seem necessary to the continued existence, in full numbers,

---

[3] *Cf.* Stewart, *Philosophy of the Active and Moral Powers*, B. II., c. 1.

of a society of human beings under actual circumstances; and that this part may easily be regarded as the whole, if we consider morality merely as a code of restrictive regulations—the aspect which has been most prominent in modern times. But this maintenance of preservative habits and sentiments surely does not exhaust our ideal of good or desirable human life. We are not content with mere Being, however secured in continuance, for ourselves or for those we love or, in so far as we are philanthropists, for humanity generally. What we demand more, may be expressed by the general notion of Culture; and though some part of what is included in this notion may fairly be interpreted as Preservative Tendencies, there is surely much that cannot possibly be so interpreted. If the Hedonistic view of Culture, as consisting in the development of susceptibilities for refined pleasure of various kinds, be rejected, it must be in favour of what I have called the Idealistic view: in which we regard the ideal objects on the realisation of which our most refined pleasures depend—Knowledge, or Beauty in its different forms, or a certain ideal of human relations (whether thought of as Freedom or otherwise)—as constituting in themselves ultimate Good, apart from the pleasures which depend upon their pursuit and attainment. I do not propose at present to criticise this view, chiefly because I am not acquainted with any philosophical exposition of it sufficiently coherent and systematic to invite criticism; though it seems to be pretty widely accepted among cultivated persons, and more or less definitely suggested in the anti-hedonistic arguments of certain philosophical writers. But it may be well to define clearly the manner in which Hedonism, as I conceive it, deals with this view.

The Hedonistic argument against the assumption of 'objective' ultimate ends, just as that against particular moral rules of absolute validity, seems to me to consist necessarily of two parts. It appeals to the immediate intuition of reflective persons; and secondly to the results of a comprehensive comparison of the ordinary judgments of mankind. The second argument comes in rather by way of confirmation of the first and obviously cannot be made completely cogent; since, as above stated, several cultivated persons do habitually judge that certain ideal goods are ends independently of the pleasure derived from them. But we may urge not only that all these ideal goods are productive of pleasure in various ways; but also that they seem to obtain the commendation of Common Sense, roughly speaking, in proportion to the degree of this productiveness. This seems obviously true of Beauty; and will hardly be denied in respect of any kind of social ideal, for it is surely paradoxical to maintain that any degree of Freedom, or any form of social order would be desirable even if it tended to impair, instead of promoting, the general happiness. The case of Knowledge is rather more complex; but certainly Common Sense is most impressed with the value of knowledge, when its 'fruitfulness' has been demonstrated. It is, however, aware that experience has frequently shown how knowledge, long fruitless, may become unexpectedly fruitful, and how light may be shed on one part of the field of knowledge from another apparently remote: and even if any particular branch of scientific pursuit could be shown to be devoid of even this indirect utility, it would still deserve some respect on utilitarian grounds; both as furnishing to the enquirer the refined and innocent pleasures of curiosity, and because the intellectual disposition which it exhibits and sustains, is likely on the whole to produce fruitful knowledge. Still in cases approximating to this latter, Common Sense is somewhat disposed to complain of the misdirection of valuable effort; so that the meed of honour commonly paid to Science seems to be graduated, though perhaps unconsciously, by a tolerably exact utilitarian scale. Certainly the moment the legitimacy of any branch of scientific enquiry is seriously disputed, as in the recent case of vivisection, the controversy on both sides is conducted on an avowedly utilitarian basis. Nor does it really make against Hedonism that knowledge and other ideal ends are often most energetically pursued by persons who do not think of the resulting happiness; if, as experience seems to show, both the concentration of effort needed for success, and the disposition most favourable to enjoyment, are promoted by this limitation of aim. Nor, finally, need the Hedonist be surprised that the enthusiasm of these pursuits should occasionally prompt to the affirmation that their ends are worthy to be chosen *per se*, even if the pursuits should result in a balance of pain over pleasure. He is only concerned to maintain that, when in a mood of calm reflection we distinguish these ideal objects from the feelings inseparably connected with them, it is the quality of these latter which we see to be the ultimate end of rational desire.

This last proposition I do not find exactly denied, in the terms in which I have stated it; but an answer is made to it by some writers, which, if valid at all, is certainly conclusive, though indirect. It is said, for example, by Mr. Green[4] that 'pleasure as feeling, in distinction from its conditions which are not feelings, cannot be conceived'; and therefore, of course, cannot be taken as an end of rational action. Whatever plausibility this argument possesses, seems to depend on that ambiguity in the term 'conceive', which has caused so much confusion in recent philosophical debate. To adopt an old comparison, Mr. Green's proposition is neither more nor less true than the statement that an angle cannot be 'conceived' apart from its sides. That is, we cannot form the notion of an angle without the notion of sides containing it; but this does not hinder us from apprehending with perfect definiteness the magnitude of any angle as greater, equal, or less than that of any other, without any comparison of the pairs of containing sides. Similarly, we cannot form the notion of any pleasure existing apart from some 'conditions which are not feelings'; but we can perfectly well compare a pleasure felt under any given conditions with any other, however otherwise conditioned, and pronounce

---

[4] I quote this sentence from Mr. Green's Introduction to the Vol. II. of Hume's *Treatise on Human Nature*, p. 9; but I have found the same argument used in almost the same words by other writers of the same school. *Cf.* (*e.g.*) Prof. Caird in *Academy*, June 12, 1874.

it equal or unequal; and we surely require no more than this to enable us to take 'amount of pleasure' as our standard for deciding between alternatives of conduct.

Mr. Green, however has another argument against the 'greatest happiness' doctrine, which it will be desirable briefly to notice; especially since it also supplies the heavy artillery in an elaborate attack on Hedonism in Mr. Bradley's *Ethical Studies* (noticed in the last number of this journal). I will give it in Mr. Green's words taken from the passage quoted above:—

Happiness 'in its full extent,' as 'the utmost pleasure we are capable of,' is an unreal abstraction, if ever there was one. It is curious that those who are most forward to deny the reality of universals in that sense in which they are the condition of all reality, viz., as relations, should yet, having pronounced these to be mere names, be found ascribing reality to a universal, which cannot, without contradiction, be supposed more than a name. Does this 'happiness in its full extent' mean the 'aggregate of possible enjoyment,' of which modern utilitarians tell us? Such a phrase simply represents the vain attempt to get a definite by addition of indefinites. It has no more meaning than 'the greatest possible quantity of time' would have. Pleasant feelings are not quantities that can be added. Each is over before the next begins, and the man who has been pleased a million times is not really better off—has no more of the supposed chief good in possession—than the man who has only been pleased a thousand times. When we speak of pleasures, then, as forming a possible whole, we cannot mean pleasures as feelings.

We may admit that if any one supposed that his 'greatest happiness' was something that could be possessed all at once, it would be important to explain to him that it was composed of elements which could only be had successively. But I must confess myself quite unable to see how it thereby becomes impossible for him to aim at it. The paradoxical character of Mr. Green's argument cannot be better shown than by taking the very analogy which he selects to enforce it. In what sense is it true that 'greatest possible quantity of time' has no meaning? Since when has it been—not merely wrong but—logically impossible to make prolongation of life an end of voluntary effort? And what is 'length of days', but 'the greatest possible quantity of time' relatively to the individual looking forward? If it is only meant that we cannot have time by itself, without some filling of time, this is of course true; just as it is true that we cannot have pleasure without the conditions on which it depends. But because Time is an abstraction, it is not therefore unreal, nor incapable of furnishing an end of action; we can aim at living as long as possible, without any regard to the manner of our living; and if we turn out centenarians, we shall commonly be thought to have succeeded in our aim. *A fortiori* we can aim at living as pleasantly as possible, without any regard to the inseparable concomitants of our 'greatest possible happiness'. Mr. Green seems to assume that because the parts of Time, and of whatever has Time for its fundamental form, must exist successively, it is therefore illegitimate to conceive them as parts at all; that a 'happy week', or a 'miserable month', is something 'which cannot without contradiction be supposed more than a name', merely because we cannot have a happy week all in one moment! Surely this is as singular a metaphysical whim as ever entered into the head of a scholastic philosopher.

I have selected these two arguments for discussion, because they are of a kind that admits of summary treatment. They are either completely cogent or totally valueless; and it does not require many words to enable the reader to decide which view to take. The case is different with other anti-hedonistic topics, such as the difficulties of estimating the amount of pleasure or pain, comparing the amount of different pleasures, &c. It is, on the one hand, impossible not to allow a certain weight to such objections: on the other hand, they hardly even claim to be decisive; and, in fact, seem rather directed against the practicability of constructing a Hedonistic Calculus, than against the truth of the Hedonistic doctrine as to the nature of Ultimate Good.

12. The Feeling-Tone of Desire and Aversion

In an article on 'The Physical Basis of Pleasure and Pain' which appeared in the last number of *Mind*, Mr. H. R. Marshall has expressed, briefly but decidedly, a view of the quality or 'feeling-tone' of Desire, Aversion, and Suspense. This view differs very markedly from that to which I have myself been led by a comparison of my own experience with what I have been able to ascertain of the experience of others. Mr. Marshall has taken note of the difference, and subjoined to his brief statement of his own view a polemical reference to mine, written with a rhetorical emphasis which indicates a strong conviction that his view is in harmony with the general experience of mankind. It is possible that this conviction may turn out to be well-founded: but I think that at any rate some further discussion of the point at issue may perhaps reduce the amount of disagreement between us. I propose accordingly in the present paper to explain the grounds on which my opposite view was founded, with more fulness than I thought appropriate in the treatise to which Mr. Marshall has referred.

As I shall have occasion to direct close attention to one or two of Mr. Marshall's phrases, I will begin by quoting in full the passages in his article that are important for my present purpose.

The important mental state which we call Desire . . . clearly involves a very important thwarting of the impulse to go out towards an object more or less vividly presented. Under such conditions we should find Desire painful, and there can be no doubt that it is invariably so. It is a complex state, however, which involves other elements than those which bring about the thwarting pain, and these other elements which involve pleasure often mask the pain . . . Aversion is a state kindred to Desire. It involves thwarted impulses relative to our separation from an object, and should bring pain of a broad kind. This pain is always found as part of an aversion, although at times difficult to isolate from other ever-present painful elements: *e.g.*, the painful representation of an object which will be painful if realised.

Now if I had had to interpret this passage in its context, apart from the polemical reference to myself in a note, I should not have felt strongly moved to disagree with it: because—as I shall presently explain—I should have thought that Mr. Marshall was knowingly using the terms Desire and Aversion in a narrower sense than that in which they are ordinarily used. But this interpretation seems to be excluded by the following polemical note:—

[From *Mind*, NS, 1 (1892), 94–101.]

Prof. Sidgwick in his *Methods of Ethics* (4th ed., pp. 182 ff.) says that he recognises 'cravings which may be powerful as impulses to action without being painful in any appreciable degree'. He actually speaks (p. 185) of 'the neutral excitements of Desire, Aversion, Suspense, Surprise'. Concerning surprise I have a word below. Here I must be allowed to say that *I* cannot see how a 'craving' can be held to be powerful as an impulse to action without being appreciably painful. As I analyse such states of mind, the so-called neutral excitement which makes the fulness of such states is in mental regions apart from the 'craving'. With certain of our most powerful cravings, for instance, there are the general conditions of high activity which joy implies—there are certain emotional elements of unrestricted love—and these and kindred states we must carefully eliminate in the consideration of the craving proper. The man who hungers gets an impulse to activities from his painful craving, which activities may so far absorb attention as to cover the craving itself entirely. To understand how Desire, Aversion, and Suspense can appear as neutral excitements to any man, requires the postulation of a degree of 'philosophic calm' which has [been] lost. Desire is that 'apathy' towards which the Greeks aimed, which has displaced all fear by an almost fatalistic trust, and which has learned to feel that, whatever the outcome of doubtful conditions, that outcome must be good.

It is evident from this passage that, in Mr. Marshall's view, the kinds of feeling which common usage denotes by the words Desire and Aversion are in no cases 'neutral excitements' but always painful. It is, then, against this sweeping statement that I propose now to argue.

Before giving my arguments, I should like to limit the field of controversy on two sides. In the first place, I am not at present concerned to maintain that there are, strictly speaking, any 'neutral excitements'. I am aware that many hold with Mr. Sully[1] that all feeling is pleasurable or painful in some degree: and although my own experience leads me to an opposite conclusion, I do not wish to complicate the present discussion with any controversy on this point. I do not here deny the proposition that Desire and Aversion, if not at least faintly painful, must be at least faintly pleasurable: what I am concerned to maintain is that these feelings are often *either* neutral *or* pleasurable, and certainly not appreciably painful. Secondly, in endeavouring to observe again the personal experiences on which this contention is primarily based, in order to ascertain, if possible, exactly where the disagreement lies between Mr. Marshall and myself, I have felt somewhat embarrassed by my opponent's qualification of his doctrine, which admits Desire to be a 'complex state containing pleasurable elements which mask the pain'. I do not quite know how far this 'masking' is supposed to go: and whether he conceives it possible for a pain to exist which the person feeling it does not recognise as such. At any rate, in the present discussion I shall assume pain so successfully 'masked' to be non-existent: and, on this assumption, I must affirm

---

[1] See *Mind*, No. 50, pp. 248–255. I may say that I am inclined to adopt Mr. Sully's view to a greater extent in the case of Suspense and Surprise than in the case of Desire and Aversion. It is partly for this reason that I confine my attention to the two latter in the present paper.

that I still find Desire, in my own case, to be more often than not an element not itself painful—and often a prominent element—in a feeling that as a whole is pleasurable.

I am inclined to explain the opposing view by a combination of four different methods. Firstly, I think that there is some difference in *definition*;—that we do not use the term 'desire' in quite the same way.

Secondly, I think that there is a certain tendency to confuse—or too closely assimilate—the ideas of Desire and Pain, owing to a real resemblance between the two, which I will presently endeavour to state precisely.

Thirdly, I think that my opponents are apt to attend too exclusively to specially marked cases of desire; for I admit that when desire is most prominent in consciousness it is most frequently also painful.

Fourthly, I think it probable that there is a real difference in the susceptibilities of different individuals; and that the proposition that desire is painful is at any rate more true of some persons than of others.

I. First, then, as to the difference of definition. It will be observed that Mr. Marshall says that desire involves a 'thwarting of the impulse to go out towards an object'. If this only means that desire involves the presence of an unrealised idea, of which the realisation would involve the extinction of the desire, I should agree that this is characteristic of all desire: but the phrase may be equally taken to imply that action for the attainment of the desired end is prevented,—in which case the characteristic only belongs to some desires and not to all. I notice this ambiguity, because I find it also in Dr. Bain's book on *The Emotions and the Will*, where it seems to me to lead to a rather confusing statement of opinion on the present question (p. 423). Chapter viii. of this book begins: 'Desire is that phase of volition, where there is a motive and *not ability to act on it*'. This certainly seems to imply that desire is only found where action tending to the realisation of what is desired is prevented: and Dr. Bain's illustration suggests the same idea. He says:—

The inmate of a small, gloomy chamber conceives to himself the pleasure of light and of an expanded prospect: the unsatisfying ideal urges the appropriate action for gaining the reality; he gets up and walks out. Suppose now that the same ideal delight comes into the mind of a prisoner. Unable to fulfil the prompting, he remains under the solicitation of the motive; and his state is denominated craving, longing, appetite, desire. If all motive impulses could be at once followed up, desire would have no place; . . . there is a bar in the way of acting which leads to the state of *conflict*, and renders desire a more or less painful frame of mind.

This certainly seems to mean 'all desire is painful, *because* desire implies a bar in the way of acting'.

Hence when Dr. Bain goes on to say that 'we have a form of desire in all our more protracted operations or when we are working for distant ends', it is not clear whether he means to affirm *this* species of desire to be painful, or, if so, why he means to affirm it: yet he goes on to speak of desire generally as a 'form of pain'.

Now I agree that desire is most frequently painful in some degree when the person desiring is inhibited from acting for the attainment of the object desired. I do not indeed think that even under these circumstances it is always painful: especially when it is accompanied with hope, and when though action for the attainment of the desired object is not possible, still some activity adequate to relieve the strain on the nerves is possible. Still I admit that when action tending to fruition is precluded, desire is very liable to be painful.

But it is surely contrary to usage to restrict the term Desire to this case. Suppose Dr. Bain's prisoner becomes possessed of a file, and sees his way to getting out of prison by a long process, which will involve, among other operations, the filing of certain bars. It would surely seem absurd to say that his Desire finally ceases when the operation of filing begins. No doubt the concentration of attention on the complex activities necessary for the attainment of freedom is likely to cause the prisoner to be so absorbed by other ideas and feelings that the desire of freedom may temporarily cease to be present in his consciousness. But as the stimulus on which his whole activity ultimately depends is certainly derived from the unrealised idea of freedom, this idea, with the concomitant feeling of desire, will normally recur at brief intervals during the process. Similarly in other cases, while it is quite true that men often work for a desired end without consciously feeling desire for the end, it would be absurd to say that they never feel desire while so working. In short, it must be allowed that the feeling of Desire is at any rate sometimes an element of consciousness coexisting with a process of activity directed to the attainment of the desired object, or intervening in the brief pauses of such a process: and I venture to think that when the feeling is observed under these conditions, it will not be found in accordance with the common experience of mankind to describe it as essentially painful. I do not affirm that under such conditions it is in itself pleasurable: I cannot carry my introspective analysis to such a pitch of refinement as would enable me to affirm this with confidence. What I do confidently affirm, as regards my own experience, is that the feeling of desire under these conditions, while not itself painful, is often an indispensable element of a complex state that as a whole is highly pleasurable. And all that I can learn of the feelings of others would lead me to think that I am not singular in this experience.

Take the case of an ardent mountaineer who wants to get to the top of a peak: desire is no less clearly an element of his consciousness when he is walking up the mountain than when he is kept at home by the weather: but in the former case it is at worst a neutral feeling and often seems to take on a pleasurable quality,—at any rate the pleasurableness of the whole state of which it is a part depends upon the presence of the desire: while in the latter case it is certainly most likely to be painful. Take, again, the case of hunger: the conscious desire to which we give this name does not change its fundamental character, does not cease to be hunger when the hungry man sits down to dinner. But it would surely be absurd to say that it is then ordinarily a painful element of feeling: it would only be so after an abnormally long fast. Perhaps Mr. Marshall would say that it is 'masked' by pleasurable anticipation of proximate satisfaction: if so, I can only say that the masking is so complete that my introspective analysis fails to penetrate it.

II. I admit, however, that hunger, and desire generally, have a certain degree of similarity to pain, in that they are both *unrestful* states: states in which we are conscious of an impulse to get out of the present state into a future one. To use a term of Locke's, we may fairly say that both desire and pain are 'uneasy' states, and thus under this common notion of uneasiness or unrest we may be led to confound the two. But I think reflexion will show the distinction clearly.[2] Both in feeling desire and in feeling pain we feel a stimulus to pass from the present state into a different one: but in the case of pain the impulse is to get out of the present state into some other which is only indefinitely and negatively represented as 'not the present'; whereas in the case of desire, the primary impulse is towards the realisation of some definite future result. One difficulty in seeing this clearly is due to the fact that when desire is painful a secondary aversion to the state of desire is generated, which blends itself with the desire and may easily be confounded with it. But we may distinguish the two impulses by observing that they do not necessarily prompt to the same conduct; since aversion to the pain of unsatisfied desire, though it may act as an additional stimulus to work for the satisfaction of the desire, may also prompt us to get rid of the pain by suppressing the desire. And, on the other hand, when desire coexists with the pleasure that attends the realisation of what is desired—as it often does in a high degree—it seems to me peculiarly easy to distinguish it from pain. I should give as a good instance of this the experience of eating after an unusually long fast. I often find that in such a case appetite is very faint—hardly a perceptible feeling— before eating is begun: then, along with the pleasure derived from the satisfaction of hunger, the feeling of appetite becomes distinct and full; and is, as I have said, peculiarly easy to distinguish from pain.

III. At the same time, I quite admit that where desire is a specially prominent element of one's mental state, so that it imperiously claims attention, it is in most cases annoying or disturbing in some degree; it becomes a feeling of which we should prefer to get rid, whether by the realisation of what is desired or in some other way. And this leads me to my third explanation of the tendency to consider desire always painful; *viz.*, that the most marked and striking instances of the feeling, those that have made most impression, and that are therefore naturally recalled in memory when we think of cases of desire—these have usually been

---

[2] I have discussed this point—partly in the same words—in my *Methods of Ethics*, bk. i. chap. iv. § 2.

painful in some degree. Of a *very intense* desire I should admit it to be commonly true in my experience that, even when the state of which it is an element is on the whole pleasurable, the desire itself is painful in some degree. It is when the desire, being combined with other prominent elements of feeling, does not reach this absorbing and overwhelming intensity that I find it in my experience at best neutral.

It may be said, perhaps, that in these latter cases the desire itself is—viewed *as feeling*—so faint that it ceases to be within our power to determine its pleasurable or painful quality by direct introspection; while it is illegitimate to draw any inference as to the 'feeling-tone' of this obscure element from the pleasurable quality of the whole state of which it is an element: it may be urged accordingly that such cases should be left out of account in the present discussion. Now I quite admit that not unfrequently during long processes of work for remote ends, the desire of the end, while remaining sufficiently strong to supply the requisite impulse to action, ceases to have a perceptible character as feeling; we only infer its presence from the actions that it stimulates, and from the satisfaction that follows on the attainment of some intermediate end which has no significance for us except as a step towards the ultimate end. But I think it is easy to give instances of pleasurable processes of activity accompanied by desires which—while not painfully intense—are strongly and distinctly felt; and at the same time are elements indispensable to the pleasurableness of the whole complex feeling that accompanies the activities stimulated by them.

Take, for instance, the case of a game involving bodily exercise and a contest of skill. I am not myself skilful in such exercises, and when I take part in them for sanitary or social purposes, I commonly begin without any desire to win the game. So long as I remain thus indifferent, the exercise is rather tedious; usually, however, I find after a time that a feeling of desire to win the game is excited, as a consequence of actions directed to this end; and that, in proportion as the feeling grows strong, the whole process becomes more pleasurable. If this be admitted to be a normal experience, I shall be surprised if it is not also admitted that desire in this case is normally either a neutral or a pleasurable feeling; certainly I am unable to detect the slightest quality of pain in it.

And it would be easy to give an indefinite number of similar instances of energetic activity carried on for an end—whether in sport or in the serious business of life—where a keen desire for the attainment of the end in view is indispensable to a real enjoyment of the labour required to attain it, and where, at the same time, we cannot detect any painfulness in the desire, however much we try to separate it in introspective analysis from its concomitant elements. In such cases, it seems to me a peculiarly unwarrantable hypothesis to suggest that the desire itself is nevertheless an extraordinarily well-masked pain.

A familiar instance is the perusal of a novel—at least of a novel in which plot is important. It will not be denied that unless the writer can rouse the reader's curiosity—his desire to know the fate of the fictitious personages—the process of reading will usually be dull, while it becomes pleasurable in proportion as the desire grows keen. At the same time the strength and prominence of the desire in the consciousness of an ordinary reader is unmistakable; it is shown (*e.g.*) by the strength of the misleading impulse—which I think most persons who enjoy this kind of literature often have to suppress by an effort of self-control—to 'look on' in order to satisfy curiosity.

IV. This last case, however, leads me to my fourth explanation of the difference of view between psychologists on this point. For I find that there is a considerable amount of variation in respect of the pleasurableness of intense curiosity in different persons. Several friends have told me that they do not care at all about the plot of a novel; that they would as soon read a novel backwards-way; that they enjoy a good novel more the second time of reading than the first. I infer from all this that either no keen desire to know how the fictitious story will turn out is aroused in such persons at all, or, if it is aroused in them, it is disagreeable rather than agreeable.

I think it possible that there may be a similar variation in the case of the bodily appetites. For instance, many persons treat hunger as a pain as a matter of course; *e.g.*, Mr. Marshall says that 'hunger and thirst are typical cases of painfulness'. Now, according to my own experience, in a state of good health the desire of food is, in its initial stages and if abstinence is not carried too far, usually not painful at all: I recognise it merely as a prompting of nature, a felt impulse to change my state, by taking food, which is strictly neutral as regards its 'feeling-tone'— though it may easily become, according to its conditions or concomitants, either disagreeable or, as I have before said, at least a prominent element of a state which as a whole is agreeable. At the same time, I can easily believe that in the experience of others it may chiefly present itself as painful; because I find that this is usually the case with myself, when I am out of health.

So far I have spoken of Desire rather than Aversion,—although in some of the instances that I have given the two feelings are in fact closely blended. I have been led to do this, because the painlessness of desire is easier to illustrate; since aversion is more often an element of a state on the whole painful, being normally connected, as we have had occasion to notice, with actual pains of all kinds; and where it is thus connected we can rarely carry introspective analysis so far as to distinguish the aversion as in itself a painless element of feeling. At the same time I think that, if Desire be once admitted to be not always painful, this will carry with it a similar admission as regards aversion: since in processes of energetic action for the avoidance of prospective evils, aversion appears to me to be often a prominent element of a state of feeling on the whole pleasurable, just as desire is in processes of action for the attainment of prospective good: and in such cases the painlessness of the aversion itself seems to me often as evident as the painlessness of desire. I need only refer briefly to the common experience of the pleasurable excitement of Danger; since this complex feeling certainly contains aversion as a prominent element.

Here, again, however, I should recognise a large amount of variation in the experiences of different persons. For instance, I myself am not ever pleasurably excited by physical danger, but always simply depressed: but I have had experience of pleasurable excitement in the case of danger to social position or reputation, where aversion has been a prominent element, not discernibly painful, of a state of feeling on the whole markedly pleasurable.

A contemplation of these differences among human beings suggests a reference to the rhetorical flourish that concludes Mr. Marshall's polemical note. He says that 'to understand how desire and aversion can appear as neutral excitements to any man requires the postulation of a degree of "philosophic calm" which has lost desire in that "apathy" at which the Greeks aimed'. This seems to me a singular view. I should have thought, on the contrary, that it is the man who regards desire and aversion as uniformly painful who is likely to aim at—and to attain; if it be attainable—the 'apathy' or 'philosophic calm' from which all desire is excluded. On the other hand, a man whose experience resembles mine is peculiarly unlikely either to seek or to find this apathy or unperturbedness; since he is likely to hold, with Hobbes, that 'the Felicity of this life consisteth not in the repose of a mind satisfied'; and that even if we can conceive a man living whose desires are at an end, we cannot conceive him living well.

13. Unreasonable Action

In the present paper I wish to examine the conception of what I think it on the whole most convenient to call the 'unreasonable action' of sane persons in an apparently normal condition; and to contribute, if possible, to the more precise ascertainment of the nature of the mental process involved in it. The subject seems to me one of great ethical importance: but I wish here to discuss it from a psychological rather than ethical point of view,—so far as the two are distinguishable.

The point is one which attracted considerable attention in Greek philosophy; since the cardinal doctrine of Socrates 'that every man wishes for his own good and would get it if he knew how' naturally brought into prominence the question 'How then is it that men continually choose to do what they apparently know will not conduce to their own good?' Accordingly the Aristotelian treatment of ethics[1] included an elaborate discussion of the 'want of self-restraint' (ἀκρασία) exhibited in such acts, considered primarily in the special case of indulgence of bodily appetites in spite of a conviction that they ought not to be indulged. The discussion, apart from its historical interest, may still be read with profit; but the combination of 'dialectical' and 'naturalistic' methods which the writer uses is somewhat confusing to a modern reader; and the *node* of the difficulty with which he deals seems to me to be rather evaded than overcome. In modern psychological and ethical treatises the question has, from various causes, usually failed to receive the full and systematic treatment which it appears to me to deserve; and this is the main reason why I wish now to draw attention to it.

I must begin by defining more clearly the phenomenon that I have in view. In the first place, I wish to include inaction as well as positive action;—the not doing what we judge that we ought to do, no less than the doing what we judge that we ought not to do. Secondly, I mean action not *objectively* but *subjectively* unreasonable; *i.e.*, not action which is contrary to *sound* judgment, but action which is consciously contrary to the practical judgment of the agent. Such practical judgment will in many cases be the result of a process of reasoning of some

[From *Mind*, NS, 2/6 (1893), 174–87.]

[1] I use this vague term because book vii. of the *Nicomachean Ethics*, which contains the discussion to which I refer, is one of the three Books which also form a part of the *Eudemian Ethics*; and as to the composition of these three Books there has been and still is much controversy. I do not propose to enter into this controversy; but I may perhaps take it as generally admitted that these Books—while certainly designed to impart pure Aristotelian doctrine—are inferior in philosophic grasp and penetration to the rest of the *Nicomachean Ethics*.

kind, either performed immediately before the act is done or at some previous time; in these cases the term 'unreasonable' seems obviously appropriate. I shall, however, extend the term to cases in which the judgment opposed to the act is apparently intuitive, and not inferential. The propriety of this extension might, I admit, be questioned; but I want a term to cover both the cases above distinguished, and I can find no other familiar term so convenient. I wish then to examine consciously unreasonable action, in this sense, from a psychological point of view, as a fact of experience capable of being observed and analysed, without reference to the validity of the judgment involved in it, or of the process (if any) of reasoning by which it has been reached; simply with the view of finding out, by reflective observation, exactly what it is that happens when one knowingly acts against one's 'better judgment'.

Again, by 'practical judgment' I do not necessarily mean what is ordinarily called 'moral judgment' or 'dictate of conscience' or of the 'moral faculty'. I mean, of course, to include this as one species of the phenomenon to be discussed; but in my view, and, I think, in the view of Common Sense, there are many cases of consciously unreasonable action where morality in the ordinary sense does not supply the judgment to which the act is opposed. Let us suppose that a man regards ordinary social morality as a mere external code sanctioned by public opinion, which the adequately instructed and emancipated individual only obeys so far as he conceives it to be on the whole his interest to do so: still, as Butler pointed out, the conflict between Reason and Unreason remains in the experience of such a man in the form of a conflict of passion and appetite with what he judges from time to time to be conducive to his interest on the whole.

But if the notion of subjectively unreasonable action is thus, from one point of view, wider than that of subjectively wrong action, it would seem to be from another point of view narrower. For action subjectively wrong would be widely held to include action which conflicts with the agent's moral *sentiment*, no less than action which is contrary to his practical *judgment*;—moral sentiment being conceived as a species of emotion not necessarily connected with a judgment as to what 'ought to be done' by the agent or what is 'good' for him. Indeed, in the account of the moral consciousness that some writers of repute give, the emotional element is alone explicitly recognised: the moral consciousness appears to be conceived merely as a species of complex emotion mixed of baser and nobler elements—the baser element being the vague associations of pain with wrong acts, due to experiences of the disagreeable effects of retaliation, punishment, and loss of social reputation, and of pleasure with acts that win praise, good-will and reciprocal services from other men; the nobler being sympathy with the painful consequences to others of bad acts, and the pleasurable consequences of good acts.

This is not my view: I regard it as an essential characteristic of moral sentiment that it involves a judgment, either explicit or implicit, that the act to which the sentiment is directed 'ought' or 'ought' not to be done. But I do not now wish to enter into any controversy on this point: I merely refer to it now to point out that conduct may be opposed to moral sentiment, according to the view of moral sentiment above given, without having the characteristic of subjective unreasonableness; and, again, this characteristic may belong to conduct in harmony with what would be widely regarded as moral sentiment. Suppose (*e.g.*) a religious persecutor yielding to a humane sentiment and remitting torture from a weak impulse of sympathy with a heretic, contrary to his conviction as to his religious duty; or suppose Macchiavelli's prince yielding to a social impulse and impairing his hold on power from a weak reluctance to kill an innocent person, contrary to his conviction as to what is conducive to his interest on the whole. In either case the persecutor or the tyrant would act contrary to his deliberate judgment as to what it would be best for him to do, and therefore with 'subjective unreasonableness'; but in both cases the sentiment that prompted his action would seem to be properly classed as a moral sentiment, according to the view above described. And in the latter case he certainly would not be commonly judged to act wrongly, —even according to a subjective standard of wrongness;—while in the former case it is at least doubtful whether he would be so judged.

By 'unreasonable action', then, I mean voluntary action contrary to a man's deliberate judgment as to what is right or best for him to do: such judgment being at least implicitly present when the action is willed. I therefore exclude what may be called 'purely impulsive' acts: *i.e.*, acts which so rapidly and immediately follow some powerful impulse of desire, anger, or fear, that there is no room for any judgment at all as to their rightness or wrongness: not only is there no clear and explicit judgment with which the will conflicts, but not even a symbol or suggestion of such a judgment. But often when there is no explicit judgment there is an uneasy feeling which a pause for reflexion might develop into a judgment: and sometimes when we recall such states of mind there is a difficulty in saying whether this uneasy feeling did or did not contain an implicit judgment that the act was wrong. For it often happens that uneasy feelings similar to ordinary moral sentiments—I have elsewhere called them '*quasi*-moral'—accompany voluntary acts done strictly in accordance with the agent's practical judgment: *i.e.*, when such acts are opposed to widely accepted rules of conduct, or include among their foreseen consequences annoyance to other human beings. Hence in trying to observe and analyse my own experiences of unreasonable action I have found a difficulty in dealing with cases in which a moral (or prudential) judgment, if present at all, was only implicitly present: since when subsequent reflexion shows a past deed to have been clearly contrary to one's normal judgment as to what is right or best, this subsequent conviction is apt to mix itself with one's memory of the particular state of mind in which the deed was actually done. In this way what was really a quite vague feeling of uneasiness may be converted in memory into a more definite judgment opposed to the volition that actually took place. I have tried, however, to be on my guard against this source of error in my own observations; and it seems possible to guard against it by temporarily suppressing, for the purpose of the present inquiry, the disposition to self-censure—which for practical purposes it is commonly desirable to encourage, in spite of the misdirection to which it is liable; and keeping one's mind as far as possible in the attitude of impartial self-observation.

Finally, I must define somewhat further the limitation of my subject to the experience of persons apparently sane, and in an apparently normal condition. I mean by this to exclude from discussion all cases of discord between voluntary act and rational judgment, when the agent's will is manifestly in an abnormal condition,—either from some distinct cerebral disease, or from some transient disturbance of his normal mental condition due to drugs, extreme heat, sudden calamity, or any other physical or psychical cause. Cases of this kind—in which there appears to be no loss of sanity, in the ordinary sense, the mental disturbance affecting the will and not the reason—are highly interesting from a psychological point of view, as well as from that of medicine or jurisprudence; whether they are cases of 'aboulia' or impotence of will, when in spite of perfect clearness in a man's practical judgment he feels it simply impossible to form an effective volition in accordance with his judgment; or whether, to use M. Ribot's[2] terms, he suffers from 'excess' and not 'defect' of 'impulsion', and appears to himself compelled to commit some atrocious crime or grotesque folly, or otherwise to act in a manner contrary to his practical judgment, under the constraint of an impulse which he feels to be irresistible. But the very characteristics that give these phenomena their striking interest render it desirable to reserve them for separate discussion. I admit that the line between 'normality' and 'abnormality' cannot be precisely drawn, and that certain phenomena, similar in kind to those just mentioned though much slighter in degree, fall within the experience of ordinarily sane persons free from any perceptible organic disorder or disturbance. I can myself recall momentary impressions of something like 'aboulia': *i.e.*, moments in which I was transiently conscious of an apparent impossibility of willing to do what I judged it right to do. And though I have not myself had any similar experience of irresistible 'excess of impulsion', I see no reason to doubt that others have had such experiences, apart from any recognisable cerebral disorder; it would seem that hunger and thirst, aversion to death or to extreme pain, the longing for alcohol, opium, &c., occasionally reach a point of intensity at which they are felt as irresistibly overpowering rational choice. But cases of either kind are at any rate very exceptional in the experience of ordinary men; and I propose to exclude them from consideration at present, no less than the more distinct 'maladies de la volonté' before mentioned. I wish to concentrate attention on the ordinary experiences of 'yielding to temptation', where this consciousness

---

[2] See *Les Maladies de la Volonté*, par Th. Ribot.

of the impossibility of resistance does not enter in; where, however strong may be the rush of anger or appetite that comes over a man, it certainly does not present itself as invincible. This purely subjective distinction seems to afford a boundary line *within* which it is not difficult to keep, though it would doubtless be difficult or impossible to draw it exactly.

To put it otherwise—though I do not at all wish to mix up the present discussion with a discussion on Free Will—it may tend to clearness to define the experiences that I wish to examine as those in which there is an *appearance* of free choice of the unreasonable act by the agent—however this appearance may be explained away or shown to be an illusion.

The connexion of 'subjective irrationality'—or at least 'subjective wrongness' —and 'freedom' is indeed obvious and natural from a jural point of view, so far as the jurist retains the popular view of punishment as retributive and the popular conceptions of Desert and Imputation: since in this view it would seem that 'subjective wrongness' must go along with 'freedom' in order to constitute an act fully deserving of punishment. For the jurist's maxim 'Ignorantia juris non excusat' is not satisfactory to the plain man's sense of equity: to punish any one for doing what he at the time did not know to be wrong appears to the plain man at best a regrettable exercise of Society's right of self-preservation, and not a realisation of ideal justice. But from a psychological point of view there is no ground whatever for mixing up the question whether acts are metaphysically speaking 'free' with the question whether they are accompanied with a consciousness of their irrationality. No Libertarian, so far as I know, has ventured on the paradox of asserting it to be essential to the conception of a rational agent that it should be possible for him to act irrationally; and no Determinist need find any difficulty in admitting that a man may be determined by a predominant appetite or passion to act in a manner opposed to what he, at the same time, still recognises as his true interest.

Nevertheless, my present wish to call attention to the characteristics and varieties of unreasonable action is largely due to the fact that its very existence appears to be not sufficiently recognised by influential writers of the most opposite schools of philosophy.

I find that such writers are apt to give an account of voluntary action which —without expressly denying the existence of what I call subjective irrationality —appears to leave no room for it. They admit, of course, that there are abundant instances of acts condemned, as contrary to sound practical principles, not only by the judgment of other men but by the subsequent judgment of the agent: but in the analysis which they give of the state of mind in which such actions are willed, they appear to place the source of error in the intellect alone and not in the relation of the will to the intellect. For instance, Bentham affirms that 'on the occasion of every act he exercises, every human being is led to pursue that line of conduct which, according to his view of the case, taken by him at the moment, will be in the highest degree contributory to his own greatest happiness':[3] and as Bentham also holds that the 'constantly proper end of action on the part of every individual at the moment of action is his real greatest happiness from that moment to the end of his life',[4] there would seem to be no room for what I call 'subjective unreasonableness'. If Bentham's doctrine is valid, the defect of a volition which actually results in a diminution of the agent's happiness must always lie in the man's 'view of the case taken at the moment': the evils which reflexion would show to be overwhelmingly probable consequences of his act, manifestly outweighing any probable good to result from it, are not present to his mind in the moment of willing; or if they are in some degree present, they are at any rate not correctly represented in imagination or thought. The only way therefore of improving his outward conduct must be to correct his tendencies to err by defect or excess in the intellectual representation of future consequences: as he always acts in accordance with his judgment as to what is most likely to conduce to his greatest happiness, if only all errors of judgment were corrected, he would always act for his real greatest happiness. (I may add that so acting, in Bentham's view, he would also always act in the way most conducive to general happiness: but with the question of the harmony of interests in human society we are not now concerned.)

I do not think that Bentham's doctrine on this point was accepted in its full breadth by his more influential disciples. Certainly J. S. Mill appears to admit important exceptions to it, both in the direction of self-sacrifice and in the direction of self-indulgence. He admits, on the one hand, that the 'hero or the martyr' often has 'voluntarily' to 'do without happiness' for the sake of 'something which he prizes more than his own individual happiness'; and he admits, on the other hand, that 'men often, from infirmity of character, make their election for the nearer good, though they know it to be the less valuable; and this no less when the choice is between two bodily pleasures, than when it is between bodily and mental. They pursue sensual indulgence to the injury of health, though perfectly aware that health is the greater good.'[5] But though Mill gives a careful psychological analysis[6] of the former deviation from the pursuit of apparent self-interest, he does not pay the same attention to the latter; and yet it is at least as difficult to reconcile the conscious self-sacrifice—if I may be allowed the term— of the voluptuary as the conscious self-sacrifice of the moral hero with Mill's general view that 'to desire anything, except in proportion as the idea of it is pleasant, is a physical impossibility'. For in a hedonistic comparison of 'sensual indulgences' and 'injury to health' the distinctions of quality, by which Mill's Hedonism is complicated, hardly come in: the prudential estimate, in which the

[3] Bentham, *Constitutional Code*, Introduction, p. 2 (vol. ix. of Bowning's edition).
[4] Bentham, *Memoirs*, p. 560 (vol. x. of Bowning's edition).
[5] *Utilitarianism*, chap. ii.   [6] *Ibid.*, chap. iv.

pleasure of champagne at dinner is seen to be outweighed by the headache next morning, is surely quantitative rather than qualitative: hence when the voluptuary chooses a 'pleasure known to be the less valuable' it would seem that he must choose something of which—in a certain sense—the 'idea' is less 'pleasant' than the idea of the consequences that he rejects. In short, Mill's general statement as to the relation of Desire to Pleasure and the Pleasant seems clearly to need some qualification; and if we attempt to give this qualification, we have to examine more closely the nature of the mental phenomenon in which what he calls 'infirmity of character' is manifested.

But before I proceed to this examination, I wish to point out that the tendency either to exclude the notion of 'wilful unreasonableness', or to neglect to examine the fact which it represents, is not found only in psychologists of Bentham's school; who regard pleasure and the avoidance of pain as the sole normal motives of human action, and the attainment of the greatest balance of pleasure over pain—to self or to other sentient beings—as the only 'right and proper' ends of such action. We find this tendency also in writers who sweepingly reject and controvert the Hedonism of Bentham and Mill. For example, in Green's *Prolegomena to Ethics*, both the psychological doctrine that pleasure is the normal motive of human action, and the ethical doctrine that it is the proper motive, are controverted with almost tedious emphasis and iteration. But Green still lays down as broadly as Bentham that every person in every moral action, virtuous or vicious, presents to himself some possible state or achievement of his own as for the time his greatest good, and acts for the sake of that good; at the same time explaining that the kind of good which a person at any point of his life 'presents to himself as greatest depends on his past experience'.[7] From these and other passages we should certainly infer that, in Green's view, vicious choice is always made in the illusory belief that the act chosen is conducive to the agent's greatest good: although Green is on this point less clearly consistent than Bentham, since he also says that 'the objects where good is actually sought are often not those where reason, even as in the person seeking them, pronounces that it is to be found'.[8] But passages in the former sense are more common in his book: and he seems to make no attempt to bring them into harmony with that last quoted.

I cannot accept the proposition 'that every man always acts for the sake of what he presents to himself as his own greatest good', whether it is offered in a hedonistic or in a non-hedonistic form. At the same time, I think that the statements which I have quoted from Bentham and Green are by no means to be treated as isolated paradoxes of individual thinkers: I think they point to a difficulty widely felt by educated persons, in accepting and applying the notion of 'wilful wrongdoing', *i.e.*, conscious choice of alternatives of action known to be in conflict with principles still consciously accepted by the agent. On the other hand, this notion

---

[7] Green, *Prolegomena to Ethics*, book ii. chap. i. f. 99.   [8] *L.c.*, book iii. chap. i. f. 177.

of wilful wrongdoing is so clearly a part of the common moral experience of mankind that it seems very paradoxical to reject it, or explain it away.

Under these circumstances it seemed to me worth while to make a systematic attempt to observe with as much care as possible—and as soon as possible after the phenomenon had occurred—the mental process that actually takes place in the case of unreasonable action. I have found some difficulty in making the observations: because action consciously unreasonable belongs to the class of phenomena which tend to be prevented by attempts to direct attention to them. This result is not, indeed, to be deprecated from a practical point of view: indeed, it might, I think, be fairly urged as a practical argument for the study of psychology, that the habitual direction which it gives to attention tends to diminish the tendency to consciously unreasonable conduct. But though perhaps practically advantageous, the result is from a scientific point of view inconvenient. This direction of attention, however, cannot be long maintained; and in the intervals in which it is otherwise directed the psychological observer is probably as liable to act unreasonably as any one else; though probably the phenomenon does not last quite as long in the case of the psychologist, since as soon as he is clearly conscious of so acting, the desire to observe the process is likely to be developed and to interfere with the desire which is stimulating the unreasonable volition.

I also recognise that I ought not to put forward the results that follow as typical and fairly representative of the experiences of men in general. It is a generally recognised obstacle in the way of psychological study, especially in the region of the intellect and the emotions, that the attitude of introspective observation must be supposed to modify to some extent the phenomena observed; while at the same time it is difficult to ascertain and allow for the amount of effect thus produced. Now in relation to the experiences with which I am here concerned, the attitude of disengaged observant attention is peculiarly novel and unfamiliar, and therefore its disturbing effect may reasonably be supposed to be peculiarly great. I have, accordingly, endeavoured to check the conclusions that I should draw from my own experience by observation and interpretation of the words and conduct of others. My conclusion on the whole would be that—in the case of reflective persons—a *clear* consciousness that an act is what ought not to be done, accompanying a voluntary determination to do it, is a comparatively rare phenomenon. It is, indeed, a phenomenon that does occur, and I will presently examine it more closely: but first it will be convenient to distinguish from it several other states of mind in which acts contrary to general resolutions deliberately adopted by the agent may be done; as most of these are, in my experience, decidedly more common than unreasonable action with a clear consciousness of its unreasonableness. These other states of mind fall under two heads: (1) cases in which there is at the time no consciousness at all of a conflict between volition and practical judgment; and (2) cases in which such consciousness is present but only obscurely present.

Under the former head we may distinguish first the case of what are commonly called thoughtless or impulsive acts. I do not now mean the sudden 'purely impulsive' acts of which I spoke before: but acts violating an accepted general rule, which, though they have been preceded by a certain amount of consideration and comparison, have been willed in a state of mind entirely devoid of any application of the general rule infringed to the particular case. Suppose, for instance, that a man has received a provocative letter in relation to some important business in which he is engaged: he will sometimes answer it in angry haste, although he has been previously led by painful experience to adopt a general resolution to exclude the influence of angry feeling in a correspondence of this kind, by interposing an interval of time sufficient ordinarily to allow his heated emotion to subside. I conceive that often, at least, in such cases the rule is simply forgotten for a time, just as a matter of fact might be: the effect of emotion is simply to exclude it temporarily from the man's memory.

The writer of the Aristotelian treatise before mentioned suggests, however, an alternative possibility, which may sometimes be realised in the case of impulsive acts. He suggests that the general rule—say 'that letters should not be written in anger'—may be still present to the mind; though the particular judgment, 'My present state of mind is a state of anger'—required as a minor premiss for a practical syllogism leading to the right conclusion—is not made. And no doubt it may happen that an angry man is quite unaware that he is angry; in which case this minor premiss may be at the time absent through pure ignorance. But more often he is at least obscurely conscious of his anger; and if he is conscious of it at all, and has the general rule in his mind, it seems to me hardly possible that he should not be at least obscurely aware that the particular case comes under the rule.

More commonly, I think, when a general resolution is remembered, while yet the particular conclusion which ought to be drawn is not drawn, the cause of the phenomenon is a temporary perversion of judgment by some seductive feeling; —such as anger, appetite, vanity, laziness. In such cases a man may either consciously suspend his general rule, from a temporary conviction, caused by the seductive feeling, that he has adopted it without sufficient reason: or he may erroneously but sincerely persuade himself that it is not applicable to the case before him. Suppose he is at dinner and the champagne comes round: he is a patient of Sir Andrew Clark* and has already drunk the limited amount allowed by that rigid adviser: but rapidly the arguments of Dr. Mortimer Granville occur to his mind, and he momentarily but sincerely becomes persuaded that though an extra glass may cause him a little temporary inconvenience, it will in the

---

* [In reprinting this essay in *Practical Ethics* (1898), Sidgwick inserted at this point the following note: 'I have left unaltered the name of this eminent physician, who was alive when the article was written; since there is no other name that would, at that time, have seemed equally appropriate.']

long run conduce to the maintenance of his physical tone. Or, as before, he has received a letter that rouses his indignation: he remembers his rule against allowing temper to influence his answer; but momentarily—under the influence of heated feeling—arrives at a sincere conviction that this rule of prudence ought to give way to his duty to society, which clearly requires him not to let so outrageous a breach of propriety go unreproved. Or having sat down to a hard and distasteful task which he regards it as his duty to do—but which can be postponed without any immediate disagreeable consequences to himself—he finds a difficulty in getting under way; and then rapidly but sincerely persuades himself that in the present state of his brain some lighter work is just at present more suited to his powers—such as the study, through the medium of the daily papers, of current political events, of which no citizen ought to allow himself to be ignorant.

I have taken trivial illustrations because, being not complicated by ethical doubts and disagreements, they exemplify the phenomenon in question most clearly and simply. But I think that in graver cases a man is sometimes sincerely though very temporarily convinced by the same kind of fallacious reasoning— under the influence of some seductive feeling—that a general resolution previously made *either* ought to be abrogated or suspended *or* is inapplicable to the present case. Such a man afterwards will see the fallacy of the reasoning: but he may not have been even obscurely conscious at the time that it was fallacious.

But, again, these examples will also serve as illustrations of a different and, I think, still more common class of cases which fall under my second head; in which the man who yields to the fallacious process of reasoning is dimly aware that it is fallacious. That is, shortly, the man sophisticates himself, being obscurely conscious of the sophistry.

Moralists have often called attention to sophistry of this kind, but I think they have not fully recognised how common it is, or done justice to its persistent, varied, and versatile ingenuity.

If the judgment which Desire finds in its way is opposed to the common sense of mankind, as manifested in their common practice, the deliberating mind will impress on itself the presumption of differing from a majority so large: if, on the other hand, the restraining dictate of reason is one generally accepted, the fallibility of common sense, and the importance of the individual's independence, will be presented in a strong light. If a novel indulgence is desired, the value of personal experience before finally deciding against it will be persuasively shown; if the longing is for an old familiar gratification, experience will seem to have shown that it may be enjoyed with comparative impunity. If the deliberating mind is instructed in ethical controversy, the various sceptical topics that may be culled from the mutual criticisms of moralists will offer almost inexhaustible resources of self-sophistication;—such as the illusoriness of intuition if the judgment is intuitive; if it is a reasoned conclusion, the fact that so many thoughtful persons reject the assumptions on which the reasoning is based. The Determinist will eagerly recognise the futility of now resisting the formed tendencies of his nature; the Libertarian will contemplate his indefeasible power of resisting them next time. The fallacies vary indefinitely; if plausible arguments are not available, absurd ones will often suffice: by hook or by crook, a *quasi*-rational conclusion on the side of desire will be attained.

Often, however, the seductive influence of feeling is of a more subtle kind than in the instances above given, and operates not by producing positively fallacious reasoning, but by directing attention *to* certain aspects of the subject, and *from* certain others. This (*e.g.*) is, I think, not uncommonly the case when an ordinarily well-bred and well-meaning man acts unreasonably from egotism or vanity: he has an obscure well-founded consciousness that he might come to a different view of his position if he resolutely faced certain aspects of it tending to lower his opinion of himself: but he consciously refrains from directing attention to them. So again, in cases where prompt action is necessary, passion may cause a man to acquiesce in acting on a one-sided view, while yet obscurely aware that the need is not so urgent as really to allow no time for adequate consideration.

In both the classes of cases last mentioned we may say that the wrongdoing is really wilful though not clearly so: the man is obscurely conscious either that the intellectual process leading him to a conclusion opposed to a previous resolution is unsound, *or* that he *might* take into account considerations which he *does* not distinctly contemplate and that he ought to take them into account. But though he is obscurely conscious of this, the sophistical or one-sided reasoning which leads him to the desired practical conclusion is more clearly present.

Finally, there remains pure undisguised wilfulness—where a man with his eyes open simply refuses to act in accordance with his practical judgment, although the latter is clearly present in his consciousness, and his attention is fully directed towards it. I think it undeniable that this phenomenon occurs: but my experience would lead me to conclude that it more often takes place in the case of negative action—non-performance of known duty: in the case of positive wrong action some process by which the opposing judgment is somehow thrust into the background of consciousness seems to me normally necessary. In other words, I should say that it was far easier for a desire clearly recognised as conflicting with reason to inhibit action than to cause it.

Even in the exceptional case of a man openly avowing that he is acting contrary to what he knows to be both his interest and his duty, it cannot be assumed that a clear conviction of the truth of what he is saying is necessarily present to his consciousness. For a man's words in such a case may express not a present conviction but the mere memory of a past conviction; moreover, one of the forms in which the ingenuity of self-sophistication is shown is the process of persuading oneself that a brave and manly self-identification with a vicious desire is better than a weak self-deceptive submission to it—or even than a feeble fluctuation between virtue and vice. Thus, even a man who said 'Evil be thou my good' and acted accordingly might have only an obscured consciousness of the awful irrationality of his action:—obscured by a fallacious imagination that his only chance of being in any way admirable, at the point which he has now reached in his downward course, must lie in candid and consistent wickedness.

Part III

Method: Truth, Evidence, and Belief

14. Verification of Beliefs

Ordinary thinking, whether vulgar and unsystematic, or systematised in special sciences, frames judgments, affirms propositions, both general and individual, in great number and of various kinds. But in the progress of thought some of these are recognised as erroneous. The ordinary mind simply discards these, and retaining the rest, continues its natural processes of acquiring, evolving, systematising beliefs with undiminished confidence. But to the reflective or philosophic mind the ascertained erroneousness of some beliefs suggests the possible erroneousness of all. Such a mind is liable to be overspread with a sweeping distrust of the processes of ordinary thinking, which attaches to them a secondary reflective uncertainty, easily distinguishable from the original uncertainty with which many of our opinions are held. It is this distrust which is the natural cause of philosophical scepticism. Such scepticism, indeed, is usually presented as a deduction from premisses accepted by philosophers; and thus each special sceptical system justifies itself not in relation to common sense, but to some special dogmatic system. But the radical, general, justification of what I have called natural scepticism is the admitted fact of error. A belief which I held certainly true, I now find doubtful, or even false; what then guarantees me against a similar discovery as to all the other beliefs which I am now holding true?

The mode in which dogmatists have tried to supply such a guarantee is by the establishment of a criterion or criteria of truth; by pointing out certain characteristics of true beliefs, which, it is asserted, have never been possessed by beliefs that have been found false. If I can show that beliefs conceived with perfect clearness, or beliefs of which the opposites are inconceivable, or beliefs derived directly from experience, or beliefs 'given in consciousness' are infallible, I exclude scepticism from at least a certain portion of my mental life. I secure a region of tranquil dogma, though its boundaries may be indefinite and fluctuating, and though it may be but an island in a sea of doubt and conflict.

The sceptic sometimes replies that this mode of regaining certainty is clearly impossible. For *quis custodiet custodem?* What is to guarantee the validity of the criterion? We seem to be involved in the well-known difficulty of the Indian cosmogony; when we have supported the earth on the elephant, we want a support for the elephant. And I should not only admit this objection; but allow generally that complete scepticism is not to be confuted by argument. This, however, is only the most comprehensive application of the familiar truth that no

[From the *Contemporary Review*, 17 (July 1871), 582–90.]

conclusion can be proved to any man who will not accept the requisite premises; the sceptic demurs to all premises, and so evades the cogency of all demonstrations. But if utter scepticism cannot be confuted, it is equally true that it cannot be defended. As soon as scepticism attempts to justify itself, it inevitably limits itself; as it assumes the truth of certain premises and the validity of some method of inference. The natural scepticism of which I just now spoke, starts with the conviction of particular errors, and argues by analogy to the possibility of universal error. But the conviction of error in certain parts of our intellectual experience is at least no more certain than the conviction of truth elsewhere; and the inference from analogy that our other beliefs are false does not destroy the force of the direct original intuition which declares them true; it at most slightly weakens it. If then we succeed in establishing criteria of truth, if we can distinguish a class of beliefs that are never found erroneous, we can repel in respect of them the faint analogy upon which the sceptic relies by a much stronger counter-analogy. For example, suppose I have discovered the beliefs, that all motion has an intrinsic tendency to cease, and that there are twelve gods residing on the top of Mount Olympus, to be false. This discovery suggests that my belief that two straight lines can nowhere enclose a space, or my belief that there is a God in heaven, may possibly be found erroneous, because there is a certain *primâ facie* resemblance between these and the former. If then I can show that these latter beliefs possess certain characteristics which have never been possessed by beliefs afterwards proved erroneous, these specific resemblances enable me to rebut the sceptical inference by a stronger inference of the same kind.

The discussion, however, of the criterion or criteria of truth is one that has been somewhat neglected in our recent philosophy. The English mind is so averse to fundamental scepticism, that it hastily presumes the most summary method of dealing with it to be the best; and thus the question is often settled offhand by a simple phrase and a single argument, or if treated at all, is treated in an incidental and fragmentary manner. It is the object of this paper to show that a more patient and complete discussion of so important a question would be desirable.

Let us inquire, then, how to verify beliefs originally certain, if their certainty be called in question on general grounds. We have first to distinguish Intuitive and Discursive certainty. The latter is apprehended by contemplating the belief not alone, but in connexion with other certain beliefs. The errors arising from wrong discursion have been carefully noted by logicians, and a machinery provided for excluding them, which is intuitively seen to be infallible where it can be applied. We may therefore, proceed at least provisionally, to the criteria of the truth of intuitively certain beliefs.

The first to be considered, whether in historical or natural order, is an *intuitive criterion*: i.e., a criterion which can be applied in contemplating the beliefs by themselves. Such a criterion has been enunciated, in forms more or less similar, by different persons. Among them Descartes is the most famous, who laid down

that 'ideas conceived clearly and distinctly were true'. There is here an unfortunate inaccuracy of expression, which has misled many persons who have since
discussed the Cartesian criterion. Truth, as Locke remarked, is an attribute of
propositions, not ideas; moreover, in this statement the intuitive certainty of the
propositions in question is merely implied. What Descartes[1] meant was, that we
may put the stamp of philosophical acceptance on judgments intuitively certain,
if the notions connected in them are found on reflection to be clear and distinct.

No one, I think, who has adequately considered the extent to which mistakes
arise from reasoning confidently with loose and vague notions can deny the practical value of this criterion. There is no doubt that the beliefs in which error and
conflict are found may be to a great extent excluded by its application. And if we
trace the progress of the exact sciences, either historically or in the apprehension
of any individual, we continually observe intuitions winning their way, by mere
virtue of superior clearness, against prejudice in favour of their opposites. Yet we
cannot unhesitatingly grant that no false intuition ever appears clear and distinct
to one who is not misled by it; still less that one who is misled could rid himself
of error by applying the Cartesian criterion. For example, the notions of men
standing, head downwards, on the other side of the globe seem clear enough, and
yet a false conviction of the incompatibility of these notions actually prevailed.
Mr. Herbert Spencer, who seems to adopt substantially this criterion, adds the
important qualification that 'it is only simple percepts or concepts', to the
relation of which immediate consciousness can satisfactorily testify: in the case
mentioned 'the states of consciousness involved in the judgment are too complex
to admit of any trustworthy verdict being given'. It is possible that Descartes
would have had no objection to explain or qualify his statement in this way,
because he gives it as an essential part of his method of answering questions,
to analyse the problem always into its elements, and take the simplest first.

Still, even thus qualified, the criterion is not always easy to apply, and if rigidly
applied seems to reduce too much the number of intuitively certain beliefs.
Indeed, the stock examples of these are propositions such as 'twice two are four',
'two straight lines cannot enclose a space', which involve notions undeniably
complex. The particular example which Mr. Spencer gives is the perception of the
inequality of two straight lines. But any spatial conception is, according to
Empirical psychologists, a complex consciousness, as Mr. Spencer least of all men
requires to be told. Again, let us take the intuition which was a fundamental
principle of the Cartesian philosophy, and had an effect that can scarcely be
exaggerated on the development of metaphysical thought since Descartes—the
principle that mind and matter cannot act directly upon one another. The notions
of 'mind' and 'matter' appeared to Descartes perfectly clear, however obscure

---

[1] It is not necessary to notice that Descartes does not distinguish analytical from synthetical
judgments: as the criterion applies equally well to both, and his obliteration of the distinction is so
complete as to cause no confusion.

they may appear to some of us; and I imagine that in his supposed clear apprehension of them he did not recognise any complexity. Or examine the proposition that 'a thing cannot act where it is not'. The notions of 'thing', 'place', 'action', appear, though very abstract, perfectly simple: simple, indeed, in virtue of their abstractness. And yet this assumption appeared irresistible to the mind of Newton; while at present no one feels any intuitive certainty in respect of it.

It seems then that this criterion, in its best form, is not one upon which we can absolutely rely to save us from error. Yet all our conclusions in the science of form and number are originally guaranteed by no other. They are no doubt confirmed by our finding that they never clash with our individual experiences; but they are not felt to require this confirmation.

I am aware of course that Empiricist thinkers deny that our certainty with regard to the principles of mathematics is properly intuitive. But much of their argument on the subject relates to the *origin* of our belief in these principles—a question which appears to me nearly irrelevant. Much trouble is spent in proving that our confident enunciation of universal propositions respecting space is due to our past experience of space. But by calling these judgments 'intuitions' I do not mean to imply anything with regard to the past, but merely state that our certainty of their truth is at present obtained by contemplating them alone, and not in connection with any other propositions. I oppose, in short, 'intuitive' to 'discursive' or 'demonstrative' certainty. The Empirical school, on the other hand, seem to use 'intuitive' as a synonym for 'innate'. This is somewhat singular in disciples of Locke; for while the best-known feature of Locke's psychology is his hostility to innate ideas, the most remarkable characteristic of his theory of knowledge is the absence of any recognition of the inductive method. His only type of science is that which proceeds by intuition and demonstration.

Still, if the logical question as to the ground of certainty were distinctly separated from the psychological inquiry into the origin of judgments, the Empirical school would explicitly repudiate the Cartesian criterion. They maintain not merely that our present universal judgments respecting space are entirely due to past individual experiences of space; but that the certainty of the former should be entirely based upon the certainty of the latter. This exclusive reference to particular 'experimental' judgments as the ultimate ground of truth we may term verification by the Baconian criterion.

Now it is observed that we naturally, in ordinary thinking, place as much reliance on universal as we do on individual beliefs, if we feel in each case an equally strong intuitive certainty. And the criterion which we have been discussing applies to both kinds of judgments alike. I can test equally my conviction that this straight line is greater than that, and my conviction that two straight lines cannot enclose a space, by considering whether the concepts (or percepts) are sufficiently clear and simple, and whether the opposite belief is strictly unbelievable. In using, therefore, the Cartesian criterion, we are not running counter to the general tendencies of human belief, but simply correcting the oversights of ordinary intuition, just as the common logic corrects the oversights of ordinary discursion. The Empiricists, on the other hand, cut sharply across the field of unphilosophic certainty. As far as individual facts go (or rather, as will appear, a certain class of these) they agree with the unsceptical thinker; while of our universal beliefs, previously regarded as certain, they begin by making total excision. Their ultimate end, however, is not sceptical, but constructive; they seem to have destroyed the highest type of science, but they propose to re-establish it on a firmer basis by means of the inductive method. Empiricism is thus a *media via* between scepticism and natural dogmatism; and has to maintain against both these the legitimacy of its method both on the destructive and on the constructive side.

First, then, let us ask why the Empiricist puts the stamp of philosophical validity on individual intuitions, naturally taken as certain, while he rejects universal intuitions that come to him with the same claim.

The only reason which Mr. Mill, who has argued the question with much earnestness, seems to allege (apart from the inquiry into origin, which is, *primâ facie*, irrelevant) is that these latter intuitions have been proved in some cases erroneous. This cannot be denied; and it must farther, I think, be admitted that we cannot hope to get an intuitive criterion in so perfect a form as entirely to exclude the possibility of error. At the same time I cannot allow that all the erroneous universal propositions to which Mr. Mill refers ('*à priori* fallacies', he calls them) are cases in point. Many, *e.g.*, of the false or misleading assumptions which dominated ancient and mediaeval physics were no more certified by clear intuition than they were by legitimate induction. The principles against which Descartes rebelled were principles accepted on authority, especially on the authority of Aristotle, whose unrivalled intellect was continually misemployed in throwing into scientific form the unsifted products of common sense; even this crude material being not taken pure, but vitiated by mistaken inferences from the language in which it was clothed. It has always been a tendency not merely of ordinary men, but of scientific inquirers who do not reflect on their methods, to accept, implicitly or explicitly, abstract principles not verified in any way, but unconsciously imbibed or caught up from the mere rumour of the speculative world. If such principles are found to mislead, it is unfair to throw the blame on the intuitional method.

However, let us grant—what Descartes himself has rendered it impossible to deny—that man's faculty for seeing truly universal facts is liable to error, and to greater error than his faculty for apprehending individual facts. The Empiricist, it would seem, is bound to maintain much more than this. In face of the success of the sciences of form and number nothing can justify his wholesale rejection of universal intuitions, except the absolute certainty of individual intuitions. And this, indeed, is generally his claim, that he alone constructs science on a firm basis of 'fact', that is, of beliefs undoubtedly true. What then are these beliefs? for it is clear that all individual judgments are not included; not, for example the judgment that one picture is more beautiful than another, or that it is wrong to disestablish the Irish Church. No, these, says the Empiricist, are not perceptions; they are emotions inadvertently thrown into the form of perceptions. 'Perception is infallible evidence for what is really perceived.' What then is 'really perceived'? At this point the profoundest difference of opinion reveals itself among the Empirical criticists. They split into two schools, the materialists and the empirical psychologists. The former assert (with common sense on their side) that the intuitive beliefs of which we may assume the legitimacy are the beliefs connected with our *external* perceptions, *viz.*, that particular portions of matter exist in particular parts of space, independently of our cognition of them. The latter maintain that the only legitimate intuitive beliefs are that certain states of consciousness, mental phenomena, exist; the belief in the existence (in any sense) of any portion of matter is always inferential, and the belief in its extra-cognitional existence an illegitimate inference,—in fact, says Professor Bain, 'a most anomalous fiction'. The materialists retort by attempting to show the total untrustworthiness of introspection. 'You are still following', says Mr. Maudsley to Professor Bain and his followers, 'the subjective method, that *ignis fatuus* of antiquity'. This irreconcilable quarrel, this mutual repudiation of methods, among such rigorous abstainers from unlawful assumptions, would in itself make me distrust the absolute certainty of these beliefs. But, besides, the assumption of either school seems to me confuted by experience. The best observer may make mistakes; it is well to repeat the experiments of the most accurate experimenter. Again every particular perception of matter is suggested by some sensation, and every sense is liable to erroneous suggestion. This is admitted at once of all senses but touch: it is no doubt rarer there: but the tongue continually exaggerates the size of things within the mouth, and if I cross my fingers and touch a marble, I have two marbles irresistibly suggested. Besides, every morning I wake up from a crowd of fallacious perceptions. That a similar waking from the long dream of life awaits us; that, therefore the material world, in a very sweeping sense, 'is not what it seems', is at least quite conceivable. If we turn to the beliefs of Empirical Psychology, it certainly seems at first sight that we must be more sure of the existence of states of consciousness than of anything else. That we should ever become convinced that we were not conscious at this present moment seems strictly inconceivable. But an ordinary introspective judgment affirms much more than that we are conscious; it affirms that we have this or that kind of feeling: which involves comparison and classification of our present feeling with other feelings: here error comes in. We cannot mistake that we are conscious; but we may very easily mistake when we try to give an account of our consciousness. Indeed, when we reflect how many metaphysical disputes have turned upon mere questions of introspectively cognizable fact, upon different accounts given by two thinkers of admittedly similar consciousnesses: *e.g.*, of the moral sentiments, the aesthetic sentiments, of volition, external perception, self-consciousness, &c.: one is almost amazed at the audacity of claiming a special trustworthiness for the intuitions of empirical psychology. I am not arguing sceptically: I do not mean that I do not rely on my own or any one's classification and description of consciousness to a certain extent: we can tell, *e.g.*, whether a state is pleasurable or painful (though a sentimental friend assures me that even this is difficult in respect of certain feelings); but the extent to which we can go without fluctuating and conflicting observations is very small. Nay, even the bare affirmation that I have a feeling, or 'there is a feeling',—*cogitatio est*, not *cogito*—implies, if it is not strictly insignificant, the existence of other entities beside feelings: which is just what the Empirical psychologist will not allow us to know intuitively.

It appears then that the Empiricist's discrimination of premisses is, however natural and plausible, yet difficult rationally to justify. Let us now examine how far he can establish upon his foundation the conclusions of science. I confess that I find it hard to understand how there can be two opinions upon this subject among competent persons. That individual premisses, however manipulated, cannot establish a universal conclusion, seems so clear, that probably no logician would have thought it necessary to prove it, unless Mr. Mill had—not *maintained* the opposite, but arranged with much care and ingenuity his original and valuable methodological speculations in such a manner as to *suggest* it. Mr. Mill, indeed, in his effort to ally old logic with new methodology, seems at first sight to involve himself in explicit contradictions. He seems to maintain at once that 'all valid, general propositions are based on induction', and that all 'valid processes of inference' (including induction, of course) 'may be thrown into a syllogistic form'. But he must be understood to allow that the ultimate induction, the inference by which the principle of the 'uniformity of nature' is obtained, is not a process which can be logically legitimated, and that this fundamental principle remains a hypothesis. 'Yes', it may be rejoined, 'but a hypothesis *confirmed* by its harmony with all our experience.' But this confirmation must fall infinitely short of what is required for certainty, as any amount of particular experience is infinitely less than universal. This principle, then, being hypothetical, all the conclusions of exactest science can have no more than a hypothetical validity; and, in fact, Mr. Mill's inductive logic may be said to be a method for making these less general propositions equally probable with the principle of the uniformity of nature. But let us observe closely the way in which this is done. In each case it is by an inference of this kind: 'A must invariably accompany or follow B, as otherwise the principle of the uniformity of nature would not be universally true.' Here is an inference of universal import; at the same time the certainty of any inference is only known to us, as Locke remarked, by intuition. It appears, then, that a logical intuition relating to universal fact, is admitted by the Empiricist. Indeed, in the more properly logical part of his treatise Mr. Mill does not appear to object to universal inferences; he is only concerned to maintain with Locke, that any particular inference is just as valid as the universal which includes it. But, if we are allowed the power of seeing universal truth in the single department of logic, on what ground is our natural claim to a similar faculty in other departments rejected?

It would seem, then, that the empirical theory of certitude is not satisfactory, either on its destructive or its constructive side. But we need not therefore reject what I have called the Baconian verification, even for propositions naturally believed as intuitively evident. If we cannot attain absolute completeness of certitude in respect either of universal or of individual intuitions, and cannot perceive any generic superiority in the one as compared with the other, our conviction of either is strengthened by perceiving a harmony between them. Only we need not limit this confirmative force to the relation between particular and general beliefs. One may say generally that as the intuitive verification cannot be made entirely trustworthy, it requires to be supplemented by a discursive verification—which consists generally in ascertaining the harmony between the proposition regarded as intuitively certain and other propositions belonging to the same department of fact, and of which the Baconian verification is the most important, but by no means the only species. For example, in the formal sciences our certainty with respect to any intuition is increased by the intimate connexion and mutual confirmation of the universal intuitions, independently of their perfect harmony with particular experiences.

15. Incoherence of Empirical Philosophy

I use the term Empirical Philosophy to denote a theory which is not primarily a theory of Being, but a theory of knowledge; nor, again, a merely psychological theory, considering the psychical fact called knowledge merely as a phenomenon of particular minds; but a doctrine that is concerned with knowledge in respect of its validity, laying down the general criteria by which true or real knowledge may be distinguished from what is merely apparent: what—using a convenient, though hardly current, term—I will distinguish as an *epistemological* doctrine. Admitting that any complete system of philosophy must include some reasoned answer—positive, negative, sceptical, or critical—to ontological questions; I still think that the term Philosophy may be fairly applied to what is primarily a doctrine of the criteria of knowledge, without reference to any ontological conclusions which such a doctrine may be held to establish. And if we try to give a precise and distinctive meaning to the term 'empirical' or 'experiential', as applied to existing schools of philosophy, without materially restricting its ordinary use, we must, I think, make it signify merely the *epistemological* doctrine that all cognitions that can be philosophically accepted as valid, whether universal or particular, must be based upon experience. In this sense we may say that Empiricism of some kind is the philosophy which students of Natural Science, at the present day, generally have, or tend to have; and also other persons who cannot be called students of Natural Science, but whose minds are impressed and dominated by the triumphant march of modern physical investigation. Such persons have a general, unanalysed conviction, independent of close reasoning of any kind, that the recent conquests of the human intellect over the world of concrete fact are mainly due to that precise, patient, and elaborate questioning of experience which has certainly been an indispensable condition of their attainment; that the extension and steady growth of these conquests constitute at the present time the most important fact for one who wishes to philosophise; and that any philosophy that is not thoroughly competent to deal with this fact has thereby a presumption against it that it is behind its age. And in order that my point of view in the remarks that follow may be understood, I should like to say at the outset that I fully admit the force of this general presumption in favour of Empiricism. Just as at the outset of modern philosophy in the age of Descartes (as well as earlier still, in the age of Plato), Mathematics naturally presented itself as the type of solid and definite knowledge, so, it seems to me, the type is now

[From *Mind*, OS, 7/28 (1882), 533–43.]

furnished by the sciences that rest on experience; to which mathematics—in the natural *primâ facie* view—stands in the subordinate relation of an instrument.

I am therefore as much disposed as anyone can be to go to experience for a test of truth; but I find myself unable—with all the aid of the eminent thinkers who have recently maintained some form or other of Empiricism—to work out a coherent theory of the criteria of knowledge on an Empirical basis. The difficulties in the way of this attempt appear to me to be of a very fundamental character; and one important group of them—those which relate rather to the premisses of empirical philosophy than to the rational procedure by which its conclusion is reached—do not seem to me to have received sufficient notice from the leading empirical writers. It is, therefore, to this part of the argument that I chiefly wish to direct attention in the present paper.

Before, however, I proceed to state these difficulties, it will be well to define somewhat more closely the fundamental doctrine of Empiricism. I understand this to be that all trustworthy congnitions[1] are either immediate cognitions of particular, approximately contemporaneous, facts, or capable of being rationally inferred from these;—let us say, for brevity, either 'immediately empirical' or 'mediately empirical'. It is only in this sense that the statement that all valid judgments are founded on experience appears to me to have a definite epistemological import, *primâ facie* tenable.

To make this clearer, I will consider briefly certain other senses in which knowledge is currently said to be 'founded on' or 'derived from' experience. In the first place, by predicating this of any piece of what presents itself as knowledge, it may be merely meant that such apparent knowledge is *caused* by certain antecedent empirical cognitions, from which, however, it is *not* rationally inferrable; or rather, strictly speaking, that it has *among* its causes such antecedent cognitions—for no one would give a mere statement of these antecedents as a complete account of its causation. The vulgar induction of a universal rule from a few particular cases is an instance of this kind of derivation of a belief from experience. It is evident that the ascertainment of the empirical antecedents of such a universal judgment, however interesting psychologically, does not in itself help us to decide the question of its truth or falsehood: for (1) *ex hypothesi* it does not supply adequate grounds for regarding the cognition so caused as philosophically established, and (2) it is no less manifest that it does not disprove the belief so arrived at—since obviously a generalisation from a few cases may be true, though it cannot be proved by reference to these cases alone. The epistemological question we have to ask about it is not from what sources it was originally derived, but upon what grounds it is now deliberately held.

---

[1] I ought perhaps to state that in this paper I use the term cognition to include intellectual states or acts which are, or involve, false judgments, as well as those which are, or involve, true judgments—or, to express it otherwise, *apparent* as well as *real* cognitions.

The result is similar if the ascertained psychical antecedents from which any judgment is said to be 'derived' are not cognitions at all but merely feelings—sensations or emotions. The ascertainment of the invariable antecedence of any such psychical facts obviously cannot validate any cognition thus ascertained to be their consequent (unless it be the cognition of these facts themselves). And it seems to me equally evident that it cannot invalidate it;—it is only by a palpable confusion between 'antecedents' and 'elements', or by a quite unwarranted transfer of chemical inferences to psychical facts, that certain Associational psychologists claim to have 'analysed into elementary feelings' apparent cognitions of what is not feeling, when they have merely shown these feelings to be invariable antecedents or concomitants of the cognitions in question. Any cognition, as introspectively contemplated, is essentially different from any mere aggregation of feelings: and I am aware of no tenable grounds for concluding that such cognition 'really consists' of elements which careful introspection does not enable us to discern in it.

Still more is the ascertainment of the (so-called) 'derivation from experience' of any piece of apparent knowledge *epistemologically* irrelevant, if the antecedents loosely referred to as 'experience' are neither cognitions nor feelings, but relations of the *bodies* of the cognising individuals (or their ancestors) to other material things: as for instance if by saying that a child can be shown to have had 'experience of space', before it can judge that a straight line is the shortest line between its extremities, it is merely meant that its limbs must have been moved about, or other matter moved across portions of its body, &c. For no empirical science professes to explain the relation between the validity or invalidity of judgments and the antecedent motions of the organism of the judging individual: so that the mere knowledge of the antecedent motions in any such case, however complete, would not give us any presumption as to the truth or falsehood of the consequent cognition. All that the most confidently dogmatic of modern biologists claim is that the cognitions of any organism capable of cognition —or rather the organic movements accompanying them—will have a certain tendency to produce motions preservative of the organism under the external conditions that normally follow those that caused the cognitions in question: and it is obvious that a cognition may have this tendency without being true.

Finally, it should be observed that the phrase 'empirical theory of the origin of knowledge' is often used to denote a doctrine which, like Locke's, is merely empirical (in a sense) as regards the *ideas* by comparing which knowledge is held to be constructed; but is essentially 'intuitional' or '*a priori*' as regards the actual synthesis of ideas that constitutes knowledge. However strongly Locke holds that ideas 'come from experience'—*i.e.*, from presentation to the mind of the realities which the ideas represent; he none the less holds that universal and immutable relations among these ideas admit of being intuitively known by abstract reflection, and that it is the apprehension of such relations that constitutes knowledge, in the highest sense of the term. And, clearly, it is the latter doctrine and not the former that must determine his *epistemological* position.

I may be allowed, however, to observe that even as regards the materials of knowledge, it does not appear to me that the ascertainment of the first origin of ideas can have any decisive effect; on account of the great changes which ideas gradually undergo, in the course of their use as instruments of scientific reasoning. We may find instances of such change in the nomenclature and terminology of almost any science. To begin with mathematics: I do not deny that my original ideas of 'straight line', 'circle', 'square' were derived from experience; in the sense that they were caused by my seeing and moving among material things that appeared straight, round, and square. But the proposition seems to me one of merely antiquarian interest; since all competent persons are agreed that, in the degree of refinement in which these notions are now used in mathematical reasonings, it is impossible to produce any objects of experience which perfectly exemplify them. In physical sciences, however, this change of meaning is often more marked. Take the notion 'Force'. This seems indubitably derived from experience of muscular exercise, and hence its original significance must have included, at least, some vague representation of the movements of muscles, or of the limbs moved by muscles, and also some of the specific feeling of muscular effort. But by 'Force', as used in physical reasonings, we mean merely a cause which we conceive obscurely through its relation to its effect, motion; which motion, again, may be merely possible, not actual. Hence, whatever be the conditions within which our knowledge of forces is confined, it does not appear that the origin or original content of the notion can have much to do with these conditions. Similarly in chemistry, the ideas of 'acid' and 'salt' must have originally represented merely the flavours experienced by tasting the things so called: but now we regard such flavours as mere accidents of the relation of the things we call 'acids' and 'salts' to our palate, and not even universally inseparable accidents. In psychology, again, the difference between the original character of the ideas by means of which we think about mental processes, and the character they ultimately acquire when our reasoning has become scientifically precise, is still more striking. For almost all our terms originally represented physical, not psychical, facts; and the physical significance often clings to the idea in such a way as to confuse our psychological reasonings, unless we take pains to get rid of it; while, at the same time, thinkers of all schools would agree that we *have* to get rid of it. Thus, 'impression' meant the physical fact of stamping or pressing, 'apprehension' meant 'grasping with the hand', 'intention' and 'emotion' suggested physical 'straining' and 'stirring up'. But we all put these physical meanings out of our view, when we are trying to think clearly and precisely about psychical phenomena; however interesting it may be to note them when we are studying the history of thought. Hence, I conclude that the settlement of the time-honoured question of the 'origin of our ideas'—so far as it admits of being settled by received scientific methods—will not really determine anything of fundamental importance, either as regards the *materials* of our actual knowledge, or as regards the mode of constructing knowledge out of them.

After this preliminary clearing of the ground, I pass to consider how the cardinal doctrine of Empiricism as above defined—that all trustworthy cognitions are either mediately or immediately empirical—is philosophically established. We may begin by laying down that this general criterion of truth must itself be based on experience—*i.e.*, upon particular cognitions of the truth of this, that, and the other empirical cognition: since it would be palpably inconsistent for Empirical Philosophy to start with the general assumption, *not* based on experience, that no general propositions are trustworthy, *except* those based on experience. If, again, we ask how these particular cognitions are to be obtained, it is obvious that they must either be proved or assumed; and that if we say that they are proved, this proof can only be given by assuming similar particulars, since it would be inconsistent with the criterion to be established if we allowed any part of its proof to rest on universal propositions as an ultimate basis; so that ultimately we must be led back to particular cognitions assumed without proof.

What, then, are these particular knowledges of which Empirical Philosophy must assume the validity at the outset of its procedure? Popular Empiricism seems to me to give at different times two different answers to this question; and by shifting about from the one to the other, and sometimes mixing the two, its argument, I think, gains in plausibility what it loses in clearness.

(1) Sometimes the answer is—whether explicitly or, as is more often the case, implicitly—that we start with what is generally admitted to be solid knowledge; that is, not the disputed and controverted matter which is found to some extent in all departments of study, and of which Metaphysics and Theology entirely consist; but the undoubted facts of history, natural and civil, and the generalisations of positive science of which, as they are commonly supposed to be based upon experience, the examination leads us *primâ facie* to the empirical criterion. Let us grant for the present that being founded on experience alone is a characteristic which we find, on examination, to belong to the majority of beliefs that are commonly admitted as constituting solid knowledge. It must still be clear that, if we make a complete survey of the classes of beliefs that are supported by the common sense of mankind, we come upon important aggregates of beliefs which, in the absolute universality with which they are commonly accepted, are certainly not based upon experience. I do not now dispute the empirical arguments used to prove that these beliefs, when duly restricted, have really a solid empirical basis—as, for instance, if we believe not (as common sense holds) that a straight line is always the shortest line between its extremities, but merely that it is so in the space with which we are familiar. But such modifications of current beliefs implicitly accuse common sense of error too extensive to leave its guarantee philosophically trustworthy: so that it becomes impossible in strict philosophical

reasoning for an Empiricist to start with assuming the validity of what is commonly taken as knowledge. We may allow him to accept for practical purposes whatever is believed by 'every sensible man' or 'every one with the least knowledge of physical science'; but he must not introduce in philosophising propositions guaranteed by this kind of warrant alone.

This seems so plain, that I need not enter into further difficulties involved in the acceptance of the criterion of General Consent,—as that the consent of the majority to science and history is ignorantly given, or not really given at all; that the consent of one age and country differs from that of another, and that in past ages the criterion would have certified many doctrines that we now reject as erroneous and superstitious, &c.—especially since these considerations have been forcibly urged by more than one empirical philosopher. In fact, empirical philosophers do not, for the most part, appeal expressly to the criterion of General Consent, so far as their philosophical procedure is concerned. If formally asked what the cognitions are which they assume to be true in the reasoning by which they establish the empirical criterion, they would usually answer (2) that they assume, first, what is immediately known, or what we are immediately conscious of, and, secondly, whatever may be cogently inferred from this.

The second part of this answer has been frequently attacked; and it certainly appears to me that no perfectly cogent inference is possible on strictly empirical principles; because no cogent inference is possible without assuming some general truth, the validity of which cannot itself be guaranteed by any canon of cogent inference. But the assumption of the validity of immediate cognitions seems to me equally open to attack; and it is to this that I now wish specially to direct attention. I must begin by removing an ambiguity in the term 'immediate'. When an Empiricist speaks of a cognition as 'immediate' he must not be understood to mean that it has not among its causes some antecedent psychical or physical phenomena—some feelings, or some movements of the matter of the organism of the cognising individual; for no empiricists maintain that *any* cognitions or any other mental phenomena are *un*caused; and if they are caused at all, they must stand in the relation of effect either to psychical or physical phenomena, or to both combined. The 'mediation' that is excluded by terming any cognition 'immediate' must therefore be logical mediation or inference.

If then it be asked, why should we make the general assumption that error is absent from non-inferred cognitions and from these alone, the answer would seem to be, first, that immediate knowledge carries with it its own warrant; that when we immediately know we also, by a secondary inseparable act of the mind,—generally latent but becoming explicit if any doubt is raised,—know that we know certainly: and, secondly, that we have no experience of error in non-inferred cognitions; error being always found to come in through inference.

But it is practically of no avail to say that immediate cognition is infallible, unless we have a no less infallible criterion for ascertaining what cognitions are immediate: and the difficulties of ascertaining this are profound and complicated. Are we to accept each man's own view of what he immediately knows? This certainly seems in accordance with empirical principles, as all experience must be primarily the experience of individual minds. But if we take, unsifted and uncriticised, what any human being is satisfied that he or she immediately knows, we open the door to all sorts of mal-observation in material matters, and to all sorts of superstition in spiritual matters,—as superstitious beliefs commonly rest, in a great measure, upon what certain persons believe themselves to have seen, heard, or otherwise personally experienced. And in fact, no empiricist adopts this alternative; there is no point upon which empirical philosophers are more agreed than on the incapacity of ordinary persons to distinguish their immediate from their mediate knowledge. Shall we, then, say that we take each man's experience so far as it commends itself to other men? But if we mean 'other men generally', this is only our old criterion of General Consent, in a negative instead of a positive aspect, and the acceptance of it would therefore bring us round again to the difficulties already discussed; with this further difficulty, that it is hard to see why, on empirical principles, any one man's experience stands in need of being confirmed by that of others. I do not see what right an empiricist has to assume that one man's immediate cognitions *ought* to coincide with the immediate cognitions of others; still less, that they ought to coincide with their inferences. And if empiricists do not trust common men's judgment as to their own immediate knowledge, they can hardly put them forward as trustworthy judges of the immediate knowledge of others.

It may, however, be said that to distinguish accurately immediate from mediate cognitions requires a skill beyond that of ordinary men, only attainable by training and practice: that, in short, it requires the intervention of psychological experts. This seems to be the doctrine of James and John Mill, and, in the main, of the school of which they, with Mr. Bain, are the founders; but, in my opinion, it is open to several fatal objections. In the first place I do not see how even an expert can claim to know another man's immediate knowledge without assuming that all human minds are similarly constituted, in respect of immediate cognition; and I do not see how this assumption is legitimate on empirical principles. And this difficulty is increased when we consider that the psychological expert, if he is an Empiricist, has to throw aside as untrustworthy the affirmations, as to their own immediate knowledge, of thoughtful persons who have given much attention to the subject—I mean the Intuitional Metaphysicians, who say that they immediately know universal truths. If we admit these to be experts, I do not see how we can hope to establish the cardinal doctrine of Empiricism. Yet how can we exclude them, except by assuming the empirical philosophers to be the only real experts? and this seems hardly a legitimate assumption in an argument that aims at proving the empirical philosophy to be true. Nor is it any answer to this objection to show that Intuitional Metaphysicians have in certain cases affirmed as immediately known propositions that are not true; since the question is not whether error is incident to non-empirical cognitions, but whether we may legitimately assume that it is not incident to empirical cognitions.

But further, even supposing that we only recognise, as experts in discriminating immediate knowledge, persons who will not allow anything to be immediately known except particular facts, serious difficulties still remain; because we find that these experts disagree profoundly among themselves. We find—not to speak of minor divergences—that there is a fundamental disagreement between two lines of empirical thought which—if I may coin a word for clearness' sake—I will call respectively *materialistic* and *mentalistic*. When a Materialistic Empiricist affirms that physical science is based upon experience he means that it is based on immediate knowledge of particular portions of something solid and extended, definitely shaped and sized, moving about in space of three dimensions. Whether he regards this matter as also coloured, resonant, and odorous, is a more doubt-ful question; but probably he would say that colour, sound, and odour are effects on the mind—or perhaps on the brain?—of the molecular movements of mater-ial particles. I can hardly profess to give a consistent account of his views on this point, if he is a thorough-going materialist, but it is enough for my present purpose that he at any rate believes himself to know immediately—through touch, if in no other way—matter with the qualities first mentioned.

The Mentalistic Empiricist, on the other hand, maintains that nothing can be immediately known except mental facts, consciousness, or feeling of some kind; and that if we are right in assuming a non-mental cause of these mental facts—which he is generally inclined to doubt—we must at any rate regard this cause as unknown in every respect except its mere existence, and this last as only known by inference.

How, then, is Empiricism to deal with this disagreement? It cannot be denied to be rather serious; since, though materialism has plenty of support among philosophising men of science, the tendency of the main line of English empir-ical philosophy, from Locke downwards, is definitely towards Mentalism. I may observe that the more thoughtful Materialists, like Dr. Maudsley, do not exactly say that there are no mental facts which we may contemplate introspectively. But they hold that no scientific results have ever been reached by such contemplation; and they say very truly that physical science has always progressed by taking the materialistic point of view, and that there is no admitted progressive science of psychology, proceeding by the introspective method, which can be set beside the physical sciences. Hence, they boldly infer that there never will be such a science; and in fact, they are inclined to lump the Mentalists along with Transcendentalists and others, under the common notion of 'Metaphysicians' (used as a term of abuse), and to charge them all together with using the Subjective Method, condemned as fruitless by experience. The Mentalists do not quite reply in the same strain; indeed, they have rather a tenderness for the Materialists, whose aid, as against Transcendentalism and Superstition, is not to be despised. But they say that the Materialists are inexpert in psychological analysis, and that what they call 'matter' is really, when analysed, a complex mental fact, of which some elements are immediately known and others added by inference. In so saying, the Mentalists appear to me to use the term 'inference' loosely, and also to fall into the confusion before pointed out between the *antecedents* (or concomitants) and the *elements* of a cognition. Certainly I find myself unable to analyse my notion or perception of matter into feelings or ideas of feelings, tactual, visual, or muscular; though I do find that such sensation-elements present themselves as inseparable accompaniments of my notion or perception of matter, when attention is directed to it introspectively. But my object now is not so much to enter into this controversy between two sets of Empiricists, as to point out the serious obstacle it opposes to a satisfactory determination of the question what is immediate cognition.

Let us suppose, however, that this controversy has been settled to the satisfaction of both parties, in the manner in which some Empiricists have tried to settle it. Let us suppose that both Materialists and Mentalists agree to affirm (1) that we immediately know the external world, so far as it is necessary to know it for the purpose of constructing physical science; (2) that we immediately know nothing but our own consciousness, and (3) that these two statements are perfectly consistent. It still remains to ask who are the 'we' who have this knowledge. Each one of us can only have experience of a very small portion of this world; and if we abstract what is known through memory, and therefore mediately, the portion becomes small indeed. In order to get to what 'we' conceive 'ourselves' to know as 'matter of fact' respecting the world, as extended in space and time—to such merely historical knowledge as we commonly regard not as 'resting' on experience, but as constituting the experience on which science rests—we must assume the general trustworthiness of memory, and the general trustworthiness of testimony under proper limitations and conditions. I do not for a moment say that we have no right to make these assumptions; I only do not see how we can prove that we have such a right, from what we immediately know.

At this point of the argument Empiricists sometimes reply that these and similar assumptions are continually 'verified' by experience. But what does 'verified' exactly mean? If it means 'proved true', I challenge anyone to construct the proof, or even to advance a step in it, without assuming one or more of the propositions that are to be verified. What Empiricists really mean, I conceive, by 'verification' in this case is that these assumptions are accompanied by anticipations of feelings or perceptions which are continually found to resemble or agree with—though not identical with—the more vivid feelings or perceptions which constitute the main stream of consciousness. Now, granting that such resemblance or agreement may be immediately known, I yet cannot see that anything is gained towards the establishment of the cardinal doctrine of Empiricism. For there is a similar agreement between actual experience and the anticipations accompanying all the general propositions—mathematical, logical, or physical—which philosophers of a different school affirm themselves to know immediately; so that this 'verification' can hardly justify one set of assumptions, as against the other.

If, finally, the reader who has got through this paper should say that my cavils cannot shake his confidence in experience, or in the aggregate of modern knowledge that has progressed and still progresses by accumulating, sifting, and systematising experience—I can only answer that my own confidence is equally unshaken. The question that I wish to raise is not as to the validity of received scientific methods, but as to the general epistemological inferences that may legitimately be drawn from the assumption of their validity. It is possible to combine a practically complete trust in the procedure and results of empirical science, with a profound distrust in the procedure and conclusions—especially the negative conclusions—of Empirical Philosophy.

16. The Philosophy of Common Sense[1]

When I received, some months ago, the invitation to address your society, my mind was carried irresistibly back to a period in the last century, in which, through my study of three eminent teachers whose works have had a permanent influence on my thought, I seem to feel more at home in the intellectual life of your famous University than in that even of my own. It is a period of about 50 years; beginning in 1730, when Francis Hutcheson was summoned from Dublin to fill in Glasgow the chair now worthily occupied by my friend Professor Jones; and ending in 1781, when Thomas Reid retired from the same chair to put into final literary form the teaching that he had given here for 17 years. Between the two, as the immediate predecessor of Reid, though not the immediate successor of Hutcheson, stands the greater name of Adam Smith. I felt 'in private duty bound' to select the work of one of the three as the theme of my address: the difficulty was to choose. I should have much liked to try to explain the attraction which the refinement, balance, and comprehensiveness of Hutcheson's ethical views have always had for me; but on such an occasion it seemed prudent to defer to the sometimes capricious judgment of history: and in face of that judgment, I felt diffident of my power of persuading you to regard Hutcheson's system with more than antiquarian interest. With Adam Smith, as I need hardly say, the case was altogether different. His doctrine has gone out into all lands, and his words unto the ends of the world: and hardly a year passes without some attempt being made somewhere to extract fresh instruction from his epoch-making work, or to throw fresh light on its method or its relations. But for this very reason I doubted whether I should not seem superfluous in adding my pebble to the imposing cairn of literary products that has thus been raised to his memory. The intermediate position of Reid, unquestionably a more important leader of thought than Hutcheson, unquestionably less familiar to current thought than Adam Smith, seemed on the whole to fit the opportunity best: I propose therefore this evening to present to you—not with the fulness and exactness of a critical historian but in the lighter and more selective style allowed to an occasional utterance —such features of Reid's philosophical work as appear to me of most enduring interest.

I will begin by endeavouring to remove a prejudice, which perhaps my very title may have produced.

[From *Mind*, NS, 4/14 (Apr. 1895), 145–58.]
[1] An address delivered to the Glasgow Philosophical Society on Jan. 10, 1895.

'The Philosophy of Common Sense', you may say, 'is not this after all an intellectual monstrosity? Philosophy is a good thing, and Common Sense in its place is a good thing too: but they are both better kept apart. If we mix them, shall we not find ourselves cutting blocks with a scalpel, and using a garden-knife for the finer processes of scientific dissection?'

And I am the more afraid of this prejudgment, because in the only passage of Kant's works in which he speaks of Reid's philosophical labours, it is this antithesis that he applies in condemnation of them: and, speaking as I do in a University where the leading expositor of Kant, to Englishmen as well as Scotsmen of our age, has taught for so many years, I cannot but feel this condemnation a formidable obstacle to my efforts to claim your sympathy for Reid.

The passage I refer to is that in Kant's *Prolegomena to any future Metaphysic* (1783) in which he 'considers with a sense of pain' how completely Hume's opponents 'Reid, Oswald, Beattie, and even Priestley' missed the point of Hume's problem. Instead of answering Hume's sceptical reasoning by 'probing more deeply into the nature of reason', as Kant believed himself to have done, 'they discovered a more convenient means of putting on a bold face without any proper insight into the question, by appealing to the common sense of mankind . . . a subtle discovery for enabling the most vapid babbler' without a 'particle of insight' to hold his own against the most penetrating thinker.

The censure you see is strong: but is it thoroughly intelligent? Reid, says the critic, has not caught Hume's point. Has Kant caught Reid's? I venture to doubt whether he ever gave himself a chance of catching it.

This for two reasons. First, look at the names he puts together, 'Reid, Oswald, Beattie';—the first a thinker of indubitable originality; the third a man of real, but chiefly literary, ability, a poet by choice and a philosopher from a sense of duty; the second a theological pamphleteer. Is it likely that Kant would have thus bracketed the three, if he had really read them? How came he then to put them on a par? That is easily explained. He had doubtless read Priestley's examination which treats the three together, and which, written as it was primarily from a theological point of view, gives even a larger space to Oswald. This explains Kant's odd conjunction of names, 'Reid, Oswald, Beattie and even Priestley',— even, that is, their critic Priestley. I imagine Kant was on general grounds more likely to be attracted by Priestley's book than by Reid's, since he had a keen interest in the progress of contemporary physical science, and Priestley had here a well-deserved reputation: and certainly the Reid who appears in Priestley's pages, misquoted, misrepresented, and misunderstood, was likely enough to be regarded as another Oswald.

My second reason is that if Kant had ever studied Reid's *Inquiry into the Human Mind* he could hardly have failed to extend his studies to the Hume to whom Reid was replying. This may startle you. 'What', you may say, 'Kant not read Hume: why any shilling handbook of the history of philosophy will tell you that Hume's scepticism woke up Kant from his dogmatic slumbers.' Certainly, but it was not the same scepticism as that which woke up Reid to construct the Philosophy of Common Sense: it was the veiled, limited, and guarded scepticism of the *Inquiry into the Human Understanding*, not the frank, comprehensive, and uncompromising scepticism of the *Treatise on Human Nature*. Kant's Hume is a sceptic who ventures modestly to point out the absence of a rational ground for his expectation that the future will resemble the past, while in the same breath hastening to assure the reader that his expectation remains unshaken by his arguments. Reid's Hume is a sceptic who boldly denies the infinite divisibility of space, who professes to have in his intellectual laboratory a solvent powerful enough to destroy the force of the most cogent demonstration, and who ventures to tell his fellow-men plainly that they are each and all 'nothing but bundles of different perceptions, succeeding each other with inconceivable rapidity'. I think that if Kant had even looked into Reid's *Inquiry*, the difference between the earlier and the later Hume must have struck him, and he must have been led on to read the *Treatise on Human Nature*; whereas it is evident and admitted that he never did read it.

Do you still want proof that Kant did not catch Reid's point? I have a witness to bring forward whom Kant himself would have allowed to be a good witness,— Mr. David Hume: who was persuaded by a common friend to peruse parts of Reid's work before it appeared, and to write his view of them to the author. Hume did not much like the task in prospect: 'I wish', he grumbles to the common friend, 'that the parsons would confine themselves to their old occupation of worrying one another, and leave philosophers to argue with moderation, temper and good manners'. In fact, he expects another Warburton: but when he has read the MS. his tone changes. 'It is certainly very rare', he writes to Reid, 'that a piece so deeply philosophical is wrote with so much spirit, and affords so much entertainment to the reader . . . There are some objections', he goes on, 'that I would propose, but I will forbear till the whole can be before me. I will only say that if you have been able to clear up these abstruse and important topics, instead of being mortified, I shall be so vain as to pretend to a share of the praise: and shall think that my errors, by having at least some coherence, had led you to make a strict review of my principles, which were the common ones, and to perceive their futility'.

Well, I think you will agree with me that this is a charmingly urbane letter, from a free-thinker of established literary reputation to a parson turned professor, as yet hardly known in the world of letters, who had hit him some smart blows and ventured to laugh at him a little as well as argue with him. But Hume recognises that the parson unexpectedly writes like a philosopher: and Hume, as we saw, has a high ideal of the manner in which philosophers should conduct their debates; and it is a pleasure to find him acting up to his ideal, a pleasure all the greater from the rarity with which it is afforded to the student of philosophical controversy.

But it was not on Hume's urbanity that I wished now to dwell: I wished to point out that it never occurs to Hume that Reid has appealed from the expert to the vulgar, and endeavoured to avoid his conclusions without answering his arguments. What rather strikes Hume is the philosophic depth that his antagonist has shown in attacking his fundamental assumptions;—which were, as he says, the common ones, and which Reid accordingly had traced back through Berkeley and Locke to the start of modern philosophy in Descartes. It is difficult, I think, for us to appreciate equally the penetration shown in this historical *aperçu*, because the connexion of ideas that Reid makes apparent now seems to us so obvious and patent. But this is the case with many important steps in the development of philosophical thought: when once the step has been taken, it appears so simple and inevitable that we can hardly feel that it required intellectual force and originality to take it. You remember, perhaps, the depreciatory remark made on Christopher Columbus by a schoolboy who 'didn't see why so much fuss should be made about his discovery of America, since, if he went that way at all, he could not well miss it'. Similarly it now seems to us that if Reid 'went that way at all' he could not fail to find the source of the Idealism of Berkeley and the pulverizing scepticism of Hume in Locke's assumption that the immediate object of the mind in external perception is its own ideas: and that finding this view equally in Malebranche, he could not fail to trace it to Descartes. His merit lay in the independence of thought required to free himself from this assumption, question it and hunt it home: and this merit Hume evidently recognised.

And now, perhaps, I may have persuaded some of my hearers that Kant entirely failed to see what Reid and his followers were driving at. But if so, I have gone too far, and persuaded them of more than I intended. The appeal to vulgar common sense *has* an important place in Reid's doctrine: he does rely on it: nor can I defend him from the charge that he relies on it too much. He does hold that the mere ridiculousness of Hume's conclusions is a good reason for disbelieving them: and even in his later and maturer treatise he speaks of the sense of the ridiculous as a guide to philosophic truth, in language that lacks his usual circumspection. For our sense of the ridiculous is manifestly stirred by the mere incongruity of an opinion with our intellectual habits: a strange truth is no less apt to excite it than a strange error. When the Copernican theory was slowly winning its way to acceptance, even the grave Milton allowed himself a jest on 'the new carmen who drive the earth about': and I can remember how, when the Darwinian theory was new, persons of the highest culture cracked their jokes on the zoologist's supposed private reasons for the absurd conclusion that his ancestor was a monkey. And this is doubtless all for the best: laughter is a natural and valuable relief in many perplexities and disturbances of life, and I do not see why it should not relieve the disturbance caused by the collision of new opinions with old: only let us remember that it is evidence of nothing except the mere fact of collision. But, though Reid does rely more than he ought on the *argumentum ad risum*, he is not so stupid as to think that a volume is required to exhibit this argument. He does say to the plain man, 'If philosophy befools her votaries, and leads them into these quagmires of absurdity, beware of her as an *ignis fatuus*': but he immediately adds, 'Is it, however, certain that this fair lady is of the party? Is it not possible that she may have been misrepresented?' and that she has been misrepresented is the thesis which he aims at proving.

In the course of the proof, no doubt, he leads us again to Common Sense, as the source and warrant of certain primary data of knowledge at once unreasonal and indubitable: but the Common Sense to which we are thus led is not that of the vulgar as contrasted with the philosopher: Reid's point is that the philosopher inevitably shares it with the vulgar. Whether a philosopher has been developed out of a monkey may possibly be still an open question; but there can be no doubt that he is developed out of a man; and, if we consider his intellectual life as a whole, we may surmise that the larger part of it is occupied with the beliefs that he still shares with the unphilosophical majority of his contemporaries. It is on this fact that Reid's appeal to him is based. He refers to Hume's account of the manner in which, after solitary reflection has environed him with the clouds and darkness of doubt, the genial influence of 'dinner, backgammon and social talk' dispels these doubts and restores his belief in the world without and the self within: and Reid takes his stand with those who are 'so weak as to imagine that they ought to have the same belief in solitude and in company'. His *essential* demand, therefore, on the philosopher, is not primarily that he should make his beliefs consistent with those of the vulgar but that he should make them consistent with his own; and the legitimacy of the demand becomes, I think, more apparent, when we regard it as made in the name of Philosophy rather than in the name of Common Sense. For when we reflect on plain Common Sense,—on the body of unreasoned principles of judgment which we and other men are in the habit of applying in ordinary thought and discourse,—we find it certainly to some extent confused and inconsistent: but it is not clear that it is the business of Common Sense to get rid of these confusions and inconsistencies, so long as they do not give trouble in the ordinary conduct of life: at any rate it is not its most pressing business, since system-making is not its affair. But system-making is pre-eminently the affair of Philosophy, and it cannot willingly tolerate inconsistencies: at least if it has to tolerate them, as I sadly fear that it has, it can only tolerate them as a physician tolerates a chronic imperfection of health, which he can only hope to mitigate and not completely to cure.

Accordingly, in Reid's view it is the duty of a philosopher—his duty *as* a philosopher—to aim steadily and persistently at bringing the common human element of his intellectual life into clear consistency with the special philosophic element. And Reid is on the whole perfectly aware,—though his language occasionally ignores it,—that for every part of this task the special training and intellectual habits of the philosopher are required. For the fundamental beliefs which the philosopher shares with the plain man can only be defined with clearness and precision by one who has reflected systematically, as an ordinary man does not reflect, on the operations of his own mind; even the elementary distinction between sensation and perception is, Reid admits, only apprehended by the plain man in a confused form. To bring the distinction into clear consciousness, to attend to 'sensation and perception each by itself, and to attribute nothing to one which belongs to the other', requires, he tells us, 'a degree of attention to what passes in our own minds, and a talent for distinguishing things that differ, which is not to be expected in the vulgar'. The philosopher alone can do it: but in order to do it, he must partially divest himself of his philosophic peculiarities. That is, he must temporarily put out of his mind the conclusions of any system he may have learnt or adopted, and merely bring his trained faculty of reflective attention to the observation and analysis of the common human element of his thought.

But if it be admitted that the philosopher alone is capable of the steady and clear attention required to ascertain the fundamental beliefs of Common Sense, what valid evidence is there of the general assent to these beliefs on which Reid says stress, and which, indeed, the term implies? He seems to be in a dilemma; either the many must be held capable of reflective analysis, or the decision on questions of fundamental belief must after all be limited to the expert few. The difficulty is partly met by pointing out that the philosophical faculty required to distinguish and state such beliefs with precision much exceeds that required to judge of such a statement when made; just as few of us could have found out the axioms required in the study of geometry, but we could easily see the truth of Euclid's at a very early age. Still, granting this, I think that Reid presses too far the competence of plain man even to *judge* of philosophical first principles. It is true, as he urges, that this judgment requires no more than a 'sound mind free from prejudice and a distinct conception of the questions': but it does not follow, as Reid seems to think, that 'every man is a competent judge, the learned and unlearned, the philosopher and day-labourer alike': because a good deal of the painful process we call 'learning' is normally needed to realise these apparently simple requirements, freedom from prejudice and distinctness of conception. I will not affirm that no day-labourer could attain a distinct conception of the positions that Reid is defending against Berkeley and Hume: but I venture to think that a day-labourer who could convince us that he had attained it would be at once recognised as a born philosopher, incontrovertibly qualified by native genius for membership of the society that I have the honour to address.

At the same time I cannot think Reid wrong in holding that the propositions he is most concerned to maintain as first principles are implicitly assented to by men in general. That for ordinary men sense-perception involves a belief in the existence of a thing perceived, independent of the perception: that similarly consciousness involves a belief in the existence of a permanent identical subject of changing conscious states: that ordinary moral judgment involves the belief in a real right and wrong in human action, capable of being known by a moral agent and distinct in idea from what conduces to his interest: that in ordinary thought about experience we find implicit the unreasoned assumption that every change must have a cause, and a cause adequate to the effect—all this I think will hardly be denied by any one who approaches the question with a fair mind. He may of course still regard it as unphilosophical to rest the validity of these beliefs on the fact of their general acceptance. But here again it must be said that Reid's own deference to general assent is of a strictly limited and subordinate kind. He is far from wishing truth to be determined by votes: he only urges that 'authority, though tyrannical as a mistress, is useful as a handmaid to private judgment'. He points out that even in the exactest sciences authority actually has this place: even a mathematician who has demonstrated a novel conclusion is strengthened in his belief in it by the assent of other mathematical experts who have examined his demonstration, and is 'reduced to a kind of suspense' by their dissent.

This is, I think, undeniable: and perhaps we may separate Reid's just and moderate statement of the claims of Authority from his exaggerated view of the competence of untrained intellects to deal with philosophical first principles; and simply take it as a cardinal point in the philosophy of Common Sense that a difference in judgment from another whom he has no reason to regard as less competent to judge them himself, naturally and properly reduces a thinker to a 'kind of suspense'. When the conflict relates to a demonstrated conclusion, it leads him to search for a flaw in the opponent's demonstration; but when it relates to a first principle, primary datum, or fundamental assumption, this resource appears to be excluded: and then, perhaps, when he has done all that he can to remove any misunderstanding of the question at issue, the Common-Sense philosopher may be allowed to derive some support from the thought that his own conviction is shared by the great majority of those whose judgments have built up and continually sustain the living fabric of our common thought and knowledge. And this, I think, is all that Reid really means to claim.

I have now, I hope, succeeded in making clear the general relation which Reid's epistemology bears to his psychology. I have not used these modern terms, because Reid himself blends the two subjects under the single notion of 'Philosophy of the Human Mind': but it is necessary, in any careful estimate of his work, to distinguish the process of psychological distinction and analysis through which the fundamental beliefs of Common Sense are ascertained, from the arguments by which their validity is justified. I do not propose to enter into the details of Reid's psychological view, which has largely become antiquated through the progress of mental science. But if Locke is the first founder of the distinctively British study, Empirical Psychology, of which the primary method is introspective observation and analysis, I think Reid has a fair claim to be regarded as a second founder: and even now his psychological work may be studied with interest, from the patient fidelity of his self-observation, the acumen of his reflective analysis, and, especially, his entire freedom from the vague materialism that, in spite of Descartes, still hung about the current philosophical conception of Mind and its operations. It is, indeed, in the task of exposing the unwarrantable assumptions generated by this vague materialism that the force and penetration of Reid's intellect is most conspicuously shown.

Let me briefly note this in the case of the beliefs involved in ordinary sense-perception, since this problem occupies a leading place in his discussion. Not, I ought to say, that he is specially interested in this problem on its own account: he makes it quite clear that it is on far greater issues that his thought is really set. God, Freedom, Duty, the spirituality of human nature,—these are, for Reid as for Kant, the grave matters really at stake in the epistemological controversy. But these greater matters, for the very reason of their supreme importance, are apt to stir our deepest emotions so strongly as to render difficult the passionless precision of analysis and reasoning which Reid rightly held to be needful for the attainment of philosophical truth: while at the same time it is clear to him that all the questions hang together, and that the decision of one in the sense that he claims will carry with it the similar determination of the rest.

Accepting this view then, and remembering that in a trivial case we are trying no trivial issue, let us examine his treatment of the cognition by Mind of particular material things. Here Reid's task, as he ultimately saw, was merely carrying further the work of Descartes. By clearly distinguishing the motions of material particles antecedent to perception from perception itself as a psychical fact, Descartes had got rid of the old psychophysical muddle, by which forms or semblances of things perceived by the senses were supposed somehow to get into the brain through the 'animal spirits' and so into the mind. But he had not equally got rid of the view that perception was the getting of an idea in the mind, from which the existence of a thing outside the mind *like* the idea had to be somehow inferred. This view is definitely held, not only by his disciple Malebranche but by his independent successor Locke. They do not see what Reid came to see, that the normal perception of an external object presents itself to introspection as an immediate cognition: that is, as a cognition which has no psychical mediation, no inference in it. What prevented them and others from seeing this was, mainly, a naïve assumption that the mind can only know immediately what is 'present' to it, and that things outside the body cannot be thus present; as the mind cannot go out to them and they cannot get into the mind, only the ideas of them can get in. It was reserved to Reid to point out the illegitimacy of this assumption, and to derive it from a confused half unconscious transfer to Mind and its function of cognition, of the conditions under which body acts on body in ordinary physical experience. When the assumption is made explicit and traced to its source, it loses, I think, all appearance of validity.

It is to be observed, that in affirming external perception to be an immediate cognition, Reid does not of course mean that it is physically uncaused. He only means that the perceiving mind has not a double object, its own percept and a non-mental thing like its percept: and accordingly that our normal conviction of the present existence of the non-mental thing perceived is not a judgment attained by reasoning, but a primary datum of knowledge. He recognises like his predecessors that it has physical antecedents, movements of material particles both without and within the organism. And he recognises, more distinctly than his predecessors, that it has psychical antecedents and concomitants, *i.e.*, sensations which he carefully distinguishes from the perception that they suggest and accompany. A consideration of these antecedents may possibly affect our reflective confidence in the cognition that follows them,—that question I will deal with presently,—but at any rate it cannot properly modify our view of the content of this cognition as ascertained by introspective observation. This, I think, remains true after duly taking account of the valuable work that has been done since Reid's time, in ascertaining more accurately the antecedents and concomitants of our common perceptions of extended matter. Whatever view we may take on the interesting but still disputed questions as to the precise manner in which visual, tactual, and muscular feelings have historically been combined in the genesis of our particular perceptions and general notions of matter and space,—there can still be no doubt of the fundamental difference in our present consciousness between these perceptions or notions and any combinations of muscular, tactual, and visual feelings.

It has indeed been held, by an influential school of British psychologists, that this manifest difference is merely apparent and illusory: it has been held that by a process of 'mental chemistry' sensations and images of sensation have been 'compounded' into what we now distinguish as perceptions and conceptions of matter in space, and that the latter really consist of sensations and images of sensation, just as water really consists of oxygen and hydrogen. But this view involves a second illegitimate transfer of physical conditions to psychical facts; and Reid would certainly have rejected 'mental chemistry' in this application as unhesitatingly as he does reject it when applied to support the conclusion that a 'cluster of the ideas of sense, properly combined may make up the idea of a mind'. He would have rejected it for the simple reason that we have no ground for holding any fact of consciousness to be other than careful introspection declares it to be. In the case of material chemistry, the inference that a compound consists of certain elements depends on experimental proof that we can not only make the compound out of the elements, but can also make the elements again out of the compound. But even if we grant that our cognitions of Matter and Space, of Self and Duty, are derived from more elementary feelings, it is certain that no psychical experiment will enable us to turn them into such feelings again: the later phenomena, if products, are biological not chemical products, resulting from evolution, not from mere composition.

Still, it may be said, granting the existence of cognitions and beliefs that cannot now be resolved into more elementary feelings, and that present themselves in ordinary thought with the character of unreasoned certitude, systematic reflection on these beliefs and their antecedents must render it impossible to accept them as trustworthy premises for philosophical reasoning. It is a commonplace that the senses deceive, and the more we learn of the psychophysical process of sense-perception, the more clear it becomes why and how they must deceive. Even apart from cases of admitted illusion, philosophical reflection on normal perception continually shows us, as Hume urges, a manifest difference between the actual percept and what we commonly regard as the real thing perceived. Thus, Hume says, 'the table which we see seems to diminish as we remove farther from it: but the real table which exists independent of us suffers no alteration. It was, therefore, nothing but its image which was present to the mind. These are the obvious dictates of reason.' In answering this line of objection Reid partly relies on a weak distinction between original and acquired perception, which the progress of science has rendered clearly untenable and irrelevant. Apart from this his really effective reply is twofold. First he points out that the very evidence relied upon to show the unreality of sense-percepts really affords striking testimony to the general validity of the belief in an independent reality known through sense-perception. It is by trusting, not by distrusting, this fundamental belief that Common Sense organised into Science continually at once corrects and confirms crude Common Sense. Take Hume's case of the table. If nothing but images were present to the mind, how could we ever know that there exists a real table which does not alter while the visible magnitude changes with its distance from us? The plain man knows this through an acquired perception, by which he habitually judges of real magnitude from visible appearances: but science carries the knowledge further, enabling us to predict exactly what appearance a given portion of extended matter will exhibit at any given distance from the spectators. Now all this coherent, precise, and unerring prediction rests upon innumerable sense-perceptions; and the scientific processes which have made it possible have been carried on throughout on the basis of the vulgar belief in the independent existence of the matter perceived. 'Is it not absurd', Reid asks, 'to suppose that a false supposition of the rude vulgar has been so lucky in solving an infinite number of phenomena of nature?'

Suppose, however, that the opponent resists this argument: suppose he maintains that, though physical science may find the independent existence of matter a convenient fiction,—as mathematicians find it convenient to feign that they can extract the square root of negative quantities,—still in truth Mind can only know mental facts—feelings and thoughts. Suppose he further urges that the common belief in the independent existence of the object of perception is found on reflection to have no claim to philosophic acceptance, because while admittedly unreasoned it cannot be said to be strictly intuitive:—granted that I may directly perceive the table before me, I cannot directly perceive that it exists independently of my perception. To this line of argument Reid has another line of reply. He points out to the Idealist that he does not escape from this kind of unreasoned belief by refusing to recognise a reality beyond consciousness. He has still to rely on data of knowledge which are open to the same objections as the belief in the independent existence of matter. For instance, he has to rely on memory. If sense-perception is fallible, memory is surely more fallible; if we do not know intuitively and cannot prove that what we perceive really exists independently of our perception, still less can we either know intuitively or prove that what we recollect really happened: if on reflection we find it difficult to conceive how the Non-ego can be known by the Ego, there is surely an equal difficulty in understanding how the Present Ego can know the Past. And yet once cease to rely on memory, and intellectual life becomes impossible: even in reasoning beyond the very simplest we have to rely on our recollection of previous steps of reasoning. A pure system of truths reasoned throughout from rational intuitions may be the philosophic ideal: but it is as true of the intellectual as of the physical life that living somehow is prior to living ideally well: and if we are to live at all, we must accept some beliefs that cannot claim Reason for their source. Is it not then, Reid urges, arbitrary and unphilosophical to acquiesce tranquilly in some of these beliefs of Common Sense, and yet obstinately to fight against others that have an equal warrant of spontaneous certitude? May we not rather say that it is the duty of a philosopher to give impartially a provisional acceptance to all such beliefs, and then set himself to clarify them by reflection, remove inadvertencies, confusions, and contradictions, and as far as possible build together the purged results into an ordered and harmonious system of thought?

If, finally, the opposing philosopher answers that he cannot be satisfied by any system that is not perfectly transparent to reason, Reid does not altogether refuse him his sympathy, though he cannot encourage him to hope. 'I confess', he says, 'after all that the evidence of reasoning, and of necessary and self-evident truths, seems to be the least mysterious and the most perfectly comprehended . . . the light of truth so fills my mind in these cases that I can neither conceive nor desire anything more satisfying. On the other hand, when I remember distinctly a past event, or see an object before my eyes', though 'this commands my belief no less than an axiom . . . I seem to want that evidence which I can best comprehend and which gives perfect satisfaction to an inquisitive mind'. And 'to a philosopher who has been accustomed to think that the treasure of his knowledge is the acquisition of his reason, it is no doubt humiliating to find' that 'his knowledge of what really exists or did exist comes by another channel' and that 'he is led to it' as it were 'in the dark'. 'It is no wonder' then 'that some philosophers should invent vain theories to account for this knowledge': while others 'spurn at a knowledge they cannot account for and vainly attempt to throw it off'. But all such 'attempts', he holds, are as impracticable as 'an attempt to fly'.

The passage from which I have quoted was published in 1785, when Reid was 75 years of age. Even before it was published, attempts at aerial navigation had suddenly come to seem less chimerical in the physical world; and, before the end of the century, in the world of thought, attempts to transcend and rationally account for the beliefs of Common Sense—more remarkable than any dreamt of by Reid—had begun to excite some interest even in our insular mind. The nineteenth century is now drawing to its close; and these attempts to fly are still going on, both in the physical and in the intellectual world; but in neither region, according to my information, have they yet attained a triumphant success. At the same time our age, which has seen so many things achieved that were once thought impossible, may without presumption contemplate such attempts in a somewhat more hopeful spirit than was possible to Reid: and I should be sorry to say anything here to damp the noble ardour or to depress the high aspirations that ought to animate a society like yours. But if there should be any one among you who, desirous to philosophize and yet fearing the fate of Icarus, may prefer to walk in the dimness and twilight of the lower region in which my discourse has moved,—then I venture to think that he may even now find profit in communing with the earnest, patient, lucid, and discerning intellect of the thinker, who, in the history of modern speculation, has connected the name of Scotland with the Philosophy of Common Sense.

17. Criteria of Truth and Error

The present essay is a partial discussion of what I regard as the central problem of epistemology. In order that its drift may be clearly seen from the outset, I will begin by explaining briefly—without argument—my view of Philosophy, Epistemology, and their relation. I take it to be the business of Philosophy— in Mr. Spencer's words—to 'unify' or systematise as completely as possible our common thought, which it finds partially systematised in a number of different sciences and studies. Now before attempting this unification, we must wish to be somehow assured that the thoughts or beliefs which we seek to systematise completely are true and valid. This is obvious; no rational being with his eyes open would try to work up a mixture of truth and error into a coherent system, without some attempt to eliminate the error.

It is *primâ facie* necessary, therefore, as a preliminary to the task of bringing into—or exhibiting in—coherent relation the different bodies of systematic thought which furnish the matter for Philosophy, to have some criteria for distinguishing truth from error. It may, however, be thought that this need—though undeniably urgent in the case of such studies as, *e.g.*, Politics and Theology—will not be practically presented, so long as the philosopher's work is confined to the positive sciences. The prevalence of error in Politics is kept prominently before our minds by the system of party government; and the effective working of this system almost requires the conviction on either side that the political programme of the other party—unhappily often in a majority—is a tissue of errors. So again in Theology, it is the established belief of average members of any religious denomination that the whole world outside the pale of the denomination lies in the darkness of error on some fundamental points; and even within the pale, the wide-spread existence of right-hand backslidings and left-hand defections from the standard of orthodoxy is continually attracting the attention of the newspapers. But no doubt, in elementary study of the positive sciences, error is commonly only brought before our minds in the strictly limited form of slight discrepancy in the results of observation, as something reducible to a minimum by an application of the theory of probabilities.

Still the danger of error is only thus kept in the background, so long as we confine our attention to the more settled parts of the established sciences in their present condition. Around and beneath these more settled portions, in the region

[From *Mind*, NS, 9/33 (1900), 8–25.]

where knowledge is growing in range or depth, and the human intellect endeavouring to solve new questions, or penetrate to a more solid basis of principles, we find continually conflict and controversy as to the truth of new conclusions —which appear established and demonstrated to the adventurous minds that have worked them out—as to the legitimacy of new hypotheses, and the validity of new methods; and wherever we find such conflict and controversy, there must be error on one side or the other, or possibly on both.

And the fact of error is still more prominently brought before our minds when we turn from the present to the past, and retrace the history of the now established sciences: since we find that in almost all cases human knowledge has progressed not merely by adding newly ascertained facts to facts previously ascertained, but also, to an important extent, by questioning and correcting or discarding beliefs—often whole systems of connected beliefs—previously held on insufficient grounds. In this way, convinced by Copernicus, the human mind dropped the Ptolemaic astronomy and reconstructed its view of the planetary and celestial motions on the heliocentric hypothesis; convinced by Galileo, it discarded the fundamental errors of Aristotle's view of matter; convinced by Lavoisier, it rectified its conception of chemical elements, and relegated the remarkable substance 'phlogiston'—that had enjoyed an imaginary existence for something like a century—to the limbo of recognised non-entities; convinced by Darwin, it abandoned its fundamental notion of the fixity of organic species, and accepted a revolution in morphological method.

Now the student of science is ordinarily not much disturbed by this evidence that his class forms no exception to Pope's oft quoted characterisation of man as 'sole judge of truth, in endless error hurled'. When, in the progress of thought, any prevalent scientific belief is recognised as erroneous, he simply discards this—with more or less endeavour to ascertain the particular causes of error and guard against their recurrence—and, on the whole, continues his natural processes of acquiring, evolving, systematising beliefs with undiminished confidence. But to the philosophical mind the ascertained erroneousness of some beliefs is apt to suggest the possible erroneousness of all. If a belief that I once held to be certainly true has turned out to be false, what guarantees me against a similar discovery in respect of any other belief which I am now holding to be true? The mind is thus overspread with a general and sweeping distrust of the processes of ordinary thinking, which is not exactly to be called philosophical scepticism—since this usually presents itself as systematically deduced from premisses accepted by philosophers—but is rather to be conceived as the naïve untechnical scepticism of a philosophic mind, which may turn out to be (as in the classical case of Descartes) a mere stage in its progress toward a dogmatic system. At any rate, it is the removal of this philosophic uncertainty—in respect of beliefs that, in ordinary thought, are commonly assumed to be true—that I regard as the primary aim of Epistemology.

I have said that this task lies in the way of philosophy; but, I ought to add, that it does not appear to lie in the way of all philosophers. Some of those who have devoted their minds to the solution of philosophical problems seem hardly to have contemplated error except as a kind of misconduct into which the rest of the human race—and especially other philosophers—are inexcusably prone to fall. It is, indeed, a common experience of mankind in all departments of theory and practice that the liability to error is more equally distributed among human beings than the consciousness of such liability. But the variations of self-confidence that we find among persons who have devoted themselves to the business of philosophy are perhaps less than elsewhere to be attributed to differences of individual temperament: it would rather seem that in the social movement of philosophic thought there are general ebbs and flows; an age of confidence followed by an age of diffidence. It is partly the fact that the philosophic mind of the modern world is now rather at the ebb, with its constructive impulses comparatively feeble, which explains the development and the prominence that the epistemological aspect or function of philosophy is now receiving; and has accordingly led to the composition of the present paper.

I will begin by somewhat limiting my subject for clearness of discussion. I have contrasted ordinary certitude with philosophic doubt; but even the plain man is not always cocksure. Sometimes he even doubts and suspends his judgment; but even when he believes and positively affirms, many of his beliefs and affirmations—most of those relating to the future—are intended to be taken as not certain but probable. By a 'probable' belief I do not now mean a belief relating to probabilities; for this may be as certain as any other—as for instance the belief that the chances are even that a penny I toss will come down tails. The theory of chances has been described as a method of extracting knowledge out of ignorance; it is undoubtedly a method of converting probable judgments into certain ones—though the certainty is of a peculiar kind, and its verification presents a special epistemological problem of some interest. But the probable beliefs that I now wish to distinguish from certain ones are beliefs which involve no attempt at a quantitative estimate of 'amount of probability'; and they are often in form of expression indistinguishable from beliefs held with certitude:—thus when a man affirms in conversation that the new plan of international arbitration will have no practical effect, or that the Liberal Party must return to power after the next general election; it will be generally understood that though the speaker may appear to express certitude on these points, he only means that the events are extremely probable. I draw attention to this ambiguity of expression, because it facilitates an indeterminateness of thought, of which we have to take note in applying the distinction that I now draw between 'certain' and 'probable' beliefs. Often in ordinary thought we do not know whether we are *sure* of what we affirm unless we are led to reflect on the point; sometimes we do not know after reflection; sometimes we are conscious of elements of uncertainty which we decide to disregard, and then we say that we are 'morally certain'—meaning that we should unhesitatingly act as if we were certain. This last state of mind I shall consider hereafter; at present I wish to confine attention to beliefs which present themselves in ordinary thought as certain without qualification. Of these I may roughly distinguish three chief classes: (1) particular beliefs about the present and recent past of the changing world of which we are part; (2) general beliefs more or less systematised in the sciences, especially the exact sciences, which we may happen to know; (3) beliefs that *primâ facie* relate not to mere matter of fact but to moral or aesthetic valuation—to what we ought to do as individuals, or what government ought to do, or what is good and bad in manners, literature, and art. Of course in these latter regions of belief any educated person is aware that there is much doubt and controversy; still there are plenty of propositions in each of the regions indicated, which it would seem in ordinary thought as absurd to dispute or qualify as propositions with regard to the most familiar matters of fact. When Charles Lamb took a candle to examine the cerebral bumps of the soap-boiler who affirmed that Shakespeare was a first-rate dramatic writer, it was, I suppose, because the irrefragable certainty of the proposition seemed to render its express statement absurdly superfluous.

Concentrating attention, then, on beliefs that in ordinary thought are certain in the sense explained, let us—with a view to a necessary limitation of our inquiry—take a second distinction. Reflecting upon the beliefs of the truth of which I have no doubt, I perceive that some of them (*e.g.*, the propositions of Euclid) have only derivative or dependent certainty—my belief in them rests on my belief in some other proposition or propositions; while in other cases (*e.g.*, most of the axioms of Euclid) my certitude may be distinguished as primary or independent. In the instance given—as I have personally followed the reasonings of Euclid and satisfied myself as to their cogency—I might employ a clearer antithesis, and say that some of my geometrical beliefs have 'intuitive' and others demonstrative certainty. But this antithesis is too narrow for my present purpose. For, firstly, I do not profess to have intuitive certainty with regard to all beliefs for which proof does not seem to be required. I am certain that I read through the three first pages of this essay before I sat down to write the fourth half an hour ago; but it would be contrary to usage to call this certainty 'intuitive', though the belief does not present itself to me as requiring proof. Secondly, I wish to include among beliefs with derivative certainty that comparatively large body of scientific conclusions which I believe to have been scientifically proved, though not to me, and which I accordingly accept on the authority of one or more other persons. Of course, in a wide sense of the word, a statement of my grounds for trusting any conclusion arrived at by some other mind might be called my 'proof' of the proposition; but at any rate it would not be scientific demonstration, and it would be odd to call the certainty of any such belief to me 'demonstrative certainty'. For simplicity, let us here provisionally disregard any doubts of the authority of others as others: then the distinction will be between beliefs which requiring proof seem to have obtained it, and beliefs which do not seem to require it.

Now the errors due to taking invalid proof for valid are the special subject of investigation in the science of Logic; and it is widely held that the labours of logicians have provided adequate criteria for excluding them: that they have discovered by analysis certain forms of reasoning into one or other of which any cogent inference may be thrown, and by the application of which the validity or invalidity of any process of inference may be made manifest. Suppose we grant this: then our epistemological problem is solved in respect of dependent or inferential beliefs—so far as the process of inference by which they are reached is capable of being thrown into a logically cogent form. That is, I can in this way obtain assurance that all my apparently proved beliefs are true if the premises from which they are inferred are true: and if these premises are themselves arrived at by inference I can similarly apply the test to the proof of them—and so on till we come to the ultimate premises. I propose to assume for the purpose of this paper that Logic has done satisfactorily what it commonly professes to have done; and that our task, accordingly, may be limited to the verification of ultimate premises, or beliefs that are in ordinary thought accepted as not requiring proof.

The importance of the task thus limited has been fully recognised by some philosophers. J. S. Mill, indeed, seems disposed to bestow on this inquiry the venerable name of 'Metaphysics'. 'The grand question', he says, 'of what is called Metaphysics is "what are the propositions that may reasonably be received without proof?"' And it is, I suppose, to propositions of this kind that Descartes' famous criterion—expressed in the formula 'that all the things which we very clearly and distinctly conceive are true'—was primarily designed to apply.

On the other hand, it seems to be also primarily to this class of propositions that Kant's unqualified rejection of 'a general criterion of truth' applies[1]—since Kant regards Logic as having adequately furnished criteria of formal truth, and therefore of all kinds of inference. In fact Kant's condemnation of the task on which I am engaged is so strong and sweeping that I think it well to examine his arguments before proceeding further. I give it somewhat abbreviated.

If truth consists—as is admitted—in the agreement of a cognition with its object, that object must, by the true cognition, be distinguished from some other object or objects. Now it is implied in the idea of a general criterion of truth that it is valid with regard to every kind of cognition, whatever the objects cognised may be. But then, as such a criterion must abstract from the particular contents of particular cognitions, whereas, as we have seen, truth concerns those very contents, it is impossible and absurd to suppose that such a general criterion can give us a sign of the truth of cognition in respect of its content or matter. Therefore a sufficient and at the same time general criterion of truth cannot possibly be found.

---

[1] See section 3 of the *Introduction to Transcendental Logic* (*Kritik der reinen Vernunft*. Hart, p. 86).

In examining this passage I may begin by pointing out that Kant's view of truth as 'consisting in the agreement of cognition with its object'—which he takes as universally accepted—cannot be applied to all propositions without a difficult extension of the notion of 'object' (Gegenstand). This will appear, if we try to apply it to strictly hypothetical propositions, or to categorical propositions of ethical import.

To this consideration I shall hereafter return; meanwhile in discussing Kant's definition, I shall assume for clearness that we are dealing with judgments that are intended to represent some fact, past, present, or future, particular or general. Thus restricted, Kant's argument is simple and at first sight plausible; but I think it contains a *petitio principii*. For it proceeds on the assumption that true cognitions cannot as such have any *common* characteristic, except that of agreeing with their objects; but that is surely to assume the very point in question. To illustrate this, let us take Descartes' criterion before referred to, as the first that comes to hand in the history of modern philosophy. How can the diversity of the objects of cognition be a logical ground for denying that 'what is clearly and distinctly conceived' is necessarily true?—since the distinction between clear and obscure, and between distinct and confused conception, does not become less applicable when we pass from one kind of object to another.

It may be answered on Kant's behalf that 'clearness and distinctness of conception' belong to the form of thought not to its matter; that clearness and distinctness of conception may prevent us from attributing to any subject an incompatible predicate, but not from attributing a predicate that though compatible does not actually belong to the subject. But it is just this dogmatic separation of form from matter that I regard as an unproved assumption. It is surely conceivable that the relation of the knowing mind to knowable things—to the whole realm of possible objects of knowledge—is such that, whenever any matter of thought is clearly and distinctly conceived, the immediate judgments which the mind unhesitatingly affirms with regard to it are always true. As will presently appear, I do not hold a brief for the Cartesian criterion; on the contrary, I have no doubt whatever that the Cartesian criterion taken by itself is inadequate. All I urge is that its inadequacy is not established by Kant's summary argument.

Let us turn to consider Kant's sweeping negation in relation to a different criterion, laid down by Empiricists.

I take the principle of Empiricism, as an epistemological doctrine, to be that the ultimately valid premises of all scientific reasonings are cognitions of particular facts; all the generalisations of science being held to be obtained from these particular cognitions by induction, and to depend upon these for their validity. I do not accept this principle; I think it impossible to establish the general truths of the accepted sciences by processes of cogent inference on the basis of merely particular premises; and I think the chief service that J. S. Mill rendered to philosophy, by his elaborate attempt to perform this task, was to make this impossibility as clear as day. But I wish now to avoid this controversy; and, in order to avoid it, I shall take the Empirical criterion as relating only to particular cognitions; leaving open the question how far we also require universal premisses in the construction of science.

The criterion is briefly discussed by Mill, *Logic*, book iv., chapter i., §§ 1, 2. It being understood that the validity of the general truths of the sciences depends on the correctness of induction from correct observation of particular facts, the question is what guarantee there is of the correctness of the observations?—in Mill's words 'we have to consider what is needful in order that the fact supposed to be observed may safely be received as true'. The answer is 'in its first aspect', very simple. 'The sole condition is that what is supposed to have been observed shall really have been observed; that it be an observation—not an inference.' The fulfilment, indeed, of this sole and simple condition is not—as Mill goes on to explain—so easy as it may appear; 'for in almost every act of our perceiving faculties, observation and inference are intimately blended; what we are said to observe is usually a compound result of which one-tenth may be observation and nine-tenths inference.' *E.g.*, I affirm that I saw my brother at a certain hour this morning; this would commonly be said to be a fact known through the direct testimony of my senses. But the truth, Mill explains, is far otherwise; for I might have had visual sensations so similar as to be indistinguishable from those I actually had without my brother being there; I might have seen some one very like him, or it might have been a dream, or a waking hallucination; and if I had the ordinary evidence that my brother was dead, or in India, I should probably adopt one or other of these suppositions without hesitation. Now, obviously, 'if any of these suppositions had been true, the affirmation that I saw my brother would have been erroneous'; but this does not, in Mill's view, invalidate the Empirical criterion, for 'whatever was matter of direct perception, namely, the visual sensations, would have been real'; my apparent cognition of this reality (he tacitly assumes) would have been a true and valid cognition. In short, only separate observation from inference and observation—or apparent knowledge obtained through observation—is absolutely valid and trustworthy; the idea that these are 'errors of sense' is itself a vulgar error, or at least a loose thought or phrase; there are no errors in direct sense-perception, but only erroneous inferences from sense.

Now I shall presently consider how far this criterion, taken in any sense in which it would be available for its purpose, is completely trustworthy. But, however that may be, it seems to me that Kant's sweeping negative argument—which we are now examining—has really no force against its validity. No doubt, according to Kant's general view of the form and matter of thought, this criterion, like the other, relates primarily to the form; for it rests on the distinction between two different functions of the knowing mind—Observation or Perception and Inference. But I see no reason to infer that it is *therefore* incapable of guaranteeing the material truth of Empirical cognition; or that the relation of the knowable world to the knowing mind cannot possibly be what Empiricism affirms it to be.

If now we contemplate together the two criteria that have been examined—the Cartesian and the Empirical—it is evident that, at least in its primary intention, neither alone covers the whole ground of the premises for which verification is *primâ facie* required. The Empirical criterion only verifies particular premises, and the Cartesian appears to be applied by its author primarily to universals—to what is 'clearly and distinctly conceived by the pure understanding'.

This leads me to suggest that Kant has perhaps taken too strictly the demand for a 'universal' (allgemein) criterion of truth. He has understood it to be a demand for some ascertainable characteristic—other than truth—always found to belong to valid cognitions, and never found in invalid ones. And no doubt a criterion of this scope is what any philosopher would like to get; but any one who has realised the slow, prolonged, tortuous process by which the human intellect has attained such truth as it has now got, will thankfully accept something less complete. If (*e.g.*) any epistemological doctrine offers, among the commonly accepted premises of scientific reasoning, to mark out a substantial portion to which the stamp of philosophic certainty may be affixed; or if, again, it offers to cut out a class of invalid and untrustworthy affirmations, to warn us off a region in which our natural impulse to affirm or believe must, if indulged, produce mere illusion and semblance of knowledge—then, if either offer is made good, we shall gratefully accept it as a philosophic gain.

Now it is remarkable that in both these ways, but especially in the latter way, Kant undoubtedly does offer general criteria of truth which, if valid, are of immense importance. Indeed it is the very aim and purpose of his *Critical Philosophy*—as its name indicates—to establish such criteria: it is its aim, by a critical examination of our faculties of knowledge, to cut off and stamp as manifest illusion the whole mass of beliefs and affirmations with regard to 'things in themselves' which common sense naïvely makes, and which—or some of which—previous dogmatic philosophers had accepted as valid. At the same time, by the same critical analysis, Kant seeks to stamp with philosophic precision and certitude the fundamental principles of physical knowledge—as that every event has a cause, and the quantum of substance in the physical world is unchangeable—while restricting the application of these principles to phenomena.

And here I would remark that the main importance for philosophy of the epistemological question brought into prominence by Kantian Criticism—the question as to the Limits of human knowledge—seems to depend upon its connexion with the question with which we are now concerned,—the inquiry after criteria. For our interest in Kant's inquiry into the limits of knowledge certainly depends on the fact that the limits which the critical thinker aims at establishing have been actually transgressed by other thinkers. It therefore implies an actual claim to validity on behalf of assertions transgressing the limits which the criticist denies:

so that he may be viewed as propounding in respect of these assertions a criterion for distinguishing truth from error, which stamps them as error. It is true that as regards a part of the assertions he discusses—e.g., as to the infinity or finiteness of Space and time, or the infinite or finite divisibility of matter—the criticist finds a controversy going on which implies error on one side or the other: but by his criterion he decides that there is error on both sides—, the 'antinomy' which leads to controversy in each case arising from a fundamental misconception common to both sides.

It is no part of my plan to criticise Kant's epistemology: what I am rather concerned to point out is that his system is embarrassed in a quite special manner by the difficulty that besets every constructive epistemology—the difficulty of finding a satisfactory answer to the question, 'Quis custodiet custodem?' For the claim of Criticism is to establish the limits of human knowledge by an examination of man's faculties of knowledge: but the proposition that we have faculties of cognition so and so constituted can only be an inference from the proposition that we have such and such valid cognitions. It would thus seem that the Critical procedure must presuppose that truth adequately distinguished from error has already been certainly obtained in some departments. And in fact this presupposition is frankly made by Kant so far as Mathematics and Physical Science are concerned. He expressly takes their validity as a *datum*. Mathematics, he tells us (*Proleg.*, § 40), 'rests on its own evidence', and Physical Science 'on experience and its thorough-going confirmation': neither study stands in need of Criticism 'for its own safety and certainty'. And he similarly assumes the validity and completeness of Formal Logic as the starting-point for his *Transcendental Analytic*.

If, therefore, we ask for a criterion of truth and error in Mathematical and Logical Judgments—and error undeniably occurs in both—or in the Empirical cognitions which confirm the general propositions of physical science, we cannot obtain this from Kantian criticism without involving the latter in a *circulus in probando*. We are therefore *primâ facie* thrown back in the former case on the Cartesian or some similar criterion for guaranteeing 'truths of reason', in the latter case on some Empirical criterion for guaranteeing 'truths of fact'.

I turn, therefore, to examine more closely these two criteria. With regard to the former, however, it may be thought that such examination is now superfluous, since the historic failure of Descartes' attempt to extend the evidence of mathematics to his physical and metaphysical principles has sufficiently shown its invalidity. '*Securus judicat orbis terrarum*'; and the inadequacy of the Cartesian criterion may be thought to be now '*res judicata*'. On the other hand, Mr. Spencer has in recent times put forward a criterion which, so far as it relates to universal cognitions, has at least a close affinity to the Cartesian. I propose, therefore, to begin by some consideration of the earlier proposition.

I may begin by saying that Descartes' statement of his criterion hardly satisfies his own requirements, *i.e.*, it is not quite clear what he means by the 'clearness' of a notion. I think that it will render Descartes' meaning with sufficient precision to drop the word 'clear', keeping 'distinct' (which, he says, involves 'clear'), and explain a distinct notion of any object to be one that is not liable to be confounded with that of any different object—'object' being taken to denote any distinguishable element or aspect of Being, in the sense in which Descartes uses 'Being' as a wider term than Existence, and includes under it the objects of mathematical thought.

One further modification of Descartes' statement seems expedient: Descartes applies the term 'clear' (or 'distinct') 'conception' to the cognition of the connexion of subject and predicate in a true judgment, as well as to the notions taken separately. But it seems desirable to make more explicit the distinction between the two; since the indistinctness that causes error may be held to lie not in the latter but in the former.

We may state our question, then, as follows: 'Is error in universal judgments certainly excluded by a distinct conception of the subject and predicate of the judgment and of their connexion?' But this at once suggests a second question: 'Why does Descartes hold it to be excluded?' And here it is noteworthy that he nowhere affirms the infallibility of his criterion to be intuitively known. He seems to have three ways of establishing it: (1) He presents it as implied in the certainty of his conscious existence (*Meth.*, iv., and *Med.*, iii.); (2) he presents it as a deduction from the veracity of God (*Princ.*, xxix., xxx.); (3) he rests it on an appeal to the experience of his readers (*Réponses aux II^des Objections*, Demande, vii.). The first two procedures appear to me obviously unsatisfactory;[2] I therefore propose only to consider the Empirical basis of the criterion.

Let us ask, then, whether, when error occurs and we are convinced of it, in mathematical or logical assertions, experience shows it to have occurred through want of distinctness in our conceptions? Now—excluding the case of reasoning in which symbols are used more or less mechanically, so that error when it occurs is usually due to a casual lapse of memory—I find that Descartes' view is confirmed by my experience in a certain sense; but not in a sense which tends to establish the adequacy of his criterion. That is, the discovery of any such error seems always to involve the discovery of a past confusion of thought; but, in some cases at least, *before* the discovery of the error the thought *appeared* to be quite free from confusion, so that the most conscientious application of the criterion would not have saved me from error. I suppose the experience of others to be similar. Let me take as an illustration a mathematical error of an eminent thinker which I transiently shared.

---

[2] The certainty of the proposition 'sum cogitans' surely does not carry with it the certainty of the only discoverable general reason for accepting it as certain; and—as the veracity of God has to be demonstrated—the second procedure involves Descartes in a logical circle as has often been observed.

In an attack on Metageometry (*Metaph.*, book ii., chapter ii.) Lotze, discussing Helmholtz's fiction of an intelligent being whose life and experience are confined to the surface of a sphere, remarks that such a being, if it moved in a small circle of the sphere, would find that 'the meridians known to it from other experiences make smaller angles with its path on the side' towards the pole of the circle, 'and greater on the opposite side'. On first reading this sentence I thought I could see clearly the fact as stated; then, on further consideration, I saw that the meridians must cut the small circle at right angles; then—reflecting on my momentary error in order to see how I had been misled—I perceived that the object I had been contemplating in idea was not a true spherical surface, but a confused mixture or *tertium quid* between such a surface and its projection on a plane. When discovered, the confusion seemed very palpable; but the opposite view had seemed clear and distinct when I agreed with Lotze's assertion, and I could not doubt that it had seemed so to Lotze himself.

I do not therefore think the Cartesian criterion useless; on the contrary, I believe that I have actually saved myself from error by applying it. But the experience to which Descartes appeals seems to me to show that judgments, universal and particular, often present themselves with an illusory semblance of distinct conception or perception which cannot be stripped from them by direct reflexion; though it often vanishes at once when the judgment is otherwise demonstrated to be erroneous. In the case of perception Descartes expressly recognises this; he speaks (*Med.*, iii.) of the existence of things outside him exactly like his ideas as something which 'I thought I perceived very clearly, though in reality I did not perceive it all'. In this case, however, the Empirical criterion offers a guarantee against error by the rigorous separation of observation from inference. This guarantee I will now proceed to examine.

I may begin by remarking a curious interchange of *rôles* between Rationalism and Empiricism as regards the evidence claimed for their respective criteria. While the Rationalist's criterion is partly supported, as we have seen, on an appeal to experience, the validity of the Empirical criterion appears to be treated as self-evident. At least this seems to be implied in Mill's language before referred to; where, after pointing out various possible sources of error in the affirmation that 'I saw my brother this morning', he says that if any of these possibilities had been realised, 'the affirmation that I saw my brother would have been erroneous: but *whatever was matter of direct perception, namely the visual sensations, would have been real*'. For his argument requires us to understand the last sentence as meaning not merely that there would have been sensations for me to perceive, but that my perception of them would certainly have been free from error: and as no empirical proof is offered of this last proposition, it seems to have been regarded as not requiring proof. But—even if we assume, to limit the discussion, that a man cannot, strictly speaking, observe anything except his own states of consciousness—it still seems paradoxical to affirm that the elimination of all inference from such observation would leave a residuum of certainly true cognition: considering the numerous philosophical disputes that have arisen from the conflicting views taken by different thinkers of psychical experiences supposed to be similar. Take (*e.g.*) the controversy since Hume about the impossibility of finding a self in the stream of psychical experience, or that as to the consciousness of free will, or the disinterestedness of moral choice, or the feeling-tone of desire; surely in view of these and other controversies it would be extraordinarily rash to claim freedom from error for our cognitions of psychical fact, let them be never so rigorously purged of inference.

The truth seems to be that the indubitable certainty of the judgment 'I am conscious' has been rather hastily extended by Empiricists to judgments affirming that my present consciousness is such and such. But these latter judgments necessarily involve an *implicit* comparison and classification of the present consciousness with elements of past conscious experience recalled in memory: and the implied classification may obviously be erroneous either through inaccuracy of memory or a mistake in the comparative judgment. And the risk of error cannot well be avoided by eliminating along with inference this implicit classification: for the psychical fact observed cannot be distinctly thought at all without it: if we rigorously purge it away, there will be nothing left save the cognition of self and of we cannot say what psychical fact. Nay it is doubtful whether even this much will be left for the Empiricist's observation: since he may share Hume's inability to find a self in the stream of psychical experience, or to maintain a clear distinction between psychical and material fact. Thus the Empiricist criterion, if extended to purge away comparison as well as inference, may leave us nothing free from error but the bare affirmation of Fact not further definable.

Here again I am far from denying the value of the Empirical criterion. I have no doubt of the importance of distinguishing the inferential element in our apparently immediate judgments as far as we can, with a view to the elimination of error. Only the assertion that we can by this procedure obtain a residuum of certainly true cognition seems to me neither self-evident nor confirmed by experience.

I pass to examine the criterion propounded by Mr. Herbert Spencer in his *Principles of Psychology* (part vii., chs. ix.–xii.): which, in his view, is applicable equally to particular and universal cognitions. It is there laid down that 'the inconceivableness of its negation is that which shows a cognition to possess the highest rank—is the criterion by which its unsurpassable validity is known'. . . . 'If the negation of a proposition is inconceivable'—*i.e.*, 'if its terms cannot by any effort be brought before consciousness in that relation which the proposition asserts between them'—we 'have the highest possible logical justification for holding it to be unquestionable'. This is, in Mr. Spencer's view, the Universal Postulate, on the validity of which the validity of all reasoning depends.

Before we examine the validity of the criterion, the meaning of the term 'inconceivable' requires some discussion. In replying to a criticism by J. S. Mill, Mr. Spencer—while recognising that 'inconceivable' is sometimes loosely used in the sense of 'incredible'—repudiates this meaning for his own use. But I agree with Mill in regarding this repudiation as hasty, so far as the criterion is applied to propositions that represent particular facts—*e.g.*, 'I feel cold'. For in most cases in which such a statement is made it would not be true to say 'I cannot conceive myself not feeling cold', since only very intense sensation excludes the imagination or conception of a feeling opposite in quality. We might, no doubt, say 'I cannot conceive that I am not feeling cold': but the form of this sentence shows that I have passed from conception, strictly taken, to belief. Spencer's contention that in this case the connexion of the predicate-notion 'feeling cold' with the subject-notion 'self' is for the time 'absolute', though only 'temporarily', seems to me to ignore the complexity of consciousness. According to my experience, disagreeable sensations, when not too violent, even tend to excite the opposite imagination: *e.g.*, great thirst is apt to be attended by a recurrent imagination of cool spring water gurgling down my throat. I cannot therefore agree that the utmost certainty in a proposition representing a transient empirical fact involves the 'inconceivability' of its negation—except in a peculiar sense of the term in which it is equivalent to 'intuitive incredibility'.

It is no doubt otherwise in the case of universal propositions intuitively known—or, in Mr. Spencer's phrase, 'cognitions in which the union of subject and predicate is permanently absolute'. I cannot imagine or conceive two straight lines enclosing a space: here 'intuitive incredibility' coincides with 'inconceivability' in the strict sense; only either attribute must be taken with the qualification that I can suppose my inability to conceive or believe to be due to a defect of my intellect.

With this explanation, I shall allow myself to use Mr. Spencer's term in a stricter or looser sense, according as the cognition in question is universal or particular. I have no doubt that 'inconceivability of negation', so understood, is normally an attribute of propositions that appear self-evident truths; I think that, in trying to apprehend distinctly the degree of certainty attaching to any such proposition, we commonly do apply—more or less consciously—Mr. Spencer's test, and that a systematic application of it is a useful protection against error. But I think that the objection before urged against the infallibility of the Cartesian criterion applies equally to Mr. Spencer's. Indeed he admits 'that some propositions have been wrongly accepted as true, because their negations were supposed inconceivable when they were not'. But he argues that this 'does not disprove the validity of the test'; chiefly because (1) 'they were complex propositions, not to be established by a test applicable only to propositions no further decomposable'; and (2) this test, like any other, is liable to yield untrue results, 'either from incapacity or from carelessness in those who use it'. The force of the second admission depends on the extension given to 'incapacity'. Casual and transient incapacity—similar to the occasional logical fallacies that occur in ordinary reasoning—would not seriously impair the value of the criterion; but how if the historical divergences of thought indicate obstinate and widespread incapacity? Mr. Spencer seems to hold that this is not the case if we limit the application of the criterion to simple propositions; thus he contrasts the complexity of the erroneous proposition maintained by those who regarded the existence of antipodes as inconceivable with the simplicity of the propositions that 'embody the ultimate relations of space'. But the proposition that 'heavy things must fall downward' is apparently as simple as the proposition that 'two straight lines cannot enclose a space'; and if analysis reveals complexity in the notions connected in the former proposition, this is equally the case with the latter, according to Spencer's own account of spatial perception: since, in his view, any perception of space involves 'an aggregate of simultaneous states of consciousness symbolising a series of states to which it is found equivalent'.

The difficulty of applying this criterion is forcibly presented when we examine the philosophical doctrine to support which it is especially propounded. For Mr. Spencer's primary aim in establishing it is to defend Realism against Idealism: this he regards as vital to his system, since 'if Idealism is true, the doctrine of Evolution is a dream'. Now, he nowhere, I think, expressly defines Realism: but his argument throughout implies that what is defended is the proposition that the Non-ego exists independently of the Ego. It is this proposition of which he seems to hold the negation inconceivable in any particular case of external perception: as (e.g.) where he speaks (*Princ. of Psych.*, § 441) of the 'primary deliverances of consciousness which yield subject and object as independent existences'; and it is in this sense, as I understand, that in his *First Principles* (§§ 44, 45) he speaks of the 'division of self from not-self' as 'the primordial datum of Philosophy'. If now we ask what 'self' and 'not-self' exactly mean, it is explained that we apply the terms *Self, Ego* to an aggregate or series of faint states of consciousness, and the terms *Not-self, Non-ego* to an aggregate or series of vivid states: 'or rather more truly—each order of manifestations carries with it the irresistible implication of some power that manifests itself, and by the words *Ego* and *Non-ego* respectively we mean the power that manifests itself in the faint forms, and the power that manifests itself in the vivid forms' (*First Principles*, § 44).

Now the proposition that an aggregate of vivid states of consciousness *plus* a power that manifests itself in them is independent of an aggregate of faint states *plus* a power that manifests itself in these is certainly not simple; while, if we try to decompose it into more elementary propositions, it seems impossible to obtain any which we can even suppose Mr. Spencer to regard as guaranteed by his criterion. For, since states of consciousness *primâ facie* imply a conscious self to which they are attributed, we cannot suppose Mr. Spencer to regard as inconceivable the negation of the independent existence of an external object so far as this is taken to be an aggregate of vivid states of consciousness; especially as he sometimes uses the term 'existence beyond consciousness' as an equivalent for the independent *non-ego*. Are we to take, then, as the fundamental doctrine of Realism, established by the criterion, the proposition that the power manifested in the vivid states exists independently of the power manifested in the faint states? But again it seems impossible to suppose that Mr. Spencer regards the negation of this proposition as inconceivable, because, first, he holds that 'it is one and the same ultimate reality that is manifested to us subjectively and objectively' (*Princ. of Psych.*, § 273); and secondly he holds that this ultimate reality or Power 'is totally and for ever inconceivable' and 'unknowable' (*First Principles*, part i., ch. v.).

I cannot indeed reconcile these two statements—I should have thought that we could not reasonably attribute either unity or duality to a totally unknowable entity: but if either of the two is maintained, it surely cannot at the same time be maintained that the negation of two independent Powers is inconceivable.

I conclude, therefore, that Mr. Spencer's Universal Postulate is inadequate to guarantee even the primordial datum of his own philosophy; and, on the whole, that—however useful it may be in certain cases—it will not, any more than the criteria before examined, provide the bulwark against scepticism of which we are in search. With this negative conclusion I must here end. In a later article, I hope to treat the problem with which I have been dealing in a somewhat more positive manner.

18. Further on the Criteria of Truth and Error

On the whole, then, I have to reject the claims of Empiricism no less than of Rationalism to put forward a simple infallible criterion for the kind of knowledge which is to be taken as the ultimately valid basis of all else that is commonly taken for knowledge. I regard both criteria as *useful*, as a means of guarding against error, but neither as infallible. I propose, then, to turn from infallible criteria to what I call methods of verification: from the search after an absolute test of truth to the humbler task of excluding error.

One of these methods I call the Intuitive Verification. It includes as two species the Rationalist and the Empiricist criteria somewhat modified. They may be regarded as two applications of a wider rule: Assure yourself of the self-evidence of what appears self-evident, by careful examination. As regards universals, especially scrutinise both the clearness and distinctness of the notions connected in a judgment, and the intuitive certainty of their connexion. As regards particular judgments, especially purge observation of inference so far as reflection enables you to do this.

These, I think, are valuable rules; but even after they have been observed as carefully as they can be observed, we may be convinced of error through *conflict* of the judgment thus apparently guaranteed with some other judgment relating to the same matter which is equally strongly affirmed by us.

This indeed is the most common way in which error is discovered. Such conflict does occur, even as regards the universal intuitions of reason or the conclusions demonstrated from them: indeed in this region it is sometimes obstinate and is then called an 'antinomy'. It is more familiar in the case of particular judgments—whether relating to matter or to mind. But perhaps the most important case of the kind is a conflict between a universal judgment accepted as self-evident, and the particular judgments of perception, or inference from these. The fate of the belief that 'a thing cannot act where it is not' may illustrate this. It was found to conflict apparently with the hypothesis of universal gravitation, which rested on a multitude of particular observations of the position of the heavenly

[Originally published in *Lectures on the Philosophy of Kant and Other Philosophical Lectures and Essays* (1905), ed. James Ward, as 'Appendix to the Preceding Essay', and preceded by the following editorial note, attached to the last sentence of the preceding essay: 'Owing to the illness and death of the author some months later this hope was never realized; but appended is the concluding portion of the second of two lectures entitled *Verification of Beliefs*, which probably furnishes in rough outline some part of what the later article would have contained. The lectures belong to a course on Metaphysics.']

bodies; and this has, I think, destroyed any appearance of intuitive certainty in it for most of us. And I may illustrate it further by the method by which in my work on Ethics Common Sense is led to Utilitarianism.[1] This was, indeed, suggested by the method of Socrates, whose ethical discussion brought to light latent conflicts of this kind. It was evident (*e.g.*) to Polemarchus that 'it was just to give every man his own'; but being convinced that it is not just to restore to a mad friend his own sword, his faith in his universal maxim was shaken.[2]

Now it is possible that what I have called the Intuitive Verification might exclude error in some of these cases, one of the conflicting intuitions being due to inadvertence. If we had examined more carefully the supposed universal truth, or the supposed particular fact of observation, we might have detected the inadvertence, or at any rate have seen that we had mistaken for an intuition what was merely inference or belief accepted on authority. But the history of thought shows that I cannot completely rely upon the Intuitive Verification alone.

It seems, then, that the Intuitive or Cartesian Verification needs to be supplemented by a second, which I will call the Discursive Verification, the object of which is to exclude the danger of the kind of conflict I have indicated. It consists in contemplating the belief that appears intuitively certain along with other beliefs which may possibly be found to conflict with it. Of course we are always liable to obtain new beliefs which will conflict with old ones; therefore this verification is necessarily fallible. Still we may reduce the danger of failure by carefully grouping the intuitions that we see to be related, and surveying them together in the most systematic order possible. It would, I think, be a gain if ethical and metaphysical writers would take more pains to state implicitly in the best attainable order the propositions they ask the reader to accept without proof. I may observe that among the chief of our particular beliefs which we commonly regard as intuitively certain—those relating to the External World—there is a natural concatenation which enables us to dispense with an artificial one; we may trust our ordinary physical beliefs with regard to the (roughly measured) size, shape, and relative position of familiar objects, because if we made a mistake we should find it out.

The most noteworthy application of the Discursive Verification is to the relations between universal propositions which appear self-evident, and the particular beliefs which they implicitly include. We continually have this verification in the case of Mathematics, though in the case of Geometry only indirectly and approximately. We see universally and necessarily that two straight lines cannot enclose a space; the lines we meet with in experience as boundaries are not exactly straight, but the more nearly straight they are the less space is it possible for two such lines to include, if they meet in two points. We might call this case

---

[1] Cf. *Methods of Ethics*, Bk. III, chaps. iii.–xi.   [2] Cf. Plato's *Republic*, Bk. I, p. 331.

of the Discursive Verification, Inductive Verification: it may be applied either to intuitive beliefs directly, or to beliefs demonstratively inferred from them.

Comparing the Intuitive and Discursive Verifications, we see that while the former lays stress on the need of clearness, distinctness, precision, in our thought, the latter—the Discursive—brings into prominence the value of *system*. The gain of system in any part of our thought is not merely (1) that it enables us to *grasp* a large and complicated mass of cognitions, or even (2) that it prevents our over-looking any hiatus, or lapse through forgetfulness, which may be either import-ant in itself or in its bearing on other cognition, but (3) that it provides against the kind of error which the conflict of beliefs reveals. And this, I may say, is the kind of service which Philosophy may be expected to render to the sciences.

I have spoken of the history of thought as revealing discrepancy between the intuitions of one age and those of a subsequent generation. But where the conflicting beliefs are not contemporaneous, it is usually not clear that the earlier thinker would have maintained his conviction if confronted by the arguments of the later. The history of thought, however, I need hardly say, affords abundant instances of similar conflict among contemporaries; and as conversions are extremely rare in philosophical controversy, I suppose the conflict in most cases affects intuitions—what is self-evident to one mind is not so to another. It is obvi-ous that in any such conflict there must be error on one side or the other, or on both. The natural man will often decide unhesitatingly that the error is on the other side. But it is manifest that a philosophic mind cannot do this, unless it can prove independently that the conflicting intuitor has an inferior faculty of envis-aging truth in general or this kind of truth; one who cannot do this must reason-ably submit to a loss of confidence in any intuition of his own that thus is found to conflict with another's.[3]

We are thus led to see the need of a third Verification, to supplement the two former; we might call it the Social or Oecumenical Verification. It completes the process of philosophical criteria of error which I have been briefly expounding. This last, as we are all aware, with many persons, probably the majority of mankind, is the Criterion or Verification practically most prominent; if they have such verification in the case of any belief, neither lack of self-evidence in the belief itself, nor lack of consistency when it is compared with other beliefs, is sufficient to disturb their confidence in it. And its practical importance, even for more reflective and more logical minds, grows with the growth of knowledge, and the division of intellectual labour which attends it; for as this grows, the proportion of the truths that enter into our systematisation, which for any individual have to depend on the *consensus of experts*, continually increases. In fact, in provisionally taking Common Sense as the point of departure for philosophical construction,

---

[3] Cf. *Methods of Ethics*, pp. 341–2. Chap. xi contains a discussion of these criteria in special application to Ethics.

it was this criterion that we implicitly applied. The Philosopher, I conceive, at the present day, starts with the particular sciences; they give the matter which it is his business—I do not say his whole business, but a part of his business—to systematise. But how is he to know what matter to take? He cannot, in this age, be an expert in all sciences; he must, then, *provisionally* accept the judgment of Common Sense. Provisionally, I say, not finally; in working out his Epistemological principles in application to the sciences, he may correct or define more precisely some fundamental conception, point out a want of cogency in certain methods, limit the scope of certain premisses and certain conclusions. Especially will he be moved to do this when he finds confusion and conflict in comparing and trying to reduce to system the fundamental conceptions, premisses, and methods of different sciences.

Let me now sum up briefly the triple exclusion of error which I have been expounding. I disclaim the pretension of establishing absolute truth or absolute exclusion of error. But if we find that an intuitive belief appears clear and certain to ourselves contemplating it, that it is in harmony with our other beliefs relating to the same subject, and does not conflict with the beliefs of other persons competent to judge, we have reduced the risk of error with regard to it as low as it is possible to reduce it.

At a later period I shall try to co-ordinate and compare the different kinds and degrees of imperfect certitude or provisional acceptance in which we have to acquiesce in cases where this triple verification cannot be obtained. Practically, the most important points are raised when one of the three verifications is wanting, while the other two are obtained entirely, or to a great extent.

Thus there are chiefly three questions:—

1. How to regard fundamental assumptions which lack self-evidence, but are confirmed or not contradicted by other beliefs relating to the same matter and accepted by Common Sense.
2. How to deal with 'antinomies', or obstinate conflicts of beliefs not peculiar to the individual thinker but shared by others.
3. How to deal with points of unsettled controversy, where, after clearing away all misunderstandings, we come upon what seems to be an ultimate difference of intuitive judgment.[4]

By way of summary, I may point out that modern Epistemology began with an inquiry for a universal criterion for distinguishing truth and error. Rationalism in Descartes propounded a simple infallible criterion (for 'truths of reason'); Empiricism the like for the particular judgments of experience which it regards as the only ultimate valid premisses. But I have not proposed any such infallible

---

[4] Another interesting question which chiefly comes into view practically in dealing with inferior grades of certainty is the relation of volition to belief, what constitutes practical or moral certainty, and whether certitudes can—and, if so, ought to be—attained by volition.

criterion. After discarding the dogmatism as to the limits of knowledge, of the *soi-disant* Critical Philosophy, I turned from criteria to Verifications: *i.e.* I converted the original 'search after an absolute test of truth to the humbler task of devising modes of excluding error'.

These verifications are based on experience of the ways in which the human mind has actually been convinced of error, and been led to discard it: *i.e.* three modes of conflict, conflict between a judgment first formed and the view of this judgment taken by the same mind on subsequent reconsideration; conflict between two different judgments, or the implications of two partially different judgments formed by the same mind under different conditions; and finally, conflict between the judgments of different minds.

Each of these experiences reveals a danger of error, and on each we may base a process for partially excluding error.

The first danger we meet by a serious effort to obtain clearness, distinctness, precision in our concepts, and definite subjective self-evidence in our judgment. The second we meet by a similar effort to attain system and coherence. The third we meet by endeavouring to attain Consensus of Experts, and so from individual variations and temporary conflicts of opinion educe the judgments of the general mind that, as Browning says, 'receives life in parts to live in a whole'. But I do not put these on a par. Indeed, it will be evident from the very words used that the second is of special and pre-eminent importance. For the ideal aim of philosophy is systematisation—the exhibition of system and coherence in a mass of beliefs which, as presented by Common Sense, are wanting therein. But the special characteristic of *my* philosophy is to keep the importance of the others in view.

Part IV

Comments and Critiques

19. Grote on Utilitarianism I

This work has more interest for the general reader than the *Exploratio Philosophica* of the same author. Indeed unlike that book it seems to have been intended for the general reader: not that there is any deliberate popularising in it, but from the natural bent of Professor Grote's mind. As he says in his preface,

my subject is not one which I should have written upon without having thought a great deal about it, and without considering that I had really something to say about it: but I have not sufficient respect, in a scientific point of view, for the moral systems which are past to have any ambition to add one to the number. My idea of moral philosophy is much more as of a thing which we all think and talk about, but often exceedingly foolishly and badly, so that what we want is good sense, discrimination and wideness of view, than as of a thing on which our minds are free and unoccupied, so that what we want is to have it set before us in the best systematic form for our holding it. *It is right manner of thought that we want about it, more than systematic knowledge.*

I have quoted this passage because it seems to me to shew the reader exactly what he may expect from the book. If all he wants from moral philosophy is 'good sense, discrimination and wideness of view'—aided by a good deal of subtle criticism of current doctrines and exposure of prevalent fallacies, then he will not be disappointed in Professor Grote's treatise. If on the contrary he wants not only good sense, but explicit principles; not only discrimination, but decision; not only wideness of view, but exactness of method: then he will find here but very indirect furtherance of his ends. For my own part I am disposed to think that to a philosophical mind it is only a 'systematic' manner of thought on such a subject that can approve itself as a 'right manner'. I quite sympathise with Professor Grote's repugnance to the exclusive systems that have prevailed hitherto, and am disposed to agree with an assertion in the last chapter, that 'in order to reason to any purpose about morals at all, we must make the supposition that all the things which can influence our action are capable, in the nature of them, of being put together in thought as a whole'—though I think it is expressed in too unqualified terms. And the suggestion that 'hedonics or hedonology is a very reasonable science for Epicurus or Bentham to construct, if they can, but that it must not put itself forward as the whole of moral philosophy' is not unconciliatory: but it is hard to see why the privilege of being scientific is to be restricted to the Benthamite

[A review of *An Examination of the Utilitarian Philosophy*, by (the late) John Grote, ed. J. B. Mayor (Cambridge: Deighton, Bell, and Co., 1870); repr. here from the *Cambridge University Reporter* (8 Feb. 1871), 182–3.]

school. The faith in the ultimate reconciliation of moral systems ought not to lead us to a lax syncretism, a languid acquiescence in oscillation between different principles, in the hope that 'it will come to the same in the end': it should rather act as a hidden spring of confidence in all the systems leading us to make the reasoning of each as clear and explicit as we can.

The principal shortcomings of the very acute and effective criticisms on Mill's 'Utilitarianism' which occupies the first half of the volume, may be traced to this want of appreciation of 'systems'. Professor Grote shews any amount of sympathy with Mr. Mill as a man, as an individual thinker: but he has no proper sympathy with utilitarianism as a system, a method of ethical thought, not exactly coincident with the opinions of any individual, but having an organic growth and development as it passes through the minds of different thinkers. Hence in his remarks on Mill's 'Neo-utilitarianism' as he calls it, he is too apt to regard any deviations from Benthamism as alien elements, introduced from other sources and not really reconcilable with the fundamental principles of the system. Thus he points out very well the great difference between the innovating utilitarianism of Bentham, which professed to reconstruct morality from (utilitarian) first principles: and the conservative utilitarianism of Mill, which takes *en bloc* the current rules of morality, as 'beliefs obtained from experience as to the effect of actions on happiness, to be accepted provisionally even by the philosopher'. But he does not see that the difference, important as it is, is yet one that may fairly exist *within* the school: both sides would agree that the question of accepting provisionally or throwing aside traditional rules of morality must be settled entirely on utilitarian grounds; and that, so far as innovation is necessary, the principle of utility must be the *principium innovandi et reformandi*. Again Mill is charged with 'importing' from Stoicism the consideration of man's social feelings as a sanction of utilitarian rules; and no doubt we have here another divergence from Bentham. But here again the difference is not ethical, but psychological: if men actually have social sympathies, with their attendant pains and pleasures, Bentham cannot without inconsistency refuse to recognise these latter as 'sanctions'; and indeed he does recognise them, in a later correction of his system (sent privately to Dumont in 1821).

But other criticisms of our author are much less easy to dispose of. Two of them especially seem to me unanswerable, and entirely destructive of Mill's system as he expounds it. Both have been stated by Mr. Lecky in a manner more concise and polished, but less subtle, close, and effective. The first of these is directed against Mill's introduction of *qualitative distinctions among pleasures*, to remove the objection taken against the older utilitarianism, that it encouraged a base and sensual view of life. Now, as Professor Grote justly says, either the qualitative distinction must be after all resolvable into a quantitative one, or pure utilitarianism is abandoned, and a point of view not distinguishable from the intuitive moralist at least partly taken. If we prefer one pleasure to another *not* because it is more pleasant, we can only express our reason for the preference by saying that it is 'higher', 'better', 'nobler' (as Mr. Mill does say): and what can these words express but the judgments of a moral faculty?—the arbitrary Sympathy and Antipathy that Bentham abhorred?[1] The other criticism to which I referred is a more obvious one: it is directed against the weakest point of Mill's system, which unfortunately happens to be the foundation. The proof that Mill offers of utilitarianism consists in arguing that it is natural: 'all men do seek pleasure, we cannot conceive ourselves aiming at anything else.' Professor Grote answers that even if the psychological proposition that I *do* always aim at my own happiness, be true, it scarcely establishes the ethical proposition, that I *ought* always to aim at the happiness of other people.

The more constructive—and less definite—portion of the treatise it would take too long to examine. In conclusion I may remark, that though the editor has not made clear how much he has done in preparing the work for publication, I should imagine, from a comparison of the style of this work with that of *Exploratio Philosophica*, that considerable credit is due to Mr. Mayor for the much greater smoothness of the former.

---

[1] It must be remembered (though Professor Grote often forgets it) that the first principle of Utilitarianism is that—not happiness of some sort, but—the greatest possible happiness is always to be preferred. This point is overlooked by the editor of the *Fortnightly Review*, in his able but very rampant answer to Mr. Lecky (May, 1869).

20. Grote on Utilitarianism II

This work, the first of a number of unpublished treatises left behind by the late Professor of Moral Philosophy at Cambridge, has been very carefully edited by his literary executor, Professor Mayor. The few alterations which he has permitted himself, without affecting the peculiar character of Mr. Grote's style, as a natural and intimate expression of very fresh and independent thought, have decidedly mitigated the perplexing prolixity in which it has always tended to luxuriate.

The style, indeed, in its good and bad qualities alike, is very well adapted to the substance of the treatise; and will lead the discerning reader to expect from the book exactly what it has to give. Mr. Grote has set himself to teach, by example and precept equally, the need and importance of being unsystematic; and that not merely as a temporary probation, but as a permanent condition of sound thinking on moral subjects. Not that we are tempted to this renunciation of system by any delusive promises. 'No person', says Mr. Grote, 'who has seriously thought about moral philosophy can expect from it a real solution of the difficulties and perplexities of human life.' All we can hope to attain, by duly recognising the 'largeness and variety of human life', is 'right manner of thought upon the subject'. Mankind in general, in so far as they act upon principle, act upon a rather random mixture and alternation of principles. The philosopher should aim at clearer apprehension and better application of these different principles; but should distrust any attempt to harmonise them, from fear of narrowing his view. We are not surprised to find that Cicero, the *bête noire* of exact reasoners, is a favourite moralist of Mr. Grote's.

Now criticism of systems and methods, at any rate in departments of thought where there is so much divergence as there is in Ethics, is continually required; and can perhaps be best performed by a thinker who has come to distrust all systems. And Mr. Grote's acuteness, subtlety, and impartiality, eager interest in human thought and life, and uniformly friendly and conciliatory temper, are qualities as rare as valuable in a critic. But to criticise methods properly, one must take an interest in them as methods, and continually try to view them in their most perfect form, carefully disconnecting their intrinsic excellencies and defects from any confusions or inaccuracies imported into them by individual expositors. Here Mr. Grote fails. He has a keen insight into the properly human element of

[A second review of Grote's *Examination of the Utilitarian Philosophy*, published in *The Academy* (1 Apr. 1871), 197–8.]

a philosophy, into the 'manner of thought' and habit of feeling of its adherents; but he has little insight into the abstract element. He can describe thinkers and discuss opinions; but is an impatient anatomist of systems, and a bad judge of their internal coherence.

Thus though many of his attacks on Mr. Mill's 'neo-utilitarianism' are very effective, and indeed quite unanswerable, they rather lose their force from being mixed with much random hitting that often falls very wide; and the whole critic-ism, though very kindly in tone and abounding in expressions of sympathy, curiously fails to be sympathetic; because Mr. Grote has never managed to look at morals as a utilitarian looks at it. The strangest example of this is that in several places he forgets that the absolute end of utilitarianism is not happiness, but maximum happiness; naturally, in such places, his argument beats the air in the blindest fashion.

This randomness is increased by the loose colloquial manner in which he writes. Such a style has, as I have said, a certain charm, and is a natural one for an original and impartial thinker to adopt, in recoil from the sham preciseness got by taking vague notions for definite, and the illusory completeness attained by ignoring difficulties, which we often find in English ethical writers. Still, the effort to be precise and complete cannot be pretermitted without serious loss. A man who writes as he would talk, however deeply he may have reflected, inevitably writes much which is inconsiderate, and which, if he is criticising, will seem captious. And some of Mr. Grote's criticisms are of this kind; sudden small cavils, which the caviller himself elsewhere half answers.

One or two of the weightiest objections against Mr. Mill's form of utilitarian-ism have been already presented to the public, though with less force and close-ness, by Mr. Lecky; who unfortunately weakened their effect by trying to argue against all modes of hedonism at once, thus confusing himself and his readers, and becoming an easy prey to the enemy. *E.g.* the criticism by either writer on Mr. Mill's 'qualitative preferableness of pleasures' is essentially sound: but Mr. Grote puts the dilemma more clearly. Either the qualitative distinction resolves itself after all into a quantitative one, or pure utilitarianism is abandoned. If one pleasure is preferred to another *not* because it is more pleasurable, but because it is 'higher', 'better', more 'dignified'; surely we have judgments in-distinguishable from those of a 'moral sense', overruling purely hedonistic comparison. It matters not that Mr. Mill makes the preference to lie between pleasures instead of actions. If the pleasures are not compared in respect of mere pleasantness, we have intuitivism in the garb of hedonism.

Another peculiarity of Mr. Mill's system is its Proof, or rather 'considerations capable of determining the intellect in its favour', as their author modestly describes them. 'The sole evidence', says Mr. Mill, 'it is possible to produce that anything is desirable is that people do actually desire it': and he has no trouble in proving that all men desire happiness as he defines happiness as the sum of objects desired: so, each man's happiness being the sole thing desirable to himself, the (greatest) happiness of the community is the sole thing desirable to all persons taken together, *i.e. per se.*

The prolonged guerilla warfare which Mr. Grote carries on against this ingenious edifice of paralogisms is a good illustration of his style. He is throughout subtle; he is much too long; he leaves nothing unsaid; he says some things twice over, makes too much of petty arguments, drops great ones too casually, and presents the whole in a bewildering spontaneity of semi-arrangement.

Still the reader is made to see very clearly that, as it belongs to human nature to frame ideals of disposition as well as of action, what each man desires is usually different from what he thinks desirable. Again, Own Happiness and Others' Happiness, though both happinesses, are in relation to the individual's appetition much more dissimilar than similar, and the desirableness of the latter does not follow from the desiredness of the former. No doubt if humanity could perform collectively an act of appetition, it would desire its own collective happiness—that being, on Mr. Mill's definition, a tautological proposition: but as it is always the individual who desires, there appears so far no reason why the aggregate of happiness should be desired or thought desirable by any one. Further, happiness, as Mr. Mill defines it, is a notion to which Benthamic measurement cannot be applied: it may be doubted whether all pleasures are commensurable, but it is quite certain that all objects of desire are not. Grant that we can compare the gratifications of Conscience and Palate; a virtuous Epicurean claims to have done the sum and brought out a clear balance in favour of Conscience; still this does not help Mr. Mill, who vindicates for utilitarianism the dignity of self-sacrifice, and says that 'virtue is to be desired for its own sake'. Virtue and its attendant pleasure are as incommensurable as a loaf of bread and the pleasure of eating it: much more is a notion which includes all four, one to which quantitative measurement is inapplicable.

It is curiously characteristic of Mr. Grote that, after showing the uselessness of 'happiness', so interpreted, for calculative purposes, he declares a strong preference for it over the old Benthamic notion of 'sum of pleasures'. In its very vagueness it seems to him 'truer to human nature'. He might at least have noticed how perfectly free Bentham is from Mr. Mill's confusions. Both alike hold the psychological proposition that a man always does seek his own happiness, along with the ethical proposition that he ought to seek the happiness of other people: but Bentham did not base the latter on the former. Indeed he can scarcely be said to have formulated it expressly. The word 'ought' was distasteful to him. He, Bentham, desired the general happiness; 'selfishness in him had taken the form of benevolence'; but he never expected such a transformation to be general. So to attain his own benevolent ends, he calls on the legislator (whom we may call a professional philanthropist) to execute a delicate and complex readjustment of the consequences of actions, so that benefit to the community may always be artificially combined with a balance of pleasure to the individual. Mr. Mill too usually requires the legislator—aided by the educator—

'to bid self-love and social be the same';

however, in the fourth chapter of his *Utilitarianism*, he has made a solitary and unfortunate attempt to dispense with both.

In the chapter on Sanctions, Mr. Mill, while relying much on the educator to produce a utilitarian conscience, gives him a powerful auxiliary in the 'social feelings of mankind', which are to 'constitute the strength of the utilitarian morality'. Mr. Grote sees here the great divergence from Bentham: but, confounding the man with the method, he fails to see that there is not necessarily any deviation from Benthamism. If the sympathetic pleasures and pains are really of great and growing influence, it is a mere oversight in Bentham not to have given them an important place among his sanctions (as he half acknowledges in a letter to Dumont, written in 1821). But when Mr. Mill describes these sympathetic sanctions as 'disinterested', and gives a psychological account of self-sacrifice, we are conscious of an effort to combine the incompatible; for if sanctions are pleasures and pains, 'disinterested sanction' is, as Bentham says, an inexact term, and self-sacrifice an abnormal tendency to fly in the face of sanctions.

Much of this and other confusion in Mr. Mill's treatise is well traced by Mr. Grote to his ethical 'Positivism'; *i.e.*, the attempt to blend views of what will be and what ought to be, while the logical relation of the two is never clearly worked out. In the common view it is the essence of morality to frame some ideal of action, varying indefinitely from the actual. 'Positivism' embodies the reaction against such ideals, and claims in some way to do without them and put 'fact' in their stead. It may take the form of a disposition to be content with things as they are, with human nature as it exists in oneself and others; such an 'esprit positif' has for maxim

'Faire ce qu'on a fait, être ce que nous sommes.'

But we rather know ethical Positivism at present in the form of a 'morality of progress'. It is rather 'faire ce qu'on fera' that our Positivist now desires; the world is moving and improving, and he will move and improve with it; if he be an enthusiast, just in front of it. In one of the most suggestive chapters in the book, Mr. Grote examines this notion of Progress, argues the necessity of an ideal standard in order to judge that movement in a given line is improvement, and criticises in detail prevalent views of the right lines of progress for speculation and society.

The non-critical part of Mr. Grote's book I can scarcely call constructive. It is not even a sketch of a system; it is a collection of sketches. He considers that utilitarians are right in the general assertion (carefully explained to be almost meaningless) that all action is aimed at happiness. But he would distinguish the study of the general effects of Conduct on happiness, from the enquiry into the principles of Duty, or right distribution of happiness, and from the investigation of the Virtues, or generous dispositions, which must be left freely to follow their special altruistic aims, and not made to depend on a utilitarian first principle. What the last two methods are to be, and how the three enquiries are to be harmonized, Mr. Grote does not clearly explain. In his desire to comprehend the diversity of human impulses, he has unfortunately neglected the one impulse (as human as any) which it is the special function of the philosopher to direct and satisfy: the effort after a complete and reasoned synthesis of practical principles. He has somewhere drawn a neat distinction between 'moralisers' and 'moralists'. With a similar antithesis, one may say of the constructive part of his treatise that it contains much excellent philosophising, but very little philosophy.

21. Fitzjames Stephen on Mill on Liberty

This is an able but unsatisfactory book. The style is throughout vigorous and interesting, though often rambling and prolix, and still more often offensively loud and overbearing: and in respect of what is practically the most important issue raised, the argument, if neither original nor exactly sound, is at least opportune and effective. Still, along with a good deal of acute reasoning, the work contains a provokingly large amount of wilful paradox and misplaced ingenuity, confusion of ideas, misrepresentation of opinions, and even downright ignorance of some very well-known facts. Perhaps the most striking instance of the latter fault is on the first page, where Mr. Stephen declares that 'Liberty, Equality, Fraternity', is the creed of a powerful religion, 'of which Positivism is the form best known to our generation', Liberty being afterwards explained to mean 'the removal of all restraints on human conduct'. What can be said of a controversialist to whom the *Politique Positive* looks much the same as the *Contrat Social?* and who attributes to the system that has 'l'ordre pour base' the very revolutionary formula for which it claims to have provided a final euthanasia? Nor is this an accidental blunder. For about half the book Mr. Stephen goes on discussing the legitimate influence of society over the individual, directing his argument against Mill and Comtism alternately, in apparent unconsciousness that his two antagonists hold diametrically opposite opinions on the point at issue. One result of this is to exhibit an entertaining and characteristic inconsistency in Mr. Stephen's own sentiments. In chapter ii he argues with much earnestness, against Mill, on behalf of 'social intolerance', and claims that 'after careful consideration and mature study' he has 'a right to say such and such opinions are dishonest, cowardly, feeble, ferocious or absurd', evidently believing that he can produce considerable effect by these epithets. But in chapter iii, against the Positivists, he maintains that their 'spiritual power'—which might fairly be called a scientific organisation of social intolerance—is 'fundamentally impotent', because when they pronounce a man 'bad and selfish', he has only to answer 'I mean to be bad and selfish and I set you and your spiritual power at defiance'. It is difficult to see in the abstract, why a weapon that is so much valued by one party should be so useless to another: or to understand why it should be so much worse to be called dishonest and cowardly by Mr. Fitzjames Stephen than to be pronounced bad and selfish by Mr. Frederic Harrison.

[A review of *Liberty, Equality, Fraternity*, by James Fitzjames Stephen (London: Smith, Elder & Co., 1873); reprinted here from *The Academy* (1 Aug. 1873), 292–4. Ed.]

But however little Mr. Stephen may know about Positivism, he has certainly studied Mill on Liberty with some care, and selected, on the whole, the right ground for attacking it. It is undeniable that in this and some other parts of his works Mill seems to forget the essential limits of the empirical utilitarian method he avowedly employs. It is not possible to obtain by this method any absolute practical axioms: but only general rules of a relative and limited validity. Of this Mill elsewhere shows himself thoroughly aware: as *e.g.* in his *Representative Government*, where he points out the error of demanding that a political constitution should be thoroughly logical, *i.e.*, should exhibit in all its details the application of some one fundamental principle. But in his treatise on Liberty he expressly says that if his arguments 'are not good for an extreme case, they are not good for any case'; which seems to show a complete misconception of the kind of proof which his subject-matter admits. And in his whole discussion of the Liberty of Thought and Discussion, as Mr. Stephen effectively shows, he strives to give a fictitious air of demonstrative cogency to what can be no more than probable reasoning. In so far then as Mr. Stephen is employed in criticising the apparent absoluteness with which Mill's practical principles are enounced his position is very strong: so long as he merely falls back on pure Benthamism as on p. 49 where he gives as his formula that 'compulsion is bad

1. When the object aimed at is bad.
2. When the object aimed at is good, but the compulsion employed is not calculated to obtain it.
3. When the object aimed at is good, and the compulsion employed is calculated to obtain it, but at too great an expense.'

But in so far as he attempts to establish any practical maxims in opposition to Mill's, he fails just as conspicuously as his opponent and in precisely the same manner. For example, he lays down that it is right to persecute socially opinions (1) if we believe them to be false, and (2) if we have bestowed on them 'careful consideration and mature study'. This second qualification considerably restricts the number of persecutors: indeed, Mr. Stephen adds that the majority of mankind have no right to any opinions at all, except for the regulation of their own affairs. Now there is obviously just as much *utilitarian* ground for persecuting a true opinion that we believe to be pernicious, unless we assume (which Mr. Stephen does not) that its truth must render persecution futile. The manner in which Mr. Stephen meets this argument is a good example of his headlong style. This 'is a suggestion', he says, 'which it is childish to discuss in public, because no one could avow it without contradicting himself and so defeating his own object'. He might as well argue that it was childish to discuss in public, whether it be right to tell lies under certain circumstances: which would no doubt be the case if the discussion bore upon some particular lie, and was held with the person to whom the lie was to be told. And as to the second qualification, it would surely be easy to assail with the reckless controversial tomahawk that Mr. Stephen wields, the proposition that a conviction sufficient 'for the regulation of one's affairs' is insufficient for action on society; and that people have no right to be intolerant of unveracity or unchastity until after 'careful consideration and mature study'.

On the one hand then it appears that Mr. Stephen's own construction is most imperfect: on the other hand, while dwelling on the formal inadequacy of Mill's arguments to prove their conclusions, he continually ignores their substantial force. *E.g.* if Mill had contented himself with pointing out that by persecuting legally or socially opinions opposed to our own, we deprive ourselves of a most important and valuable guarantee for the truth of our own convictions, *viz.* that given by the free consensus of experts, I conceive that his position would have been unassailable. At any rate Mr. Stephen does not assail it, but contents himself with showing that the guarantee is not strictly indispensable. Such criticism is by no means useless: still, taken by itself it is not only jejune but misleading.

Similarly, he never seems to have understood the very simple argument for Mill's view that the penalties of social disapprobation ought to be confined to offences against society. In the case of these acts—if for any reason they lie out of the reach of the law—the force of the social sanction is generally required to counterbalance the immediate gain to the agent accruing from the act, which otherwise would be actually recommended by rational self-love. But where the consequences of an act fall primarily on the agent himself, a properly enlightened self-love would forbid it: and though we may agree with Mr. Stephen in thinking the social sanction more or less useful in some even of these cases, its influence here is only supplementary to considerations of self-interest.

When we pass to chapter v, on 'Equality', we find at the outset a very singular account of justice. Judicial justice, our author thinks, is something altogether different from legislative justice: we call a judge just when he applies a law impartially to all persons included under its general terms, but in calling the law itself just we mean only that it is expedient. Mr. Stephen may mean what he likes by his terms at the risk of being unintelligible; but it seems clear that in both cases alike the common notion of justice implies equal consideration for the reasonable claims of all persons concerned. If justice does not simply direct equality of treatment, it clearly excludes arbitrary inequality. Indeed Mr. Mill shows (in a passage which Mr. Stephen quotes but fails to understand) that even in pure utilitarian ethics the idea of expediency requires this element of justice to explain or supplement it, in order that a complete criterion of right conduct may be furnished: for the same amount of happiness may be distributed in an indefinite number of ways, and therefore we require to be told how to distribute the 'greatest happiness' at which we are told to aim.

Our author then begins a discussion of Mill's *Subjection of Women*; but is unexpectedly checked by the consideration that any minute examination of the differences between men and women is—not exactly indecent, but—'unpleasant in the direction of indecorum'. We should be sorry to encourage any remarks calculated to raise a blush in the cheek of a Queen's Counsel: but as the only conceivable ground for subjecting women, as a class, to special disabilities, must lie in the differences between them and men, it is obviously impossible to decide on the justice—or if Mr. Stephen prefers it, the 'expediency'—of those disabilities, without a careful examination of these differences. And in fact Mr. Stephen's sudden delicacy does not suffice to hinder him from deciding the question with his usual rough dogmatism: it only renders his discussion of it more than usually narrow and commonplace.

The third part of the treatise is so far original that it attacks the one element in Christian teaching which the most virulent antagonists of Christianity have hitherto left unassailed—the sentiment of human brotherhood. In discussing 'Fraternity' Mr. Stephen seems to confound two very distinct issues, how far men actually do love each other, and how far it would be for their mutual benefit that they should. Sometimes, indeed, the discussion seems to be almost narrowed to the question whether Mr. Fitzjames Stephen loves his fellow-men: which, he assures us, is only the case to a very limited extent. Life, to Mr. Stephen, would be intolerable without fighting: a millennium where the lion is to lie down with the lamb, presents to him a very flat and tedious prospect: he has no patience with the sentimentalists who insist on pestering him with their nauseous affection. These facts are not without interest for the psychological student: and we may admit that they exhibit forcibly the difficulty of realising the evangelical ideal. But we can scarcely treat them as serious arguments against the practical doctrine that any possible increase of mutual goodwill among the members of the human family is likely to be attended with an increase of their common happiness. 'Yes, but what do we mean by "happiness"?' Mr. Stephen would reply. Certainly he does not clearly know what he means by it. He generally assumes that every one must necessarily wish to impose his own idea of happiness upon every one else: indeed in one place he goes so far as to say that if two persons' views of what constitutes happiness are conflicting, they cannot have a mutual wish for each other's happiness. Yet Mr. Stephen is elsewhere perfectly aware that 'every man's greatest happiness is that which makes him individually most happy, and of that he and he only can judge'. What confusion this double view introduces into his utilitarian arguments, we need scarcely indicate. And there are many similar confusions: in fact we continually find Mr. Stephen assuming in one place without hesitation a common opinion against which he elsewhere directs page after page of more or less ingenious sophistry. Throughout the book, too, there is a great want of clearness of method: applications of utilitarian principles and appeals to popular prejudices, the logic of Bentham and the rhetoric of Carlyle, succeed each other with bewildering incoherence.

22. Bradley's *Ethical Studies*

I find some difficulty in describing the general aim and character of this collection
of Essays: since the account given of it by the author differs materially from the
impression produced on my mind by its perusal. Mr. Bradley informs us that
his 'object in this work has been mainly critical', and that it is 'very far from
attempting a systematic treatment of ethical questions': I should have thought,
on the contrary, that his chief aim was not merely directly dogmatic, but even
vehemently propagandist; and that he had used all the rhetorical resources at his
command—more perhaps, than the canons of good taste would permit—to
bring his reader to the acceptance of a set of doctrines, chiefly derived from
Hegel, which if they are not really coherent were at least believed by himself to
be so. At any rate, whatever the author may have intended, I venture to think that
uncritical dogmatism constitutes the largest and most interesting element of
Mr. Bradley's work. It is true that his polemical writing, especially his attack on
ethical and psychological Hedonism in Essays III and VII, is always vigorous, and
frequently acute and suggestive: but often again, just at the *nodes* of his argument,
he lapses provokingly into mere debating-club rhetoric; and his apprehension
of the views which he assails is always rather superficial and sometimes even
unintelligent. This last defect seems partly due to his limited acquaintance with
the whole process of English ethical thought, partly to the contemptuous asper-
ity with which he treats opposing doctrines: for really penetrating criticism,
especially in ethics, requires a patient effort of intellectual sympathy which
Mr. Bradley has never learned to make, and a tranquillity of temper which he
seems incapable of maintaining. Nor again, does he appear to have effectively
criticised his own fundamental positions, before presenting them to the public.
His main ethical principle is that Self-Realisation is the ultimate end of practice:
but in Essay II (p. 59) the reader is startled by the communication that Mr. Bradley
'does not properly speaking know what he means when he says "self" and "real"
and "realise" '. The frankness of this confession disarms satire: and the reader will
probably be rather glad to find that Mr. Bradley, in spite of the Hegelian colour of
his teaching, has not yet definitely enrolled himself among the

> überwitzigen Leuten
> Die Gott, und Welt, und was sie selbst bedeuten
> Begriffen längst mit Hegelschem Verstande.

[A critical notice of F. H. Bradley, *Ethical Studies* (Oxford: Oxford University Press, 1876), published
in *Mind*, OS, 1/4 (1876), 545–9.]

At the same time one cannot but wish that he had reduced the different accounts that he does explicitly give of this central notion of 'self' into somewhat clearer coherence. In Essay I., for example, everything turns on his conception of 'self' and its relations. Here Mr. Bradley, while professing to compare the 'vulgar notion of responsibility' with the 'theories of Free-Will and Necessity', of course suggests his own view of the causation of voluntary actions, as the true philosophical way of *thinking* what the vulgar *believe*. As against the advocates of Free Will he maintains that 'a man of healthy mind has no objection to the prediction of any actions which he looks on as issuing from his character' and does not find such prediction incompatible with his notion of his responsibility for his actions. He considers that what the 'plain man' repudiates is not an internal necessity linking himself and his volition, so that if he be known as having this or that character his actions may be foreknown as the result of his character, but such a causal connection of his character with antecedent phenomena as implies a possibility of explaining himself into his elements, *i.e.*, into what is not himself. And as against the Determinist Mr. Bradley urges that such explanation is impossible, since 'the character of the man is not what is made, but what makes itself out of and from the disposition and environment'. How, as regards the series of volitions by which character thus 'makes itself' we are to avoid the dilemma between Determinisn and Indeterminism, I cannot see: but at any rate it is clearly held that each mature individual—when he begins to philosophise and inquire into the ultimate end of action—has, or rather *is*, a certain definite character (*plus* a certain amount of 'raw material of disposition' not yet manufactured into character) which under given circumstances will express itself in acts of a certain kind.

Hence when in Essay II on the question 'Why should I be Moral?' our author tells us that 'self-realisation is the end in itself', we naturally think of the realisation or development into act of the potentialities constituting the definite formed character of each individual. It is indeed evident that this, as it stands, can hardly serve as the Summum Bonum: but we might expect Mr. Bradley to take this notion and somehow modify it for ethical purposes. Instead of this, however, he starts afresh, and offers us various new meanings of his cardinal term. He tells us first that for 'morality' or 'the moral consciousness', the end is something to be done by me, *my* act—not something beyond it to which the act is a means—and so is the realisation of myself. He tells us secondly that what we desire is always 'self', 'for all objects or ends have been felt in and as ourselves or we have felt ourselves therein; and the only reason why they move us now is that we feel ourselves affirmed in them'. Without discussing the metaphysical issue here raised, we may at least say that a term which equally denotes the fulfilment of any of my desires by some one else and my own accomplishment of my duty, will hardly avail us much in a definition of the Highest Good. At this point Mr. Bradley tries to help us by the further statement that 'the self we try to realise is a whole': that is, as he explains, we have some main end which embraces other ends, 'some general wish which would include and imply all our particular wishes'. I hardly think that the lives of ordinary men are actually as much systematised as Mr. Bradley supposes: indeed it seems to be chiefly their absence of system which renders them such easy subjects for cynical treatment. But undoubtedly we all recognise that this systematisation is demanded of us as reasonable beings: indeed it is with a view to this that we set out on our inquiry for an ultimate end of conduct; the question then is whether we gain anything by calling the object of our search 'the true whole which is to realise the true self'. According to Mr. Bradley's interpretation of his formula, we gain at least an argument against Hedonism. The notion of Maximum Pleasure is certainly sufficient for systematising conduct, as it gives us a universally applicable standard for selecting and regulating our activities. But it does not give us an end which can ever be realised as a whole, in Mr. Bradley's sense, that is, all at once: for obviously there is and can be no moment at which a 'greatest possible sum of pleasures' can be enjoyed.

If Hedonism, then, be rejected on this ground and because of its conflict with the common moral consciousness and practical experience of mankind (Essay III), where are we to seek for such an ultimate end as Mr. Bradley requires, a 'universal present throughout its particulars?' Can we find it in Kant's interpretation of the moral consciousness, announcing that 'there is nothing good but a good will'. If the 'common moral consciousness' does assent to this, it is, I think, because it overlooks the dialectical trap into which it is falling: it means by a good will a will that wills the good, and does not see that the negative part of the proposition to which it has assented deprives the affirmative part of its usual content, and leaves as the sole good a will that wills itself. This notion is obviously empty if we only contemplate a single volition: we can only put a meaning into it by thinking of many different volitions, and so understanding it as a self-consistent will: and it only appears to be adapted for a moral principle, when we further introduce a plurality of voluntary agents. We can then give as characteristic of the 'good wills' of any number of individuals that they are perfectly harmonious: each wills what all others would will in its place; each, we may say, is merely the expression of one universal will, realising itself in different concrete particulars. It was perhaps the sublimity of the ideal of moral order thus presented that blinded Kant to its incompleteness. Mr. Bradley has no difficulty in showing (in Essay IV) that we cannot logically pass from the mere notion of a self-consistent universal will to the determination of a particular concrete good act: but when, in order to supply the deficient particularity and concreteness, he accepts a merely relative universality as a sufficient criterion of goodness, his reasoning seems dangerously loose and rash. He tell us in Essay V that this 'concrete universal' is given in the society to which each individual belongs. 'We have found self-realisation, duty, happiness in one, when we have found our function as an organ in the social organism.' The reader may perhaps understand by this no more than the old doctrine—to which modern sociology has given a new form and a new emphasis—that the individual man is essentially a social being, a member of a larger whole or system, and that his life and work must be accounted good in so far as it tends to the good of the whole. Mr. Bradley, I think, has not clearly distinguished this view from his own: and the effectiveness of his argument against Individualism depends chiefly on the non-distinction. But it is obvious that this doctrine does not get us beyond the point at which Kantism was found wanting. What is this 'good of the whole' which is to determine 'good for me?' If the latter notion gives us a problem to be solved, how can the former be already known? It is Mr. Bradley's answer to this question which constitutes the difference between his view and that of modern sociology. He attributes to the social organism not merely a common life which the individual shares, but a rational will, expressed in the laws, customs, and common moral judgments of his society, the realisation of which is the realisation of his true self. Good life for me is life lived according to the moral spirit of my community: which is to be learnt not from the theories of 'thinkers', but from the intuitive judgment on concrete cases of honest unreflective persons. This judgment, no doubt, varies from age to age and from community to community, and so far morality is 'relative': but for me in my own age and country it is absolutely good to do what unsophisticated common sense regards as my duty. 'To wish to be better than the world is to be on the threshold of immorality.'

I have given this view as Mr. Bradley's, because—however unsatisfactory it may seem to those who have been stimulated to ethical inquiry by the palpable inadequacy of the very common sense which is here offered as the solution of their difficulties—he certainly expounds it in Essay V with an air of earnest conviction and an unusual outburst of triumphant rhetoric. I should add, however, that he immediately proceeds to point out some of the many obvious objections that might be made against it, and qualifies it to an important extent in the Essays that follow. In Essay VI on 'Ideal Morality', he recognises not only an ideal of social behaviour beyond what common sense imposes as a duty, but also ultimate ends, such as Beauty and Truth, the pursuit of which is morally incumbent on certain persons, though it cannot be fairly included in the 'will of the social organism'. Nor does he merely regard this pursuit as superadded to the performance of common social duty: he allows that 'some neglect of common morality' is, to the aspirant after the ideal, 'unavoidable': and even that 'open and direct outrage on the standing moral institutions which make society and human life what it is' may be 'justified on the plea of overpowering moral necessity'. But here he plainly comes into conflict with 'unsophisticated common sense': and surely if that authority be thus found *falsus in uno*, it must be at least *fallibilis in omnibus*: and thus we have still to seek for some criterion of the validity of its dictates. Indeed Mr. Bradley himself elsewhere acknowledges the legitimacy of 'cosmopolitan morality' which has a 'notion of goodness not of any particular time and country': and again in Essay VIII, which deals with the transition from Morality to Religion, he appears to recognise a universal will, higher than the will of any particular social organism. In this way, no doubt, the doctrine expounded in Essay V loses its paradoxical character; but it is also stripped of its apparent definiteness and completeness, and reduced to little more than a vague and barren ethical commonplace, dressed in a new metaphysical formula.

I have been obliged to confine my notice to the main ethical argument of Mr. Bradley's *Studies*, neglecting a good deal of metaphysical discussion which he has connected with it. Much of the latter, I must confess, seems to me either irrelevant or inadequate: and the author, though he has a considerable turn for smart and epigrammatic writing, hardly possesses the gift of lucid exposition. Yet on the whole his book, though crude and immature, is certainly interesting and suggestive: perhaps all the more from its marked antagonism to current philosophical opinion.

23. Sidgwick *vs.* Bradley

23A. Mr. Sidgwick on 'Ethical Studies', by F. H. Bradley

In the last number of *Mind*, Mr. Sidgwick did me the honour to review my *Ethical Studies*. His remarks were on the whole welcome to me, for they showed clearly the necessity there was, and is, for some work of the kind. I am not surprised that my reviewer did not *see* that necessity: that he *felt* it I think his article shows. 'Really penetrating criticism, especially in ethics, requires a patient effort of intellectual sympathy', and I am sorry that such an effort should be made in vain. But that in this instance it has been so I should like to be allowed to show. I am prepared to go through the article point by point, but cannot ask from the readers of *Mind* so much space for matters partly personal. Indeed if the reviewer had confined himself to remarks of a personal or generally depreciatory nature, I would not have trespassed on their forbearance at all. As it is I must ask leave to correct some misunderstandings which are calculated to prejudice my views by representing them to be other than they are.

And (1) I must impress on the reader that I disclaimed the attempt to solve the problem of individuality in general; and in particular that of the origin of the Self in time, and the beginning of volition. But so far as I have said anything, I will endeavour to show that it is not incoherent, as soon as objections against it are distinctly formulated. I can not do so before. However, I may say that I have no quarrel with Determinism if only that view will leave off regarding the Self as a collection, and volitions as 'resultants' or compositions of forces, and will either reform or cease to apply its category of cause and effect. The problem, as Mr. Sidgwick states it, on p. 46 of his *Methods of Ethics*, I consider to involve a false alternative.

(2) The fact that when I speak of self-realisation 'we naturally think of the realisation or development into act of each one of the potentialities constituting the definite formed character of each individual' is not surprising, until we have learnt that there are other views than those which appear in the *Methods of Ethics* (p. 72 foll.). And this we very soon do if we proceed. I have written at some length on the good and bad selves (Essay VII); and on p. 146, I have repudiated distinctly Mr. Sidgwick's understanding of the term. I thought that I had left no doubt

[From *Mind*, OS, 2/7 (1877), 122–5 (Bradley), 125–6 (Sidgwick).]

that characters might be partly bad, and that this was *not* what I meant by self-realisation, as = end.

(3) 'We may at least say that a term which equally denotes the fulfilment of any of my desires by some one else and my own accomplishment of my duty, will hardly avail us much in a definition of the Highest Good.' Perhaps. But I emphatically repudiate the doctrine that the mere bringing about by some one else of anything desired by me is my self-realisation. If the reviewer wishes the reader and myself to believe that I put this forward, he owes us a reference. If it be meant as a *deduction* from my premises, he owes us an argument. He has given us neither; and as I think, nothing but a sheer misunderstanding.

(4) Mr. Sidgwick must be aware that I have endeavoured to define self-realisation, as = end. He proceeds to remark, 'the question then is whether we gain anything by calling the object of our search "the true whole which is to realise the true self"'. I think we do: but then I have not left the matter here as my reviewer seems to indicate. That point of view is reached on p. 67, and the whole remainder of the discussion down to p. 74 is quietly ignored by him. I call particular attention to this.

The passage on Hedonism which follows I will take hereafter.

(5) I do not know whether in what is said about Kant there is an objection to my views, nor, if so, what that is; but when the reviewer says of me, 'he accepts a merely relative universality as a sufficient criterion of goodness', I must remark that this is what I do *not* say. I say relative *and* absolute (p. 174); and this appears even from my reviewer's next page.

(6) 'Mr. Bradley, I think, has not clearly distinguished this view from his own; and the effectiveness of his argument against Individualism depends chiefly on the non-distinction.' The view is 'the old doctrine . . . that the individual man is essentially a social being'. But (*a*) if my view is partly the same as another, what is that against it? (*b*) If Mr. Sidgwick will point out confusion, I will admit it or answer it. I cannot do either until he does. (*c*) At any rate, 'that the individual man is essentially a social being' *is* my view, and is *not* my reviewer's. If it be 'a vague and barren ethical commonplace', yet in his book he must be taken to deny it, for he finds the end, and, I suppose, the essence of man by examining a supposed 'single sentient conscious being' (p. 374).

(7) 'He allows . . . even that "open and direct outrage on the standing moral institutions which make society and human life what it is," may be "justified on the plea of overpowering moral necessity"'. Here I must earnestly beg the reader to consult the context in my book (pp. 204–5). I cannot ask for space to quote it. The question I was discussing was the extent to which *in theory* we must hold that collisions may proceed (*cf.* p. 142). On p. 143 I distinctly denied that 'moral theory' is 'meant to influence practice' (*cf.* p. 205 foot-note). And I do think this ought not to have been ignored.

(8) My reviewer continues—'But here he plainly comes into conflict with "unsophisticated common sense": and surely, if that authority be thus found *falsus in uno*, it must be at least *fallibilis in omnibus*: and thus we have still to seek for some criterion of the validity of its dictates'. First, I must ask for a reference for 'unsophisticated common sense'. It is given as a quotation from me, but I do not recognise it. Next, I have maintained that I do *not* really come into collision with common morality, but, when understood, am at one with it (p. 204, *cf.* 142–3). And my reasoned exposition, ignored by the reviewer, may stand I hope against his 'plainly'. Thirdly, he argues, What is *falsus in uno* is *fallibilis in omnibus*. The falseness in this one thing I deny. Next, if I admitted it, I should like to see the steps by which the conclusion follows. Next, I have never hinted that the moral consciousness is *not* fallible in particulars. Mr. Sidgwick really should give references for what he attributes to me. Next, I deny that it is fallible in all points. Lastly, even if it were false throughout, I say we have *not* 'to seek for some criterion of the validity of its dictates'; for none is possible.

This is all I think it necessary to say in answer to that which my reviewer has urged against the doctrine I have put forward. The rest which I have not noticed, I must not be taken to admit. And now, seeing that a large part of my book was directed against Hedonism in general, and one or two pages even against Mr. Sidgwick in particular, I naturally hoped for some discussion of the matter. This is all I can find. 'The notion of Maximum Pleasure is certainly sufficient for systematising conduct, as it gives us a universally applicable standard for selecting and regulating our activities. But it does not give us an end which can ever be realised as a whole, in Mr. Bradley's sense, that is, all at once: for obviously there is and can be no moment at which a "greatest possible sum of pleasures" can be enjoyed.'

First, as was said above, the reviewer ignores my interpretation of self-realisation. Next, he suggests that my argument against Hedonism is that pleasures cannot be enjoyed all at once. True, that is *an* argument; but is it possible that Mr. Sidgwick can really believe that in other respects Maximum Pleasure answers to my conception of the end? This is so wholly at variance with the doctrine I hold that I confess I was not prepared for it. Thirdly, that the notion of Maximum Pleasure can systematise conduct and give a standard, is a proposition I have formally contested. Mr. Sidgwick not only gives me an assertion for an answer, but by the way he introduces the assertion suggests to the reader that I believe it myself.

I can find no other defence of his opinions but the (unsupported) charge against me that I use rhetoric for argument, and that my apprehension of the views which I assail 'is always rather superficial and sometimes even unintelligent'. Those views I think should be securely founded, if they are to bear being defended in this way.

23B. Sidgwick's Reply

Mr. Bradley seems to be under a strange impression that, while professing to write a critical notice of his views on ethics, I have been or ought to have been— defending my own. I entertain quite a different notion of a reviewer's 'station and duties'. In criticising his book (or any other) I put out of sight my own doctrines, in so far as I am conscious of them as peculiar to myself: and pass my judgments from a point of view which I expect my readers generally to share with me. Hence the references in his reply to my opinions would be quite irrelevant, even if he understood those opinions somewhat better than he does. I passed lightly over his attack on Hedonism in Essay III for the simple reason—which I gave— that I thought it less interesting and important than other parts of his work. Much of it, as he must be perfectly aware, either has no bearing on Hedonism as I conceive it, or emphasises defects which I have myself pointed out: the rest consists chiefly of familiar anti-hedonistic commonplaces: the freshest argument I could find was one with which I had made acquaintance some years ago in Mr. Green's Introduction to Hume. This, as stated by Mr. Green, I have taken occasion to answer in the course of an article in the present number of this journal. The attack on my book appended to Essay III, though not uninstructive to myself, is far too full of misunderstandings to be profitable for discussion. It is criticism of the kind that invites explanation rather than defence: such explanation I proposed to give in its proper place—which was certainly not my notice of Mr. Bradley.

On the special points which he raises, the very briefest reply will suffice.

(1) (2) (3) He scarcely attempts to answer my charge of 'want of clear coherence' in his exposition of 'Self'. He does not deny that the 'self' presented in Essay I is dropped without explanation when we pass to Essay II, and other accounts are given of the same notion. Among them is the statement that 'all we can desire is self'; from which I drew the immediate inference that the fulfilment of any desire is a kind of self-realisation: if he did not intend this inference, pp. 61, 62 are confusing and somewhat irrelevant.

(4) The discussion on 'finite' and 'infinite' (pp. 68–73) is a part of the metaphysics of which, in general terms, I notified my omission. I thought and think still, that it was comparatively unimportant to the ethical discussion. A critical notice does not profess to be a table of contents.

(5) He misunderstands my 'relative universality'. I say that the social organism, of which the individual in Essay V is explained to be essentially a part, is a *relative* and not an *absolute* whole. That is, it is not the universe: and we have no reason to identify its will—granting this to be real and cognisable—with the universal or Divine Will to which our wills should conform.

(6) I did not absurdly complain that he combined in his *positive* doctrine the common view of society as a natural organism with his peculiar view of this

organism as possessing a reasonable will: I criticised him for not distinguishing them in his polemic against Individualism. The result of the non-distinction is that much of this polemical argument—as far as I can trace it through its folds of rhetoric—is directed against an individualism which will find no defenders: the individualism, namely, to which the 'Social Compact', belongs, and to which Utilitarianism long since gave the *coup de grâce*.

(7) (8) I still maintain that the non-theoretical unreflective person who is exalted in Essay V as furnishing the moral standard will be considerably startled to find his encomiast justifying, with whatever qualifications, 'open and direct outrage on the standing moral institutions which make society and human life what it is'. He will regard Mr. Bradley as almost a 'thinker', and at least 'on the threshold of immorality'. And I doubt whether he will be quite consoled by learning that this justification is not 'meant to influence practice': though I admit that the consolation is well adapted to the average philosophical capacity of the non-theoretical person.

But I need not press this point: because Mr. Bradley, as I understand, admits the possibility of a conflict between common sense and his private moral consciousness; and is prepared, in case of such conflict, to rely entirely on his own particular moral intuition, allowing no appeal to any express principle or external standard. If this be so, his apparent reference to an external standard in Essay V is found (as I said) to be devoid of precise meaning or scientific value.

To sum up, then, I have nothing to retract or qualify on any of the points raised by Mr. Bradley—except a pair of inverted commas which were accidentally attached to a phrase of my own. But I should prefer to part from him in a friendly manner; and therefore I am glad to find something to concede to him in the phrase in which I characterised his style as over-rhetorical. I still dislike the quality of his rhetoric, whether it be satirical, pathetic, or declamatory: and I think it is sometimes introduced, at important points, so as to interfere with the closeness of his reasoning. But I find that the sentence in which I combined these two judgments was too strongly worded: and am glad to substitute for it the milder phrases just given.

24. Bentham and Benthamism in Politics and Ethics

In the critical narrative, equally brilliant and erudite, which Mr. Leslie Stephen has given us of the course of English thought in the eighteenth century, there is one gap which I cannot but regret, in spite of what Mr. Stephen has said in explanation of it. The work of Bentham is treated with somewhat contemptuous brevity in the chapter on Moral Philosophy; while in the following chapter on Political Theories his name is barely mentioned. The present paper is an attempt in some measure to supply this deficiency. I should not have ventured on it if Bentham's teaching had become to us a matter of merely historical interest; as I cannot flatter myself that I possess Mr. Stephen's rare gift of imparting a sparkle to the dust-heaps of extinct controversy. But no such extinction has yet overtaken Bentham: his system is even an important element of our current political thought; hardly a decade—though an eventful one—has elapsed since it might almost have been called a predominant element. Among the other writers to whom Mr. Stephen has devoted many entertaining pages in his tenth chapter, there is not one of whom this can be said. It would be almost ostentation, in polite society at the present day, to claim familiarity with Bolingbroke; it would be even pedantry to draw attention to Hoadly. The literary sources of the French Revolution are studied with eager and ever-increasing interest; but they are studied, even by Englishmen, almost entirely in the writings of France: the most ardent reader of revolutionary literature is reluctant to decline from Rousseau to Tom Paine. Mr. Kegan Paul's entertaining biography has temporarily revived our interest in Godwin, otherwise *Political Justice* would be chiefly known to this generation through the refutation of Malthus; and Malthus's own work is now but seldom taken from the shelf. There are probably many schoolboys feeding a nascent taste for rhetoric on the letters of Junius; but Mr. Stephen has felt that the inclusion of these in an account of Political Theories requires something like an apology. Burke lives, no doubt, not merely through the eloquence which immortalises even the details of party conflicts, but through a kind of wisdom, fused of intellect and emotion, which is as essentially independent of the theorising in which it is embedded as metal is of its mine. But though Burke lives, we meet with no Burkites. The star of Hume's metaphysical fame has risen steadily for a

[From *Fortnightly Review* (May 1877), 627–52; repr. here from its reappearance in *Miscellaneous Essays and Addresses*, 135–69.]

century; but his warmest admirers are rather irritated by his predominant desire for literary popularity, and are perhaps too much inclined to turn aside from the philosophic material that was wasted in furnishing elegant essays on National Character and The Idea of a Perfect Commonwealth. In short, of all the writers I have mentioned, regarded as political theorists, it is only the eccentric hermit of Queen's Square Place whose name still carries with it an audible demand that we should reckon with his system, and explain to ourselves why and how far we agree or disagree with his opinions.

Mr. Stephen, it should be said, is so far from denying this exceptional vitality of Benthamism, that he even puts it forward as an explanation of his cursory treatment of this system. 'The history of utilitarianism as an active force belongs', he tells us, to the new post-revolutionary era, on the threshold of which his plan compels him to stop. This argument would have been sound if Bentham had really been a man of the nineteenth century, born before his time in the eighteenth, and thus naturally not appreciated till later, when the stream of current thought had at length caught him up. Such freaks of nature do sometimes occur, to the very considerable perplexity of the philosophical historian, in his efforts to exhibit a precise and regular development of opinion. But this is so far from being the case with Bentham, that when J. S. Mill, in his most eclectic phase, undertook to balance his claims as a thinker against those of Coleridge, he described the conflict between these two modes of thought as the 'revolt of the nineteenth century against the eighteenth'. The appropriateness of the phrase is surely undeniable. No doubt it is also true, as Mr. Stephen says, that Benthamism as an active force—and Benthamism is nothing if it is *not* an active force—belongs rather to the nineteenth century. It is just because both these views are equally true that Bentham deserves the special attention of the historian of opinion. In England, at least in the department of ethics and politics, Benthamism is the one outcome of the Seculum Rationalisticum against which the philosophy of Restoration and Reaction has had to struggle continually with varying success. It is, we may say, the legacy left to the nineteenth century by the eighteenth; or rather, perhaps, by that innovating and reforming period of the eighteenth century in which Enlightenment became ardent, and strove to consume and recreate. In his most characteristic merits, as well as his most salient defects, Bentham is eminently a representative of this stirring and vehement age: in his unreserved devotion to the grandest and most comprehensive aims, his high and sustained confidence in their attainability, and the buoyant, indefatigable industry with which he sought the means for their attainment—no less than in his exaggerated reliance on his own method, his ignorant contempt for the past, and his intolerant misinterpretation of all that opposed him in the present.

It must be admitted that, though distinctly a child of its age, Benthamism was not exactly a favourite child. The *Fragment on Government* (1776), and the *Principles of Morals and Legislation* (published 1789), had found comparatively few sympathising readers at the time when *Political Justice* and *The Rights of Man* were being greedily bought. At the age of forty-two (1790) Bentham speaks, in a letter to his brother, of 'the slow increase of my school'. Yet we observe very clearly that from the first Bentham appears as a teacher and master of political science—one who has, or ought to have, a 'school'—and is accepted as such by competent judges. In 1778, only two years after the publication of the *Fragment*, D'Alembert writes to him, in the style of the time, as a philosopher and professional benefactor of the human race. Two years later he was taken up by Lord Lansdowne, who seems to have had the eager receptivity for abstract theory which is often found in powerful but imperfectly trained intellects, even after the fullest acquisition of all that experience can teach. The retired statesman bore with really admirable patience the humours of the sensitive and self-conscious philosopher: and in the circle at Bowood Bentham found—besides the one romance of his life—invaluable opportunities for extending his influence as a thinker. It was there that he first met Romilly, the earliest of the band of reformers who, in the next century, attempted the practical realisation of his principles; and there, too, he laid the foundation of his remarkable ascendency over Dumont. The self-devotion with which a man of Dumont's talents and independence of thought allowed himself to be absorbed in the humble function of translating and popularising Bentham was a testimony of admiration outweighing a bushel of complimentary phrases: of which, however, Bentham had no lack, though they came from a somewhat narrow circle. 'The suffrages of the few', writes Dumont in one of his earlier letters, 'will repay you for the indifference of the many . . . Write and bridle my wandering opinions.' Through Dumont he became known to Mirabeau: and a good deal of Benthamite doctrine found its way into that hero's addresses to his constituents, which Dumont assisted in composing. Brissot again, who saw a good deal of Bentham in London, some years before 1789, always spoke and wrote of him with the utmost enthusiasm: to which it may be partly attributed that, in August 1792, a special law of the National Assembly made him (as he tells Wilberforce afterwards) 'an adopted French citizen, third man in the universe after a natural one'; Priestley and Paine being the first two. As soon as Dumont published the *Principes de la Code Civile et Pénale* (1802), expressions of even hyperbolical admiration were sent to the philosopher from different parts of Europe. A Swiss pastor subscribes himself, rather to Bentham's amusement, 'un homme heureux, regéneré par la lecture de vos ouvrages'. A Russian general writes that his book 'fills the soul with peace, the heart with virtue, and dissipates the mists of the mind'; and conjures him to dictate a code to Russia. Another Russian admirer ranks him with Bacon and Newton as the 'creator of a new science', and writes that he is 'laying up a sum for the purpose of spreading the light which emanates' from his writings. Nor is he without similar honour even in his own country. Lord Lansdowne, answering good-humouredly a reproachful epistle of sixty pages, says that it is a letter which 'Bacon might have sent to Buckingham'.

In 1793 a gentleman whom he has asked to dinner writes expressing 'a woman's eagerness to meet a gentleman of so enlightened a mind'. A few years later we find that the great Dr. Parr is never tired of praising his 'mighty talents, profound researches, important discoveries, and irresistible arguments'. On the whole we may say that as even in his revered old age he never attained the kind of popularity that adapts a man's name for utterance on platforms: so even in the earlier part of his career he often met with respect that almost amounted to homage from men more or less influential and representative.

The degree and kind of influence which Bentham exercised in the revolutionary period corresponds tolerably well to the degree of affinity between his teaching and the principles on which the revolutionary movement proceeded. In the combat against prejudices and privileges any ally was welcome; and Bentham was as anxious as any revolutionist to break with the past, and reform all the institutions of society in accordance with pure reason. It is true that, from our point of view, the reason of Bentham appears the perfect antithesis of the reason of Rousseau; but it is very doubtful whether this would have been evident to Rousseau himself. The mainspring of Bentham's life and work, as his French friends saw, was an equal regard for all mankind: whether the precise objects of this regard were conceived as men's 'rights' or their 'interests', was a question which they would not feel to be of primary concern. He himself, indeed, was always conscious of the gulf that separated him from his fellow-citizens by adoption. 'Were they', he writes in 1796, 'to see an analysis I have by me of their favourite Declaration of Rights, there is not perhaps a being upon earth that would be less welcome to them than I could ever hope to be'. But the *Anarchical Fallacies*, like some other fruits of Bentham's labours, remained on the philosopher's shelves till the end of his life; only a meagre fragment of them found its way into Dumont's *Principes*; and by the time that this came out, anarchical theories were somewhat obscured behind military facts. And unless the 'principle of utility' explicitly announced itself as hostile to the fundamental principles of the common revolutionary creed, it certainly would not be generally perceived to be so. I should almost conjecture from what Mr. Stephen says of Bentham, compared with the references to utilitarianism in his discussion of earlier writers, that he has hardly enough recognised that Bentham's originality and importance lay not in his verbal adoption of utility as an end and standard of right political action, but in his real exclusion of any other standard; in the definiteness with which he conceived the 'general good'; the clearness and precision with which he analysed it into its empirically ascertainable constituents; the exhaustive and methodical consistency with which he applied this one standard to all departments of practice; and the rigour with which he kept its application free from all alien elements. Merely to state 'utility' as an ultimate end was nothing; no one would have distinguished this from the 'public good' at which all politicians had always professed to aim, and all revolutionary politicians with special amplitude of phrase. The very Declaration of the National Assembly, that solemnly set forth the maintenance of the 'natural, imprescriptible, and inalienable' rights of man, as the sole end of government, announced in its very first clause, that 'civil distinctions, *therefore*, can be founded only on public utility'. It was not then surprising that Morellet, Brissot, and others, recognising the comprehensiveness of view and clearness of grasp that were so remarkably combined in Bentham's intellect, the equal distribution of his sympathies, and the elevated ardour of his philanthropy, should have hailed him as worthy to 'serve in the cause of liberty'.

And yet the almost comical contrast that we find between Bentham's temper and method in treating political questions, and the habitual sentiments and ideas of his revolutionary friends, could hardly fail to make itself felt by the latter. Let us take, for example, the *Essay on Parliamentary Tactics* which he offered for the guidance of the new Assembly in 1789; and let us imagine a French deputy—a member of the 'Tiers' that has so recently been 'Rien' and is now conscious of itself as 'Tout'—attempting its perusal. He finds in it no word of response to the sentiments that are filling his breast; nothing said of privileged classes whose machinations have to be defeated, in order that the people may realise its will; instead of this, he is met at the outset with an exhaustive statement of the various ways in which he and other servants of the people are liable to shirk or scamp their work, or otherwise to miss attainment of the general good. The object of the treatise, as the author explains, is—

To obviate the inconveniences to which a political assembly is exposed in the exercise of its functions. Each rule of this tactic can therefore have no justifying reason, except in the *prevention of an evil*. It is therefore with a distinct knowledge of these evils that we should proceed in search of remedies. These inconveniences may be arranged under the ten following heads:—

1. Inaction.
2. Useless decision.
3. Indecision.
4. Delays.
5. Surprise or precipitation.
6. Fluctuations in measures.
7. Quarrels.
8. Falsehoods.
9. Decisions, vicious on account of form.
10. Decisions, vicious in respect of their foundation.

We shall develop these different heads in a few words.

Under the head of delays, we find—

may be ranked all vague and useless procedures—preliminaries which do not tend to a decision—questions badly propounded, or presented in a bad order—personal quarrels— witty speeches, and amusements suited to the amphitheatre or the playhouse.

The last and most important head is thus further analysed:

When an assembly form an improper or hurtful decision, it may be supposed that this decision incorrectly represents its wishes. If the assembly be composed as it ought to be, its wish will be conformed to the decision of public utility; and when it wanders from this it will be from one or other of the following causes:—

1. *Absence.*—The general wish of the assembly is the wish of the majority of the total number of its members. But the greater the number of the members who have not been present at its formation, the more doubtful is it whether the wish which is announced as general be really so.
2. *Want of Freedom.*—If any restraint have been exercised over the votes, they may not be conformable to the internal wishes of those who have given them.
3. *Seduction.*—If attractive means have been employed to act upon the wills of the members, it may be that the wish announced may not be conformable to their conscientious wish.
4. *Error.*—If they have not possessed the means of informing themselves—if false statements have been presented to them—their understandings may be deceived, and the wish which has been expressed may not be that which they would have formed had they been better informed.

And so on for page after page of dull and beggarly elements, methodised no doubt in a masterly manner, and calculated to have a highly salutary and sobering effect on the mind of any legislator who can be persuaded to read them. One defect which Bentham is most seriously concerned to cure is the imperfect acquaintance that legislators are liable to have with the motions on which they vote.

'Nothing is more common', he says, 'than to see orators, and even practised orators, falling into involuntary errors with respect to the precise terms of a motion.' This evil, he thinks, may be obviated by 'a very simple mechanical apparatus for exhibiting to the eyes of the assembly the motion on which they are deliberating.'

'We may suppose a gallery above the president's chair, which presents a front consisting of two frames, nine feet high by six feet wide, filled with black canvas, made to open like folding doors;—that this canvas is regularly pierced for the reception of letters of so large a size as to be legible in every part of the place of meeting. These letters might be attached by an iron hook, in such manner that they could not be deranged. When a motion is about to become the object of debate, it would be given to the compositors, who would transcribe it upon the table, and by closing the gallery, exhibit it like a placard to the eyes of the whole assembly.'

One would think that these suggestions were sufficiently particular; but Bentham feels it needful to give a page more of minute directions as to size of letters, method of fixing them, composition of the table, etc.

The salutary working of this machinery is obvious:—

When the orator forgets his subject, and begins to wander, a table of motions offers the readiest means for recalling him. Under the present régime, how is this veil remedied? It is necessary for a member to rise, to interrupt the speaker, and call him to order. This is a provocation—it is a reproach—it wounds his self-love. The orator attacked, defends himself; there is no longer a debate upon the motion, but a discussion respecting the application of his arguments. . . . But if we suppose the table of motions placed above [the president], the case would be very different. He might, without interrupting the speaker, warn him by a simple gesture; and this quiet sign would not be accompanied by the danger of a personal appeal.

The faithful Dumont is unbounded in his eulogy of this 'absolutely new and original' work, which 'fills up one of the blanks of political literature', and reports that Mirabeau and the Duc de la Rochefoucauld admired this 'truly philosophical conception'. Still the reader will hardly be surprised to learn that Morellet thinks it not likely to be appreciated by 'light-minded and unreflecting persons' in the crisis of 1789. Bentham, we feel, must often have appeared to his French friends as a perfect specimen of the cold unsentimental type of Englishman; though with an epistolary prolixity which Sir Charles Grandison could hardly surpass. On one occasion the admiring Brissot cannot repress a murmur at the 'dryness and drollery' with which he responds to sentiment. 'You have then never loved me!' he exclaims,—'me whose sensibilities mingle with legislation itself!' And in truth, though Bentham had plenty of sensibilities beneath his eccentric exterior, he was not in the habit of letting them mingle with legislation.

The above extracts have sufficiently illustrated another marked characteristic of Bentham's work in politics, besides his severe exclusion of fine sentiments: his habit, namely, of working out his suggestions into the minutest details. This tendency he often exhibits in an exaggerated form, so that it becomes repellent or even ridiculous; especially as Bentham, with all his desire to be practical, is totally devoid of the instinctive self-adaptation which most men learn from converse with the world. Still the habit itself is an essential element of the force and originality of his intellectual attitude. 'A man's mind', says the representative scientific man in *Middlemarch*, 'must be continually expanding and shrinking between the whole human horizon and the horizon of an object-glass'. Bentham's mind was continually performing a similar 'systole and diastole'; and thus, in spite of the unduly deductive method that he generally employs, he really resembles the modern man of science in the point in which the latter differs most strikingly from the ancient notion of a philosopher. His apprehension, whether of abstract theory or of concrete fact, has marked limitations; but as regards the portion of human life over which his intellectual vision ranges, he has eyes which can see with equal clearness in the most abstract and the most concrete region; and he as naturally seeks completeness in working out the details of a practical scheme as in defining the most general notions of theoretical jurisprudence. He aims at a perfectly reasoned adaptation of means to ends in constructing a 'frame of motions', no less than in constructing a code of laws; and he passes from the latter to the former without any abatement of interest or any sense of incongruity.

Thus, for twenty years (from 1791 to 1811), while his fame as a philosophical jurist was extending through the civilised world, he was probably better known to the Government at home as belonging to the rather despised class of beings who were then called 'projectors', from his favourite plan of a 'Panopticon' Penitentiary, which was continually urged on their notice by himself and his friends.

Panopticon or Inspection House was a circular building, in which prisoners' cells were to occupy the circumference and keepers the centre, with an intermediate annular wall all the way up, to which the cells were to be laid open by an iron grating. This construction (which with proper modifications could be adapted to a workhouse) fills a much larger space in Bentham's correspondence than all his codes put together. Indeed, among the numerous wrongs, great and small, on which the philosopher in his old age used to dilate with a kind of cheerful acrimony peculiar to himself, there was none which roused so much resentment as the suppression of Panopticon, which he always attributed to a personal grudge on the King's part. He composed a whole volume on 'the war between Jeremy Bentham and George III., by one of the belligerents'. 'But for George III.' the narrative begins, 'all the prisons and all the paupers in England would long ago have been under my management.' For the administration of his prisons he had devised a complete scheme, to the realisation of which he was prepared to devote himself. The expense of prisoners was to have been reduced ultimately to zero by a rigid economy, which yet, when mitigated by the indulgences that were to be earned by extra labour, would only produce about sufficient discomfort to make the punishment deterrent. Idle prisoners were to be fed on potatoes and water *ad lib.*, clothed in coats without shirts, and wooden shoes without stockings, and made to sleep in sacks in order to save the superfluous expense of sheets. Existence being thus reduced to its lowest terms, a means of ameliorating it was provided in a certain share of the profits of industry; and Bentham was sanguine enough to suppose that fifteen hours a day of sedentary labour and muscular exercise combined, could be got out of each prisoner by this stimulus. Contract-management was an essential feature of the scheme; it must be made the manager's interest to extract from his prisoners as much work as he could without injuring them; while the prisoners would be sufficiently protected against the manager's selfishness by the terms of his contract, by the free admission of the public to inspect the prison, and by a fine to be paid for every prisoner's death above a certain average.

The amount of labour that Bentham spent in elaborating the details of this scheme, defending it against all criticisms, urging it on ministers and parliamentary friends, and vituperating all whom he believed to have conspired to prevent its execution, would have alone sufficed to fill the life of a man of more than average energy; while the total disappointment of the hopes of twenty years, after coming within sight of success—for in 1794 Parliament had authorised such a contract as Bentham proposed—would have damped any ordinary philanthropic zeal. But Panopticon and all that belongs to it, including all that he wrote on the Poor Law and Pauper Management, might be subtracted from Bentham's intellectual labours, without materially diminishing the impression produced on the mind by their amount and variety. Nay, even if the whole of his vast work on Law and its administration, including innumerable pamphlets on special points and cases, were left out of sight,—if we knew nothing of Bentham the codifier, or Bentham the radical reformer,—his life would still seem fuller of interests and activities than most men's. Besides his well-known pamphlet in defence of usury, he composed a *Manual of Political Economy*, in which the principles of *laisser-faire* are independently expounded and applied. The Bell and Lancaster method of instruction inspired him to enthusiastic emulation: he immediately planned an unsectarian Chrestomathic day-school to be built in his own garden in Queen's Square Place. The school itself never came into existence; for this, like some other educational schemes, was wrecked on the rock of theology. But Bentham fulfilled his part in composing a *Chrestomathia*, which contained, besides a full and original exposition of pedagogic principles, a sort of manual of geometry, algebra, and physics, and an encyclopaedic discussion of scientific nomenclature and classification. And this is only one striking specimen of his habitual practice. *Quicquid agunt homines*—whatever men do for men's happiness—is certainly the farrago of his inexhaustible MSS. Whatever business suggests to him an idea of amelioration he immediately studies with minute and intense interest, until he believes himself to have perfectly penetrated it by his exhaustive method, and is ready with a completely reasoned scheme of improvement. Currency projects, banking regulations, proposals for an 'unburthensome increase of the revenue', reform of the Thames police, a new mode of taking the census, a device for preventing forgery, a prospect of abolishing the slave-trade, a plan for morally improving Irish labourers in New York—each subject in its turn is discussed with a fresh eagerness and an amplitude of explanation that seem to belong to the leisured amateur of social science. Nor is his attention confined to matters strictly social or political. He is not too much engaged in applying his method of study to expound it in an *Essay on Logic*, supplemented by a characteristic dissertation on Language and Universal Grammar. Chemistry and botany, from their rich promise of utility, are continually attractive to him. He is never too busy to help in experiments which may enrich mankind with a new grass or a new fruit. At one time he is anxious to learn all about laughing gas; at another he corresponds at length about a Frigidarium, in which fermentable substances may be preserved from pernicious fermentation while remaining unfrozen. Nothing seems to him too trivial an object for his restless impulse of amelioration; and he cannot understand why it should seem so to any one else. There is an amusing instance of this in one of his letters to Dumont at the crisis of a negotiation in which the latter, having won Talleyrand's patronage for the *Civil and Penal Codes*, is delicately endeavouring to secure a favourable notice for Panopticon. Dumont has asked his master to send Talleyrand a set of economical and political works. It occurs to Bentham that it will be a stroke of diplomacy to forward along with the books 'a set or two sets of my brother's patent but never-sold fire-irons of which the special and characteristic property is levity'. They would serve, he thinks, 'as a specimen of the Panopticon system. One might be kept by T. (Talleyrand), the other, if he thought fit, passed on to B. (Bonaparte).' Even the sympathetic Dumont declines to extend his interest to patent fire-irons, and coldly intimates that he is 'not familiar with such instruments'. The humblest games, we find, are not unworthy of utilitarian consideration, and may be treated in the same confident deductive fashion as governments. At Ford Abbey—where Bentham lived from 1814 to 1817, and where the youthful J. S. Mill found the 'sentiment of a larger and freer existence' in the 'middle-age architecture, baronial hall, and spacious and lofty rooms'—battledores and shuttlecocks were kept in frequent exercise; and any tendency in manufacturers to deviate from the true type of shuttlecock was severely repressed. 'Pointed epigrams, yes,' writes the philosopher; 'but pointed shuttlecocks never were, nor ever will be, good for anything. These, it is true, have not been tried; but trial is not necessary to the condemnation of such shuttlecocks as these.' Bentham was strictly temperate in his diet: he ate meat but once a day, and then very moderately, and was almost a teetotaller. But the pleasures of the table were too important to be diminished by a stupid adherence to custom; and being particularly fond of fruit, he used often to maximise his prandial happiness by commencing with the dessert, before the sensibility of his palate had been impaired by coarser viands.

I have dwelt at some length on this side of Bentham's character, because it seems to me that we get the right point of view for understanding his work in politics and ethics, if we conceive it as the central and most important realisation of a dominant and all-comprehensive desire for the amelioration of human life, or rather of sentient existence generally. A treatise on deontology, a code, an inspection-house, a set of fire-irons, may all be regarded as instruments more or less rationally contrived for the promotion of happiness; and it is exclusively in this light that Bentham regards them. Thus, perhaps, we may partly account for the extreme unreadableness of his later writings, which are certainly 'biblia abiblia'. The best defence for them is that they are hardly meant to be criticised as books; they were written not so much to be read as to be used. Hence if, after they were written, he saw no prospect of their producing a practical effect, he kept them contentedly on his shelves for a more seasonable opportunity. In his earlier compositions he shows considerable literary faculty: his argument is keen and lucid, and his satirical humour often excellent, though liable to be too prolix. But the fashion in which he really liked to express his thoughts was the proper style of legal documents—a style, that is, in which there are no logically superfluous words, but in which everything that is intended is fully expressed, and the most tedious iteration is not shunned if it is logically needed for completeness and precision. And as years went on, and Dumont saved him the necessity of making himself popular, he gave full scope to his peculiar taste. Such a manner of expression has indeed a natural affinity to the fullness of detail with which his subjects are treated. But the tedium caused by the latter is necessarily aggravated by the former; and therefore the 'general reader' has to be warned off from most of Bentham's volumes; or perhaps such warning is hardly needed. Those, how-ever, who study him as he would have wished to be studied, not for literary gratification, but for practical guidance, will feel that his fatiguing exhaustiveness of style and treatment has great advantages. It to some extent supplies the place of empirical tests to his system; at least, whatever dangers lurk in his abstract deductive method of dealing with human beings, we certainly cannot include among them the 'dolus' which 'latet in generalibus'. If in establishing his prac-tical principles he has neglected any important element of human nature, we are almost certain to feel the deficiency in the concrete result which his indefatig-able imagination works out for us. Often, indeed, the danger rather is that we shall be unduly repelled by the mere strangeness of the habits and customs of the new social organisation into which he transports us.

Thus from different points of view one might truly describe Bentham as one of the *most* or the *least* idealistic of practical philosophers. What is, immediately suggests to him what ought to be; his interest in the former is never that of pure curiosity, but always subordinated to his purpose of producing the latter; there is no department of the actual that he is not anxious to reconstruct systematically on rational principles, and so in a certain sense to inform and penetrate with ideas. While again his ideal is, to borrow a phrase of John Grote's, as much as pos-sible *de-idealised*, positivised, some might say philistinised, his good is purged of all mystical elements, and reduced to the positive, palpable, empirical, definitely quantitative notion of 'maximum balance of pleasure over pain'; and his concep-tion of human nature and its motives—the material which he has to adapt to the attainment of this good—is not only un-ideal, but even anti-ideal, or idealised in the wrong direction. While he is as confident in his power of constructing a happy society as the most ardent believer in the moral perfectibility of mankind, he is as convinced of the unqualified selfishness of the vast majority of human beings as the bitterest cynic. Hence the double aspect of his utilitarianism, which has caused so much perplexity both to disciples and to opponents. It is as if Hobbes or Mandeville were suddenly inspired with the social enthusiasm of Godwin. Something of the same blending of contraries is found in Helvetius; and he, perhaps, rather than Hume, should be taken as the intellectual progenitor of Bentham. In Helvetius, however, though utilitarianism is passing out of the critical and explanatory phase in which we find it in Hume, into the practical and reforming phase, the transition is not yet complete. Still the premisses of Bentham are all clearly given by Helvetius; and the task which the former took up is that which the latter clearly marks out for the moralist. Indeed, if we imagine the effect of *L'Esprit* on the mind of an eager young law-student, we seem to have the whole intellectual career of Bentham implicitly contained in a 'pensée de jeunesse'.

Helvetius puts with a highly effective simplicity, from which Hume was precluded by his more subtle and complex psychological analysis, these two doctrines: first, that every human being 'en tout temps, en tout lieu' seeks his own interest, and judges of things and persons according as they promote it: and secondly, that, as the public is made up of individuals, the qualities that naturally and normally gain public esteem and are called virtues are those useful to the public. Observation, he says, shows us that there are a few men who are inspired by 'un heureux naturel, un désir vif de la gloire et de l'estime', with the same passion for justice and virtue which men generally feel for wealth and greatness. The actions which promote the private interest of these virtuous men are actions that are just, and conducive, or not contrary, to the general interest. But these men are so few that Helvetius only mentions them 'pour l'honneur de l'humanité'. The human race is almost entirely composed of men whose care is concentrated on their private interests. How, under these circumstances, are we to promote virtue? for which Helvetius really seems to be genuinely concerned, though he is too well bred to claim for himself expressly so exceptional a distinction. It is clear, he thinks, that the work will not be done by moralists, unless they completely change their methods. 'Qu'ont produit jusqu'aujourd'hui les plus belles maximes de la morale?' Our moralists do not perceive that it is a futile endeavour, and would be dangerous if it were not futile, to try to alter the tendency of men to seek their private happiness. They might perhaps gain some influence if they would substitute the 'langage d'intérêt' for the 'ton d'injure' in which they now utter their maxims; for a man might then be led to abstain at least from such vices as are prejudicial to himself. But for the achievement of really important results the moralist must have recourse to legislation. This is a conclusion which Helvetius is never tired of enforcing. 'One ought not to complain of the wickedness of man, but of the ignorance of legislators who have always set private interest in opposition to public.' 'The hidden source of a people's vices is always in its legislation; it is there that we must search if we would discover and extirpate their roots.' 'Moralists ought to know that as the sculptor fashions the trunk of a tree into a god or a stool, so the legislator makes heroes, geniuses, virtuous men, as he wills: . . . reward, punishment, fame, disgrace, are four kinds of divinities with which he can always effect the public good.' In short, Helvetius conceives that universal self-preference might by legislative machinery be so perfectly harmonised with public utility that 'none but madmen would be vicious': it only wants a man of insight and courage, 'échauffé de la passion du bien général', to effect this happy consummation.

Such, then, was the task that Bentham, at the age of twenty-five, undertook; and perhaps his bitterest opponent, surveying his sixty years of strenuous performance, will hardly blame him severely for presumption in deeming himself to possess the requisite qualifications. The young Englishman, indeed, with his faith in our 'matchless constitution' as yet unshaken, conceives himself to be in an exceptionally favourable position for realising this union of morals and legislation. 'France', he writes in his commonplace-book for 1774–75, 'may have philosophers. The world is witness if she have not philosophers. But it is England only that can have patriots, for a patriot is a philosopher in action.' Such a 'philosopher in action' might hope not merely to delineate, but actually to set on foot that reformation in the moral world which could only come from improvement in the machine of law. But in the moral no less than in the physical world one cannot improve a machine without understanding it; the study of it as it exists must be separated from the investigation of what it ought to be, and the former must be thoroughly performed before the latter can be successfully attempted. This is to us so obvious a truism that it seems pedantic to state it expressly; but it is a truism which Bentham found as much as possible obscured in Blackstone's famous *Commentaries*. The first thing then which he had to do was to dispel that confusion between the expository and the censorial functions of the jurist, which seemed to be inherent in the official account of the laws and constitution of England. The clearness and completeness with which this is done are the chief merits of the *Fragment on Government*. In this elaborate attack on Blackstone's view of municipal law Bentham does not as yet criticise the particulars either of the British constitution or of British administration of justice: his object is merely to supply the right set of notions for apprehending what either actually is, together with the right general principles for judging of its goodness or badness. His fundamental idea is taken, as he says, from Hume; but the methodical precision with which it is worked out is admirable; in fact, the *Fragment* contains the whole outline of that system of formal constitutional jurisprudence which the present generation has mostly learnt from his disciple John Austin. Among other things we may notice as characteristic the manner in which he throws aside the official nonsense about the 'democratic element' in the unreformed British Parliament, which half imposed even on the clear intellect of Paley. 'A duke's son', he says, 'gets a seat in the House of Commons; it needs no more to make him the very model of an Athenian cobbler.' In a similar spirit he banters Blackstone's account of the 'wisdom and valour' for which our lords temporal are selected. He remarks that in Queen Anne's reign, in the year 1711, 'not long after the time of the hard frost', there seems to have been such an exuberance of these virtues as to 'furnish merit enough to stock no fewer than a dozen respectable persons, who upon the strength of it were all made barons in a day'; a phenomenon, he adds, which a contemporary historian has strangely attributed to the necessity of making a majority. It is evident that whatever constitution Bentham may prefer, he will not be put off by any conventional fictions as to the relations of its parts; his preference will depend entirely on what he believes to be their actual working.

More than thirty years, however, were to elapse before Bentham seriously turned his attention to constitutional construction. Indeed nothing is more characteristic of the Benthamite manner of thought, in its application to politics, than the secondary and subordinate position to which it relegates the constitutional questions that absorbed the entire attention of most English politicians of the eighteenth century. Such politicians, even when most theoretical, seem to have had no notion that the political art properly includes a systematic survey of the whole operation of government, and a thorough grasp of the principles by which that operation should be judged and rectified. Their philosophy was made up of metaphysico-jural dissertations on the grounds and limits of civil obedience, and loose historical generalisations as to the effects of the 'three simple forms' of government, conceived as chemical elements out of which the British constitution was compounded. What they habitually discussed was not how laws should be made or executed, but what the terms of the social compact were, and whether the balance between Crown and Commons could be maintained without corruption. It is perhaps some survival in Mr. Stephen's mind of this now antiquated way of viewing politics which has led him, while speaking respectfully of Bentham's labours in the sphere of jurisprudence, to refer so slightly to him in describing the course of political thought. And no doubt Bentham's determination to maintain a purely and exhaustively practical treatment in all his writings on law and its administration, render it almost necessary to leave the greater part of his work to the criticism of professional experts. But the general principles by which the whole course of his industry was guided; that government is merely an organisation for accomplishing a very complicated and delicate work, of which the chief part consists in preventing, by the threatened infliction of pain or damage for certain kinds of conduct, some more than equivalent pain or loss of happiness resulting from that conduct to some of the governed; that the primary end of the political art is to secure that this work shall be done in the best possible way with the utmost possible precision and the least possible waste of means; and that the rules controlling the appointment and mutual relations of different members of the government should be considered and determined solely with a view to this end,—these were surely worth mentioning among political theories. For it is this fundamental creed that has given Benthamism its vitality; when once these principles were clearly and firmly apprehended by a man with the 'infinite capacity for taking trouble' which has been said to constitute genius, though the eighteenth century, ideally speaking, was not yet over, the nineteenth had certainly begun. A theory that is exclusively positive and unmetaphysical, at the same time that it is still confidently deductive and unhistorical, forms the natural transition from the 'Age of Reason' to the period of political thought in which we are now living.

When we consider that Bentham's early manhood coincided with the intensest period of revolutionary fervour, and that he was in close personal relations with some influential Frenchmen of this age, it seems a remarkable evidence of his intellectual independence that he should have so long kept his attention turned away from constitutional reform. Probably the aversion he felt for the metaphysics in which the conception of rational and beneficent government seemed to be commonly entangled, co-operated to concentrate his attention on that department of reform in which alone he felt himself in full sympathy with the party of movement. At the outset of the American war he was altogether hostile to the colonists, owing to the 'hodge-podge of confusion and absurdity' which he found in their Declaration of Rights. Six years later he was content to regard the English constitution as 'resting at no very great distance, perhaps, from the summit of perfection'. In 1789 he went so far with his French friends as to offer the cause of liberty his treatise on Parliamentary Tactics. Still, as we have seen, the dry practicality of this dissertation could hardly be surpassed; it does not touch on a single 'burning question' except Division of Chambers, which it treats very abstractly and neutrally. In 1793 whatever sympathy he may have felt for the revolutionists had quite vanished. 'Could the extermination of Jacobinism be effected', he writes to his cousin Metcalf, 'I should think no price that we could pay for such a security too dear'; and about the same time he tells Dundas that though some of the MSS. he sends him might 'lead to his being taken for a republican', he is 'now writing against even Parliamentary Reform, and that without any change of sentiment'. It is evident that he is thoroughly absorbed in schemes of legislative and administrative improvement: his interest in the French Revolution was due to the unexampled opportunity it seemed to offer for new codes, new judicial establishments, Panopticons, etc.; he has no desire to quarrel with the English Tory Government if it will find employment for his inventions in this line. Until 1791 he seems to have hoped that Lord Lansdowne would place him in Parliament; he even obtained a vague promise to that effect, though for some reason or other the idea was afterwards dropped. Then during the twenty years (from 1791 to 1811) in which Panopticon was in suspense, he would naturally shrink from risking its prospects by any open breach with the Government. Still it is pretty clear that his opinion of the practical efficiency of the Matchless Constitution was growing rapidly worse during the latter part of this period, until in 1809 he wrote his first plan of Parliamentary Reform. This, however, remained unpublished till 1817; and in a letter to President Madison in 1811, in which he proposes to codify for the United States, he takes care to say that 'his attention has not turned and is not disposed to turn itself' to changes in the form of their government. Indeed, since the enthusiastic reception which his Civil and Penal Codes, in Dumont's rendering, had met with throughout Europe, his hopes of benefiting the human race by codification had taken so wide a range as almost necessarily to keep him neutral even towards the most despotic kind of rule. In no country was this reception more enthusiastic than in Russia. Accordingly in 1814, Panopticon being finally suppressed, and code-making being in hand in

Russia, Bentham considers that the time has come to offer his services for this purpose. The Emperor, with every expression of courtesy and respect, requests him to communicate with the Commission that is sitting on legislation. But this seems to him useless. Alone he must do it; and he somewhat sourly rejects all compliments not accompanied with legislative *carte blanche*. When he is convinced that he cannot be employed on these conditions, his last reason for keeping terms with the traditional forms of government would seem to have vanished; and he prepares, when already verging on threescore and ten, to crown the edifice of his jurisprudence with a Constitutional Code.

It is not often that an energetic practical philanthropist throws himself into constitutional reform at the age of sixty-eight. When he does so, it is likely to be with the accumulated bitterness resulting from a lifetime of baffled attempts to benefit his fellow-men under their existing constitution. And all that Bentham writes after 1817 is full of the heated and violent democratic fanaticism which is incident to the youth of many Liberals who in later years become 'tempered by renouncement', but which, as we have seen, was conspicuously absent from the earlier stages of Bentham's political activity. No doubt this may be partly attributed to the spirit of the time. From 1817 to 1830 the tide of Liberalism was rapidly rising, and the flavour of the rising Liberalism was peculiarly bitter. Still a man of sixty-eight is not usually carried away by an upsurging wave of opinion; and we can hardly explain Bentham's mood without taking into account the acrimony of the disappointed projector. It is the persistent rejection of Panopticon and many other fair schemes which has inspired him with so intense a conviction that governments of One or Few invariably aim at the depredation and oppression of the Many. He tells us himself, in the 'historical preface' (published 1828) intended for the second edition of the *Fragment on Government*, that it is only after the experience and observation of fifty years that he has learnt to see in the imperfections of the British constitution 'the elaborately organised and anxiously cherished and guarded products of sinister interest and artifice'. Had George III., any time between 1793 and 1811, made peace with Panopticon, had Alexander in 1814 allowed free play to the great codifier's energies, the Constitutional Code, we may well believe, would have remained unwritten, and the philosophy of modern English Radicalism would have acknowledged a different founder.

And yet, when we examine the rational basis of his constitutional construction, whether as given in the introduction to his *Plan of Parliamentary Reform* (1817), or more fully and characteristically developed in the elaborate work just mentioned, we find that it consists in a few very natural inferences from the ethical and psychological premises on which his whole social activity proceeded; inferences, indeed, so simple and obvious, that we can hardly suppose him not to have tacitly drawn them, even in the earliest stage of his career. If once we regard the administration of law as a machinery indispensable for identifying the interest of individuals with the conduct by which they will most promote the general happiness, so that through a skilful adjustment of rewards and punishments the universally active force of self-preference is made to produce the results at which universal benevolence would aim, it is plain that our arrangements are incomplete unless they include means for similarly regulating the self-preferences of those who are to work and repair the machine. And this, of course, must be done by a combination of rewards and punishments; the problem is, how to apply these so as to produce an adequate effect. It is obviously a far more difficult problem than that with which Bentham had to deal in regulating private relations. For what the private man, in his view, has for the most part to *do*, in order to promote the general happiness, is to consult the interests of himself and his family; whatever private services it is desirable he should render to others should rarely be made legally obligatory, except when he has freely bound himself by special and definite contracts. But from governors, if government is to be well performed, we require the energetic and sustained exercise of all their faculties in the service of their fellow-citizens generally—even more sustained energy than most men spend on their own affairs, in proportion as government is a more difficult business; while at the same time this business is of such a nature that it is necessary to give the managers of it an indefinite power of interfering with the liberty, property, and even life of their fellow-citizens generally. For to set definite limits to this power in the prescriptions of a constitutional code is, from a utilitarian point of view, manifestly irrational. The only rational limits—those which utility would prescribe in any case—cannot be foreseen and fixed once for all; hence any such constitutional restrictions, if observed, are likely to prevent salutary laws and ordinances as well as mischievous ones; while, if they are to be overruled by the 'salus populi', their announcement was worse than useless—it was an express incitement to groundless rebellion. The only plan that remains, and the only one that can possibly secure the requisite junction of interests, is to provide that government, while supreme over individuals, shall be under the continual vigilant control of the citizens acting collectively. Every citizen who is not childish, insane, etc., should *primâ facie* have a share in this control, otherwise his interests will presumably be neglected; and every one an equal share, in so far as we have no ground for considering one man's happiness of more importance than any other man's.

We are thus led to the familiar system of Representative Democracy, with universality and equality of suffrage; but, be it observed, without any of the metaphysical fictions which had commonly been involved in the construction of this system. Bentham's system is not a contrivance for enabling every one to 'obey himself alone': such an end would have seemed to him chimerical and absurd: it is merely an arrangement for securing that every one's interests shall be as well as possible looked after. To this difference of *rationale* corresponds naturally a difference of constitutional sentiment. Bentham's supreme legislative assembly is not a majestic incarnation of the sovereignty of the people; it is merely a collection of agents, appointed by the people to manage a certain part of their concerns, liable, like other agents, to legal punishment if they can be proved to have violated their trust, and to instant dismissal if it seem probable that they have done so.

Another important difference appears at once in comparing the *rationale* of utilitarian democracy with that based on natural rights. The former, however dogmatically it may be announced, depends necessarily upon certain psychological generalisations, the truth of which may be continually brought to the test of experience. Between traditional legitimacy and natural freedom there was no common ground, and therefore really no argument possible. If I maintain that I and my fellow-citizens have an imprescriptible right to be governed only by laws to which we have consented, I can find no relevancy in the answer that certain persons have inherited a prescriptive right to govern me. But if I maintain that our common interests are most likely to be well looked after by managers whom we can dismiss, however confident I may be in my deduction of this probability from the 'universality of self-preference', I must admit arguments from experience tending to prove the opposite. And when these are once admitted, the descent from the position of Bentham and James Mill, that democracy is absolutely desirable, to John Stuart Mill's relative and qualified assertion of its desirability, is logically inevitable; though, like many other logically inevitable steps, it took a generation to make it.

The chief peculiarities, however, in the main outline of Bentham's constitution are due not to his conception of the political end, but to his intense sense of the need of guarding his government against the danger of perversion: a danger which democrats of the older type, from their confidence in ordinary human nature, had commonly overlooked. If the oppressions of kings and aristocrats are connected with the prevalence of prejudice and superstition, it is natural to suppose that when these are removed the business of government is as likely to go on well as any other business. But in Bentham's view governors, under however enlightened a constitution, will be ordinary human beings exposed to extraordinary temptations, to which, therefore, we must presume that they will certainly yield unless very exceptional securities are provided. All the members of government will have natural appetites for power, wealth, dignity, ease at the expense of duty, vengeance at the expense of justice, which are obviously all forces acting in the direction opposed to the general happiness. And since for the exercise of their normal functions governors, or at least the chief among them, must have power not definitely limited, and must have at their disposal a similarly indefinite amount of wealth, it cannot but be profoundly difficult to prevent them from satiating—if it be possible to satiate—all their mischievous appetites. To set one part of government to watch another will avail little: corrupt mutual connivance is too obviously their common interest. The utmost frequency in the elections of the members of the legislative assembly is a desirable, but not an adequate security: it will be the interest of each legislator to corrupt his leading constituents by patronage, and it will be their interest to be corrupted; and the claim of experience which the sitting member can put forward will be so plausible that it will be easy for the leading constituents to hoodwink the rest. How then shall we prevent legislators, administrators, and leading constituents from being thus driven by the combined force of their self-preferences into a conspiracy against the general happiness? We must do what we can by 'minimising confidence and maximising control', through the concentration of responsibility, together with arrangements for securing to the public easy and complete cognisance of all official acts. We must 'minimise the matter of corruption' by continually keeping down the amount of wealth and power disposable by each official: in order to reduce salaries, Bentham proposes to institute a pecuniary competition among the properly qualified candidates for any office, on the principle of choosing the man who will take least, or perhaps will even pay, to perform its functions. We must render bargains with electors difficult by secret voting. But, above all, we must be in a position to stamp out the virus of corruption as soon as it appears by immediately dismissing—or, as he prefers to say, 'dislocating'—the peccant official. He considers that direct 'location' by the people is incompatible with good government, except in the case of members of the legislature; even the appointment of the head of the executive, who has to make or sanction other administrative appointments, he would give to the supreme assembly; but 'universal dislocability' by a vote of the majority of citizens seems to him absolutely indispensable: all other securities will be inadequate without this.

After all is done, the readers of the *Constitutional Code* will probably feel that, when Helvetius proposed to ardent philanthropy the noble task of moralising selfish humanity by legislation, he had not sufficiently considered the difficulty of moralising the moralisers, and that even the indefatigable patience and inexhaustible ingenuity of Bentham will hardly succeed in defeating the sinister conspiracy of self-preferences. In fact, unless a little more sociality is allowed to an average human being, the problem of combining these egoists into an organisation for promoting their common happiness is like the old task of making ropes of sand. The difficulty that Hobbes vainly tried to settle summarily by absolute despotism is hardly to be overcome by the democratic artifices of his more inventive successor.

Bentham's final treatise on politics was never absolutely completed. Only about one half had been printed or revised for the press when his long career of intellectual toil was terminated. On the 6th of June 1832, there remained for the indefatigable old man but one last contribution to the balance of human happiness, which was faithfully rendered: to 'minimise the pain' of the watchers round his dying bed. His treatise on private ethics, or, as he calls it, *Deontology* (the place of which in his system had been indicated fifty years before in his *Treatise on*

Morals and Legislation), was left a mere mass of undigested fragments. The task of preparing it for publication was, however, at once undertaken by Bowring, the favourite disciple of the master's later years; and so much of Bentham's work had been given to the world through the medium of a disciple, that there seemed no reason why the *Deontology* should not take rank with *The Civil and Penal Codes* as a generally trustworthy exposition of Benthamite doctrine. But the book had no sooner appeared than it was formally repudiated by that section of the school whose opinions were likely to have most weight with the public. J. S. Mill, writing [in] August 1838, in the *London and Westminster Review*, urged that, considering its dubious origin and intrinsic demerits together, it should be omitted from any collected edition of Bentham's works; its demerits being that instead of 'plunging boldly into the greater moral questions', it treated almost solely of 'the *petite morale*, and that with pedantic minuteness, and on the *quid pro quo* principles which regulate trade'. That the *Deontology* corresponds to this description is undeniable; the only question is whether a disciple of Bentham's ought to have been surprised at it. The surprise, at any rate, is a phenomenon demanding explanation; for Bentham is not a Hegel, to be understood by one disciple only, and misunderstood by him; he is commonly liable to be wearisome from obtrusive consistency, and unreadable from an excessive desire to be unmistakable.

The truth is that an ethical system constructed on Bentham's principles is an instrument that may be put to several different uses; so that it is not unnatural that his disciples, employing and developing it each in his own way, should insensibly be led to widely divergent views as to the really essential characteristics of the master's doctrine. The theory of virtue which he received from Helvetius has two aspects, psychological and ethical. Psychologically analysed, common morality appears as a simple result of common selfishness. 'Each man likes and approves what he thinks useful to him; the public (which is merely an aggregate of individuals) likes and praises what it thinks useful to the public; that is the whole account of virtue.' How, on this theory, men's moral judgments come to agree as much as they actually do is not sufficiently explained; and in any case there is no rational transition possible from this psychological theory to the ethical principle that 'the standard of rectitude for all actions' is 'public utility'. Nor does Bentham really maintain that there is: when he is pressed, he explains frankly that his first principle is really his individual sentiment; that, in fact, he aims at the general happiness because he happens to prefer it. Still, for all practical purposes, he does accept 'greatest happiness'[1] as (to use his own words) 'a plain as well as true standard for whatever is right or wrong, useful, useless, or mischievous in human conduct, whether in the field of morals or of politics'. The

---

[1] The phrase which he used during the greater part of his life, and which has become current—'The greatest happiness of the greatest number'—he found, at the age of twenty-two, in an early pamphlet of Priestley's. In the *Deontology*, however, he proposes to drop the latter half of the phrase, as superfluous and liable to misinterpretation.

primary function, then, of the utilitarian[2] moralist is to apply this standard to the particulars of human life, so as to determine by it the different special virtues or rules of duty, so far as such determination is possible in general terms; and, in fact, several of the fragments put together in the *Deontology* were written with this aim. But suppose this has been accomplished, and the code of duty clearly made out: we have still to ask what the exact use of it will be. It will, of course, give a complete practical guidance to persons whose ruling passion is a desire to promote universal happiness; but Bentham, no less than Helvetius, regards such persons as so exceptional that it would be hardly worth while to print a book for them. What, then, is the relation of the utilitarian moralist to the great mass of mankind, in whose breasts universal benevolence holds no such irresistible sway? This is the practically important question. One answer to it is that given by Paley (and afterwards by John Austin), which treats the rules of utilitarian duty as a code of Divine Law, adequately supported by religious sanctions. Such an answer avoids some of the objections to utilitarianism, at the cost, perhaps, of introducing greater ones; but in any case it is not Bentham's, though it is not expressly excluded by him. If we put this aside, there remain two entirely different ways of dealing with the question, each of which, from a utilitarian point of view, is perfectly appropriate. In the first place, the code as above deduced may be offered to mankind as a standard for rectifying their ordinary judgments of approbation and disapprobation, clearing them from a certain amount of confusion and conflict which now perplexes them, and so increasing their beneficent effect. Even if few persons are sufficiently benevolent to take the general happiness as the one ultimate end of their own conduct, it may still be generally accepted as a standard for apportioning praise and blame to others; and much would be gained for the general happiness if the whole force of these powerful motives could be turned in the direction of promoting it. In all Bentham says of the 'moral sanction' in his *Morals and Legislation*, this conception of morality as a system of distributing praise and blame is implied; and such, I gather, was the view taken by James Mill of the practical function of the utilitarian moralist (except in so far as his associational psychology led him to recognise the love of virtue as a distinct though derivative impulse). But this view, though not absent from the *Deontology*, is certainly not prominent there; and it is plain from Bentham's earlier treatise[3] that he conceived 'private ethics' not merely as an art of praising and blaming, but rather as an art of conduct generally, from the individual's point of view—'art of self-government' he calls it. But in counselling individuals Bentham thought, like Helvetius, that it was useless to 'clamour about duty'; the only effective way of persuading a man to its performance was to show him its coincidence with

[2] J. S. Mill tells us in his *Autobiography* that he introduced this term into currency from one of Galt's novels. It was, however, suggested by Bentham, in a letter to Dumont in June 1802, as preferable to 'Benthamite'.

[3] Cf. esp. c. xix. of the *Principles of Morals and Legislation*, §§ 2, 3, 6, 7.

interest. In such a demonstration the pleasures of pure benevolence are, of course, not neglected: but he obviously cannot lay much stress on them. Hence the necessity for the '*quid pro quo*' treatment of which Mill complains. The erroneousness of the estimate which the vicious man makes of pains and pleasures has to be shown in every possible way; honesty has to be exhibited as the best policy, extra-regarding beneficence as an investment in a sort of bank of general good-will, etc. We can see at the same time why, from this point of view, the *petite morale* is so prominent. For the more important part of the coincidence between interest and duty it belongs to the legislator to effect and enforce; and his share of the code ought to be written, to use a Platonic image, in large print, needing no comment; the moralist's task is to decipher and exhibit the minor supplementary prescriptions of duty. And that Bentham, when he had once undertaken this task, should have performed it with a 'minuteness' which a hostile critic might call 'pedantic', can hardly have surprised any one so familiar with his works as Mill was.

So far, I think, there can be no doubt that Bowring has given us the genuine Bentham, and that the faithful historian must refuse to follow Mill in rejecting the *Deontology*. But it is one thing to hold that the moralist ought chiefly to occupy himself in showing men how much of their happiness is bound up with their duty: it is quite another thing to maintain that the two notions are universally coincident in experience, and that (from a purely mundane point of view) 'vice may be defined to be a miscalculation of chances'. This latter is the ground implicitly taken throughout the greater part of the *Deontology*, and expressly in one or two passages. No doubt the step to this from the former position is a very natural one for an enthusiastic and not very clear-headed disciple; for if it is tenable, the moralist's task can be much more triumphantly achieved. But that Bentham himself would ever have deliberately maintained this position is very difficult to believe. Certainly in the passage of his earlier treatise above referred to, where he defines the relation of 'private ethics' to legislation, he distinctly avoids taking it. 'It cannot but be admitted', he says, 'that the only interests which a man at all times and on all occasions is sure to find adequate motives for consulting are his own'. All he can maintain is that 'there are no occasions on which he has not *some* motives for consulting the happiness of other men'. And with his purely practical view of the moralist's function, he would naturally, in writing his notes for the *Deontology*, exhibit these motives without dwelling on their occasional inadequacy, and would thus encourage his editor to take the critical step from the actual to the ideal, and assert that they are always adequate. But if, as we have seen, the author of the *Principles of Morals and Legislation* shrank from asserting this, we can hardly suppose that the author of the *Constitutional Code* had seen reason to change his mind. For if it is always every man's interest, on a rational computation of chances, to promote the general happiness, what becomes of his anti-monarchical and anti-oligarchical deductions from the principle of self-preference? It may of course be said that monarchs and oligarchs may and do mistake their true interests. But Bentham's argument goes far beyond this. He repeatedly states it as certain and inevitable that, without such artificial junction of interests as is provided by the *Constitutional Code*, governors will sacrifice the happiness of the governed to their own appetites for power, wealth, ease, and revenge. There are some inconsistencies so flagrant that even a philosopher should be held innocent of them till he is proved guilty; and to hold the serene optimism of the *Deontology* as to human relations generally, together with the bitter pessimism of the *Constitutional Code* as to the relation of rulers and subjects, would surely be an inconsistency of this class.*

At the same time I must admit that there were other utilitarians besides Bowring who did not perceive the incongruity, and that even after it had been explained to them by a writer who generally succeeded in making his explanations pretty clear. In the famous passage of arms between the *Edinburgh* and the *Westminster* in 1829–30, Macaulay no doubt ventured into a region where he was not altogether at home; still his clear common sense, wide knowledge of historical facts, and a dialectical vigour and readiness which few philosophers could afford to despise, rendered him by no means ill matched even against James Mill; in fact, both combatants, on the ground on which they met, were better equipped for offensive than for defensive warfare; and if the author of the *Essay on Government* had himself replied to his assailant, the conflict would probably have been bloody, but indecisive. But when Macaulay's article came out, the split between Bowring and the Mills had taken place, and the management of the *Westminster* had passed into the hands of Colonel Perronet Thompson, who accepted to the full Bowring's view of utilitarian ethics, and in fact regarded the coincidence of utilitarian duty with self-interest properly understood as

---

* [The editors of the *Miscellaneous Essays and Addresses* added on p. 374 of that work a note to be inserted at this place. The note reads as follows: [In the preface to the third edition of his *Outlines of the History of Ethics*, published in 1892, Professor Sidgwick says: 'I have . . . changed my opinion on a point of some importance in the history of Utilitarianism: I am now disposed to accept the posthumously published *Deontology* of Bentham, as giving a generally trustworthy account of his view as to the relation of Virtue to the virtuous agent's Happiness.' And on p. 244 of the same work he says: 'In the *Deontology* . . . it is distinctly assumed that, in actual human life as empirically known, the conduct most conducive to general happiness *always* coincides with that which conduces most to the happiness of the agent; and that "vice may be defined as a miscalculation of chances" from a purely mundane point of view. And it seems probable that this must be accepted as Bentham's real doctrine, in his later days; since he certainly held that the "constantly proper end of action on the part of every individual at the moment of action is his real greatest happiness from that moment to the end of life," without retracting his unqualified acceptance of the "greatest happiness of the greatest number" as a "plain but true standard for whatever is right and wrong in the field of morals" (see Bentham's *Works*, vol. x (*Life*), pp. 560, 561, and 79); and the assumption just mentioned is required to reconcile these two convictions, if the empirical basis on which his whole reasoning proceeds is maintained.'—Ed.] Although the editors don't, we should note that Sidgwick adds: '. . . since it is at least very difficult, in the actual conditions of human society, to give adequate empirical proof of this universal harmony of interests, it is not surprising that several of Bentham's disciples have endeavoured to avoid this mode of supplying the gap in his system. . . .'.]

Bentham's cardinal doctrine. Colonel Thompson was a writer of no mean talents, and if he had only had to defend his own view of the 'greatest happiness principle' he might have come off with tolerable success. Unfortunately the conditions of the controversy rendered it incumbent on him to defend James Mill's at the same time; and against the compound doctrine that it is demonstrably the interest of kings and aristocracies to govern well, and yet demonstrably certain that they will never think so, Macaulay's rejoinder was delivered with irresistible force.

Macaulay's articles had other consequences, more important than that of exhibiting the ambiguities of the greatest happiness principle. His spirited criticism of the deductive politics of James Mill, though it was treated with contempt by its object, had a powerful effect on the more impartial and impressible mind of the younger Mill; and the new views of utilitarian method which were afterwards propounded in the latter's *Logic of the Moral Sciences*[4] owe their origin in some measure to the diatribes of the *Edinburgh*. If space allowed, it would be interesting to trace the changes that Bentham's system underwent in the teaching of his most distinguished successor, under the combined influences of Comtian sociology, Associational psychology, and Neo-Baconian logic. But such an undertaking would carry us far beyond the limits of the present historical sketch, and right into the midmost heats of contemporary controversy.

[4] *Cf.* J. S. Mill's *Logic*, Bk. vi. cc. vii. viii.; and his *Autobiography*, p. 158.

25. Mr. Spencer's Ethical System

The aim of Mr. Herbert Spencer's recently published book on the *Data of Ethics* is, as the author tells us in his preface, 'the establishment of rulès of right conduct on a scientific basis'. And though the volume itself is not a complete treatise on the subject to which it relates—being, in fact, only the first division of such a treatise—it claims to imply the specific conclusions to be set forth in the entire work 'in such wise that definitely to formulate them requires nothing beyond logical deduction'. We may take it therefore as containing in outline Mr. Spencer's ethical system; and it has all the more interest, as the exposition of this system is regarded by the author as the culmination of his Synthetic Philosophy, the 'part of his task to which all preceding parts are subsidiary'. The influence of a book, so prefaced, on the numerous disciples of this Synthetic Philosophy will undoubtedly be great; and as it is to be hoped that Mr. Spencer will find time to complete the work of which this is an instalment, it seems opportune to examine one or two fundamental points in his system, on which, as it appears to me, some further explanation or justification is required. In performing this examination, I shall find it most convenient not to follow closely the order of Mr. Spencer's exposition; but rather to ask, in what seems to me their natural sequence, the chief questions to which every ethical system has to supply an answer, and then to ascertain—by a comparison, if necessary, of different chapters—how these questions are answered by Mr. Spencer.

In the first place, we have to notice a certain ambiguity in the general notion of 'establishing rules of conduct on a scientific basis'. Writers who discuss moral rules either from what Mr. Spencer calls 'the evolution point of view', or in the earlier manner of the Associationist school, frequently mean by a 'scientific' treatment of morality merely an investigation of the laws according to which the ethical beliefs and sentiments of our own or any other society have come into existence. Such an investigation is obviously a legitimate branch of Sociology or Psychology; and those chapters (cc. vii. and viii.) of Mr. Spencer's book which treat of the 'Psychological View' and the 'Sociological View' seem to be largely concerned with speculations of this kind. So far as this is the case, I do not propose to criticise either the method or the conclusions of these chapters; what I wish to point out is that this species of inquiry, however successfully conducted, has not necessarily any tendency to 'establish' the *authority* of the morality of which it explains the existence. More often, I think, it has an effect of the opposite

[From *Mind*, OS, 5/18 (1880), 216–26.]

kind; the 'law so analysed', as Bishop Blongram says, is felt after the analysis not to 'coerce us much'. A scientific explanation of current morality which shall also be an 'establishment' of it, must do more than exhibit the causes of existing ethical beliefs; it must show that these causes have operated in such a way as to make these beliefs true. Now this Mr. Spencer certainly does not attempt; for the sufficient reason that he does not admit the final authority of existing ethical beliefs. In the chapters which contain (*inter alia*) his account of the origin of current moral conceptions he is continually criticising them as 'defective', 'one-sided', 'vitiated', destined to give way to a 'truer ethics'. In short it is this 'truer ethics'—Mr. Spencer's morality, not the current morality—which it is his ultimate aim to 'establish'.

In what way then does Science—that is, Biology, Psychology, and Sociology—provide a basis for this 'truer ethics'. Mr. Spencer's answer seems to be that these sciences show us, in the first place, a supreme or ultimate end, to the realisation of which human actions are universally or normally directed; and that they enable us, in the second place, to determine the kind of conduct by which this end may be attained in the highest possible degree. Let us begin with the establishment of the end. Mr. Spencer seems to be leading us to this in his two first chapters; in which he considers the conduct to which ethics relates, that is, the voluntary actions of human beings, commonly judged to be right and wrong, as a portion of 'universal conduct—conduct as exhibited by all living creatures'. He defines conduct, in this wider sense, as the 'adjustment of acts to ends'; acts being more precisely defined as external motions of animate beings. He points out how the conduct of the lower animals as compared with the higher, in a scale ascending up to civilised man, 'mainly differs in this, that the adjustment of acts to ends are relatively simple and relatively incomplete'. What, then, in the case of these lower forms of life, are we to regard as the ultimate end, to which the special ends of catching food, avoiding foes, &c., are subordinate? Mr. Spencer unhesitatingly says that the 'general' or 'supreme' end of the adjustments which constitute life is the continuance and further development of these adjustments themselves. Life, in short, is for life's sake; only we are instructed not to measure life merely by its length, but by what is called its 'breadth' also; that is, we must take into account the different 'quantities of change' that different living beings pass through in the same period of time. We have also, of course, to bear in mind that the actions of any individual may be partly adjusted to the initiation, prolongation and enlargement of other lives besides its own; and we observe that this is to a continually greater extent the case, as we ascend in the scale of living beings. Still, notwithstanding this doubleness of measurement and this complexity of adjustment, 'quantity of life' none the less remains the ultimate end of 'universal conduct'; and we naturally expect that, when we pass to consider the particular part of this conduct to which ethics relates, this same end will be taken as the final standard for judging actions as right and wrong: especially since, even in speaking of the lower animals, Mr. Spencer does not hesitate to describe actions that fail to sustain life as 'conduct falling short of its ideal'.[1] And in fact, when he comes to treat of human actions, Mr. Spencer does argue that we commonly regard conduct as good in proportion as it conduces to 'the greatest totality of life in self, in offspring, and in fellow-men'. But he does not accept this view as final; on the contrary, he is concerned to point out that it involves 'an assumption of extreme significance'. It is assumed that life 'brings a surplus of agreeable feeling'; and this he emphatically declares to be the only possible justification for maintaining it, or for judging conduct to be good that conduces to its preservation. The Ethical End, therefore, in relation to which moral rules are to be established, turns out to be not merely quantity of life, 'estimated by multiplying its length into its breadth', but quantity of agreeable feeling, pleasure, or happiness.[2]

Now, after all that has been said of the importance of considering human conduct in connexion with the 'universal conduct' of which it is a part, I think that this transition from 'quantity of life' which was stated to be the end of the latter to 'quantity of pleasure' is too rapidly and lightly made. Pessimism, as Mr. Spencer himself says, stands in the way, declaring that life does not bring with it a surplus of agreeable feeling. We expect therefore a scientific confutation of Pessimism; and I am unable to perceive that this expectation is ever adequately realised. Indeed I am unable to find any passage in which Mr. Spencer expressly undertakes such a confutation. And yet he can hardly think that pessimism is sufficiently confuted by demonstrating that the common moral judgments of mankind imply the assumption that life, on the average, yields a surplus of pleasure over pain. This is not establishing morality on a scientific basis; such an appeal to common sense merely indicates the *pis aller*, the provisional support, with which moralists have to content themselves when they cannot provide a scientific basis for their doctrines.

From a comparison of different passages[3] I am inclined to think that, in Mr. Spencer's view, pessimism is indirectly confuted by the argument—given as an 'inevitable deduction from the hypothesis of evolution'—which shows that 'necessarily throughout the animate world at large, pains are the correlatives of actions injurious to the organism, while pleasures are the correlatives of actions conducive to its welfare'. But, granting this connexion to be established, I do not see how we can strictly infer from it that life on the whole is pleasurable rather than painful. It seems to me that we can only infer that actions preservative of the

[1] The frankly teleological point of view from which, in this book, Mr. Spencer contemplates the phenomena of Life generally, seems worthy of notice; since in his *Principles of Biology* he seems to have taken some pains to avoid 'teleological implication'. Cf. Pr. of Bi. c. v. p. 27.

[2] Mr. Spencer seems to use 'pleasure' and 'happiness'—or at least 'quantity of pleasure' and 'quantity of happiness'—as convertible terms. I should concur in this: but I think he is rather hasty in condemning Aristotle—who could not foresee how he would be translated into English—for not taking a precisely similar view of the relation of εὐδαιμονία to ἡδονή.

[3] Cf. pp. 33, 56, 63, 67 among others.

individual or the race will be generally speaking less painful than those which have an opposite tendency; and that the pains normally endured will not be sufficiently intense to destroy life. The connexion, in fact, leaves nature a choice of alternative methods in her business of adjusting the actions of living beings to the preservation and continuance of life; she may either attract them in the required direction by pleasure, or deter them from divergent courses by pain: it is undeniable that, hitherto at least, her plan of management has combined the two modes of guidance, and I do not see how the proportion in which the two methods are actually mixed can be ascertained by *a priori* inference. Still less do I see how Mr. Spencer is justified in assuming that conduct tending to make 'the lives of each and all the greatest possible, alike in length and breadth' is simply identical with conduct of which the 'ultimate moral aim' is 'gratification, enjoyment, happiness'. I think that we may fairly ask him, in any future instalment of the present treatise, to give us something more like a proof of the Optimism which is so essential a feature in his ethical construction.

Meanwhile, let us suppose that Pleasure or Happiness has been established—scientifically or otherwise—as the ethical end. Before we come to consider the appropriate means for the realisation of this end, one fundamentally important point remains to be settled, *viz., whose* pleasure we have in view. Is the ultimate aim of Mr. Spencer's Ethics to make pleasure or happiness in general a maximum? or is it rather to advise the individual human being how to gain the greatest possible amount of happiness for himself? Of course these two ends will be to a great extent attained by the same means; and many utilitarians have held that this is altogether the case, and that it is impossible for any individual to attain his own happiness in the greatest possible degree by any conduct other than that which is most conducive to the aggregate happiness of all whom his conduct affects. But in any case the extent to which Egoistic Hedonism and Universalistic Hedonism[4] practically coincide will have to be carefully investigated in a scientific exposition of either system: we have first to settle whether we take the happiness of the individual or happiness generally as the *ultimate* end; and then when our choice is made, there arises a second and quite distinct question in either case—*viz.*, how far this ultimate end will be best attained indirectly by taking the other end as the direct object of pursuit. Now I cannot but think that Mr. Spencer has somewhat confounded these two questions in the chapters (cc. xi.–xiv.) in which he first discusses the claims of 'Egoism' and 'Altruism', and then proposes a 'Compromise' between the two, and an ultimate 'Conciliation'. For instance, in arguing the case of 'Egoism *versus* Altruism', he appears to assume general happiness as an ultimate end, a final criterion by the application of which we are to determine the limits of Egoism as a subordinate practical principle; his contention seems to be

---

[4] I venture to adopt my own nomenclature—to which Mr. Spencer does not seem to have any objection.

merely (to use his own words) that the 'pursuit of individual happiness within those limits prescribed by social conditions is the final requisite to the attainment of the greatest general happiness', and that in various ways 'diminutions of general happiness are produced by inadequate egoism'. On the other hand, in c. xiii., he expressly attacks Bentham and his followers for holding that general happiness should be the ultimate end and final standard of right conduct; and refuses to admit 'that from the stand-point of pure reason, the happiness of others has no less a claim as an object of pursuit for each than personal happiness'. But he seems to treat this position as identical with the 'theory which makes general happiness the sole [or almost the sole] *immediate* object of pursuit'; a theory very remote from Bentham's—whose practical view was characteristically expressed in the sentence that 'self-regard alone will serve for diet, though sympathy is very good for dessert'—and not maintained, so far as I am aware, by any of his leading disciples. And it is only against this latter doctrine, which he more frequently and more properly designates as 'pure altruism', that Mr. Spencer's arguments are in any way effective; the issue (as he himself states it) is whether 'equitable egoism' or 'pure altruism' will produce the 'greatest sum of happiness' on the whole; and his conclusion is that 'general happiness is to be achieved mainly through the adequate pursuit of their own happiness by individuals'—which, as I have just said, was precisely Bentham's conclusion. I think therefore that Mr. Spencer's apparent antagonism to the Utilitarian school, so far as the ultimate end and standard of morality is concerned, depends on a mere misunderstanding; and that in all this part of his treatise his quarrel is not really with the very sober and guarded 'altruism' of Bentham and the Benthamites, but with certain hard sayings of the prophet of the Positivist religion, from whom the term Altruism is taken.

Provisionally, then, I shall conclude that in Mr. Spencer's Ethics the ultimate criterion used in establishing rules of Conduct is Happiness or Pleasure, taken generally.[5] Let us now pass to consider his method of scientifically determining the rules themselves.

---

[5] I do not wish here to put prominently forward the difficulties that I find in working with the notion of a 'sum of pleasures'—difficulties which I have explained at sufficient length in my *Methods of Ethics* (B. II. c. iii). But since Mr. Spencer has referred (in c. ix.) to this part of my treatise, I may perhaps observe that he has not altogether apprehended the scope of my argument. I did not merely urge that in many cases when we try to compare two different pleasures (or pains) we are unable to ascertain which of the two is the greatest. The answer, that we ought to choose the greatest surplus of pleasure *so far as we can ascertain it*, is sufficiently obvious, and if I had meant no more than what can be thus answered, I should not have dwelt so long on the point. But I thought it important to point out further that the very notion of a 'sum of pleasures' implies that the pleasures spoken of are capable of being summed; that is, that they are things quantitatively determinate in respect of their quality as pleasures; and that this assumption, however natural and even irresistible it may be, certainly lacks empirical verification.

I must just add that Mr. Spencer's argument on this point suggests that I am not aware that the objections urged by me against the Hedonistic method apply with even greater force to Universalistic, than they do to Egoistic Hedonism. I certainly thought that I had stated this in the clearest possible language. (*Cf. Meth. of Eth.* B. IV., c. iv., § 1.)

The apprehension of this method is rendered, I think, more difficult for the reader by the fact that a definite statement of it is given for the first time in the two concluding chapters of the treatise. It is true that the general nature of it has been gradually elucidated in various earlier passages. For instance, its scientific claims are plainly declared in chapter v., on 'Ways of judging Conduct'; from which we learn that Mr. Spencer's way of judging it is to be a high *priori* road. He will not rely on mere generalisation from observation of the actual consequences of different kinds of conduct; it is the defect of current utilitarianism that it does not get beyond these merely empirical generalisations; Mr. Spencer, on the other hand, proposes to 'ascertain necessary relations' between actions and their consequences, and so to 'deduce from fundamental principles what conduct *must* be detrimental and what conduct *must* be beneficial'. Those are brave words, and they will perhaps raise the reader's hopes to the pitch of expecting to find this demonstrated morality in the four chapters that follow, giving respectively the Physical, Biological, Psychological, and Sociological views of conduct. If so, I fear he will be disappointed to learn (c. vi., § 31) that he is to 'avoid the tendency' to judge Mr. Spencer's conclusions 'by their applicability to humanity as now existing'; and he will be perplexed as to the extent to which he is to avoid this tendency; since a good deal of the discussions in this and the two following chapters plainly relate to human beings that actually exist or have existed. I certainly think that Mr. Spencer ought to draw a clearer line between the actual and the ideal in this part of his treatise; until this is done, it seems to me difficult to criticise these reasonings closely, though they contain much that suggests criticism.

In the concluding chapters, however, these perplexities are cleared away. It is there made quite plain that the rules of conduct, of which Mr. Spencer undertakes to provide a deductive science, are rules that 'formulate normal conduct in an ideal society': a society so ideal that in it such conduct will 'produce pure pleasure—pleasure unalloyed with pain anywhere'. Indeed, in his view, it is only conduct of which the effects are thus unmixed that can be called 'absolutely right'; 'conduct that has any concomitant of pain, or any painful consequence, is partially wrong'. Ethical science, then, is primarily 'a system of ideal truths expressing the absolutely right'; and we are to note that it is only this 'Absolute Ethics' of which the method rises above the merely empirical procedure, previously condemned as defective; for 'Relative Ethics', which has to deal with all practical questions as to what we ought to do here and now, is 'necessarily empirical' in its judgments—at least in all cases that present any difficulty.

The questions then arise (1) How far are we able to form a sufficiently definite conception of the constitution of Mr. Spencer's ideal society to enable us to frame a system of rules for it? and (2) How much guidance would such a system give us in solving the problems of conduct presented by our actual conditions of social life? I have argued against Mr. Spencer's view on these points, in a brief and general way, in my book on the *Methods of Ethics* (B. I., c. ii., § 2). I refer to this passage because Mr. Spencer has replied to me at some length in the present work (c. xv., § 105); but has unfortunately omitted to answer my arguments, owing to a misapprehension which I must now explain. My reasoning was not addressed directly to such a statement of the relation of Absolute and Relative Ethics as I have above endeavoured to abridge from the two last chapters of the treatise before us; what I tried to combat was the far more paradoxical doctrine on the same subject which I found in Mr. Spencer's *Social Statics*. It was there maintained not merely that Absolute Ethics ought to 'take precedence of Relative Ethics'; but that Absolute Ethics was the only kind of Ethics with which a philosophical moralist could possibly concern himself. To quote Mr. Spencer's words:—

The moral law must be the law of the perfect man . . . any proposed system of morals which recognises existing defects, and countenances acts made needful by them, stands self-condemned. . . . Moral law . . . requires as its postulate that human beings be perfect. The philosophical moralist treats solely of the *straight* man. . . . a problem in which a *crooked* man forms one of the elements, is insoluble by him. (c. i.)

Still more definitely is Relative Ethics excluded in the concluding chapter of the same treatise:—

It will very likely be urged that, whereas the perfect moral code is confessedly beyond the fulfilment of imperfect men, some other code is needful for our present guidance . . . to say that the imperfect man requires a moral code which recognises his imperfection and allows for it, *seems at first sight reasonable. But it is not really so*[6] . . . a system of morals which shall recognise man's present imperfections and allow for them *cannot be devised; and would be useless if it could be devised.*

I observe that Mr. Spencer, in replying to me, refers to his *Social Statics*, as though he still held the opinions there expressed; but I must confess that I cannot reconcile these passages, and others that might be quoted from the same context, with the view of Relative Ethics given in the concluding chapters of the present treatise. At any rate, it was in opposition to this earlier view and not to the later one that I thought it fair to adduce the analogy of astronomy, and to suggest the absurdity of a 'philosophical astronomer' declining to deal with any planets that did not move in perfect ellipses. Mr. Spencer, in his rejoinder, takes the suggested analogy to relate to the question whether the study of Absolute Ethics should precede that of Relative Ethics. Had this been my meaning, the reference to astronomy would have been manifestly inappropriate. But in fact it was only in the paragraph succeeding that to which Mr. Spencer has replied that I began to discuss this latter question, as is evident from the following sentences with which my second paragraph opens:—

This inquiry into the morality of an ideal society can therefore be at best but a preliminary investigation, after which the step from the ideal to the actual remains to be taken. We have to ask, then, how far such a preliminary construction seems desirable.

---

[6] The italics are mine.

After which I proceed to state my objections to that more moderate view of the claims of Absolute Ethics which is expounded in the treatise before us. These objections Mr. Spencer has not noticed: in fact his interest in my argument seems to have ceased exactly at the point at which it began to be really relevant to his present position. My criticisms, no doubt, were tolerably obvious; but as they still appear to me substantially valid, I have nothing to do but to re-state them briefly, with such variations as his present treatise suggests.

In the first place, granting—a large grant—that Mr. Spencer's ideal society, in which the voluntary actions of all the members cause 'pleasure unalloyed by pain anywhere' to all who are affected by them, is one which we can conceive as possible, it seems to me quite impossible to ascertain a priori the nature of the human beings comprising such a society with sufficient definiteness and certainty to enable us to determine their code of conduct. It has not come within Mr. Spencer's plan to delineate this code in the present treatise, otherwise than in the scantiest and most general way; but among the meagre generalities that he has given us, I can find nothing that is in any degree important which is not also in a high degree disputable. The most important is undoubtedly the formula of Absolute Justice as the fundamental principle for regulating social co-operation. Of this Mr. Spencer, in the concluding chapter, gives the following statement:—

Individual life is possible only on condition that each organ is paid for its action by an equivalent of blood, while the organism as a whole obtains from the environment assimilable matters that compensate for its efforts; and the mutual dependence of parts in the social organism necessitates that, alike for its total life and the lives of its units, there similarly shall be maintained a due proportion between returns and labours: the natural relation between work and welfare shall be preserved intact . . . That principle of equivalence which meets us when we seek its roots in the laws of individual life, involves the idea of measure; and on passing to social life, the same principle introduces us to the conception of equity or equalness, in the relation of citizens to one another; the elements of the questions arising are quantitative, and hence the solutions assume a more scientific form.

Here, in speaking of a 'due proportion between returns and labours', Mr. Spencer does not mean merely—as the analogy of the individual organism might lead us to suppose—that each labourer will receive the means of carrying on his labour in the most efficient manner; his meaning is, as several other passages show, that he will receive a share of wealth proportioned to the value of his labour. But so far as this share is more than our ideal labourer needs for labouring efficiently, I see no ground for affirming a priori that he will receive it, since it is quite conceivable that the surplus would produce more happiness if distributed among other ideal persons. To this Mr. Spencer would probably answer (Cf. c. xi., § 69) that unless 'superiority profits by the rewards of superiority' the struggle for existence, to which 'the progress of organisation and the reaching of a higher life' have hitherto been due, can no longer continue. This is doubtless a weighty consideration in dealing with the practical problems of existing societies; but I cannot admit its relevancy in 'Absolute Ethics', until it is shown how we are to get the advantages of the struggle for existence without their attendant disadvantages, that is, without some pain to those who are defeated in the struggle; for all such pain is *ex hypothesi* excluded from Mr. Spencer's ideal society, in which all voluntary actions produce unalloyed pleasure. Again, I cannot see any validity in the conception of 'equalness', as governing the relations of ideal citizens, except so far as it means merely that similar persons will be treated similarly; for we cannot know *a priori* how far our ideal citizens will be dissimilar, and therefore reasonably subjected to dissimilar treatment. The progress of Evolution, Mr. Spencer elsewhere tells us, is to increase heterogeneity; though he nowhere attempts to define the degree of heterogeneity which the ideal society will exhibit. This point is very important in reference to a further question that Mr. Spencer indicates— as to the legitimate ends and limits of government authority. I cannot conceive how this question is to be definitely answered, unless we know in what varying degrees political wisdom is distributed among our more or less heterogeneous ideal citizens; and how can we precisely know this *a priori?*

In short, it seems to me that the imagination which Mr. Spencer has exercised in constructing his ideal society has none of the characteristics of a really scientific imagination; he has not succeeded in leading us logically to a precise and consistent conception of the mutual relations of the members of this society.

But, secondly, even if it were otherwise—even if we could construct scientifically Mr. Spencer's ideal code, I do not think such a code would be of much avail in solving the practical problems of actual humanity. For a society in which— to take one point only—there is no such thing as punishment, is necessarily a society with its essential structure so unlike our own, that it would be idle to attempt any close imitation of its rules of behaviour. It might possibly be best for us to conform approximately to some of these rules; but this we could only know by examining each particular rule in detail; we could not know it generally and *a priori*. We cannot even affirm that it would be best for us to approximate to it as far as is practicable. For even supposing that this ideal society is ultimately to be realised, it must at any rate be separated from us by a considerable interval of evolution; hence it is not unlikely that the best way of progressing towards it is some other than the apparently directest way, and that we shall reach it more easily if we begin by moving away from it. Whether this is so or not, and to what extent, can only be known by carefully examining the effects of conduct on actual human beings, and inferring their probable effects on the human beings whom we may expect to exist in the proximate future; that is, by the humble and imperfect empirical method which Mr. Spencer may be right in despising, but for which he has not yet provided an efficient substitute.

26. Leslie Stephen's *Science of Ethics*

Mr. Stephen's book is an elaborate and important—though not, in my opinion, a thoroughly successful—attempt to 'lay down an ethical doctrine in harmony with the doctrine of evolution'. Its merits and defects combine to render it a difficult book to review: as its chief merit appears to me to be its sustained vigorous thoughtfulness, its abundance of pertinent and pointed observations and reflections, to which it is impossible to do justice within the limits of a notice: while on the other hand I find it wanting in clearness of method and systematic arrangement, both as regards the conduct of particular arguments and the organisation of the whole set of discussions which it contains. These discussions are of three kinds: one portion of them belongs to subjective psychology, being concerned with an analysis—from the individual's point of view and mainly introspective—of the kind of consciousness that precedes and determines volition; another part is occupied with the development of positive morality regarded as a property of the social organism, and here the procedure is sociological observation and induction, aided largely by the deductive application of the Darwinian theory; while again the treatise also seems to aim at a result strictly ethical (in the narrower sense), at the systematic determination of an ideal code of morality. But what precisely the method of reasoning is by which this third result is attained, I find it difficult to say; especially since the treatment of this subject is made to run rather confusingly through the parts of the other discussions, like a thread of logically alien texture. Again, there seems a certain awkwardness in the arrangement by which (as we shall see) the sociological part of the treatise is interpolated between two discussions that belong to subjective psychology; and the ascertainment and analysis of the facts of the ordinary moral consciousness as at present existing are hardly enough distinguished from the history—necessarily somewhat hypothetical—of the manner in which it has been developed.

These sources of confusion and perplexity I will try to indicate more fully as I proceed; they do not, I think, detract materially from the interest of the work.

Mr. Stephen's problem, as he originally states it, is 'to discover the scientific form of morality . . . the general characteristic, so far as science can grasp it, of the moral sentiments' . . . the part they 'play in the general system of human society'. He begins by an account of human motives generally, considered from the subjective point of view. All human conduct is determined by feelings; and

[Critical Notice of *The Science of Ethics*, by Leslie Stephen (London: Smith, Elder & Co., 1882), published in *Mind*, OS, 7/28 (1882), 562–86.]

this, according to Mr. Stephen, is equivalent to saying that it is determined by pleasure and pain. The ethical importance of this proposition is, however, less than at first appears: since Mr. Stephen does not mean that when a man chooses between two alternatives of conduct the consequences of the course that he chooses are always represented at the moment of choice as more pleasant or less painful than the consequences of the course that he rejects. 'No feeling can affect us except so far as it is felt'; that 'the estimate of future pleasure does not always produce a corresponding pleasure . . . will be admitted on all hands'; and we find later on that the pleasures and pains of others are liable to affect us so much as to lead us to sacrifice knowingly our own happiness to theirs. Still, it is affirmed that 'the will is always determined by the actual painfulness or pleasantness of the choice at the moment of choosing'; or, in a different phrase, 'by the simple process of feeling one course to be the easiest', according to 'the principle of least resistance'.

I cannot accept this account; and the criticism that I shall make on it illustrates what Mr. Stephen elsewhere says of the lack of agreement on elementary points in psychology. In my view, the feelings that normally cause action are not pleasures and pains as such, but desires and aversions, which may be very strong without being definitely either pleasurable or painful; while, again, the desire of an intense pleasure may be a painful feeling, and the aversion to formidable pains, if not distinctly recognisable as itself a pleasure, is at any rate sometimes an indispensable element of a consciousness on the whole pleasurable—as in enterprises of which the charm depends upon their danger. It further appears to me that, while the satisfaction of a desire is always a pleasure, this pleasure is not necessarily or even normally the result which the desire moves the will to aim at; and that we often desire results which are not conceived as the pleasures (or relief from pains) either of ourselves or other sentient beings. In particular, the aversion normally accompanying the moral judgment that an act is wrong is not, in the main, aversion to the foreseen pain of remorse; nor is it, in many cases at least, aversion to the painful consequences of the wrong act to others;—aversion (*e.g.*) to unveracity or injustice is often felt when the consequences of the act contemplated appear on the whole desirable. Mr. Stephen, as I understand him, is concerned to maintain that such moral judgments cannot, any more than any other operation of the intellect, move the will, apart from emotion. This seems to me rather a subtle psychological question; but at any rate I should say that in the case of moral judgments I am frequently not conscious of any emotion other than what is implied in the mere consciousness that the judgment carries with it a motive. And it is, I suppose, this consciousness, in cases where we feel some powerful emotion prompting in an opposite direction, that has led to the phrase 'conflict of reason with passion' to which Mr. Stephen objects. In his view, what is called the government of passion by reason is simply the effect of represented [non-rational] emotion, or symbols of emotion operative through habit and association—'latent emotion' being converted into actual so far as is needed for the resistance of passion. Intellectual development of course influences emotion so far as it is accompanied by the development of new sensibilities; and influences volition so far as it leads to the more accurate representation of facts—including among facts the agent's future feelings: in this way it tends to reduce vagaries and caprices and give continuity and consistency to the conduct. Though, as Mr. Stephen subtly argues, the condition of logical consistency does not strictly enable us to condemn any feeling as unreasonable: since 'there is always some cause for the wildest vagary or the most unreasonable prejudice', and 'to give a merely formal consistency to my conduct it is sufficient that this cause should become a reason'; still, the development of reason does tend to bring about a certain harmony of action: 'for, instead of allowing each impulse to operate exclusively in turn, it subjects each to the implicit and explicit control of the others'. But 'we may still ask, how is the relation between the different instincts determined? what settles the influence exerted by each member?' to which the only answer that he can give, from the point of view of subjective psychology, is that it will be settled by the balance of instincts which constitutes at the time the character of the individual; 'we have so far no means of saying why one character should not be just as reasonable as another'.

In all this Mr. Stephen seems to me, first, to ignore the psychological phenomenon of divergence which the play of represented and actual feelings continually causes between the resulting *judgment* as to what is right or best to do, and the resulting action,—the 'video meliora proboque deteriora sequor'. This is surely too important a fact to be overlooked in discussing the relation of reason and feeling even from a purely psychological point of view. And, secondly, his conclusion here seems to be inconsistent with what he afterwards says (c. vi., p. 254) as to the 'only assignable rule of conduct'—sympathy apart—'prescribing action for a maximum of happiness': since it follows that when we find the balance of instincts in any individual leading to misery, and in another to happiness, the reason cannot but prefer the latter character. In short, I can see no good reason why the psychological discussion should be thus broken off here and taken up again in c. vi.: the transition effected to the sociological point of view, and the comparison of types of character by the standard of conduciveness to social well-being, appears to me sudden and forced.

However, let us pass to the sociological discussion. Here, as has been said, the general assumption is that natural selection tends to produce, in human character as in other departments of life, the type of maximum efficiency for life under given conditions: but the application of this principle to the particular case of human character is very carefully conducted, and forms, I think, the most interesting part of the treatise. We note first that evolution—in the case of man—is concerned with the vitality not of single individuals, as such, but of a class of beings that have to be continually reproduced and exist only in more or less organised societies. We may therefore distinguish, as susceptible of improvement by evolution, qualities tending to preserve (1) the individual, (2) the race, and (3) the organised community; recognising that all are required and that any improvement in (1) accompanied by greater deterioration in (2) or (3) would not really be useful to the kind, and would not therefore be produced by natural selection. *Ceteris paribus*, any improvements in the efficiency of living individuals are of course useful to the kind, so far as they tend to be transmitted through physical propagation, and to the community, which is an aggregate of individuals though not a mere aggregate. But what we are specially concerned to observe is the important class of qualities which are not possessed by the individual through physical inheritance, requiring only interaction with his material environment for their development, but are acquired after birth through social intercourse.

To this class belong knowledge and all that is implied in language, skills, and arts of all kinds, and, in particular, a moral code. An account of the changes that take place in these qualities gives us the life of human society as such: and history shows these changes to be vast, while the constitution of human individuals, as born, remains approximately constant: one of these changes being the growth of a recognised and formulated moral law. (Mr. Stephen, I think, goes beyond the evidence in assuming the physical similarity of the infants of pre-moral savages with civilised infants, since we know so little of the brains of either; but the point is not of fundamental importance.) We have then to ask how the general course of this social history is determined by the principle of natural selection. Here Mr. Stephen draws attention to a difficulty often overlooked in this kind of discussion. Man—at least civilised man—is not a member of one community but of many: we usually think of his 'social organism' as a state; but members of different states may belong to the same industrial or ecclesiastical organisation, and members of the same state may belong to different clubs, companies, &c., each having its own corporate existence. Now which of these societies is the 'unit upon which the process of evolution impinges'? If political communities were so separate in their lives that improvements could not be diffused from the one to the other, the unit of evolutional improvement would be the nation: but in 'any moderately civilised state of the world' this is not the case, as 'war is then a comparatively subordinate phenomenon'; even when a conquest takes place, the conquered group is 'not extirpated but incorporated'. Hence we must take as the unit in the struggle for existence, which 'necessarily implies the supplanting of the weaker by the stronger', what Mr. Stephen calls the *race*—how he defines it I do not quite understand—which forms what he prefers to call 'social *tissue*'[1] rather than 'organism'; since a race is not, as a state is, capable of combined action for a common end. 'The unity which we attribute to it consists in this, that every individual is dependent upon

---

[1] The relation of 'race' and 'tissue' seems, however, rather vaguely conceived; as Mr. Stephen afterwards speaks of different races as having identical tissue.

his neighbours, and every modification arising in one part is capable of being propagated directly in every other part'; the organisation of such a tissue into different states not destroying its continuity. The effect of the competition for existence is of a mixed and complicated kind; it partly consists in different degrees of success in efforts to survive under material conditions without direct mutual struggle; so far as the latter comes in, it is no doubt possible that a large political community of inferior tissue may extirpate a superior though smaller nation; but, generally speaking, the 'tendency is to the predominance of races having intrinsically the strongest tissue'. We have then in considering the properties of social man to distinguish three kinds: (1) those he would equally have, if he had been transported as an infant into a different society; (2) those he has as a member of a certain social tissue; and (3) those he has as a member of a state or other special organ of human society. And since the dissolution of the states does not involve the destruction of the individuals composing them, we must take the social tissue as the 'primary unit upon which the process of evolution impinges': we must understand the social evolution, which has produced among other things an explicit moral code, to mean the evolution of a strong social tissue.

What, then, is the exact place of morality in this process? When we speak of morality as a Law or Code, we mean that there are certain 'organic customs' essential or useful to the society; which would not exist unless the mature members of the society generally had developed instincts of conformity to them, but which we may call a 'law' relatively to any particular individual, meaning that he is under 'a pressure tending to enforce a correspondence between his actions or feelings and those of his neighbours'—the sanction of this law being 'whatever consequences other than the legal ones result from imperfect harmony with his social medium'. Morality, then, consists of the most important of these customs maintained, and habits or instincts generated, by social pressure in members of any social tissue generally—as distinct from the customs or habits belonging to any particular organ of this tissue. It contains 'the essential conditions of the vitality of this tissue'—or rather the *actual* moral law must be 'an approximate statement' of such essential conditions. It must be this, because 'the process by which society has been developed implies that the most important characteristics developed in the individual by social pressure correspond approximately to the conditions of existence of the society'.

Mr. Stephen's main distinctions, in the long analysis that I have briefly summarised, seem to me interesting and valuable in a general way; but I think that they are drawn somewhat too sharply for his special purpose, and, further, that he is hardly aware of the extreme vagueness of the only conclusion attainable by his method. In the first place, I should conjecture that the organisation in political communities must have had more importance than he attaches to it, at least in the earlier part of the evolution that he describes; *e.g.*, I should trace the prominence given to military valour in early estimates of human excellence to the struggle for existence between tribes before war became a 'comparatively subordinate phenomenon'. And it is only in this earlier period that I can regard the natural selection of social 'tissues' as a really important factor in the development of morality; I do not see, for instance, how any of the important changes that have taken place in the morality of civilised Europe during the last twenty centuries can be properly attributed to this cause. But secondly, accepting 'social tissue' as the unit which the struggle for existence tends to improve, I think Mr. Stephen's conclusion that the actual morality of any society represents 'approximately' the essential conditions of its existence is only admissible—as a mere deduction from the 'evolution theory'—if we take 'approximately' in a very loose sense. It might equally well be deduced from the same theory that the individual's organism was 'approximately' adapted to its conditions of existence, and therefore that all men were always in approximately good health, with a balance of instincts that could be approximately trusted to lead to health-preserving conduct. And in a certain sense this would be true; but it is in the interval between the 'approximation' and perfect adaptation that the whole art of medicine finds its field; and surely the moralist—whom Mr. Stephen afterwards compares to a physician—must be prepared for at least an equal hiatus between the customs actually enforced by praise and blame in any society and the truly 'essential conditions of its social existence'.

Mr. Stephen proceeds to explain from the same point of view the chief characteristics recognised as belonging to morality generally; and to exhibit the chief branches of duty or virtue—courage, temperance, truth, justice, and benevolence—as essential conditions of social existence. The truth of his conclusions, broadly taken, no one is likely to gainsay; nor is he unsuccessful in explaining, in harmony with his general view, certain commonly recognised exceptions to particular rules—such as the rule of veracity. I think, however, that in this part of the treatise the mixture of methods which I before mentioned is a source of confusion: the view of morality at which Mr. Stephen arrives by direct analysis of existing moral sentiments, and effort to reduce them to a clear and consistent system, mingles itself perplexingly with the application of his sociological doctrine to the history of the growth: in consequence of which certain characteristics that explicitly belong only to morality in its latest stage are apparently thrown back into the earlier periods of its development. Thus the distinction between the 'prudential' and the 'moral' codes is given as though it were necessarily apprehended throughout the whole evolution; whereas it is only found in germ at so late a stage as that of Greek ethical reflection. Again, Mr. Stephen gives as an essential characteristic of morality proper its 'internality': 'the moral law has to be expressed in the form "be this," not in the form "do this": it prescribes character primarily not conduct'. Admitting the vast gain in general effectiveness that is obtained when morality advances from the mere regulation of outward actions to the regulation of feelings or dispositions—I still think Mr. Stephen's statement misleading even as regards the latest stage of moral development; since there is an important class of virtues, such as (*e.g.*) veracity and justice, which, though I may regard them as qualities of character rather than conduct, I yet cannot definitely conceive except as tendencies to produce certain external effects. At any rate the primary effect of 'social pressure' must be to produce outward conformity to the approved type of conduct. And this leads me to say that I desiderate, in this part of the treatise (cc. iv., v.), a more thorough and systematic analysis of the inner causes of moral development, the existence of which is necessarily presupposed in applying the theory of natural selection. It is perhaps from want of this analysis that Mr. Stephen sometimes falls, as I think, into the error of the older utilitarian school, in their historical explanations, of attributing the emergence of new moral approvals or disapprovals to conscious calculations of utility. For instance, the following explanation of asceticism is surely unhistorical: 'The growth of a rich and powerful class . . . in which great men plunge themselves into sensuality with indifference to the sufferings of their dependents, suggests the doctrine that sensuality is the great enemy of mankind. . . . The best teachers see that the passions are strong enough to take care of themselves . . . and therefore they denounce [sensuality] unsparingly without supplying those qualifications which will be sufficiently supplied by the facts.' Surely this calculated overcharging of the condemnation of sensuality is utterly alien to the temper of such men as those who, in any age or country, have led mankind in the direction of asceticism!

In the three following chapters (vi.–viii.) the psychological discussion of motives is taken up afresh. Taking the individual man now as a member of a society having a moral code, and taking morality, as distinct from prudence, to prescribe a character tending to act for the good of others, we have yet to ask (1) 'what is the quality in respect of which the individual is susceptible to the social pressure, (2) what is the form taken by that pressure, and (3) what is the nature of the character that must be impressed on the individual'. In answering the first of these questions, Mr. Stephen seems to me to ignore unduly the part played by what Mr. Spencer aptly distinguishes as the 'ego-altruistic' sentiments, the fear of the disapprobation of one's fellows and pleasure in their approval: probably because he does not consider the external conformity produced by these feelings as properly deserving the name of morality. True 'morality, taken as implying the existence of certain desires which have for their immediate objects the happiness of others', can only find a basis in distinctly altruistic sentiments: that is, in the sympathy by which an individual derives pleasure or pain from the mere representation of the pleasures and pains of others. Mr. Stephen draws attention to the necessary implication of sympathy in cognitive processes generally; knowledge even of a non-sentient object involves an implicit recognition of other consciousnesses to which it is objective, while knowledge of anything sentient more obviously includes representation of its feelings. But in saying that the 'pain due to the pain of others is a direct and necessary result of the very process of thinking about others' Mr. Stephen surely goes too far; since, as he himself recognises, if we think about others in a malevolent mood, we derive pleasure—up to a certain point—from a vivid representation of their pains; and, apart from malevolence, men often gain a purely pleasing excitement from the narrative of others' sufferings, and still more often cognise pain as an external fact without any perceptible emotion. Still it must be admitted that the intellectual representation of the feelings of others normally tends, if vivid, to be accompanied by some emotional sympathy with them: and therefore that conduct *to a certain extent* 'altruistic'—promotive of the happiness of others—is natural on the part of such a being as man. But I am unable to follow the transition by which Mr. Stephen proceeds to argue that the complete subordination of self-interest to the interest of society is 'reasonable'—thus, I may remark, taking up the snapped thread of the earlier chapter on motives. His argument is as follows:—

To become reasonable . . . is to act on general principles, and to act consistently; and this, as I have said, includes the condition that a statement of the real cause of my actions should equally assign the reason for my actions. The law which my feelings actually follow must coincide with the principle which commends itself to my reason. In order, then, that a being provided with social instincts should act reasonably, it is necessary, not that he should take the course of conduct which gives the greatest chance of happiness [to himself], but that which gives the greatest chance of happiness to the organisation of which he forms a constituent part.

I have nothing to say against this ethical conclusion; but I cannot see the force of the reasoning by which it is reached. For no one's actions conform perfectly either to the prudential or to the social axiom; and yet, as Mr. Stephen has himself argued, the 'real cause' of every one's actions is not therefore less intrinsically capable of being represented as its reason. It may be answered that the actual conduct of civilised man at any rate approximates more closely to the social than to the prudential axiom: but (1) this answer does not justify the inference above given, and (2) I hardly think that Mr. Stephen can consistently make it. He holds that the two axioms approximately coincide in the conduct that they prescribe: and so far as they diverge, so far as individuals have to choose between their own greatest happiness and that of the community, Mr. Stephen will hardly maintain that they actually more often sacrifice the former than the latter.

I return to the explanation of actual morality. Taking sympathy as the element of virtue, we observe, next, that virtue 'implies more than simple altruism or benevolence', *viz.*, 'the elaboration and regulation of the sympathetic character which takes place through the social factor'. Through sympathy we not only seek the happiness of others, but also 'catch the contagion of their complex sentiments': this, however, explains how individuals acquire moral sentiments rather than how these arise in a society. 'If virtue were identical with altruism we might identify moral approval with gratitude'; but as it is not, this approval requires explanation. In the explanation, however, that Mr. Stephen offers (in c. vii.) I find it hard to disentangle his exposition and justification of his own notion of merit from his account of the development of the ordinary notion: and yet the two conceptions do not seem to be identical. According to Mr. Stephen, a man 'is meritorious, so far as he is so constituted as to obey the moral law unconditionally': but the ordinary notion of merit he defines as 'the exchange value set upon virtue'; it varies, therefore, with the supply and demand of the latter, and carries with it a reference to an assumed average standard of 'conduct'—there is a zero point of merit below which the moral law would be obeyed even by average persons without extrinsic motives. Again, in Mr. Stephen's view, the desire of others' praise must, I suppose, be classed as an extrinsic motive; but this does not seem to be the ordinary view as expounded by himself, since he expressly says that we only give praise to conduct with the view of stimulating it.

The greater part of this chapter, however, is occupied in clearing away certain fallacies which obscure the conception of merit, being, according to Mr. Stephen, distortions of its proper characteristics. Thus the fact that merit only attaches to actions as exhibiting character—exhibiting that is a disposition to choose actions socially beneficial apart from any extrinsic motive—is distorted into the supposed condition that merit involves free-will in the metaphysical sense; while, again, the relativity of the ordinary standard of merit has led to the erroneous doctrine that merit is proportioned to effort: the true view being that 'the man is most meritorious who is virtuous with the least effort, provided always that he has the normal passions of a man'. There is much that I should like to say in answer to Mr. Stephen's acute arguments in support of these conclusions; but I must pass to consider the yet more important question as to the nature of the 'intrinsic motive for right doing'. From Mr. Stephen's view of the essence of morality, it manifestly follows that actions may be virtuous although done without any conscious reference to a moral law; for if an individual enjoys such a balance of instincts as naturally impels him to acts preservative of his social tissue, he will do right, though he may never think of right and wrong as such. Still Mr. Stephen holds that an explicit recognition of the law is 'the crown and final outcome of the moralised character'; so long as this is wanting 'we are without the full guarantee for a regular observance of the moral law'. But he is at the same time concerned to maintain (in c. viii.) that the faculty to which this recognition is commonly referred, under the name of conscience, is not 'separate', 'elementary', or 'primitive'. If we admit the gradual development of morality out of a pre-moral state of human existence, it follows that the faculty of moral cognition cannot be, in a historical sense, 'primitive': but I can find no significance in the assertions that it is 'separate' and 'elementary', except so far as they import what seems to me a clear result of reflection—viz., that the notions of right and wrong, as peculiar to moral cognition, are unique and unanalysable. On the other hand, I should quite agree with Mr. Stephen's statement that 'the law is given much more distinctly than the feeling by which it is enforced', understanding it to mean that the cognition or judgment of rightness and wrongness is more distinct than the accompanying emotions: but then it is the cognition especially that I regard as the manifestation of the moral faculty, which in its special application to the agent's own conduct we call conscience. The emotions attending this special application seem to me complex, variable, and difficult to analyse exhaustively. The sense of shame, to which Mr. Stephen calls attention, is doubtless one element of the emotions that generally attends a condemnatory judgment; but it is not universally present; and, as he points out, it is even more strongly excited by breaches of social decorum too trivial to be within the pale of morality, and when it attaches to breaches of the moral law is by no means proportioned to their magnitude. Again the contemplation of virtue produces aesthetic emotion, very intense and vivid in certain minds and under certain circumstances; and perhaps an ideally cultivated taste would derive most pleasure from the type of character most preservative of social tissue; but actually the play of this emotion diverges very much from this ideal—which is of less practical consequence since it is not an important element of the ordinary moral consciousness.

The emotion most essential to conscience, in Mr. Stephen's view, is a kind of 'corporate sentiment' or feeling of 'loyalty', which grows up normally towards any association of human beings and carries with it 'a sense of obligation'. The sentiment of duty 'has the same relation to the social tissue as the various special sentiments corresponding to each organ or association have to the body to which they correspond'; and the narrower associations—especially that of the family—are a school in which the mind is trained for the wider sentiment. I do not quite understand what is meant by 'having the same relation': that virtue tends unconditionally toward preservation of social tissue we have been already told; and Mr. Stephen does not mean that in the ordinary judgments of conscience this preservation is explicitly recognised as the ultimate end. Nor does the 'sense of obligation' seem to be adequately explained when it is referred to the 'perception that the rule is formed by something outside us, that we imbibe it from the medium in which we live'; since so long as we observe the rule merely as external, and not from an intrinsic motive, our action is not, in Mr. Stephen's view, properly moral.

In c. ix., Mr. Stephen passes definitely from psychology and sociology to ethics, and discusses the fundamental question of the criterion of morality. By this time the careful reader will have come to feel a certain curiosity as to the choice which the author means to make between the two ultimate ends and standards of moral conduct to which the two lines of reasoning conducted in the preceding chapters seem respectively to lead. As we have seen, from the point of view of subjective psychology he has arrived at the conclusion that it is reasonable for the individual to aim at maximum general happiness; while from the sociological point of view preservation of social tissue has throughout been presented as the end to which the whole development of positive morality is a means. Which of these, then, will he take as the ultimate end for a true or ideal morality—happiness or preservation? Mr. Stephen fully recognises that he has to 'justify morality both as happiness-giving and as life-preserving', and that if the ends diverged he would 'get into considerable difficulties': but he thinks it sufficient to say that 'the very principle of evolution implies that there must be at least an approximate coincidence, and there is no apparent *a priori* reason why the coincidence should not be indefinitely close'. I submit that, in the first place, this is much too short a cut to Optimism. The principle of evolution, as I understand it, decides nothing as to the issue between Optimism and Pessimism: Von Hartmann and Mr. Herbert Spencer may equally hold it. All it involves is that, when preservative and destructive actions are presented as alternatives, the preservative must be, generally speaking, the less painful: but whether life on the whole has a balance of inevitable pain is a question to which evolution has nothing to say. Now Mr. Stephen admits that if he were a pessimist, 'if the preservation of the race meant a continuance of misery', he could not reasonably take preservation as his criterion of morality; hence, as he does practically choose the evolutionist criterion in preference to the utilitarian, his ethical system is logically bound to include an adequate con-futation of Pessimism—which he has certainly not given us. And I would suggest that the real need of this proof has been partly concealed from the reader by Mr. Stephen's continual use of the terms 'social welfare', 'wellbeing', and even 'health', instead of mere 'preservation', in speaking of his evolutional criterion: since all these terms naturally imply that the existence preserved is a desirable existence.

But secondly, even supposing Pessimism confuted, the complete coincidence of conditions tending to general happiness with conditions tending to social preservation is very far from being made out; since, so far as we know, of two social states which equally tend to be preserved, one may be indefinitely happier than the other. We may grant that in the early history of morality—when to live at all was a difficult task for human communities—the maintenance of preservat-ive habits and sentiments was its most important function: but it is not therefore reasonable that we should permanently be content with the mere securing of existence for ourselves or for humanity generally, and should confine ourselves to efforts at making this security greater, instead of seeking to make the secured existence more desirable. Nor can I even grant that the criterion of 'tendency to preservation of social tissue' is necessarily more easy to apply than that of 'tendency to happiness', even so far as the two ends are coincident; still less that it 'satisfies the conditions of a scientific criterion'. Were Sociology a science really constructed, this would doubtless be the case: but Mr. Stephen has himself told us—in stronger language than I should have ventured to use—that sociology at present 'consists of nothing more than a collection of unverified guesses and vague generalisations, disguised under a more or less pretentious apparatus of quasi-scientific terminology' (p. 10). If this be so, I submit that the practical superiority of the evolutional to the utilitarian criterion, is not established even by the most vigorous exposition of the defects of the latter.

I quite admit the effectiveness of Mr. Stephen's criticisms on the utilitarianism which treats society as a 'simple combination of independent atoms of uniform and constant nature', among whom 'happiness is a kind of emotional currency capable of being calculated and distributed in lots', which have 'a certain definite value independent of any special tastes of the individual'. But the system thus criticised seems to me to be a caricature even of Bentham's, who has a great deal to say about the variations of the individual's sensibilities, and to have very little resemblance to any system that has flourished since the influence of J. S. Mill— and, chiefly through Mill, of Comte—has been strong. And here I may remark, that Mr. Stephen seems to me throughout to exaggerate the novelty, not of his own speculations, which he is rather disposed to underrate, but of those of the English Evolutionist school: he seems hardly aware that the ideas of 'sociology', of the 'social organism' and its relation to its environment, of the need of a positive and historical study of ethics and politics, were familiar to Englishmen from Comte's writings, long before the theory of natural selection was invented.

From the discussion of the true criterion of morality, Mr. Stephen passes (in c. x.) to examine the adequacy of its sanction: or, in other words, the extent of the coincidence of Virtue and Prudence. That the two 'approximately coincide' —in the wide sense Mr. Stephen gives to this adverb—will not probably be denied: nor will any one who accepts the general doctrine of evolution doubt that the progress of society has a certain tendency to produce healthy individuals whose characters conform approximately to the prudential ideal, and also individuals who have the social affections strong. But it does not necessarily follow that the two developments tend to coincide very closely; for though doubtless in a society where sympathy is generally vigorous, a man markedly defective in this respect is likely to be less happy, we cannot therefore argue that the precise development of sympathy which will be most useful to society will also be most conducive to the happiness of the sympathetic individual.

Nor does Mr. Stephen try to prove this. He points out in the first place that the type best adapted for social tissue includes many qualities besides those in which popular morality recognises merit, because they are qualities which do not comparatively require the encouragement of praise. 'Nature', says Mr. Stephen, characteristically, 'wants big, strong, hearty, eupeptic, shrewd sensible human beings; and would be grossly inconsistent if she bestowed her highest reward of happiness upon a bilious, scrofulous, knock-kneed saint', &c. This, however, is really rather an argument against popular morality—as in fact Mr. Spencer uses it: except so far as the useful qualities in question are connate superiorities, in which case they are not really relevant to the question at issue: since—taking

Mr. Stephen's comparison—in order to prove the coincidence of Virtue and Prudence, we are not bound to show that a naturally bilious saint is happier than a naturally eupeptic sinner, but merely that he is happier than a sinner of the same unfortunate physical constitution. But in fact, as Mr. Stephen goes on to explain, though we may show that ordinary virtue tends generally to the interest of the virtuous individual, we cannot fairly deduce from the doctrine of evolution even this general presumption in respect of the virtue that is before its age. So again, if we consider the question from the point of view of the man who is not yet virtuous and ask if it is his interest to become so, the conclusion seems to be 'that, as a very general rule at least, obedience to the external moral law is a matter of prudence for everybody; that it can be proved to almost any man that it is safer for him not to be at war with his fellows or indulge his appetites to excess; but that, on the other hand, it cannot be said with any confidence that if we were to consult the happiness of the agent exclusively, we should always try to instil into him habits of virtue which transcend this rather moderate limit'. Still more clear is it that we cannot establish the coincidence in particular exceptional cases: that, to take the old stock instance, we cannot deny that Regulus may have been imprudent in returning to Carthage; 'it may be true both that a less honourable man would have had a happier life, and that a temporary fall below the highest strain of heroism would have secured for him a greater chance of happiness'. And Mr. Stephen is even inclined to think that not merely heroism but 'even virtue of the ordinary kind demands real sacrifices upon some occasions'. He sums up, indeed, by saying that the acquisition of altruistic sentiments may be recommended on merely prudential grounds; but he does not deny that from the point of view of the individual's happiness it would be better to cultivate them—like other tastes and impulses—in such a way that they would submit when necessary to the supreme control of the prudential reason. Whether he is right in holding that this conclusion 'does not diminish the intrinsic motives to virtue, inasmuch as those motives are not really based upon prudence', is a profoundly important question, which I have not space to argue adequately; but Mr. Stephen would not deny that the development of civilised morality has, throughout its history, been accompanied by a general belief in the coincidence of virtue with the happiness of the virtuous agent, though with very different views as to the precise manner in which this coincidence is to be realised: and I cannot but think that he much underrates the support which ordinary morality has received from this belief.

Before leaving this topic, I must dispute Mr. Stephen's assertion that the problem presented by the relations of virtue and prudence is 'bound up in the old one of the origin of evil'. I should rather say that if the former were satisfactorily settled, the latter would still remain, but would cease to have more than a merely speculative interest. I do not explain why I am in a world full of misery by proving that my own happiness would always be maximised by the same conduct that would maximise happiness generally; but if I were convinced of this latter proposition, and could ascertain the conduct that would have these consequences, the solution of the former problem would have no practical importance.

In a concluding chapter Mr. Stephen deals briefly with what some would call the Metaphysic of Ethics—not that he himself would use the term, since it is his avowed aim to separate his 'scientific' treatment of ethics from all metaphysical admixture. A writer who makes this his aim is usually liable to leave something wanting in the statement of his first principles: and Mr. Stephen seems to me no exception to this rule. If I had to state the basis of his ethical system, I should describe him as holding that the general happiness of human beings was, in the abstract, the right ultimate end of human action, but was inapplicable as a criterion for the determination of actual rules; for which purpose, therefore, preservation of social tissue, being necessarily coincident with general happiness, must be taken as the practically ultimate criterion, and the end that ought to be consciously aimed at. But no such statement as this—in which the term 'right' or 'ought' is necessarily introduced in an absolute sense—is explicitly made by Mr. Stephen; and he often makes statements which seem to me incompatible with a clear apprehension of the necessary nature of an ethical first principle. He says, for instance, that the question 'which man would on the whole observe the genuine moral code with the fewest exceptions' is 'a question of fact, to be settled by psychologists and direct observation' (p. 38); and again 'it is a simple objective fact that a man acts rightly or wrongly in a given case'. Now, undoubtedly, the conduciveness of an action to human happiness is a fact ascertainable—at least theoretically—by psychological observation and inference: its conduciveness to the preservation of social tissue is a fact similarly capable of being brought to the test of sociological observation; but neither psychologist nor sociologist can observe that either general happiness or preservation of tissue is the true ultimate standard for determining right and wrong, the true ultimate end to the realisation of which the 'genuine' or 'ideal' moral code is the best means. Such propositions as these are purely ethical and do not represent 'facts' either of psychical or physical experience. Similarly, when Mr. Stephen maintains that it is capable of 'scientific proof' to a murderer that murder is 'wrong, as being opposed to that underlying moral code which expresses the conditions of social welfare', I must again answer that it may doubtless be scientifically proved that murder is not generally conducive to the preservation of social tissue, but that if it can be scientifically proved that the murderer ought to adopt the preservation of social tissue as his ultimate end, the proof must be different in kind from any reasoning that Mr. Stephen has used; and I am unable to conjecture how he would set about constructing it. In a later passage (p. 448) Mr. Stephen seems to suggest that the historical method may lead us to such a proof. He says that we 'may look for some approximation to agreement' in ethics and politics as the historical 'method is more generally adopted and more systematically carried out . . . when we cease to ask "what is the moral" and ask "what men have actually admired" '; since the 'true nature of the thing' may then reveal itself. But the 'true nature of the thing' is in this case the true answer to the ethical (or political) question 'what is ultimately right or good': and if Mr. Stephen holds that the examination—on however large a scale—of men's opinions as to what is right or good will supply a cogently reasoned answer to this question, I can only entreat him to state explicitly and fully the steps of the reasoning by which this result is reached; since I have long and vainly sought for such a statement in the most elaborate treatises of the historical school.

27. Green's Ethics

Green's *Prolegomena to Ethics* is a highly interesting and impressive book; and no one who makes the study of morality a matter of serious concern—to whatever school he may belong—can read it without instruction and edification. At the same time I do not find myself able to obtain from it a clear and consistent conception of the author's ethical system, even in outline. It may be said that the book does not profess to give such a system; its title indicates that it consists merely of 'Prolegomena' to a future or possible systematic exposition of ethics; and the calamity which prevented its completion has left it imperfect in the very part in which the plan of such a systematic treatise might have been expected to be at least foreshadowed. I admit the force of these considerations; and therefore I do not put forward the following arguments as a formal criticism of what has perhaps not been formally attempted: I merely think it worth while to state the reasons why—though fully appreciating both the philosophical importance of this work and its remarkable literary qualities—I am unable to put together into a coherent whole the different expressions of Green's ethical view which I find in it.

Green's doctrine as to the basis of morality, in the most comprehensive account which he gives of it, is stated to be a 'Theory of the Good as Human Perfection'. The Perfection which is thus taken to be the ultimate end of rational conduct is otherwise described as the 'realisation', 'development' or 'completion' of human 'faculties' or 'capabilities'. If we ask further to what part of man's apparently composite nature these 'faculties' or 'capabilities' belong, we are told that they are 'capabilities of the spirit which is in man' to which, again, a 'divine' or 'heaven-born' nature is attributed. The realisation of these capabilities is, in fact, a 'self-realisation of the divine principle in man'; that is, of the 'one divine mind' which 'gradually reproduces itself in the human soul'. 'God', we are elsewhere told, 'is a being with whom the human spirit is identical, in the sense that He *is* all which the human spirit is capable of becoming' (p. 198). Hence the conception of the Divine Spirit presents to the man who is morally aspiring an 'ideal of personal holiness' with which he contrasts his own personal unworthiness.

If, however, we are to obtain from these notions anything more than a vague emotional thrill, which, however salutary it may be, cannot carry with it any ethical instruction, we must go on to ask how this relation of man to God is

[A discussion of Thomas Hill Green, *Prolegomena to Ethics*, ed. A. C. Bradley (Oxford: Oxford University Press, 1883), in *Mind*, OS, 9/34 (Apr. 1884), 169–84.]

philosophically known, and what definite and reasoned content can be given to this notion of a Divine Spirit. It would appear from the order of Green's treatise, and the proportions of its parts, that an answer to these questions was intended to be given in Book i., on the 'Metaphysics of Knowledge'. Here we are certainly introduced to a 'spiritual principle in nature' corresponding to the spiritual principle implied in all human knowledge or experience. It is argued (pp. 30, 32) that to constitute the 'single, all-inclusive, unalterable system of relations', which we find in nature, properly understood, something beyond nature is needed: 'something which renders all relations possible', and supplies the 'unity of the manifold' which is involved in the existence of these relations. 'A plurality of things cannot of themselves unite in one relation, nor can a single thing of itself bring itself into a multitude of relations . . . there must therefore be something other than the manifold things themselves which combines them.' Such a 'combining agency' in each one's experience is his own intelligence, his intelligent self which unites the objects of his experience while distinguishing itself from them. Hence if we suppose nature to be real 'otherwise than merely as for us', we must 'recognise as the condition of this reality the action of some unifying principle analogous to that of our understanding'. Indeed, Green passes—I do not precisely understand how—from the affirmation of *analogous action* to the affirmation of *identical quality*, and says that nature in its reality implies not only an all-uniting agency which is not natural, but a thinking self-distinguishing consciousness like our own. We further find that this principle of synthesis or unity is 'eternal', in the sense that it is not in time, and 'complete', in the sense that its combining agency extends to all conceivable objects; and that our own empirical knowledge can only be explained as an imperfect reproduction in us of this eternally complete consciousness.

I am obliged to summarise very briefly the results of an elaborate and complicated argument; but I am not now concerned with the argument itself, merely with the ethical bearing and value of its results; and I venture to think that the above meagre statement gives substantially all the characteristics which Green explicitly attributes to the 'spiritual principle' disclosed to us in Book i.—and all, I submit, that can possibly be known about it by the lines of reasoning there developed. And I am confirmed in this view by the passage in Book iii., ch. 2 (p. 189), in which the 'conclusions so far arrived at are summarised'; since there also the 'one divine mind' which 'gradually reproduces itself in the human soul' is not represented with any other 'constant characteristics' beyond those of being a unifying, self-distinguishing, self-objectifying consciousness. 'If', says the author expressly, 'we mean by personality anything else than the quality in a subject of being consciously an object to itself, we are not justified in saying that it necessarily belongs to God.' But how, I would ask—with all reverence for the deep religious emotion of our author,—can we possibly get an 'ideal of holiness', of an 'infinitely and perfectly good will', out of this conception of a combining, self-distinguishing, and self-objectifying agency? What perfection can the human spirit aim at, so far as it is merely conceived as the reproduction of such an agency, except the increase of knowledge, extensively or intensively? the presence to the combining intelligence of a more extensive manifold of combined objects, or the presence of them as more effectively combined? I need not say that nothing can be more unlike this conception than Green's moral ideal; in which, indeed, as I shall presently argue, knowledge rather occupies a too subordinate place.

It may be said perhaps that though the Divine Mind cannot be *known* to us as more than a combining intelligence, the source of the systematic unity of nature, we may and ought to *believe* it to be more; and that Green must be supposed to mean this when he describes the 'attitude of man towards an infinite spirit' as 'not the attitude of knowledge' but only of 'awe and aspiration' (p. 329). But the reason he gives for excluding the attitude of knowledge is a reason which, so far as it is valid at all, applies precisely to that conception of the spiritual principle which is given in Book i.: 'knowledge', he says, 'is of matters of fact or relations, and the infinite spirit is neither fact nor relation'; and since the net result of the 'Metaphysics of Knowledge' is at any rate to establish the necessary existence of an eternally complete thinking consciousness which is 'neither fact nor relation', but yet 'needed to constitute' facts and relations, it seems to me merely an eccentric subtlety of metaphysical terminology to say that we have no 'knowledge' of such an eternal mind. We have at any rate, if we have followed assentingly a hundred pages of close argument, a reasoned conviction with regard to it; and my point is that Green seems unaware of the barrenness of this conviction for his ethical purposes, and nowhere offers us a suggestion of any other reasoning by which his philosophical conception of the Divine Mind might be turned into one capable of furnishing us with an adequate ethical ideal. I, at least, can find no grounds in the argument of Book i. for attributing to the spiritual principle any such characteristic as the term 'holiness' expresses: I cannot even find adequate reasons for attributing to it anything analogous to Will. It is merely, so far as I understand, an eternal intellect out of time, to which all time and its contents are eternally and (we may say) indifferently present: being equally implied in the conception of *any* succession, it is not shown to carry with it the conception of progress towards an end in the series of motions or changes of which the process of the world in time consists. And even if we grant that such a progress is implied in the development of the eternal consciousness in *us*, it is, as I have already said, still a purely intellectual progress, a growth of that which knows in knowledge alone.

I have so far proceeded on the assumption that the 'human perfection' which we are trying to define is the perfection of that spiritual principle which is said to be in a manner identical with God, being an imperfect reproduction of the eternal divine consciousness. But, the classically instructed reader of the *Prolegomena*, remembering the ethical psychology of Aristotle, and noting the large share of influence which the study of Aristotle has obviously had on Green's speculation, may perhaps surmise that our ideal of human perfection—so far as it is practical and (in a narrow sense) ethical, and not scientific or merely intellectual—belongs rather to the human soul as a function of an animal organism, modified by being made a vehicle of the eternal consciousness, and not to that eternal consciousness itself, as making the animal organism the vehicle. And this surmise would certainly find considerable support in the analysis and exposition of the psychological elements of moral action—desire, intellect, volition—which Green has given in Book ii. The author, indeed, is specially concerned to maintain the real unity between the effort of the self-conscious soul in learning to know, and its effort 'in the way of giving to or obtaining for objects, which various susceptibilities of the self-conscious soul suggest to it, a reality among matters of fact' (p. 138). But he recognises that its efforts of this latter kind, to a large extent, 'originate in animal wants or the susceptibility to animal pleasure, in the sense that without such want or susceptibility they could not be' (p. 129); and though he denies that the desires most important in the moral life of civilised man—such as love, envy, ambition—are directly dependent on animal susceptibilities, I do not understand him to deny that they may be traced ultimately to animal feelings, as modified by the supervention of self-consciousness carrying with it a consciousness of the individuality of other persons. Certainly animals feel love, envy, jealousy; and no reason is suggested why a reproduction of the eternal consciousness should have these emotions, independently of the conditions of the animal organism to which it is subject. Admitting Green's account of the manner in which the self-conscious self reacts upon the desires thus organised, so that they become something differ-ent from what they would be in a merely animal soul: admitting that it presents to itself objects of desire, distinct from itself and from each other, and that in seeking the realisation of any particular object it is always seeking its own satisfac-tion; I should still have inferred that it is only because it has 'supervened upon the appetitive life' of an animal organism that the self-conscious self has such desires for the realisation of objects at all. And since the essential characteristic of moral action, as explained in Book ii., consists in the presence of this self-distinguishing and self-seeking consciousness, identifying itself with different particular desires —or rather usually with a complex resultant of several distinguishable desires; I should have expected that man's pursuit of perfection would be traced to some combination of natural desires modified by self-consciousness.

But the account of the moral ideal, which the author proceeds to give in Book iii., does not correspond to this expectation: the impulse of the spirit to seek 'moral good' is rather represented as being in profound contrast and antagonism to the impulses of the animal soul. We are told that though self-satisfaction is continually *sought* by moral agents in the realisation of the objects of particular desires—due to the conditions under which the self-conscious subject exists in the human organism—it cannot be really found there. 'The conditions of the animal soul, "servile to every skiey influence", no sooner sated than wanting, are such that the self-determining subject cannot be conscious of them as conditions to which it is subject . . . without seeking some satisfaction of itself that shall be independent of these conditions.' Accordingly though 'good' is defined as 'that which satisfies some desire', 'moral good' or the 'true good' is defined as 'an end in which the effort of a moral agent may really find *rest*' (p. 179)—or, as Green elsewhere expresses it, 'an abiding satisfaction of an abiding self' (p. 250).

That is, this appears to be Green's view on the whole, though there is a certain ambiguity or hesitation in his language. In some passages he rather confuses the reader by apparently using 'good' to denote the object in which self-satisfaction is sought, whether or not it is really found in it. Thus he speaks (p. 99) of a moral agent presenting to himself a certain idea of himself as an 'idea of which the realisation *forms*'—not *seems*—'for the time his good'. So again, p. 166—'The man who calmly faces a life of suffering in the fulfilment of what he conceives to be his mission could not bear to do otherwise. So to live is his good'; where the context shows that such a man is not therefore conceived to find satisfaction in so living. But supposing we understand 'good' in such passages to mean 'apparent' or 'anticipated' good, another difficulty remains. Green holds, of course, that particular desires are continually being satisfied; and since he speaks of the moral agent as 'identifying itself' with such desires (or their objects) and even speaks of a 'particular *self*-satisfaction' to be gained in attaining one of these objects (p. 108), I do not see how he can consistently deny that the good even of a moral agent is *temporarily* gained in such 'particular self-satisfactions'. Still, the passages in which such denial is explicitly or implicitly made are too numerous and unmistakable to leave any doubt that they express a doctrine deliberately held. Such a doctrine indeed is indispensable as a basis to the intermittent controversy with Hedonism which Green carries on throughout the treatise; since, so far as I can see, his only substantial objection to the Hedonistic end relates to its transient quality: it is not a 'permanent' or 'abiding' good. He still indeed clings to the paradox maintained by him on previous occasions of controversy[1] that 'a greatest sum of pleasures' is 'intrinsically unmeaning'; but a Hedonist, I think, need not seriously concern himself with the refutation of this paradox, since in another passage Green explains that he does not intend to 'deny that there may be in fact such a thing as desire for a sum or contemplated series of pleasures, or that a man may be so affected by it as to judge that some particular desire should not be gratified'; and I need hardly say that he does not intend to deny that certain courses of action 'tend to make life more pleasant on the whole', or that 'an overbalance of pain on the whole would result to those capable of being affected by it' from certain other courses of action—in fact he expressly affirms both these propositions in the very words that I have used. In these propositions it is implied

---

[1] Cf. *Mind*, VI., 267–9; and the Introduction to Hume's *Treatise on Human Nature*, § 7.

that pleasure and pain, as distinguished from their conditions, can be subjected —in some degree at least—to quantitative measurement; and therefore, when in another passage Green lays down that 'pleasure (in distinction from the facts conditioning it) is not an object of the understanding', the Hedonist need not be troubled at the strange statement; for he will perceive that it is to be understood in some subtle metaphysical sense with which he is not concerned.[2] In short, the one anti-hedonistic argument on which our author now appears seriously to rely is that pleasures are of 'perishing nature' and 'do not admit of being accumulated in enjoyment':[3] that, therefore they are not in any sense permanent or 'abiding', so that no amount of them can give real satisfaction to a moral agent, and constitute his true good. The pleasure-seeker, like the 'animal soul', is 'no sooner sated than wanting', the satisfaction of any particular desire is no sooner attained than a desire, similar or different, emerges again; and therefore true self-satisfaction is not attained; the effort of the moral agent does not 'find rest'.

Now, I have given this argument—which Green urges with a very impressive earnestness of conviction—my best consideration; and I am obliged to conclude that there must be very fundamental differences in the constitution of moral agents, if I may be allowed to count myself one. For if I understand what Green means by 'rest', I can only say that I desire it as little as I expect it, in this life or in any other. The happiness that I have enjoyed has been conditioned by the perpetual presence—or rather the continually fresh emergence—of desire; and whether this condition is to be referred to the 'animal soul' or not, I have no aversion to it and do not aspire to be independent of it. I recognise this dislike of desire and this contempt for transient satisfactions which Green expresses as characteristic of the conscious experience of certain meditative minds; but I can confidently deny that these feelings are necessary or universal, and I have no adequate ground for regarding them as even common among human beings generally. I admit that men frequently, under the influence of strong desire, are liable to the illusion that the agreeable 'repose of a mind satisfied' will be at least

[2] I must confess that I cannot even conjecture in what sense Green lays down this proposition; since it appears to me that in this very discussion he conducts long arguments which are only intelligible if the distinction between pleasure and the facts conditioning it is thoroughly grasped and steadily contemplated by the understanding. And I may add that this distinction is carried to a degree of subtlety far beyond that which the Hedonist requires, or would be disposed to adopt; for Green insists on his distinguishing 'pleasure' from the 'satisfaction' involved in the conscious realisation of a desired object.

[3] In some passages I incline to think that Green's argument proceeds on the tacit—and surely quite unwarrantable—assumption that an 'end', in the ethical use of the term, ought to mean something to which we gradually get nearer and nearer—some sort of goal or consummation. But all that I, and (I conceive) most ethical writers, mean by the term is an object of rational aim—whether attained in successive parts or not—which is not sought as a means to the attainment of any ulterior object, but for itself. And so long as any one's prospective balance of pleasure over pain admits of being made greater or less by immediate action in one way or another—which Green does not deny—there seems no reason why 'Maximum Happiness' should not provide a serviceable criterion of good.

a comparatively permanent consequence of attaining the desired object, and are temporarily disappointed when they find that this is not the case; but neither the expectation nor the disappointment is inevitable or universal: indeed, they seem to me rather experiences of the immature mind, which riper reflection on the relation of desire to life tends to suppress. The man who has philosophised himself into so serious a quarrel with the conditions of human existence that he cannot be satisfied with the prospect of never-ending bliss, because its parts have to be enjoyed successively, and under the condition of being successively desired—such a man. I venture to think, is not a typical φρόνιμος.

I have digressed somewhat from the main line of my discussion, because I could hardly avoid noticing the anti-hedonistic controversy which occupies so large a space in the *Prolegomena*: but as my primary object is not to criticise Green's view from the outside, but rather to exhibit the difficulties of framing a clear and consistent notion of it, I will assume for the present that the true good of man must be a 'permanent' or 'abiding' good, and therefore cannot be pleasure. What then is it? and what ground have we for supposing it attainable by man? It does not appear that the path of moral progress, even as pursued with the most stoical contempt for attendant pleasures and pains, is one in which the effort of the moral agent finds 'rest', at least in this earthly sphere. Green, at any rate, does not maintain this: he says of the 'man who calmly faces a life of suffering in the fulfilment of what he conceives to be his mission', that '*if* he could attain the consciousness of having accomplished his work, . . . he would find satisfaction in the consciousness', but adds that '*probably just in proportion to the elevation of his character he is unable to do so*' (p. 166): it would seem therefore that he no less than the voluptuary is always pursuing and never attaining.

Perhaps it may be said that if the 'abiding good' is not *found* by the man who is seeking perfection, it is at any rate approached by him; the moral aspirant who is daily growing less imperfect may not experience the satisfaction of attainment, but at any rate he is getting towards it.[4] But (1) what can this avail him if he never actually attains? and (2) even granting that the consciousness of approximation is the best substitute available to him for the consciousness of attainment in this earthly life, I cannot conceive in what sense this can be regarded as an 'abiding satisfaction', unless there is a reasonable prospect of the continuance of his personal existence after death,—and I do not see that Green's reasonings give him any justification for such an expectation. We are told, indeed, that 'a capacity consisting in a self-conscious personality cannot be supposed to pass away. It partakes of the nature of the eternal.' But granting this, still everything depends on the extent and manner in which this participation is conceived: however true it may be that the human spirit is in a sense identical with the Divine Being, it is undeniably

---

[4] P. 256. 'But of particular forms of life we may say that they are better, because in them there is . . . a nearer approach to the end in which alone man can find satisfaction for himself.'

different from it as a self-conscious individual; and the question whether its participation in the nature of the eternal involves immortality of its distinct individual self is one which Green does not seem to me to have definitely faced. In the passage (pp. 193–5) in which he comes nearest to discussing it, the question that primarily seems to interest him is not whether the individual John or Thomas has reason to expect continued existence as an individual after death, but whether we have reason to expect that the life of the spirit will always be realised in *some* individual persons. What he is concerned to maintain is, that 'the human spirit cannot develop itself according to its idea except in self-conscious subjects . . . the spiritual progress of mankind is an unmeaning phrase, unless it means a progress of which feeling, thinking, and willing subjects are the agents and sustainers'. Considering the 'promise which the spirit gives of itself, both in its actual occasional achievement and in the aspirations of which we are individually conscious'; we may, he thinks, 'justify the suppositions that the personal life, which historically or on earth is held under conditions which thwart its development, is continued in a society, with which we have no means of communication through the senses, but which shares in and carries further every measure of perfection attained by men under the conditions of life that we know. Or we may content ourselves with saying that the personal self-conscious being, which comes from God, is for ever continued in God. Or we may pronounce the problem suggested by the constant spectacle of unfulfilled human promise to be simply insoluble.'

Now doubtless the consideration of these alternatives, the weighing of the *pros* and *cons* for each of them, is an interesting and elevating speculation; but I fail to perceive that any one of them meets the difficulty with which I am now dealing. If

> The high that proved too high, the heroic for earth too hard,
> The passion that left the ground to lose itself in the sky

present us only with an insoluble problem, I do not see how the philosopher is to fulfil the task he has undertaken of showing the effort after an 'abiding self-satisfaction' to be rational. Nor, again, do I see how this is achieved by adopting the second alternative, and supposing that the personal self-conscious being, now designated as John or Thomas, is to be 'for ever continued in God'. For God, or the eternal consciousness—according to the definition given in Book i.—is necessarily conceived as unalterable: it is eternally in reality all that the human spirit is in possibility, and there are no conceivable perfections that could be added to it; and the process of man's moral effort is surely futile if it is to end in nothing but the existence of that which exists already.[5] It may be said that objections

---

[5] It may perhaps be said that I ought not to apply such a conception as 'already existing' to a Being whose existence is expressly stated to be out of time. And, though I cannot profess to be able to reason about such a Being without tacitly conceiving it in some relation to time, I should not have ventured to use the phrase in the text if Green had not set me the example; *e.g.*, in speaking (p. 181) of a 'best state of man already present to some divine consciousness'.

of this kind may be brought against every philosophical theology, unless it diverges widely from religious common-sense: a plain man cannot but conceive the world-process, divinely ordered, as designed to bring about some good not yet realised which must be good from a divine or universal point of view, and yet he cannot conceive the Divine existence as at any time defective or wanting in any respect. I admit the force of the rejoinder; only, unlike Green, I should draw from it the inference that we ought not to use these theological notions, while yet unpurged of such palpable inconsistencies, as the basis of a philosophy of practice.

If, however, we leave on one side these theological difficulties, can we find the 'abiding self-satisfaction' which a moral agent is supposed to seek, in the first of the alternatives above suggested—in the conception, that is, of a society of persons who somewhere, somehow, in the indefinite future, are to carry further that movement towards perfection which is so seriously impeded among the human beings whom we know? We might perhaps accept the solution—it being granted that the human spirit can be abidingly satisfied with movement instead of rest, progress instead of perfection—if a 'better state of humanity' could be taken as a convertible term for the 'better state of myself' at which, as a moral agent, I necessarily aim. In several passages Green seems to pass backwards and forwards between these two notions as if they might be used indifferently in his reasonings; but I cannot see how his moral psychology justifies this procedure. He has laid it down that 'in all desire, or at any rate in all that amounts to will, it is self-satisfaction which the self-conscious agent necessarily seeks . . . a certain possible state of himself which in the gratification of the desire he seeks to reach' (pp. 177, 182): and since he has also explained how the most characteristic human desires depend on the conscious distinction between the desirer's own individuality and that of other persons, I presume that we must maintain this distinction in interpreting the account above given of 'all desire'; and therefore that the 'better state of myself' which I necessarily seek cannot be the better state of any other person as such. But if so, we must know exactly how the one comes to be identified or indissolubly connected with the other under the comprehensive notion of the 'bettering of man' or 'humanity'; by what logical process we pass from the form of unqualified egoism under which the true end of the moral agent is represented to us on one page, to the unmediated universalism which we find suddenly substituted for it on another. I admit, of course, that the Divine Spirit, so far as it can be rightly conceived to aim at the realisation or reproduction of itself in men, must be conceived as aiming at its realisation in 'persons', not in 'this person', in humanity, not in me; but this only brings out more forcibly the difference that has to be bridged over between the aim of my one indivisible conscious self at its own satisfaction, and this aim of the Divine Spirit at a satisfaction or realisation which may just as well be attained in anyone else as in me. The mere fact that I am aware of myself as a self-distinguishing consciousness and attribute a similar consciousness to other men, does not necessarily make me regard their good as my own; some rational transition is still needed between the recognition of them as ends to themselves, and the recognition of them as ends to myself.

Can this transition be obtained by dwelling on the essential sociality of men, the universal or normal implication, through sympathy, of each one's interest or good with the interests of some others—according to the plain man's conception of 'interest' no less than the philosopher's? In some parts of his discussion (*e.g.*, in Book iii., ch. 3) Green seems to rely to some extent on this line of reasoning, with which the looser optimism of eighteenth-century moralists appears to have been often entirely satisfied; but I think that an exact consideration of it will show its inadequacy to establish the required conclusion. For granting all that is claimed, it only proves that I cannot realise good for myself without promoting the good of others in some degree; it does not show that my own good is in any sense identical with the good of others who are to live after me, so that it will 'abide' in another form when my individual existence has terminated. And even if we give up the characteristic of 'permanence' and merely consider whether my good during life can be identified with the good of humanity at large, I still fail to see how this identification can be justified by anything that we know of the essential sociality of ordinary human beings. The 'better state of himself' as conceived even by a voluptuary, who aims at dining well, is a social state: his dinner must be a convivial dinner if it is to be good; but it does not follow that he contemplates the waiters who hand round the dishes as ends-in-themselves or has any interest in future good dinners of which he will not partake. This is a coarse illustration; but the proposition that it illustrates seems to me equally, if less palpably, true of all the ordinary exercises and functions of cultivated social existence: the mere fact that I am a social being, that my life is meagre and starved if I do not enlarge it by sympathy, and live the life of the community of which I am a member, does not necessarily constitute the good of humanity my good: it brings me a certain way towards this, but it has not necessarily any force or tendency to carry me the rest of the way. Granting that 'to any one actuated by it the idea of perfection for himself will involve the idea of a perfection for all other beings, *so far as* he finds the thought of their being perfect necessary to his own satisfaction', it remains true that to most persons the dissatisfaction caused by the idea of the imperfection of other beings, not connected with them by some special bond of sympathy, is at any rate an evil very faintly perceptible; and the question why in this case they should sacrifice any material part of their own good or perfection to avoid it remains unanswered.

I shall be told, perhaps, that the true good of man is so constituted that no competition can possibly arise between the good of one individual and the good of any other. And, doubtless, Green often affirms with sufficient distinctness that 'the idea of a true good does not admit of the distinction between good for self and good for others'. I think, however, that he does not steadily keep before his mind the gulf that he has placed between himself and common sense by the adoption of this important proposition; and that, in consequence, he wastes his energies in trying to establish the untenable paradox that civil society is 'founded on the idea' of a common good of this kind. He admits, indeed, that 'we are very far, in our ordinary estimates of good, whether for ourselves or for others, from keeping such a standard before us ... the conviction of the community of good for all men has little positive influence over our practical judgments'; good being, in fact, 'sought in objects which admit of being competed for'. But he does not seem to see that the acceptance of this proposed standard would radically alter the common notions of virtue, even the notions to which he himself adheres most unquestioningly in his delineation of the moral ideal. Consider, for example, his description of the ideally just man, who is 'so over-curious, as it seems to the ordinary man of the world, in inquiring, as to any action that may suggest itself to him, whether the benefit which he might gain by it for himself or for some one in whom he is interested would be gained at the expense of anyone else'; and so determined not to 'promote his own wellbeing or that of one whom he loves or likes, from whom he has received service or expects it, at the cost of impeding in any way the wellbeing of one who is nothing to him as a man, or whom he involuntarily dislikes' (p. 244). Surely all this scrupulous investigation, all this resolute impartiality, implies that, in the opinion of Green's ideally just man, it is at least possible that he and his friends may be benefited at the expense of others, that the promotion of one's own well-being may really involve the cost of impeding the well-being of others: in short, that good really consists—at least to some extent— in 'objects that admit of being competed for'. How, after writing this description of an ideally just man, Green could go on to say that 'the distinction of good for self and good for others has never entered into that idea of a true good upon which moral judgments are founded', I cannot imagine. That the distinction ought to be banished from our moral judgments is an intelligible proposition— though I think a moralist who makes it is rather bound to reconstruct our notions of justice and injustice, and show us the form they will take when the distinction is eliminated—but the statement that it has 'never entered in' I contemplate with simple amazement.

So again, the 'habitual self-denial', the 'self-sacrificing will' which form an essential element of Green's moral ideal, seem to me notions with regard to which Kant's question *Quid juris?* is very obviously raised by Green's theory of the true good; and the question one that never finds an answer. If all self-conscious agents are always aiming each at his own good or self-satisfaction, and the most virtuous man only differs from the most vicious in that he seeks it with a truer insight into its nature, how can he—in the strictness of philosophical discourse —be said to 'deny' or 'sacrifice' himself in so seeking it? What he denies is not 'himself'—according to Green's psychology as expounded in Book ii.—but those 'impulses', 'influences', or 'tendencies' due to his animal soul with which he does *not* identify himself,[6] 'by which he is consciously affected but which are not he'; and which Green, indeed, with a certain eccentricity of terminology, is reluctant even to call 'his desires'. I trust the reader will not think that I am disputing about words; the question, I take it, is not of language but of the correctness of a certain psychological analysis; I seem to discern, in Green's account of moral action, pagan or neo-pagan forms of ethical thought combined with Christian or post-Christian forms without any proper philosophical reconciliation.

It may be said, however, that these objections are purely formal, or at least that they do not affect the substance of our author's own doctrine: let us leave them, therefore, and try if, when we examine in detail the content of Green's conception of a 'true good' for the individual, we find it really so constituted that it cannot possibly come into competition with the true good of any other individual. It is difficult to see how this can be maintained with reference to the wide ideal of human perfection which is put forward in many passages of the treatise. The 'realisation of human capabilities' at which we ought to aim is repeatedly stated to include 'art and science' as well as 'specifically moral virtues': we must suppose 'all that is now inchoate in the way of art and knowledge' to have reached completion in it (p. 309): the development of arts and sciences is 'a necessary constituent' of any life which 'the educated citizen of Christendom' presents to himself as one in which he can find satisfaction (p. 415). But if I am right in thinking the development of artistic faculty and taste a part of my true good, I surely cannot be wrong in regarding the latter as including 'objects that admit of being competed for', so long as the material conditions of our spiritual existence remain at all like what they are at present: indeed I should have thought that a writer like Green, who steadily refuses to take a hedonistic view of ordinary human aims and efforts, must regard the 'realisation of scientific and artistic capacities', taken in a wide sense, as constituting the main motive of the keen struggle for material wealth which educated and refined persons generally feel themselves bound to keep up, for their children even more than for themselves. The thoughtful trader knows that wealth will enable him to provide himself and those he loves with books, pictures, prolonged education, varied travel, opportunities of intellectual society: and, knowing this, he allows himself to adopt methods of dealing which sometimes, perhaps, are hardly compatible with Green's ideal of justice. Similarly the hardest choice which Christian self-denial imposes is the preference of the work apparently most socially useful to the work apparently most conducive to the agent's own scientific and aesthetic development.[7]

---

[6] *Cf.* especially Bk. ii. ch. 2, p. 151.

[7] I think Green unconsciously evades the difficulty which this choice presents, on his theory, when he speaks (pp. 292–3) of 'the conscientious man sacrificing *personal pleasure* in satisfaction of the claims of human brotherhood . . . the good citizen has no leisure to think of developing his own faculties of *enjoyment*'. Of course his good man, being anti-hedonistic, has no theoretical difficulty in sacrificing his own pleasure or enjoyment—or indeed that of anyone else: but we may still ask whether and why and how far he is called upon to sacrifice the realisation of his scientific and artistic capabilities.

It may be replied that Art and Science are good, but Virtue better; that the self-devotion which leads a man to postpone to duty the fullest possible realisation of his scientific or artistic faculties is an exercise in which a fuller development of his nature as a whole is attained. I cannot conceive any empirical criterion of 'fulness of development' by which this could be made to appear even probable as a universal proposition: but if we grant it to be true, in all cases in which the occasion for such a sacrifice may be presented, it can only be because the superiority in importance of the 'specifically moral virtues', as compared with

> All other skills and gifts to culture dear,

is held to be so great that the alternatives may be regarded as practically incommensurable. But if this be so, it seems to me that the promotion of the specifically moral virtues—considering the amount that remains to be done in this direction—ought in consistency to occupy so large a share of the practical philanthropist's attention that Green's inclusion of Art and Science will turn out to have hardly any real significance. In short Green seems to me to have unconsciously tried to get the advantages of two distinct and incompatible conceptions of human good: the one liberally comprehensive, but palpably admitting competition, the other non-competitive but stoically or puritanically narrow.

If, again, we concentrate our attention on the narrower conception of 'specifically moral virtue', we find a similar difficulty in combining, as Green wishes us to do, formal and material criteria of virtuous action: nor do I think that matters are improved by the trenchant and dogmatic solution of the difficulty which Green here offers. Sometimes the formal criterion is put forward in language which would satisfy the most orthodox Kantian: 'the only good', we are told, 'which is really common to all who pursue it is that which consists in the universal will to be good' (p. 262): the good will is 'the one unconditional good . . . the end by reference to which we estimate the effects of an action' (p. 316). On the other hand, it is explained that the 'good will' must not be understood to be 'a will possessed by some abstract idea of goodness or moral law', which would 'amount to a paralysis of the will for all effectual application to great objects of human interest'. We conclude therefore that a will is not good, as with Kant, merely through its motive being pure regard for duty, but through its leading to good effects; and accordingly Green expressly says that a man 'cannot have been good unless he has done what is good in result' (p. 332). It immediately occurs to us that, if this be true, in order to be good a man must have more than a mere will to be good; his zeal must be according to knowledge; he must have the power of foreseeing what actions will lead to good results. 'A dominant interest in the perfection of mankind' will avail him little, if he erroneously supposes that it may be best promoted by a free use of dynamite. And besides mere knowledge there are various other qualities, caution, presence of mind, instinctive sympathy and tact, &c., the want of which, as is commonly thought, may seriously impair the good effects of the most well-intentioned acts. How then can we say that a good will is the 'one unconditional good'? Green meets this difficulty by dogmatically enunciating that 'there is no real reason to doubt that the good or evil in the motive of an action is exactly measured by the good or evil in its consequences as rightly estimated' (p. 320). 'With the whole spiritual history of the action before us on the one side, with the whole sum and series of its effects before us on the other, we should presumably see that just so far as a good will . . . has had more or less to do with bringing the action about, there is more or less good . . . in its effects.'

Nothing that can be called evidence is offered on behalf of this startling presumption, and I cannot conjecture on what grounds Green considered himself justified in thus dogmatically affirming it: especially when I find him saying later on that it is 'obvious that the exact measure in which my conduct has fallen short of . . . perfection', in any particular action, 'cannot be speculatively ascertained, till we can see all moral effects in their causes'. If it is obviously impossible to ascertain how far the effects of any action are good, how can I possibly tell that they are certain to be exactly as good as the agent's motives were? The perplexity is made greater when Green goes on to admit expressly (p. 334) that evil consequences of actions may have been due to a 'want of the requisite knowledge and ability to foresee' (pp. 333, 334); without expressly maintaining or even implying that such ignorance and want of foresight are always traceable to want of good will. The perplexity reaches its height when we consider wherein the goodness of these good effects consists and how it is to be known. It must ultimately lie, as Green repeatedly tells us, in the tendency of the immediate consequences of actions to promote good character, that 'perfection of mankind of which the essence is a good will on the part of all persons'. It is true that this promotion can be only indirect, since 'every one must make his character for himself. All that one man can do to make another better is to remove obstacles and supply conditions favourable to the formation of a good character.' Still it remains true that the promotion of a good character in others and ourselves must, according to Green, be the sole ultimate end and standard of the goodness of the effects of our actions. On the other hand, Green explains in another passage (pp. 318, 319) that 'we are on very uncertain ground' when we try, in judging the actions of contemporaries, to 'ascertain the state of character on the part of the agents which the actions represent': and hence concludes that it is wiser 'to confine ourselves to measuring the value of actions by their effects without reference to the character of the agents'. But, as we have seen, these effects can only be effects on the character of other persons; and since, I presume, our judgments as to effects on character must ultimately be inferred from observations of conduct, there would seem to be precisely the same kind of difficulty in measuring the value of actions by their effects as there is in trying to ascertain the character of the agent; only that in the former case the unknown quantity comes in at a later stage of the calculation.

I cannot but think that these and other fundamental difficulties of method would have pressed themselves more strongly on Green's attention, and would therefore have obtained from him at least a consistent solution, if he had ever felt strongly the practical importance of improving men's knowledge or reasoned conviction as to what they ought to do. But—in face of the vehement jar and conflict of principles and methods continually exhibited by contemporary schools and sects of social reformers, whose sincerity and earnestness cannot be doubted —he remains firmly persuaded that practically the tendency of actions to pro- duce a perfection of human society will be 'within the ken of any dispassionate and considerate man'; and hence, though he recognises that it is the function of philosophy to supply men with a *rationale* of the various duties' prescribed to them, I cannot perceive that the enthusiasm for human well-being which the whole treatise breathes has actually impelled him to furnish such a *rationale*, or even to provide his readers with an outline of a coherent method by which a system of duties could be philosophically worked out. There is much instructive description and discussion, in the concluding Book of the treatise, of the general attitude which a moral man should adopt in dealing with practical problems, much subtle analysis and distinction of different elements presented for his con- sideration; but if the reader expects to be guided to a cogently reasoned solution of any such problems—proceeding from unambiguous ethical premises to definite practical conclusions—the expectation will hardly be fulfilled.

This, at least, is the conclusion at which I have arrived, after a careful perusal of the treatise: but I expect that it will be widely disputed. Considering the grow- ing prevalence of the manner of thought of which Green was a leading represen- tative, the great influence exercised by himself personally, the amount of close and powerful reasoning which his book contains, and the singularly elevated and inspiring ethical mood which pervades it from first to last—it is hardly possible that such a work should not meet with many readers to whom it will give, as a whole, more intellectual satisfaction than I have been able to find in it. Indeed, had I thought otherwise, it would have seemed to me more suitable—as it would certainly have been more consonant with my own feelings—to treat this post- humous book in a less polemical manner; to dwell more upon its literary merits, and upon those aspects or elements of its doctrine with which I am in cordial sympathy. But, regarding the treatise as one about which our ethical discussion is likely for sometime to turn, I have thought it best to urge the fundamental difficulties that I find in its teachings as frankly and fully as I should have done if the author had been living to reply. There are many, I doubt not, ready—if they should think it needful—to come (as Plato says) 'to the aid of the orphaned doc- trine, the father of which had he lived would have struck many a good stroke in its behalf': or let me rather say—since he never wrote for victory—that he would have set himself to remove such difficulties as he thought worthy of consideration in the candid, earnest, careful, exhaustive style of controversy which was peculiarly his own. That this source of further instruction is now for ever closed to us, no one can regret more sincerely than the writer of this article.

28. Fowler's *Progressive Morality*

This book is 'an attempt to exhibit a scientific conception of morality in a popular form, and with a view to practical applications rather than the discussion of theoretical difficulties'. It is therefore not primarily intended for the students of ethics who may be supposed to be readers of this Review: at least, in the present notice, I am rather called upon to examine the adequacy and coherence of Prof. Fowler's scientific conception than the degree of success attained by him in popular exposition. Still, before I proceed to the criticisms that I have to offer from the former point of view, it is only fair to say that the book appears to me, in style and manner of treatment, excellently adapted for the purposes for which it is primarily intended. When I disagree with the author, it is almost inevitable, from the nature of the subject, that I should sometimes attribute to him confusion or obscurity of thought or expression; but whenever I find myself in agreement with his views, he seems to me to have very successfully packed much instructive matter into lucid and unburdensome paragraphs.

Thus nothing can be better, for its purpose, than the greater part of ch. i., in which the moral motive or sanction, regarded as the 'internal feeling of approbation or disapprobation with which, on reflection, we look back upon our own acts', is distinguished not only—as by Bentham—from the physical and legal sanctions, but also from the social sanction (which Bentham and others have called 'moral') and from the 'lower' and 'higher' religious sanction. I do not myself think that what is here characterised as the 'higher' religious motive, which operates when 'we simply do good and act righteously, because God, who is the supreme object of our love and the supreme ideal of conduct, is good and righteous'— comes strictly under the head of 'sanctions' as defined by Prof. Fowler: that is, I do not think it is clearly a case of pleasure attracting or pain deterring: but probably this psychological question is one of the controversial points which the author has wished to avoid.

In ch. ii., after effectively pointing out how the moral sanction 'varies as applied not only by different individuals but by the same individual at different times', Prof. Fowler raises the fundamental question, How then, in spite of the variation, can we 'justify the application of this sanction' as the 'supreme and final sanction in case of conflict'? His answer consists of two parts. He first urges that 'in the main we approve of ourselves for having done what we thought right at

[Critical Notice of Thomas Fowler, *Progressive Morality* (London: Macmillan and Co., 1884), in *Mind*, OS, 10 (1885), 266–71. Replied to by Professor Fowler in *Mind*, 10 (1885), 481–6.]

the time, even though we may have come to think it wrong'. This is, I conceive, true as regards the moral judgments of reflective persons: but if we are considering the moral *sanction*, *i.e.*, the pleasure and pain attending judgments of approbation and disapprobation respectively—I think it must be admitted that the emotional satisfaction with which we contemplate a past act, performed under a sense of duty which we have come to regard as mistaken, is at best a very feeble pleasure. At any rate, the proposition that this feeling should always prevail in conflict with others demands some further justification, besides a mere demonstration that it approves its own predominance. This further justification Prof. Fowler finds in the fact that 'human nature, in its normal condition, is so constituted that the remorse felt, when we look back upon a wrong action, far outweighs any pleasure we may have derived from it, just as the satisfaction with which we look back upon a right action far more than compensates for any pain with which it may have been attended'. I infer, however, from a later passage (ch. iv., p. 139) that by a 'normally constituted' mind Prof. Fowler means a mind where the feelings of self-approbation and self-disapprobation are 'very strong'— since it is only in the case of such a mind that he is prepared to affirm 'that a man *always* gains more happiness in the long run by following the path of duty'. This view, at any rate, importantly limits the application of Prof. Fowler's justification of the moral sanction; and this limitation, I think, should be more carefully explained in ch. ii. But, further, if the claim of moral sentiments to prevail is justified on the ground that they are 'more intense and durable than other pleasures and pains', some qualification seems to be needed in the account subsequently given (ch. iii.) of 'sacrifice' as an essential characteristic of acts morally approved. I do not see how, according to Prof. Fowler, it is possible for a 'normally constituted mind' really to sacrifice its 'own good to the greater good of others': I do not even see how moral action can even *appear* to such a mind under the form of 'sacrifice', provided that it has duly apprehended the greater intensity and durability of moral pleasures and pains.

I have, however, a more fundamental difficulty with regard to the analysis of the moral sentiment given in ch. iii. Prof. Fowler aims at 'discriminating carefully between the intellectual and emotional elements in an act of approbation or disapprobation': and following Hume's 'peculiarly lucid treatment' of this distinction, he explains that 'whether we are reviewing the actions of ourselves or of others, what we seem to do, in the first instance, is to refer them to some class or associate them with certain actions of a similar kind which are familiar to us, and then, when their character has thus been determined, they excite the appropriate feeling of approbation or disapprobation, praise or censure'. Here, however, there is a fundamental question to ask, with regard to which Hume's answer seems to me different from Prof. Fowler's. In this intellectual reference of an action to a class which precedes the feeling of approbation or disapprobation, is the class conceived as having *ethical* characteristics—I mean, as being good or bad, right or wrong—or is it not? That Hume means to answer this question in the negative is quite clear; but if Prof. Fowler means to answer it in the same way, I think his language should be more carefully chosen. He speaks of this intellectual or logical process—when distinguished from the '*feeling* of moral approbation or disapprobation'—as a 'moral judgment', a 'decision upon conduct': and he gives as illustrations of it that 'as soon as we have recognised an act as brave or generous, we regard with esteem or admiration the doer of it . . . no sooner is the act duly labelled as a lie, a theft, or a fraud, or an act of cruelty or ingratitude, or the like, than the appropriate ethical emotion is excited'. No doubt it is; only, I conceive, in this 'labelling' the acts are implicitly judged to be good or bad. When a plain man recognises an act as 'brave' he implicitly recognises it as good or deserving of praise, at least in some respects if not absolutely; and in the same way 'theft', 'fraud', 'cruelty', as commonly used, are dyslogistic terms—*e.g.*, in saying that a vivisector is cruel it is commonly meant not merely that he inflicts a great deal of pain in order to advance knowledge, but also that he ought not to inflict it. If then Prof. Fowler means to use the terms with their ordinary connotation, his view is different from Hume's; if not, such connotation should be more scrupulously excluded.

To a certain extent, I think, the book shows a hesitation or oscillation between these two incompatible views. Throughout the interesting discussion in ch. iii. (pp. 47–80), in which the distinctive characteristics of the object of moral approbation and disapprobation are determined, Prof. Fowler seems to be considering exclusively moral *sentiments*; as if he held with Hume that 'the final sentence which stamps on characters and actions the mark of approbation or censure' depends on some 'internal sense or feeling'. And in accordance with this view he explains that 'the feelings of moral approbation and disapprobation can never be properly described as erroneous . . . the error attaches to the preliminary process of reasoning, reference, or classification'. In ch. iv., however, we are told that in the logical process of which the moral judgment is the result, 'there are two possible sources of error. In the first place, the act of reference or association may be faulty . . . but even if the action be referred to its right head, there remains the second question whether we are really justified in regarding the class of actions itself as right and wrong.' This second question clearly relates to a judgment or opinion, not a mere sentiment: there are, as Prof. Fowler goes on to say, 'wide divergences of *opinion* on matters of conduct', so that it is of vast importance to 'discriminate between those acts which are really and those which are only reputed, right and wrong'. For this kind of discrimination Hume's view, as I understand it, leaves no room: in attempting it, Prof. Fowler seems to me to have left Hume behind, and to have accepted the fundamental assumption of an objective rightness and wrongness in actions, which is strictly incompatible with Hume's system. Where Hume only explains, Prof. Fowler is prepared to justify.

Where then is the justification to be obtained? Prof. Fowler agrees with Utilitarians in holding that it 'must be derived from the observation of the effects and tendencies of actions': and the manner in which he traces the progress of morality as the result of the continued application of this test, at first in a merely semi-conscious and almost instinctive way, and afterwards, in the later stages of civilisation, by the consciously reflective action of philosophers and reformers, affords a good specimen of his terse, fluent, and generally judicious exposition. It appears to me, indeed, over-dogmatic to affirm that 'wherever any change of moral conduct takes place, unless it be dictated by blind passion, or mere submission to authority. . . . the change is *invariably* due to some change of opinion on what constitutes the advantage of the persons whom it affects'; since—to take Prof. Fowler's own instance—I should attribute such a change as that which has brought about the abolition of slavery rather to an increased general concern for the feelings of slaves than to a changed opinion as to what constituted their advantage. But I have a difficulty in criticising closely Prof. Fowler's view of moral progress, since I am unable to conceive with any precision the application of the test which he proposes. He holds, with Bentham, that 'we may rightly regard the tendency to produce a balance of pleasure over pain as the test of the goodness of an action'; but he considers that in estimating pleasure and pain we must 'frankly acknowledge that there are some pleasures and pains which are incommensurable with one another', and also 'recognise the fact that our pleasures differ in quality as well as in volume'. Now I cannot myself remember to have experienced any pleasure or pain strictly incommensurable with any other feeling definitely recognised as pleasurable or painful: *i.e.*, I cannot recall any one pleasure so immeasurably greater than some other that I should prefer the former, however limited in duration, to an indefinitely prolonged pleasurable consciousness of the latter kind: and similarly *mutatis mutandis* of pains. And if such incommensurabilities are really found in the conscious experience of others, it seems fundamentally important to know—what Prof. Fowler does not tells us—how many grades of incommensurability there are, and what pleasures and pains belong to each grade; since it is obvious that, in testing rules of conduct by a rational estimate of their effects, wherever any pleasure of an incommensurably higher grade comes in, the whole aggregate of pleasures of a lower grade, however prominent they may be in our forecast of consequences, will have to be discarded from practical consideration. Surely a calculation conducted on this plan would turn out very unlike that ordinary regard for consequences which Prof. Fowler represents as being historically the spring of moral progress.

But the calculation becomes still more perplexing if besides these incommensurables we are to take into account differences in 'quality' as contrasted with differences in 'volume'. By what standard are we to compare superiority in quality with superiority in volume? and why is it to be assumed that men's common judgments as to the 'high' or 'low' quality of pleasures are less open to the charge of 'prejudice, fancy and caprice' than their common judgments as to the goodness or badness of actions? I observe that Prof. Fowler prefers to call his ultimate standard of morality 'welfare' or 'well-being' rather than happiness, partly because it 'corresponds almost exactly with the εὐδαιμονία of Aristotle'. I am afraid that this is, in my view, a reason for objecting to it; since I find that Aristotle, in determining the particulars of εὐδαιμονία, appeals to just those common moral opinions as to virtue and vice for which a test, in Prof. Fowler's view, is required. Now if, when we ask how to distinguish what is really 'good' in conduct from what is reputed such, we are referred to the effects of actions on social well-being, it is clear that the test will be illusory if the notion of well-being is to be, in its turn, wholly or partially identified with that of good conduct; but it is just this identification that is the prominent characteristic of Aristotle's treatment of εὐδαιμονία.

I have hardly space to comment on the last chapter, in which Prof. Fowler gives 'some examples of the manner in which the test of conduct may be applied to practical questions, either by extending existing rules to cases which do not obviously fall under them, or by suggesting more refined maxims of conduct than those which are commonly prevalent'. But I may observe that the particular duties which he proceeds to enforce are to a great extent such as ordinary men would admit to be obligatory in any theoretical discussion, however much they may practically neglect them; at least I cannot recall any grave arguments in favour of smuggling, evading taxes, accepting or offering bribes, reckless gambling, inconsiderate almsgiving, borrowing without a reasonable prospect of repaying, or the minor social faults of impertinent curiosity, impertinent advice, and the like. And in those cases in which Prof. Fowler has pronounced on points that are really matters of serious controversy, it seems to me that his reasoning is liable to lack cogency from excessive brevity. Thus it is not made clear why 'under all circumstances' suicide involves the 'evil example of cowardice' more than any other avoidance of useless pain: nor, again, why 'cock-fights and bull-fights' are to be summarily dismissed as admitting of no justification, if the 'beneficial effects in enjoyment' to the fox-hunter are to be adduced to justify foxhunting. Still, in spite of this undue abbreviation of the arguments, the frank, earnest, practical survey of neglected duties which this chapter presents is a commendable feature in Prof. Fowler's treatise; and contains instruction for readers of all classes.

29. Idiopsychological Ethics

In *Mind* No. 39 I reviewed Dr. Martineau's *Types of Ethical Theory*. A reply from Dr. Martineau, somewhat longer than my review, appeared in the next number. On reading this reply, it seemed to me desirable to deal in different ways with the historical and the theoretical portions of it. Dr. Martineau's answers to my criticisms on his historical work convinced me that there was nothing to be gained by a prolonged and enlarged controversy on this part of the subject: a brief and immediate rejoinder, which I gave in the following number, was all that seemed desirable. The case was otherwise with the further explanations which Dr. Martineau had been led to give of his own views: since, on the one hand, these threw new lights on certain parts of Dr. Martineau's doctrine, which rendered necessary a partial modification of my objections to it; while, on the other hand, they suggested to me that possibly a fuller statement of these objections might render them more intelligible to Dr. Martineau, and to any others who may share his ethical views.

The appearance of a second edition of Dr. Martineau's book seems to afford a favourable opportunity for this fuller statement; and, for the convenience of the reader, I shall take up the question *de novo*, and shall not refer—except in one note—to my original article; while, at the same time, I shall try to avoid any mere repetition of arguments there urged.

I will begin by criticising an unwarranted assumption—as it appears to me—which underlies Dr. Martineau's whole procedure. He characterises his ethical system as 'idiopsychological': that is, he professes to give the 'story' that the 'moral consciousness tells of itself', or 'what the moral sentiment has to say of its own experience'. And he appears generally to entertain no doubt that there is one and the same 'story' to be told in all cases; that if the same question be definitely put to the moral consciousness of any number of different individuals, they will return definitely the same answer as his own. He holds, at any rate,[1] that all men in their particular moral judgments judge primarily and essentially of the moral preferability of particular impulses or incentives to action, and that so far as the impulses presented are similar men's judgments of their moral value will also be similar. 'However limited the range of our moral consciousness, it would lead us all to the same verdicts, had we all the same segment of the series [of impulses] under our cognisance' (p. 61) . . . 'the instant that any contending principles press

[From *Mind*, OS, 12 (1887), 31–44.]
[1] ii. 16, 17. The references are throughout to the second edition (vol. ii).

their invitations on [a man], *there* too is the consciousness of their respective rights . . . his duty consists in acting from the right affection, about which he is *never left in doubt'* (p. 72)—unless, that is, he wilfully neglects to use the faculty of moral insight with which he is endowed, for 'the inner eye is ever open, unless it droops in wilful sleep'.

Now I do not find that Dr. Martineau has adduced any sufficient reasons for making this fundamental assumption. He can hardly rest it on the agreement of the accounts given of the moral consciousness by the persons who have most systematically reflected on it; since this class includes, as I shall presently show, moralists who disagree fundamentally with Dr. Martineau. And I see no sign that his assumption is based on a careful induction from the accounts actually given by plain men of their moral experience. Indeed in other passages Dr. Martineau seems to admit that the moral judgments of mature men do not actually manifest an undeviating harmony with his own scale of preferability. 'To find the true instinct of conscience', he says, 'we may more often go with hope to the child than to the grandparents. . . . of most men the earlier years are nobler and purer . . . unfaithfulness inevitably impairs and corrupts the native insight'. That there is an element of truth in this I would not deny: it does not, however, appear that Dr. Martineau has made any such careful and extensive observation of the moral judgments of children as would justify him in affirming broadly that they are more in harmony with his own scale than those of mature men; and, in any case, the assumption that the divergences of the latter are due to 'unfaithfulness' is one that seems to me to require a kind of justification that he has not attempted.

I have been led—both from observation of my contemporaries and from examination of the morality of other ages and countries—to take an essentially different view of the variation and conflict in men's moral judgments and sentiments which their discourse appears to reveal. I agree, indeed, with Dr. Martineau that such variations are to a considerable extent due to differences in the objects contemplated; but I hold that they cannot entirely or even mainly be referred to this cause: that when we have made full allowance for this, an important element of difference still remains which it appears to me unwarrantable to attribute to 'unfaithfulness', or 'wilful drooping of the inward eye' in one or other of the differing individuals. Among reflective persons, who belong to the same age of history and are members of the same civilised society, the amount of difference that is disclosed by a comparison of moral opinions bears usually a small proportion to the amount of agreement; but it is probably rare that some material difference is not discernible, whenever two such persons compare frankly and fully the results of the spontaneous, unreflective play of their moral sentiments. And if we survey the views of the whole aggregate of persons who devote serious thought to moral questions at any given time, we cannot but see that systematic ethical reflection,—while it tends to group individuals together into so-called schools, and so to intensify the consciousness of a common morality among members of the same group,—has so far tended to develop profounder differences between one group and another.

As an illustration of the irreducible differences of which I am speaking, I may note a point of some importance on which I find myself in disagreement with Dr. Martineau. In stating what he calls the 'fundamental ethical fact of which we have to find the interpretation' (p. 18), he affirms that 'wherever disapprobation falls, we are impelled to award disgrace and such external ill as may mark our antipathy, with the consciousness that we are not only entitled but constrained to this infliction'. Now I find that the sense of being 'constrained to award external ill' to a fellow-man of whose conduct I disapprove, not in order to prevent worse mischief to him or to others, but merely to 'mark my antipathy', is entirely absent from my moral consciousness; and, what is more, I feel an instinctive moral aversion to the impulse thus characterised which goes decidedly beyond my reflective and deliberate disapprobation of it. But I do not therefore affirm that Dr. Martineau has wrongly analysed his own moral consciousness; still less do I suggest that it has been corrupted through unfaithfulness. I should rather say that his sentiment appears to me to belong to that earlier stage in the development of morality in which legal punishment is regarded as essentially retributive, instead of preventive. Nor do I affirm that the common sense even of civilised mankind has as yet passed out of this stage; but I think that it is beginning to pass out of it, and that a continually increasing number of reflective persons are conscious of no *moral* impulse to 'award external ill' to their fellow-creatures, except as a means to some ulterior good.

I have made these preliminary remarks, because, while the main object of this paper is to show the erroneousness of Dr. Martineau's account of the moral judgments which we, here and now, habitually pass, it is important to make clear at the outset that the question discussed does not seem to me to admit of being answered so decisively as Dr. Martineau assumes. I think that the assumption of a common moral consciousness which we all share, and which each of us can find in himself by introspection, is to a great extent true; that to a great extent we—educated members of the same society—tend, in our ordinary thought and discourse, to pass similar judgments of approbation and disapprobation, feel similar sentiments of liking or aversion for the conduct so judged, and similar promptings to encourage or repress it. But, after carefully reflecting on my own moral sentiments and comparing them with those of others—to whom I have no reason to attribute a less careful reflection—I do not find in the result anything like the extent of agreement which Dr. Martineau assumes. This is the explanation of the 'hesitation' that Dr. Martineau finds in my attempt to formulate the morality of common sense: on any point on which opposing opinions appear to me tolerably balanced, so that neither can fairly be described as eccentric, I represent common sense as hesitating: to decide any such point either way would be an improper substitution of my own judgment for that common judgment of educated and thoughtful persons which I am trying to ascertain and formulate. Nor do I consider the verdict of common sense, so far as it is clearly pronounced, as final on the question of ethical truth or falsehood; since a study of the history of human opinion leads me to regard the current civilised morality of the present age as merely a stage in a long process of development, in which the human mind has—I hope—been gradually moving towards a truer apprehension of what ought to be. As reflection shows us in the morality of earlier stages an element of what we now agree to regard as confusion and error, it seems reasonable to suppose that similar defects are lurking in our own current and accepted morality; and, in fact, observation and analysis of this morality, so far as I have been able to ascertain what it is, has led me to see such defects in it. How to eliminate, if possible, these elements of error, confusion, and uncertainty is, in my view, the fundamental question of ethics, which can only be answered by the construction of an ethical system. With this task I am not at present concerned—further than to explain that I do not expect to find this true moral system where Dr. Martineau looks for it; that is, by introspection directed to the moral sentiments and apparently immediate moral judgments caused in my mind by the contemplation of particular acts, apart from systematic consideration of these acts and their consequences in relation to what I adopt as the ultimate end of action. That I should have such sentiments, and, where prompt action is needed, should act on such judgments, is at once natural and, in my opinion, conducive to the ultimate end; but I continually find that these immediate pronouncements have to be corrected and restrained by a careful consideration of consequences.

To sum up: there are, in my view, three fundamentally distinct questions, which ought to be investigated by essentially different methods: (1) what the received morality was in other ages and countries, which is to be answered by impartial historical study; (2) what the received morality is here and now, which is to be ascertained by an unprejudiced comparison of one's own moral judgments with those of others; (3) what morality ought to be—a problem which can only be solved by the construction of an ethical system. It is the answer which Dr. Martineau has given to the second of these questions—and this alone—which I propose now to consider.

According to Dr. Martineau, the 'broad fact' of the moral consciousness is that 'we have an irresistible tendency to pass judgments of right and wrong' (p. 17): when I pass such judgments 'as an agent' on my own conduct 'I speak *of my duty*' —a word which 'expresses the sense we have of a debt which we are bound', or 'obliged', to pay. This sense of obligation implies, of course, a conflict between the moral judgment and some impulse prompting us to conduct disapproved by our moral judgment. But in Dr. Martineau's view it necessarily implies more than this; it necessarily implies the recognition of 'another person', who has authority over us: the dictates of conscience, he holds, are unmeaning unless we give them a Theistic interpretation.

Now I quite admit that a Christian Theist must necessarily conceive of the dictates of conscience as Divine commands; but I think it rash and unwarrantable in him to affirm that they cannot be regarded as authoritative unless they are so conceived. To me, indeed, it is inconceivable that the authoritativeness or bindingness of moral rules should depend essentially on the fact that they emanate from 'another Person'. Dr. Martineau himself admits—or I should rather say emphatically declares—that it is not a Person regarded apart from moral attributes that can be conceived as the source of the authority of which we are speaking; it is, he says, 'an inward rule of Right which gives law to the action of God's power . . . which first elevates into authority what else would only operate as a necessity or a bribe' (p. 113). If, then, moral rules, when conceived as Divine commands, are thought to have authority not because they emanate from an Omnipotent Person, but because they emanate from a person who wills in accordance with a rule of Right, I cannot conceive how they should lose this authority even if the 'other person' is eliminated altogether, provided that the 'rule of right' is left.

I may perhaps make this clearer by referring to an analogy which Dr. Martineau elsewhere draws between mathematical and moral truth. 'There is', he says, 'as much ground, or as little, for trusting to the report of our moral faculty as for believing our intellect respecting the relations of number and dimensions. Whatever be the "authority" of Reason respecting the true, the same is the "authority" of Conscience respecting the right and the good'[2] (p. 114).

Now I presume that Dr. Martineau does not maintain that the 'authority of Reason respecting the relations of number and dimension in regard to time' cannot 'really exist' for an atheistic mathematician—one who has, in Laplace's phrase, had no 'besoin de l'hypothèse de Dieu' in his system of the physical universe. But if he does not maintain this, I think he is bound in consistency to admit that the 'authority of Conscience respecting the right' may similarly exist for the atheistic moralist.

---

[2] In dealing with this point in my former article I quoted passages in which, as it appeared to me, Dr. Martineau committed himself to a 'definitely and confidently anthropomorphic conception of the Divine mind'. In his reply, Dr. Martineau affirmed that in the passages quoted he intended to 'explain an anthropomorphic habit' of which he had 'exposed the error', not to adopt it as his own. I accept, of course, Dr. Martineau's account of his intentions; but, having carefully re-read the passages from which I quoted—especially p. 86 (1st ed.) with its context, which remains unaltered (as p. 92) in the present edition—I feel bound to say that they are not calculated to convey to the mind of an ordinary reader what he now declares to be his meaning. Dr. Martineau writes throughout from an avowedly Christian point of view: hence, when he describes 'Christianity' and 'Christian feeling' as taking 'naturally' a certain view of the Divine Nature, without which 'the negative element requisite for every ethical conception, the antagonism to something resisted and rejected, would be wanting; and the evangelical and the heathen Theism would be without further essential distinction'—I do not think any ordinary reader will suppose that Dr. Martineau is intending to 'expose the error' of the view in question.

I have accepted, for the sake of argument, Dr. Martineau's distinction between 'Reason' and 'Conscience'. But, to prevent misunderstanding, I ought to explain that, in my view, the 'authority of Conscience' is the authority of Reason in its application to practice: 'authority' or 'obligation', in my view, expresses the relation that we recognise on reflection between a judgment as to what ought to be willed by us and a non-rational impulse prompting in a direction opposed to this judgment.

Let us now consider more closely the general nature of the judgment to which this authority—however understood—is recognised as belonging. I find that in discussing this question Dr. Martineau, on the one hand, labours needlessly a point not likely to be disputed; and, on the other hand, confuses or slurs over the distinction which I regard as fundamentally important. We shall all, I conceive, agree that moral approbation, strictly taken,[3] relates to what Dr. Martineau loosely calls the 'inner spring or inner principle' of an action—i.e., that it relates to the mental or psychical element of the complex fact which we call action; as distinct from the muscular movement that follows the psychical volition, or any external consequences of this movement considered as external and not as foreseen by the agent. Further, I agree with Dr. Martineau in defining the object of the common moral judgment as volition or choice of some kind. Our difference begins when we ask what the object is which is willed or chosen. In Dr. Martineau's view the choice is always between particular impulses to action—whether 'propensions', 'passions', 'affections' or 'sentiments'; in my view it is, in the largest and most important class of cases, among different sets of foreseen external effects, all of which are conceived to be within the power of the agent. That Dr. Martineau has not clearly seen the point at issue may, I think, be inferred from the language (cp. pp. 129–30) in which he criticises my own procedure. He says that I, among others, 'by no means call in question the general principle that moral worth or defect is to be estimated by the inward *affection or intention* whence actions flow'; and implies that I have thereby 'admitted the necessity' of 'enumerating' and 'classifying' motives or impulses to action, though I afterwards 'run away from the work as unmanageable and superfluous'. But it is plain that if I am right in regarding the choice of right outward effect as being, in the most important cases, the primary object of ordinary moral judgment, my primary business is to enumerate and classify, not the propensions or passions that prompt to choice, but the outward effects that ought to be chosen and intended. It is always the choice or intention, and not its actual result, that is approved or disapproved; but the differences of choice or intention, on which the

---

[3] I say 'strictly taken', because in a wider sense of the terms we approve or disapprove of a human being and his actions without distinguishing between their voluntary and involuntary elements; just as—in Dr. Martineau's words—we 'approve a house' or 'condemn a ship', from a consideration of its fitness or unfitness for some accepted end.

moral judgment turns, can only be conceived as differences in the objects chosen; and can therefore, on my view, only be sought in that 'field of external effects of action' which Dr. Martineau would relegate to a separate and subsequent investigation.

Nor is the case practically altered by that condition of our approval of right choice to which I have (in my *Methods of Ethics*, bk. iii., ch. i., p. 3) called attention under the term 'subjective rightness'; *viz.*, that the outward effects which we judge to be the right objects of choice must not be thought by the agent to be wrong. The condition is, in my view, an essential one; if, in any case—owing to what we regard as a mistake of conscience—the agent makes what we hold to be the right choice of foreseen outward effects, himself conceiving it to be wrong, we certainly withhold our moral approbation. If we are asked whether in this unhappy situation a man ought to do what he mistakenly believes to be his duty, or what really is his duty if he could only think so, the question is found rather perplexing by common sense; and—so far as it can ever be a practical question—it would, I think, be answered differently in different cases, according to the magnitude and importance of the error of conscience. But the difficulties of this question need not now be considered; for, obviously, they arise equally whether the mistake of conscience relates to choice of motives or to choice of outward effects; and, however essential it may be that a moral agent should do what he believes to be right, this condition of the object of moral approbation does not require or admit of any systematic development. Thus the details with which ethics is concerned still remain to be sought elsewhere; and, on my view, they are found by common sense primarily in the region of external effects, and not among the different propensions, passions, affections or sentiments impelling the agent.

It may be said, perhaps, that the issue as I have stated it cannot be fundamental, because the effects as foreseen must operate as motives—as causing desires or aversions—otherwise action would not result.[4] But my point is that the effects

---

[4] Dr. Martineau would not exactly urge this; because he considers it fundamentally important to lay stress on the absence of any conscious foresight of effects in the case of what he distinguishes as 'primary springs of action', which urge us, 'in the way of unreflecting instinct', to seek blindly ends not preconceived. I agree that such blind impulses have a considerable place among the normal causes of our voluntary action, though I think he has exaggerated their place; according to my experience, they cannot be at all powerful or prolonged without arousing some representation of the effects to which they prompt. But, in any case, I cannot understand how they can be morally judged *as blind*; I conceive that the effects of the action to which such unreflecting impulses prompt, however absent or faintly represented when the impulse operates, are necessarily represented when it becomes the object of a moral judgment. This will appear, I think, if we reflect on any example included in Dr. Martineau's exposition of the 'scale of springs of action'—*e.g.*, in comparing the appetite for food with the desire of the pleasure of eating, he says, 'it is surely meaner to eat for the pleasure's sake than to appease the simple hunger': well, it seems to me clear that, so far as I pass this judgment, it is not on hunger, *quâ* blind impulse, but on hunger conceived as an impulse directed towards the removal of an organic want.

which, in our judgment, make an action bad may not have been desired at all, but only accepted as inevitable accompaniments of what was desired, and that the effects which make it good may have only been desired as a means to some further end; and that it is not to the desired effects of volition, *quâ* desired, but to the effects foreseen as certain or highly probable—and so chosen instead of other possible consequences—that our judgments of approbation and disapprobation are commonly directed under the heads of justice, temperance, good faith, veracity and other leading branches of duty. I contend that the approbation implied by the designation of agents or acts as truthful, just, temperate—and the disapprobation implied by the opposite terms—are commonly given independently of any consideration of motive, as distinct from intention or choice to produce certain external effects (using 'external' to include effects on the agent's physical system). I do not say, as Dr. Martineau has understood me to say, that we regard the motives of such acts as ethically unimportant: I recognise that common sense distinguishes motives as higher and lower, and even positively as good and bad; and if we definitely conceive of (say) truth-speaking as prompted by a motive recognised as bad, we do not approve of the agent's state of mind, though I should say that we still approve of the act. We think that the veracious agent has willed what he ought to have willed, though he ought to have willed something else too, *viz.*, the suppression of the bad motive—so far, at least, as it was within his power to suppress it while doing the act. I introduce this last qualification, because I think that it is not always within the power of the will—and therefore not always strictly a duty—to get rid of an objectionable motive.

Take the case of the motive which Dr. Martineau places last,—Vindictiveness, or the desire of malevolent pleasure. Bentham and Sir James Stephen[5] regard it as an important part of the benefits of criminal law that it provides the 'pleasure of revenge', or, as Sir J. Stephen says, a 'legitimate satisfaction for the passion of revenge'. These phrases, I think, give some offence to our common moral consciousness; and, in my *Methods of Ethics*, I have suggested that 'perhaps we may distinguish between the impulse to inflict pain and the desire of the antipathetic pleasure which the agent will reap from this infliction, and approve the former in certain circumstances, but condemn the latter absolutely'. I suggest this, however, with some hesitation, on account of the great difficulty of separating the two impulses. A man under the influence of a strong passion of resentment can hardly exclude from his mind altogether an anticipation of the pleasure that he will feel when the passion is gratified; and, if so, he can hardly exclude altogether the desire of this gratification. It is, I think, clear to common sense that a man ought not to *cherish* this desire, to gloat over the anticipated gratification; but it is, perhaps, too severe to say that the desire of malevolent pleasure should be excluded altogether. If, as Sir James Stephen says, the 'deliberate satisfaction

---

[5] Cp. *General View of the Criminal Law of England*, ch. iv.

which criminal law affords to the desire of vengeance' excited by gross crimes is an indispensable means of preventing such crimes—human nature being what it is; if it is important for the well-being of society that men should derive 'hearty satisfaction' from the hanging of a cold-blooded murderer, or the infliction of penal servitude on an unscrupulous swindler; then it is, perhaps, going too far to condemn absolutely the desire of this satisfaction. In any case, it seems to me contrary to common sense to say that the prosecution of such a murderer or swindler becomes a bad act if the prosecutor is conscious of desiring the malevolent pleasure that he will receive from the criminal's punishment: we commonly judge such an act to be right, even though partly done from a motive which we think ought to be excluded as far as possible. It is sometimes said that, though a man cannot help *having* the inferior motive, he can and ought to avoid *yielding* to it, or 'identifying himself' with it; but here there seems to me some psychological confusion or error. I cannot understand how a man can avoid 'yielding to' a desire, if he cannot exclude it from his mind while doing precisely the act to which it prompts.[6] Even if the motive of an externally right act were entirely bad—*e.g.*, if a man were strictly veracious with a view to gain and ultimately misuse the confidence of his hearers—common sense, I conceive, would still decide that his veracious volition was right *quâ* veracious; only that it coexisted with a wrong intention as to future conduct, and did not indicate any moral worth—*i.e.*, any general tendency to right actions—in the agent.[*]

It is still more clear to common sense that bad acts may be done from the best conceivable motives; indeed we are all familiar with historical examples of men prompted by religion, patriotism, or philanthropy to acts that have excited most general and intense moral disapprobation. When we contemplate Torquemada torturing a heretic for the eternal good of souls, Ravaillac assassinating a monarch in the cause of God and his church, a Nihilist murdering a number of innocent persons in order to benefit his country by the destruction of an emperor, a pastor poisoning his congregation in the sacramental wine in the hope of securing their eternal happiness—we recognise that such acts are (so far as we know) not only subjectively right, but done from the very highest motives; still common sense does not therefore hesitate to pronounce them profoundly bad.

It may be said, however, that my argument admits that the distinction of 'good' and 'bad', or 'higher' and 'lower', motives is recognised by common sense as important; it must, therefore, be the duty of the moralist to make this distinction as precise as possible, in its application to different classes of motives; and in doing

---

[6] Very often the course of action prompted by a bad motive would differ palpably in details from that prompted by a pure regard for duty; and such differences would afford occasions for 'not yielding' to the bad motive. But I know no reason for assuming that palpable differences of this kind would be found in all cases.

[*] [From approximately this point on, the argument of this paper appears in the 4th edn. of *The Methods of Ethics* (1890), 370–2. Ed.]

this he will be led to frame such a scale as Dr. Martineau's. But a careful reflection upon our common judgments or motives will lead us, I think, to interpret and systematise them in a manner fundamentally different from Dr. Martineau's. According to him, the springs of human action may be arranged in an ethical scale, so constituted that if any of its 'propensions',[7] 'passions', 'affections', and 'sentiments' thus classified ever comes into conflict with one higher in the scale, right volition consists in choosing the 'higher' in preference to the 'lower'. The view of common sense appears to me rather that, in all or most cases, a natural impulse has its proper sphere, within which it should be normally operative, and that the question whether a higher motive should yield to a lower is one that cannot be answered decisively in the general way in which Dr. Martineau answers it: the answer must depend on the particular conditions and circumstances of the conflict. For a higher motive may intrude unseasonably into the proper sphere of the lower, just as the lower is liable to encroach on the higher; only since there is very much less danger of the former intrusion, it naturally falls into the background in ethical discussions and exhortations that have a practical aim. The matter is complicated by this further consideration: we recognise that as the character of a moral agent becomes better, the motives that we rank as 'higher' tend to be developed, so that their normal sphere of operation continually enlarges at the expense of the lower. Hence there are two distinct aims in moral regulation and culture, so far as they relate to motives: (1) to keep the 'lower' motive within the limits within which its operation is considered to be legitimate and good on the whole, so long as we cannot substitute for it the equally effective operation of a higher motive; and at the same time (2) to effect this substitution of 'higher' for 'lower' gradually, so far as can be done without danger, up to a limit which we cannot definitely fix, but which we certainly conceive, for the most part, as falling short of complete exclusion of the lower motive.

[7] For the reader's convenience, I give the table of the springs of action in which Dr. Martineau has collected the results of his survey:—

LOWEST.

1. Secondary Passions—Censoriousness, Vindictiveness, Suspiciousness.
2. Secondary Organic Propensions—Love of Ease and Sensual Pleasure.
3. Primary Organic Propensions—Appetites.
4. Primary Animal Propension—Spontaneous Activity (unselective).
5. Love of Gain (reflective derivation from Appetite).
6. Secondary Affections (sentimental indulgence of sympathetic feelings).
7. Primary Passions—Antipathy, Fear, Resentment.
8. Causal Energy—Love of Power, or Ambition; Love of Liberty.
9. Secondary Sentiments—Love of Culture.
10. Primary Sentiments of Wonder and Admiration.
11. Primary Affections, Parental and Social—with (approximately) Generosity and Gratitude.
12. Primary Affection of Compassion.
13. Primary Sentiment of Reverence.

HIGHEST.

I may illustrate by reference to the passion of resentment of which I before spoke. The view of reflective common sense is, I think, that the malevolent impulse so designated, as long as it is strictly limited to resentment against wrong and operates in aid of justice, has a legitimate sphere of action in the social life of human beings as actually constituted: that, indeed, its suppression would be gravely mischievous, unless we could at the same time so intensify the ordinary man's regard for justice or for social well-being that the total strength of motives prompting to the punishment of crime should not be diminished. But, however much it were 'to be wished', as Butler says, that men would repress wrong from these higher motives rather than from passionate resentment, we cannot hope to effect this change in human beings generally except by a slow and gradual process of elevation of character: therefore—to come to the point on which Dr. Martineau appears to me to be at issue with common sense—supposing a conflict between 'Compassion', which is highest but one in Dr. Martineau's scale, and 'Resentment', which he places about the middle, it is by no means to be laid down as a general rule that compassion ought to prevail. We ought rather—with Butler—to regard resentment as a salutary 'balance to the weakness of pity', which would be liable to prevent the execution of justice if resentment were excluded.

Or we might similarly take the impulse which comes lowest (among those not condemned altogether) in Dr. Martineau's scale—the 'Love of Ease and Sensual Pleasure'. No doubt this impulse, or group of impulses, is continually leading men to shirk or scamp their strict duty, or to fall in some less definite way below their own ideal of conduct; hence the attitude habitually maintained towards it by preachers and practical moralists is that of repression. Still, common sense surely recognises that there are cases in which even this impulse ought to prevail over impulses ranked much above it in Dr. Martineau's scale; we often find men prompted—say by 'love of gain' or 'love of culture'—to shorten unduly their hours of recreation; and in the case of a conflict of motives under such circumstances we should judge it best that victory should remain on the side of the 'love of ease and pleasure', and that the unseasonable intrusion of the higher motive should be repelled.

Perhaps it may be said that in neither of these instances would the conflict of motives remain such as I have described: that though the struggle might begin, so to say, as a duel between resentment and compassion, or between love of ease and love of gain, it would not be fought out in the lists so marked out; since still higher motives would come in in each case, regard for justice and social well-being on the side of resentment, regard for health and ultimate efficiency for work on the side of love of ease; and that it would be the intervention of these higher motives that would decide the struggle so far as it was decided rightly and as we should approve. This certainly is what would happen in my own case, if the supposed conflict were at all serious and its decision deliberate; and it is for this reason that such a scale as Dr. Martineau has drawn up, of motives arranged according to their moral rank, can never, in my view, have more than a very subordinate ethical importance. It may serve to indicate in a rough and general way the kinds of desires which it is ordinarily best to encourage and indulge, in comparison with other kinds which are liable to compete and collide with them; and we might perhaps settle, by means of it, some of the comparatively trifling conflicts of motive which the varying and complex play of needs, habits, interests, and their accompanying emotions continually brings forth in our daily life. But if a serious question of conduct is raised, I cannot conceive myself deciding it morally by any comparison of motives below the highest: the case must, as I have elsewhere said,[8] be 'carried up' for decision 'into the court' of the motive which I regard as supreme—*i.e.*, the desire to promote universal good, understood as happiness of sentient beings generally. Thus the comparison ultimately decisive on the particular question raised would inevitably be not a comparison between the motives primarily conflicting, but between the effects of the different lines of conduct to which they respectively prompt, considered in relation to whatever we regard as the ultimate end of reasonable action. And this, I conceive, is the course which moral reflection will naturally take in the case not only of utilitarians, but of all who follow Butler in regarding our passions and propensions as forming naturally a 'system or constitution', in which the ends of lower impulses are subordinate as means to the ends of certain governing motives, or are comprehended as parts in these larger ends. So far as any view of this kind is taken, any tabulation of the moral rank of motives other than the governing ones can, at best, have only a quite subordinate interest: it cannot possibly furnish a method of dealing with the fundamental problems of ethical construction.

[8] *Methods of Ethics*, bk. iii., ch. xii., p. 372. [3rd ed., 1884].

30. Spencer on Justice

Mr. Spencer's book on 'Justice' is stated in his *Preface* to be Part IV. of a comprehensive work on *The Principles of Ethics*, of which Part I. was published in 1879 as *The Data of Ethics*. 'Led', he says, 'by the belief that my remaining energies would probably not carry me through the whole, I concluded that it would be best to begin with the part of most importance. Hence, passing over Part II., "The Inductions of Ethics," and Part III., "The Ethics of Individual Life," I devoted myself to Part IV., "The Ethics of Social Life: Justice".'

The contents of the new book may be summarily described by saying that the first seven chapters are ethical, the last seven mainly political, while the intervening fifteen are concerned with a subject common to ethics and politics—the determination on general grounds of the rights of individuals. In the present notice, it seems best to direct attention chiefly to the ethical aspect of the treatise.

Mr. Spencer begins by recalling briefly his general view of ethics, as given in *The Data of Ethics*. 'The primary subject-matter of ethics is conduct considered objectively as producing good or bad results to self or others or both.' The primary question, therefore, relates to the determination of the ultimate end and standard by which 'goodness' and 'badness' of results are to be estimated. In *The Data of Ethics* a double conception was presented of this ultimate end or standard. Regarded from a biological point of view the End was recognised as 'Life estimated by multiplying its length into its breadth', *i.e.*, by taking into account, not simply duration, but also quantity of change. 'The conduct called good rises to the conduct conceived as best', when it 'simultaneously achieves the greatest totality of life, in self, in offspring, and in fellow-men'. But regarded from the point of view of subjective psychology, a different ultimate end was presented, *viz.*, 'desirable feeling called by whatever name—gratification, enjoyment, happiness'. Accordingly, Mr. Spencer's system, as expounded in this earlier book, appeared open to the criticism that it assumed too easily a practically complete coincidence between Life and Pleasure; *i.e.*, it assumed that actions conducive to Maximum Life would always be no less conducive to Maximum Pleasure, and *vice versâ*. This fundamental assumption Mr. Spencer seems still to maintain; but, on the whole, we may say that, in the treatise now before us, the hedonistic aspect of his system drops somewhat into the background. Thus in the first chapter, on 'Animal Ethics', the ultimate end—not only of human conduct but of animal

[Critical Notice of *Justice*, part IV of the *Principles of Ethics*, by Herbert Spencer (London: Williams & Norgate, 1891), in *Mind*, NS, 1/1 (1892), 107–18.]

'conduct at large'—is stated to be 'the greatest length, breadth, and complete-ness of life'; while 'relatively to the species' acts are said to be good 'which are conducive to the preservation of offspring or of the individual'. Such acts may be 'egoistic' or 'altruistic': thus there are 'two cardinal and opposed principles of animal ethics': for (1) 'within the family group most must be given where least is deserved', while (2) 'after maturity is reached benefit must vary directly as worth'—'worth' being measured by 'fitness for the conditions of existence'. The second of these principles or laws is limited by the first; since so far as adults act for the sustentation of their children, they do not receive from their own acts 'benefit' in proportion to their worth: and it is further limited by the considera-tion that 'if the constitution of the species and its conditions of existence are such that sacrifices, partial or complete, of some of its individuals so subserve the welfare of the species that its numbers are better maintained than they would otherwise be, then there results a justification for such sacrifices'.

This third point, however, is not, in Mr. Spencer's view, an essential one: he recognises only 'two essential but opposed principles of action by pursuance of which each species is preserved', and in considering successively (in chaps. ii. and iii.) 'sub-human' and 'human' Justice, he concerns himself only with one of these principles, 'passing over the law of the family as composed of adults and young'. It would seem that this limitation of view is not unlikely to lead to error, when an attempt is subsequently made to analyse and trace the growth of the 'sentiment' and 'idea' of Justice among men, and to determine its fundamental formula: since the common sense of mankind certainly recognises family relations as a part of the sphere of Justice. And in fact when Mr. Spencer comes in later chapters (xx. and xxi.) to treat of the mutual rights or claims of husbands and wives, and of parents and children, the inadequacy of the principle of Justice formulated in his earlier chapters becomes manifest.

For the present, however, let us 'consider the law of the species as composed of adults only'. Considering this first in the case of 'sub-human life', Mr. Spencer lays down as the 'law of sub-human justice' that 'each individual shall receive the benefits and the evils of its own nature and its consequent conduct'. In a certain sense, this law is said to 'hold without qualification in sub-human life': in another sense, it is explained that 'sub-human justice is extremely imperfect, both in general and in detail'. In general, it is imperfect 'in the sense that there exist multitudinous species the sustentation of which depends on the wholesale destruction of other species': which, according to Mr. Spencer, implies that 'the species serving as prey have the relations between conduct and consequences habitually broken'.

But surely the existence of a predatory species is a part of the conditions of existence of the species preyed upon; and if the former eats up the latter, it would seem that the latter's unfitness to the conditions of its existence would be demonstrated, and Spencerian Justice perfectly realised in its annihilation. It may be said, as Mr. Spencer goes on to say, that 'enemies are causes of death which so operate that superior as well as inferior are sacrificed': and that other 'accidents' —'inclemency of weather', 'scarcity of food', 'invasions by parasites'—fall 'indiscriminately upon superior and inferior individuals'. Here, however, the term 'superior' seems ambiguous: it may mean (1) more highly organised, or (2) more qualified to preserve itself and its species under hypothetical conditions—e.g., with extremes of frost and heat, exceptional famines, foes and parasites left out— or (3) more qualified to live under actual conditions, though not sufficiently vigorous to resist the destructive forces. The two former meanings seem hardly relevant, when we are basing ethical principles on biological laws; for the adaptation of the species in accordance with biological laws must be adaptation to an actual, not an ideal, environment. And if the third meaning be taken, I do not see that 'sub-human justice' can be said to be imperfect, according to Mr. Spencer's statement of its law, because it is not finely graduated. Suppose that, in a given region, two-thirds of a certain species of animal are killed by extreme cold: each individual is none the less 'subject to the effects of his own nature' because some are hardier than others. The point is that no one is hardy enough.

Proceeding, we learn that the individualistic 'law of sub-human justice' is further qualified by the conditions of gregariousness. Firstly, each member of a group of gregarious animals receives the benefits and evils not only of 'his own nature and its consequent conduct' but of the nature and consequent conduct of some or all of the other members of the group: even 'an occasional mortality of individuals in defence of the species' may further the preservation of the species 'in a greater degree than would pursuit of exclusive benefit by each individual'. This last 'limitation of sub-human justice', however, is, in Mr. Spencer's view, solely due to the coexistence of living enemies of the species in question. Secondly, a condition 'absolute for gregarious animals' is that 'each member of the group, while carrying on self-sustentation and sustentation of offspring, shall not seriously impede the like pursuits of others'. This condition, in the case of some gregarious creatures, even becomes a law enforced by sanctions, —as Mr. Spencer affirms on the authority of observers of beavers, bees, crows, and rooks.

In the illustrations that he gives of this enforcement, however, Mr. Spencer seems to me to put together cases that should be carefully distinguished. In some cases *abnormal* action on the part of a member of a gregarious group, tending to interfere with the sustentation of other members, is punished by those other members—as when 'among rooks, a pair which steals the sticks from neighbouring nests has its own nest pulled to pieces by the rest'. But the case of a class in the gregarious community only organised for the performance of a certain function, and destroyed when this function is performed that it may not be a burden on the community—as when the drones of a hive are massacred by worker-bees—is surely quite different. I dwell on this because 'sub-human justice' is introduced to lead up to 'human justice'; and, while the former kind of repression of acts inconvenient to the community is certainly analogous to the mainly individualistic legislation of actual civilised societies, the latter suggests a drastic treatment of those who neither 'toil nor spin' such as the most blood-thirsty socialist has never yet recommended. Moreover, when Mr. Spencer says that 'conditions such that by the occasional sacrifices of some members of a species, the species as a whole prospers' are 'relative to the existence of enemies', he seems to ignore this normal destruction of drones by workers.

I pass now to 'Human Justice'; which Mr. Spencer regards as a 'further development of sub-human justice', the two being 'essentially of the same nature' and forming 'parts of a continuous whole'. Of man, as of all inferior creatures, we are told that 'the law by conformity to which the species is preserved is that among adults the individuals best adapted to the conditions of their existence shall prosper most, and that individuals least adapted to the conditions of their existence shall prosper least. . . . Ethically considered, this law implies that each individual ought to receive the benefits and evils of his own nature and subsequent conduct.' But, in the case of man, the operation of this law is admitted to be modified by the condition of gregariousness in a manner only 'faintly indicated among lower beings'. For 'as communities become developed' the 'limits to each man's activities necessitated by the simultaneous activities of others' become more and more 'recognised practically if not theoretically': also in the case of this 'highest gregarious creature' the principle of individualistic justice has to be qualified, to a greater extent than in the case of lower gregarious creatures, by admitting the sacrifice of individuals for the benefit of the community. This highest creature is distinguished by the characteristic of fighting his own kind; and 'the sacrifices entailed by wars between groups' of human beings have been 'far greater than the sacrifices made in defence of groups against inferior animals'. But 'the self-subordination thus justified, and in a sense rendered obligatory, is limited to that which is required for defensive war'. It may indeed be contended that 'offensive wars, furthering the peopling of the earth by the stronger, subserve the interest of the race'. But, in Mr. Spencer's view, 'it is only during the earlier stages of human progress that the development of strength, courage, and cunning are of chief importance; . . . the arrival at a stage in which ethical considerations come to the entertained is the arrival at a stage at which offensive war ceases to be justifiable'. And he holds that even defensive war, and the qualifications of the abstract principle of justice which it involves, belong to a transitional condition, and 'must disappear when there is reached a peaceful state'. Such qualifications therefore belong to 'relative' not 'absolute ethics'. In absolute ethics, the law that 'each individual ought to receive the benefits and evils of his own nature' is true without qualification; and Mr. Spencer affirms that it is 'obviously that which commends itself to the common apprehension as just'.

It seems to me that the effects of gregariousness, in the highly developed form in which it appears in the human race, are too lightly treated in this argument.

It is too hastily assumed that the necessity for subordinating the welfare of the individual to that of the species arises solely from war: and in the consideration of war and its consequences Sociology and Ethics are too much mixed. Granting that it would be for the advantage of the human race that war should disappear, it does not follow that it will disappear; it might similarly be better for sub-human life that beasts of prey and parasites should disappear, but Mr. Spencer's faith in sub-human evolution does not lead him to assume that this will be its ultimate result. Granting, again, that industrialism will put an end to militancy, it is not shown that conflicts of interest among industrial groups—such as we see at present in apparently growing intensity—will not continue, and that the exigencies of such conflicts will not impose on individuals a severe subordination to the interests of their respective groups. Granting, finally, that such industrial conflicts are ultimately to cease, it seems rash to assume that when this consummation is reached, Mr. Spencer's individualistic principles of justice will be found reigning unchecked: for it may be that this result will be brought about by an implication of interests and a development of sympathy which will render all men 'members one of another' to a degree beyond our present experience: so that when any one suffers the rest will inevitably suffer with him and the rule that 'each is to bear the evils of his own nature' will become impracticable or unmeaning. I do not prophesy that these things will be: but if Mr. Spencer is allowed to 'fancy warless men' and lay down *a priori* rules of conduct for a world lapped in universal peace, I do not see why Mr. Bellamy, or any one else, may not with equal legitimacy fancy more unselfish men, and construct a still more Absolute Ethics for a non-competitive Utopia.

And I cannot admit that Mr. Spencer's principle is 'obviously that which commends itself to the common apprehension as just'. Doubtless the popular phrases that a man 'has no one to blame but himself', that 'he has made his own bed and must now lie in it', or that another has 'fairly earned his reward', indicate the consciousness that justice demands a proportion between effort and advantage. But we commonly recognise that equal efforts do not produce equal results: and it is not 'obvious' to the common sense of civilised men that Justice requires a man to suffer for failures not due to wilful wrong-doing or neglect. I agree with Mr. Spencer that it would be practically disastrous to adopt the communistic principle that 'each shall make the same effort, and that if by the same effort, bodily or mental, one produces twice as much as another he is not to be advantaged by the difference'. Still I think that this principle is in accordance with the prevalent view of ideal justice, so far as the comparatively inefficient individual is not to blame for his comparative inefficiency;—though, as the impracticability of realising the principle under the actual conditions of human life is generally recognised, it presents itself as a principle of Divine rather than of human justice.

Making these reserves, I recognise much truth in Mr. Spencer's account (in chaps. iv. and v.) of the origin and growth of the 'sentiment' of Justice, and also in his characterisation of the 'idea' of Justice, which the individualistic development of modern civilised society has tended to render prevalent. He begins with what he rather strangely calls the 'egoistic sentiment of justice'—the individual's resentment of interference with the pursuit of his private ends—and proceeds to explain how the 'altruistic sentiment of justice' comes into existence by the aid of a 'pro-altruistic sentiment having several components'. He explains how the egoistic resentment of interference combines with fear of similar resentment and retaliation on the part of others if they are interfered with, and also with the dread of social reprobation, the dread of legal punishment and the dread of Divine vengeance for such interference: and how, society being held together by the 'pro-altruistic' sentiment thus compounded, the development of sympathy through gregariousness gradually produces the genuine 'altruistic' sentiment of justice. In this way the 'conception of a limit to each kind of activity up to which there is freedom to act' gradually 'emerges and becomes definite' in human thought. The idea of Justice that thus emerges contains two elements. 'Inequality is the primordial ideal suggested. For if the principle is that each shall receive the benefits and evils due to his own nature and consequent conduct, then since men differ in their powers, . . . unequal amounts of benefit are implied.' On the other hand, the recognition of the need of 'mutual limitations of men's actions' involves the conception of Equality; since 'experience shows that these bounds are on the average the same for all'. But the appreciation of these two factors in human justice has long remained unbalanced. Thus 'in the Greek conception of justice —which admitted slavery as just—there predominates the idea of inequality', and 'the inequality refers not to the natural achievement of greater rewards by greater merits but to the artificial apportionment of greater rewards to greater merits'. On the other hand, in the dictum of Bentham that 'everybody is to count for one, nobody for more than one' the idea of inequality entirely disappears. It has, in short, been left for Mr. Spencer to give the true conception of Justice by 'co-ordinating the antagonistic wrong views', and showing that the ideas of equality and inequality 'may be and must be simultaneously asserted', being 'applied the one to the bounds and the other to the benefits'. The formula of justice, so conceived, may be precisely expressed as follows: 'Every man is free to do that which he wills provided he infringe not the equal freedom of another man.'

In an Appendix (A) Mr. Spencer recognises that Kant's 'Universal Principle of Right'—with which he was till recently unacquainted—is closely allied to his own: but he points out that Kant 'enunciates an *a priori* requirement, contemplated as irrespective of beneficial ends', whereas Mr. Spencer's 'law of equal freedom' is to be regarded as 'the primary condition which must be fulfilled before the greatest happiness can be achieved by similar beings living in proximity'. But when the 'greatest sum of happiness' is thus expressly stated to be the 'remote end' to which Mr. Spencer's formula simply prescribes the indispensable means, I think it becomes clear that his criticism of Bentham's dictum above quoted involves a misunderstanding. For, as Mill says, 'the greatest happiness principle is a mere form of words without rational significance, unless one person's happiness, supposed equal in degree,[1] is counted for as much as another's'. The dictum, in short, is merely designed to make the conception of the end precise, not to determine anything as to the legal rules by which the end may be best attained.

How then is it known that Equal Freedom thus understood is unconditionally the best means to the attainment of the greatest sum of human happiness? Several lines of argument in Mr. Spencer's view combine to give this principle the highest imaginable 'warrant'. First there are the biological considerations, yielded by a survey of life or conduct at large, which we have before examined. Secondly, Mr. Spencer tries to show, in the history of human institutions and ideas, a gradual growth of this conception into distinctness. I think he has some right to claim as an example of this the doctrine of natural law, as held by a succession of jurists from Roman times to the eighteenth century; along this line of thought we may fairly trace a development towards the modern individualistic ideal. Other parts of Mr. Spencer's historic argument have less force; e.g., a reference to the 'Christian maxim—Do unto others as ye would that others should do unto you'—is hardly relevant to a definition of strict Justice. It is not, however, on a biological or a historical basis alone that Mr. Spencer rests the Formula of Justice. The Law of Equal Freedom is, in his view, 'an immediate dictum of the human consciousness after it has been subjected to the discipline of prolonged social life'. It is an ethical intuition, comparable in self-evidence with the axioms of geometry, though 'relatively vague' and needing, far more than the mathematical intuitions, to be subjected to 'methodic criticism'. It does not, indeed, seem to be a dictum of every developed human consciousness: since, as Mr. Spencer tells us with much emphasis, the 'reigning school of politics and morals' treats it with scorn, and 'daily legislation' serenely overrides it. Nevertheless, Mr. Spencer maintains (in chap. viii.) that all 'rights truly so-called are corollaries deducible from it'; and these corollaries will be found 'one and all' to correspond with legal enactments of modern States.

Then, in ten successive chapters, he works out this correspondence in detail, by deducing from the Law of Equal Freedom 'the right to physical integrity', the 'rights to free motion and locomotion', the 'rights to the uses of Natural media', the rights of property, corporeal and incorporeal, the rights of gift and bequest, of free exchange, free contract, free industry, free belief and worship, free speech and publication. In each case Mr. Spencer appends a brief account of the historic process by which, as civilisation has progressed, these rights have come to be recognised with increasing clearness and fulness. No one is more skilful than

---

[1] Mill here adds 'with the proper allowance made for kind'. The addition seems to me either superfluous or erroneous: but the question whether it is so or not is not relevant to the present issue.

Mr. Spencer in exhibiting the cumulative force of a comprehensive and complex argument: and many parts of these chapters are both interesting, though dealing with trite topics, and effective for Mr. Spencer's purpose. I think, however, that in several cases the deductions from Mr. Spencer's principle are not performed with sufficient exactness; and that, if they were made more exact, the discrepancy between the results obtained by deduction and the established laws of modern States would be more marked. This would not, indeed, necessarily invalidate Mr. Spencer's conclusions; since, firstly, actual law may be wrong, and secondly, it may be right but not ideal, a compromise inevitable at the present stage of social development: for Mr. Spencer's idea of Justice, as he is careful to state, is 'appropriate to an ultimate state, and can be but partly entertained during transitional states'. But it would be an advantage to have the three things—the ideal rights of an ideal society, the legal rights as they ought to be here and now, and the actual legal rights—more clearly and fully compared. As it is, I fear that the reader will not always thoroughly distinguish the three questions: (1) 'How far can we know the relations of members of an ideal society?' (2) 'How far ought we to imitate these relations here and now?' (3) 'What changes in our actual law would this imitation involve?'

One cause of inexactness in Mr. Spencer's deductions lies in the unpreciseness of his fundamental formula. The simplest statement of the 'Law of Equal Freedom' is that 'the liberty of each' should be 'limited only by the like liberties of all'. This, however, as Mr. Spencer sees, might be interpreted as allowing A to knock B down if he were willing to take his chance of being knocked down by B. To exclude this, Mr. Spencer defines the formula as meaning 'that each in carrying on the actions which constitute his life for the time being and conduce to the subsequent maintenance of his life, shall not be impeded further than by the carrying on of those kindred actions which maintain the lives of others'. But he does not seem always to keep to this definition, vague as it is: for instance, in discussing the 'Rights to the uses of Natural Media' he lays down that 'vitiation of air' which is 'mutual' 'cannot constitute aggression': though it would seem that such vitiation might easily impede the maintenance of the lives of the mutual vitiators. Sometimes, again, a wider and more purely utilitarian meaning is given to the formula. Thus we are told that 'considered as the statement of a condition by conforming to which the greatest sum of happiness is to be obtained, the law forbids any act which inflicts physical pain'. But if it is so 'considered' why does it take account of *physical*[2] pain only, and why does it forbid any act inflicting such pain, and not merely acts that cause a balance of pain on the whole? Mr. Spencer would perhaps reply that, in an ideal society, all right acts cause 'pleasure unalloyed by pain anywhere':[3] but then such a society is so unlike that in which our

---

[2] Of course, in a sense all pain is 'physical', but I presume Mr. Spencer is using the term in a narrower sense.   [3] *Data of Ethics*, p. 101.

ancestors have lived that their experiences can hardly have generated any trust-worthy intuitions with regard to it.

The vagueness of Mr. Spencer's fundamental formula is strikingly illustrated by the manner in which he applies it (chap. xi.) to the burning question of Right to the Use of Land. For here the 'law of equal freedom' is allowed to drop the idea of 'freedom': it is converted into the proposition that 'men have equal claims to the use of land'. Equality, not Liberty, is here the point; for, obviously, the admis-sion of 'equality of claims' does not in any way determine how much freedom is to be allowed to any one in using land: indeed, as Mr. Spencer goes on to argue, the principle is realised by 'the people's supreme ownership of the land' as asserted in the right of 'appropriation of land for public purposes' claimed and exercised by modern Governments. But if the 'law of equal freedom' as applied to the use of land is satisfied by 'the people's ownership' of the commodity, it would seem to admit a completely communistic system, in which all manage-ment and cultivation of land would be strictly public, and private use would only begin after the product was divided. And in fact Mr. Spencer's deduction of the Right of Property (chap. xii.), as established in modern civilised societies, is singularly the reverse of cogent. After describing the manner in which private ownership grows up, he says that, 'though we cannot say that ownership of prop-erty, thus arising, results from actual contract between each member of the com-munity and the community as a whole, yet there is something like a potential contract; and such potential contract might grow into an actual contract if one part of the community devoted itself to other occupations, while the rest con-tinued to farm; a share of the produce being in such case payable by agreement to those who had ceased to be farmers, for the use of their shares of the land'. But he adds that 'we have no evidence that such a relation between occupiers and the community has ever arisen'; and merely suggests that hereafter 'there may again arise a theoretically equitable right of property'. I am therefore unable to see why in subsequent discussions he allows himself to treat existing rights of property as though they had been adequately justified by his formula.

In an Appendix (B) Mr. Spencer suggests that in England the sums paid in poor-relief since 1601 may be reasonably held to satisfy the just demands of the landless, as they have not an equitable claim to more than 'the original prairie value of the land'. But, granting that the Law of Equal Freedom can be properly fulfilled by this method of what has been called 'ransom', it may surely be con-tended that, on his own principles, the claim of the landless extends at least to *all* the present value of the land after subtracting what would now have to be paid to bring it from its original condition to its present degree of utility,—i.e., not the prairie value alone, but the prairie value *plus* the 'unearned increment'; and it may be contended further that the existing landless ones cannot reasonably be held to have been compensated by poor-rates paid to their ancestors.

It would, however, be out of place to argue here the economico–political issue thus raised. I notice it here chiefly in order to point out how clearly the whole discussion shows the inadequacy of the single formula of justice offered by Mr. Spencer. When we are inquiring what compensation is justly due to persons whose rights have admittedly been encroached upon, supposing the encroachments have been sanctioned by law and custom and complicated by subsequent exchange, it is evident that the Law of Equal Freedom cannot help us; we want some quite different principle of Distributive or Reparative Justice.

A similar conclusion is suggested by the discussion, in chapters xx. and xxi., of the Rights of Women and Children. Firstly, in considering the position of married women, Mr. Spencer seems to assume, without justifying the assumption, that it is not to be settled simply by free contract between men and women. But surely the question of the Marriage-Law ought to be more frankly faced by a thorough-going individualist pursuing a high *priori* road. If he intends to allow perfect freedom of contract in determining conjugal relations, he ought to admit openly his breach with the law and morality of all civilised societies; if not, he ought to make quite clear how he justifies restrictions on freedom of contract. Again, assuming that the State has to determine a division of power and responsibility between husbands and wives, surely it is manifest that this must be done on some principle of justice quite different from Mr. Spencer's formula. We are told, for instance, that 'justice appears to dictate' that 'the power of the mother may fitly predominate during the earlier part of a child's life, and that of the father during the latter part'. But what kind of Justice? Certainly not the Law of Equal Freedom. Similarly when we are told that 'since, speaking generally, man is more judicially-minded than woman, the balance of authority should incline to the side of the husband', the proposition—however sound—seems to have no connexion with Mr. Spencer's Formula: though we may perhaps trace in it a connexion with the Greek conception of Justice, as 'inequality established by authority', which has been repudiated in a previous chapter.

After civil rights, the reader may perhaps expect to pass, in chapter xxii., to a discussion of constitutional rights, on the basis of Absolute Justice. He finds, however, that in Mr. Spencer's view 'there are no further rights, truly so called', than the civil rights already set forth: 'so-called political rights' being 'but an instrumentality for the obtainment and maintenance' of these civil rights. The conception (*e.g.*) of the 'power of giving a vote' as 'itself a right' involves a 'confusion of means with ends'. Hence, in the discussion that follows on the structure of Government, the *a priori* method is almost entirely abandoned. Mr. Spencer, indeed, implies obscurely that there is a 'constitution of the State justified by absolute Ethics'; but he makes no attempt to determine it otherwise than by the vague suggestion that it 'must be a constitution in which there is not a representation of individuals but a representation of interests'. The only topic under the head of the constitution of the State, on which Justice again becomes the governing conception, is the 'distribution of State-burdens'; but here again we feel strongly the need and the absence of some principle other than Mr. Spencer's formula. For instance, it may be true that 'as life and personal safety are, speaking generally, held equally valuable by all men', such public expenditure as is entailed by use of these shall 'fall equally on all': but the conclusion is hardly deducible from the Law of Equal Freedom.

The *duties* of the State, on the other hand, can be simply determined by the fundamental formula, applied positively and negatively: it must 'prevent interferences with individual action beyond such as the social state itself necessitates'. Justice requires it to do this adequately: and Justice requires it to do nothing further, —at any rate if the further action is either coercive or expensive; since either coercion or expenditure, beyond what is needed for the protection of individual rights, is itself an infringement of these rights. It would hardly be suitable in the present notice to discuss adequately Mr. Spencer's application of this simple principle, which will be, in the main, familiar to readers of his previous writings. I will only say, briefly, that the consequences of the political empiricism that disregards this principle are severely expounded, and impressively illustrated by modern instances, in the concluding chapters.

Notes on Sources

1. 'Utilitarianism' (1873) Previously unpublished; privately printed for discussion at a meeting of the Metaphysical Society, 16 Dec. 1873.
2. 'The Theory of Evolution in its Application to Practice', *Mind*, OS, 1/1 (1876), 52–67.
3. 'Professor Calderwood on Intuitionism in Morals', *Mind*, OS, 1/4 (1876), 563–6.
4. 'Mr Barratt on "The Suppression of Egoism"', *Mind*, OS, 2 (1877), 411–12.
5. 'The Establishment of Ethical First Principles', *Mind*, OS, 4 (1879), 106–11.
6. 'Some Fundamental Ethical Controversies', *Mind*, OS, 14 (Oct. 1889), 473–87.
7. 'Law and Morality', ch. 13: 200–16 of Sidgwick's *Elements of Politics* (2nd edn.; London: Macmillan & Co., 1897).
8. 'The Distinction Between "Is" and "Ought"', originally published under the title 'Is the Distinction Between "Is" and "Ought" Ultimate and Irreducible?' in the *Proceedings of the Aristotelian Society*, NS, 2/1, part II (1892), 88–92; the lead paper in a symposium; the other speakers were J. H. Muirhead, G. F. Stout, and Samuel Alexander.
9. 'The Relation of Ethics to Sociology', *International Journal of Ethics*, 10/1 (Oct. 1899), 1–21; repr. in *Miscellaneous Essays and Addresses*, 249–69.
10. 'Pleasure and Desire', *The Contemporary Review*, 19 (Apr. 1872), 662–72.
11. 'Hedonism and Ultimate Good', *Mind*, OS, 2 (1877), 27–38.
12. 'The Feeling-Tone of Desire and Aversion', *Mind*, NS, 1 (1892), 94–101.
13. 'Unreasonable Action', *Mind*, NS, 2/6 (1893), 174–87; repr. in *Practical Ethics*, 235–60; Oxford edn., 129–42.
14. 'Verification of Beliefs', *Contemporary Review*, 17 (July 1871), 582–90. A somewhat different version (unpublished) entitled 'The Verification of Beliefs', privately printed, was presented to the Metaphysical Society, 27 Apr. 1870.
15. 'Incoherence of Empirical Philosophy', *Mind*, OS, 7/28 (1882), 533–43; repr. in *Lectures on the Philosophy of Kant, and Other Philosophical Lectures and Essays (LPK)*, 372–91.
16. 'The Philosophy of Common Sense', *Mind*, NS, 4/14 (Apr. 1895), 145–58; repr. in *LPK*, 406–29.
17. 'Criteria of Truth and Error', *Mind*, NS, 9/33 (1900), 8–25; repr. in *LPK*, 430–60.
18. 'Further on the Criteria of Truth and Error', *LPK* (1905), 461–7.
19. 'Grote on Utilitarianism I', review of John Grote's *Examination of the Utilitarian Philosophy*, *Cambridge University Reporter* (8 Feb. 1871), 182–3.
20. 'Grote on Utilitarianism II', second review of Grote, *The Academy* (1 Apr. 1871), 197–8.
21. 'Fitzjames Stephen on Mill on Liberty', review of James Fitzjames Stephen's *Liberty, Equality, Fraternity*, *The Academy* (1 Aug. 1873), 292–4.
22. 'Bradley's *Ethical Studies*', review, in *Mind*, OS, 1/4 (1876), 545–9.
23. 'Sidgwick *vs*. Bradley', Bradley's reply to Sidgwick's review of *Ethical Studies* and Sidgwick's 'Rejoinder', *Mind*, OS, 2/7 (1877), 122–6.

24. 'Bentham and Benthamism in Politics and Ethics', *Fortnightly Review* (May 1877), 627–52; repr. in *Miscellaneous Essays and Addresses*, 135–69.
25. 'Spencer's Ethical System', review of Herbert Spencer's *Data of Ethics*, *Mind*, OS, 5/18 (1880), 216–26.
26. 'Leslie Stephen's *Science of Ethics*', Critical Notice, in *Mind*, OS, 7/28 (1882), 562–86.
27. 'Green's Ethics', discussion of T. H. Green's *Prolegomena to Ethics*, in *Mind*, OS, 9/34 (Apr. 1884), 169–84.
28. 'Fowler's *Progressive Morality*', Critical Notice, in *Mind*, OS, 10 (1885), 266–71.
29. 'Idiopsychological Ethics', the last item in an exchange with James Martineau on Martineau's *Types of Ethical Theory*, in *Mind*, OS, 12 (1887), 31–44. Sidgwick's initial discussion of the book appeared in *Mind*, 10 (1885), 426–42; Martineau's 'Professor Sidgwick on "Types of Ethical Theory"' appeared in *Mind*, 10 (1885), 628–39; Sidgwick's response to this, 'Dr. Martineau's Defence of "Types of Ethical Theory"' was published in *Mind*, 11 (1886), 142–5, to which Martineau appended a brief rejoinder on pp. 145–6, followed by the paper included here.
30. 'Spencer on Justice', Critical Notice of Herbert Spencer's book *Justice*, in *Mind*, NS, 1/1 (1892), 107–18.

Bibliography and Bibliographical Notes

I. Books by Sidgwick

Only the first five were published during Sidgwick's lifetime.

The Methods of Ethics (ME) (London: Macmillan & Co., which published all of Sidgwick's books with the exception of *Practical Ethics*), 1st edn., 1874; 2nd edn., 1877; 3rd edn., 1884; 4th edn., 1890; 5th edn., 1893 (this is the last edition Sidgwick was able to see through the press himself); 6th edn., 1901; 7th edn., 1907. An index appears for the first time in the 4th edn., the work of E. E. Constance Jones, who shepherded the 6th and 7th edns. through the press. The 7th edn. is the one that is canonical and has been reprinted several times since; it is practically equivalent to the 6th. (Schneewind reports a Japanese translation in 1898, and a German translation in 1909. I have been unable to examine the Japanese translation.) Reprinted 1962 by the University of Chicago Press; and in paperback the same year by Dover Publications. Reprinted 1981 by Hackett Publishing, Indianapolis, with a foreword by John Rawls.

(A Supplement to the First Edition of the Methods of Ethics, 1878.)

(A Supplement to the Second Edition of the Methods of Ethics, 1884.)

The Principles of Political Economy (PPE), 1st edn., 1883; 2nd edn., 1887; 3rd edn., 1901.

Outlines of the History of Ethics for English Readers (HE), 1st edn., 1886; 2nd edn., 1888; 3rd edn., 1892; 4th edn., 1896; 5th edn., 1902. (Italian translation, 1902.)[1] Reprinted 1988 by Hackett Publishing.

The Elements of Politics (EP), 1st edn., 1891; 2nd edn., 1898; 3rd edn., 1908; 4th edn., 1919.

Practical Ethics: A Collection of Essays and Addresses (PE) (London: Swan Sonnenschein, 1898). Repr., with an introd. by Sissela Bok (New York: Oxford University Press, 1998), with different pagination.

---

[1] In 1931 Macmillan published an enlarged, or 6th edn., with an additional chapter, V, by Alban G. Widgery, who said in his 'Note to the Enlarged Edition', 'Since its publication in 1886 this book has remained the best brief historical survey of Ethics in English. It has seemed, however, that a short account of the ethical thought of the last fifty years might contribute to its continued usefulness. Sidgwick's own work has been left untouched.' Widgery's account of Sidgwick's ethics is on pp. 298–302 of the enlarged edition. This enlarged edition has now become the standard edition of the work.

Philosophy, its Scope and Relations: An Introductory Course of Lectures (*Phil.*), 1902, ed., with an editorial note, by James Ward. Repr. (Bristol, England: Thoemmes Press, 1998).

Lectures on the Ethics of T. H. Green, H. Spencer, and J. Martineau (*GSM*), 1902, ed. E. E. Constance Jones.

The Development of European Polity (*DEP*), 1903, ed. Eleanor Mildred Sidgwick. Havard, *Henry Sidgwick & Later Utilitarian Political Philosophy* (cited *inf.*, Sect. IV) quotes Max Lerner as saying that 'on Greek political institutions . . . Sidgwick's *Development of European Polity* . . . has not to my mind been supplanted by later books' (p. 148). And Havard adds that '*The Elements of Politics* deserves, but has not . . . received, praise equal to that bestowed by Broad and Lerner on the other books'.

Miscellaneous Essays and Addresses (*MEA*), 1904, ed. Eleanor Mildred Sidgwick and Arthur Sidgwick.

Lectures on the Philosophy of Kant and Other Philosophical Lectures and Essays (*LPK*), 1905, ed. James Ward. (Cf. *inf.*) In addition to the lectures on the metaphysics of Kant, contains lectures on the metaphysics of T. H. Green and on the philosophy of Herbert Spencer, as well as five other essays on similar topics.

Henry Sidgwick: A Memoir (*Mem.*), by A. S. and E. M. S., 1906. The most authoritative account of his life, written by his wife and his brother; contains entries from a journal kept by Sidgwick, excerpts from his letters, some reprinted poetry of Sidgwick's, and a couple of unpublished papers, so partly by Sidgwick as well as about him.

Edited, with a preface, *Introduction to Political Science: Two Series of Lectures*, by (the late) John Robert Seeley (London, New York: Macmillan, 1896, 1902). 'I have . . . here and there omitted repetitions more suitable to an oral lecture than to a book, and once or twice altered the position of sentences; and generally speaking, have made such corrections as I thought it probable that the author would have made before publishing the lectures. In the books prepared by him for publication, Seeley was . . . unsparing of pains in rewriting such portions as did not come up to his ideal. I have felt, therefore, that it would be unjust to his memory to let this posthumous book go forth without such correction of inadvertencies as I was able to make. No reader can feel more strongly than I do how inadequate a substitute this is for his own revision' (p. ix). On p. 3 Seeley says that he uses 'the word [paradox] in its original sense of a proposition which is really true, though it sounds false'. Compare this conception of paradox with Sidgwick's in Ch. 6, *sup.*; see also Sect. VI of the editor's Introd.

Schultz, Bart, ed., *The Complete Works and Select Correspondence of Henry Sidgwick* (a data base), on CD-ROM (Charlottesville, Va.: Intelex Corp., 1997).

II. Essays, Pamphlets, Reviews, etc., by Sidgwick

This bibliography is based largely on the excellent one in *Mem.*, 616–22. It is, as the authors of *Mem.* say, 'probably incomplete', especially with respect to some early pieces published anonymously, letters to the press, and some contributions to the *Journal of the Society for Psychical Research*, etc., but it is complete enough, certainly, for philosophical purposes. It is here supplemented by information—especially information on privately printed but unpublished essays—contained in the excellent and even more complete bibliography in

J. B. Schneewind's *Sidgwick's Ethics and Victorian Moral Philosophy* (cited *inf.*). It is perhaps needless to say that I have not been able to examine all the items listed; I have, however, examined nearly all the philosophical essays listed, and I have supplied page numbers where I could. Essays included in this book are indicated by an asterisk.

1860   'Goethe and Frederika' (verses, pub. anon.), *Macmillan's Magazine* (Mar. 1860), 353; repr. in *Mem.*, 51.

1861   'Eton', *Macmillan's Magazine* (Feb. 1861), 292.

'The Despot's Heir' (verses, anon.), *Macmillan's Magazine* (Mar. 1861), 361; repr. in *Mem.*, 64.

Review: of Ranke's *History of England*, *Macmillan's Magazine* (May 1861), 85.

'Alexis de Tocqueville', *Macmillan's Magazine* (Nov. 1861), 37; repr. *MEA*.

1866   'Ecce Homo', *Westminster Review* (July 1866); repr. in *MEA*. A discussion of the book, *Ecce Homo: A Survey of the Life and Works of Jesus Christ* (1st edn., 1865; 4th edn., London: Macmillan, 1866). Both the book and Sidgwick's discussion were published anonymously; it turned out that the book had been written by J. R. Seeley (1834–95), one of Sidgwick's friends.

1867   'Liberal Education', *Macmillan's Magazine* (Apr. 1867), 40–58 (referred to in *Mem.*, 164).

'The Prophet of Culture', *Macmillan's Magazine* (Aug. 1867), 271; repr. *MEA*. A critique of Matthew Arnold, written prior to the publication of Arnold's *Culture and Anarchy* (1869). Cf. Strachey and Trilling, *inf.*

'The Theory of Classical Education', in *Essays on a Liberal Education*, ed. F. W. Farrar (Macmillan, 1867); repr. *MEA*, 270–319.[2]

1869   'Mr Roden Noel's Poems', *Spectator* (13 Feb. 1869).

Review: Courthope's *Ludibria Lunae*, *Spectator* (7 Aug. 1869).

'The Poems and Prose Remains of Arthur Hugh Clough', *Westminster Review* (Oct. 1869); repr. *MEA*.

Review: Baring Gould's *Origin and Development of Religious Belief*, *Cambridge University Gazette* (15 Dec. 1869).

1870   Review: F. N. Broome's *Stranger of Seriphos*, *Spectator*, 19 Feb. 1870.

'Clerical Engagements', *Pall Mall Gazette* (6 Jan. 1870).

Pamphlet: *The Ethics of Conformity and Subscription* (London: Williams and Norgate, 1870), 36 pp.; repr., in part only and with some revisions, under the title 'The Ethics of Religious Conformity' (1896).

'The Verification of Beliefs' (unpub.; privately printed to be read to the Metaphysical Society, 27 Apr. 1870). (Cf. Ch. 14 this vol.)

1871   Review: Courthope's *Paradise of Birds*, *Spectator* (18 Feb. 1871).

*Review: J. Grote's *Examination of the Utilitarian Philosophy*, *Cambridge University Reporter* (8 Feb. 1871), 182–3. (Ch. 19 this vol.)

Review: Swinburne's *Songs Before Sunrise*, *Cambridge University Reporter*, 22 Feb. 1871.

Review: Maguire's *Essays on the Platonic Ethics*, *Cambridge University Reporter* (1 Mar. 1871).

---

[2] I include the page numbers here to give the reader an idea of the length of this piece, almost that of a monograph.

*Review: J. Grote's *Examination of the Utilitarian Philosophy*, *The Academy* (1 Apr. 1871), 197–8. (Ch. 20 this vol.)

Review: Conway's *Earthly Pilgrimage*, *Academy* (15 Apr. 1871), 215.

Review: Hutton's *Essays, Theological and Literary*, *Academy* (1 July 1871), 325.

Review: Maguire's *Essays on the Platonic Ethics*, *Academy* (15 Sept. 1871), 441.

Review: Beale's *Life Theories and their Influence on Religious Thought*, *Academy* (15 Oct. 1871), 481.

Review: G. H. Lewes's *History of Philosophy*, *Academy* (15 Nov. 1871), 519.

Critique: Professor Fraser's edn. of Berkeley, *Athenaeum* (17 and 24 June 1871).

*'Verification of Beliefs', *Contemporary Review*, 17 (July 1871), 582–90. (Ch. 14 this vol.)

1872   Obituary Notice: 'Professor Trendelenburg', *Academy* (1 Feb. 1872), 53.

Review: Zimmerman's *Professor Clarke's Life and Doctrine*, *Academy* (1 Apr. 1872), 132.

Review: Miss Cobbe's *Darwinism in Morals and Other Essays*, *Academy* (15 June 1872), 231.

Review: Barzelotti's *La Morale nella Filosofia Positiva*, *Academy* (1 July 1872), 256.

Review: Spicker's *Die Philosophie des Grafen von Shaftesbury*, *Academy* (15 Aug. 1872), 313.

Review: Mahaffy's *Kant's Critical Philosophy for English Readers*, *Academy* (15 Sept. 1872), 357.

Review: Jodl's *Leben und Philosophie David Humes*, *Academy* (15 Oct. 1872), 388.

Review: Leifchild's *Higher Ministry of Nature viewed in the Light of Modern Science*, *Athenaeum* (6 Apr. 1872).

'Lord Ormathwaite's *Astronomy and Geology Compared*', *Athenaeum* (20 Apr. 1872).

'Monck's *Space and Vision*', *Athenaeum*, 18 May 1872.

Review: Dr Bree's *Exposition of Fallacies in the Hypothesis of Mr Darwin*, *Athenaeum* (20 July 1872).

Review: Bikker's and Hatton's *Ethics for Undenominational Schools*, in *Athenaeum* (27 July 1872).

Note in Reply to Dr Bree's Vindication of his Book, *Athenaeum* (3 Aug. 1872).

*'Pleasure and Desire', *Contemporary Review*, 19 (Apr. 1872), 662–72. (Ch. 10 this vol.)

'The Sophists, I', *Journal of Philology*, 4/8 (1872); repr. *LPK*. (Rev. by Dr Henry Jackson for reprinting in *LPK*.)

1873   'The Sophists, II', *Journal of Philology*, 5/9 (1873); repr. *LPK*.

Review: Spencer's *Principles of Psychology*, *Academy* (15 July 1873), 131.

Obituary notice: 'John Stuart Mill', *Academy* (15 May 1873), 193.

Review: Mansel's *Letters, Lectures, and Reviews*, *Academy* (15 July 1873), 267.

*Review: J. F. Stephen's *Liberty, Equality, Fraternity*, in *The Academy* (1 Aug. 1873), 292–4. (Ch. 21 this vol.)

Review: Dr Tuke's *Effect of the Mind upon the Body*, *Athenaeum* (12 July 1873).

Review: Spencer's *Principles of Psychology*, *Spectator* (21 June 1873).

Review: Prof. Cairnes's *Political Essays*, *Spectator* (8 Nov. 1873).

*'Utilitarianism' (unpub.; privately printed to be read to the Metaphysical Society, 16 Dec. 1873). (Ch. 1 this vol.)

1874   'On a Passage in Plato's *Republic*', *Journal of Philology*, 5/10 (1874).

Review: Green and Grose's Edition of Hume's *Treatise*, *Academy* (30 May 1874), 608.

1875   Review: Green and Grose's Edition of Hume's *Essays*, *Academy* (7 Aug. 1875), 146.

Review: Green and Grose's Hume, *Spectator* (27 Mar. 1875).

'The Late Professor Cairnes', *Spectator* (31 July 1875).

'The Theory of Evolution in its Application to Practice' (unpub.; privately printed for presentation to the Metaphysical Society, 13 July 1875; cf. Ch. 2 this vol.).

'The Eton Dispute', *Spectator* (27 Nov. 1875).

1876   *'The Theory of Evolution in its Application to Practice', *Mind*, 1/1 (1876), 52–67. (Ch. 2 this vol.)

'Philosophy at Cambridge', *Mind*, 1/2 (1876).

*Critical Notice: 'Bradley's *Ethical Studies*', *Mind*, 1/4 (1876), 545–9. (Ch. 22 this vol.)

*'Professor Calderwood on Intuitionism in Morals', *Mind*, 1/4 (1876), 563–6. (Ch. 3 this vol.)

'Idle Fellowships', *Contemporary Review* (Apr. 1876); repr. *MEA*.

1877   *'Hedonism and Ultimate Good', *Mind*, 2/5 (1877), 27–38. (Ch. 11 this vol.)

*Rejoinder to Bradley's Reply, *Mind*, 2/7 (1877), 125–6. (Ch. 23B this vol.)

Critical Notice: John Grote's *Treatise on the Moral Ideals*, *Mind*, 2/6 (1877), 239–44.

*Reply to Mr Barratt on 'The Suppression of Egoism', *Mind*, 2/7 (1877), 411–12. (Ch. 4 this vol.)

*'Bentham and Benthamism in Politics and Ethics', *Fortnightly Review*, 125 (1 May 1877), 627–52; repr. *MEA*. (Ch. 24 this vol.)

1878   Article: 'Ethics', *Encyclopedia Britannica*, 9th edn (1878). Enlarged version published as *HE*, 1886.

'Dr Georg von Gizycki on Hume's Ethics', *Academy* (5 Oct. 1878).

'The Relation of Psychogony to Metaphysics and Ethics' (unpub.; privately printed for presentation to the Metaphysical Society, 15 Jan. 1878).

1879   *'The Establishment of Ethical First Principles', *Mind*, 4/13 (1879), 106–11. (Ch. 5 this vol.)

'Incoherence of Empirical Philosophy' (privately printed for presentation to the Metaphysical Society, 14 Jan. 1879; later version published in 1882; cf. Ch. 15 this vol.).

'The So-called Idealism of Kant', *Mind*, 4/15 (1879).

Critical Notice: Guyau's *La Morale d'Epicure et ses Rapports avec les Doctrines Contemporaines*, *Mind*, 4/16 (1879), 582.

'Economic Method', *Fortnightly Review* (Feb. 1879).

'What is Money?', *Fortnightly Review* (Apr. 1879).

'The Wages Fund Theory', *Fortnightly Review* (Sept. 1879).

1880   'On Historical Psychology', *The Nineteenth Century*, 7 (Feb. 1880), 353–60.

'Kant's Refutation of Idealism', *Mind*, 5/17 (1880), 111.

'The Scope of Metaphysics' (unpub.; privately printed for presentation to the Metaphysical Society, 10 Feb. 1880).

Review: Fouillée's *L'Idée moderne du droit*, *Mind*, 5/18 (1880), 135.

*'Mr Spencer's Ethical System', *Mind*, 5/18 (1880), 216–26. (Ch. 25 this vol.)

1882   Inaugural Address, as President, to the Society for Psychical Research, *Proceedings of the SPR*, 1, part I (July 1882), 7.

Address to the Society for Psychical Research (reply to criticisms), *Proceedings, SPR*, 1, part II (1882), 65.

'On the Fundamental Doctrines of Descartes', *Mind*, 7/27 (1882), 435.

*'Incoherence of Empirical Philosophy', *Mind*, 7/28 (1882), 533–43. (Ch. 15 this vol.) (Cf. 1879 *sup.*)

*Critical Notice: Leslie Stephen's *Science of Ethics*, *Mind*, 7/28 (1882), 572–86. (Ch. 26 this vol.)

1883   'A Criticism of the Critical Philosophy I', *Mind*, 8/29 (Jan. 1883), 69–91.

'A Criticism of the Critical Philosophy II', *Mind*, 8/31 (July 1883), 313–37.

'Kant's View of Mathematical Premises and Reasonings', *Mind*, 8/31–2 (1883), 421–4, 577–8.

Address to the Society for Psychical Research (on the relation of Psychical Research to Science), *Proceedings, SPR*, 1, part IV (1883), 152.

1884   Address to the Society for Psychical Research (on the general scientific position of the Society), *Proceedings, SPR*, 2, part VI (1884), 152.

*'Green's Ethics', *Mind*, 9/34 (Apr. 1884), 169–87. (Ch. 27 this vol.)

1885   *Critical Notice: Thomas Fowler's *Progressive Morality*, in *Mind*, 10/38 (1885), 266–71. (Ch. 28 this vol.)

Critical Notice: James Martineau's *Types of Ethical Theory*, *Mind*, 10/39 (1885), 426–42.

'The Scope and Method of Economic Science', 'An address delivered to the Economic and Statistics Section of the British Association as President of the Section in 1885'; pub. in *MEA*.

1886   'Dr Martineau's Defence of *Types of Ethical Theory*', *Mind*, 11/41 (1886), 142–5.

'The Historical Method', *Mind*, 11/42 (1886), 203–19.

Review: Bluntschli's *Theory of the State*, *English Historical Review* (Apr. 1886).

Note: 'The Possibilities of Mal-Observation', *Proceedings, SPR*, 9, part X (1886).

'Bi-metallism (No. 1): theory of international bi-metallism', *Fortnightly Review* (Oct. 1886).

'Economic Socialism', *Contemporary Review* (Nov. 1886); repr. in *MEA*.

1887   *'Idiopsychological Ethics', *Mind*, 12 (1887), 31–44. (Ch. 29 this vol.)

1888   'The Kantian Conception of Free-Will', *Mind*, 13/51 (1888), 405 ff.; reprinted as appendix to *ME*, 7th edn.

Review: Pulszky's *Theory of Law and Civil Society*, *English Historical Review* (Oct. 1888).

Introduction to Dr Aschrott's *The English Poor Law System*, London 1888 (2nd edn., London: Knight & Co., 1902), pp. vii–xiii.

Address to Society for Psychical Research (a survey of the work of the Society), *Proceedings SPR*, 5, part XIII (July 1888), 271.

'The Scope and Limits of the Work of an Ethical Society', address delivered 18 May 1888, to the Cambridge Ethical Society; published in *PE*.

1889   Address to the SPR on the Physical Phenomena of Spiritualism, *Proceedings, SPR*, 5, part XIV (May 1889), 399.

'Canons of Evidence in Psychical Research', *Proceedings, SPR*, 6, part XV (May 1889), 1.

'The Census of Hallucinations', *Proceedings, SPR*, 6, part XV (1889), 7.

'Experiments in Thought Transference' (written with Mrs Sidgwick), *Proceedings of SPR*, 6, part XV (1889), 128.

'Plato's Utilitarianism: A Dialogue by John Grote and Henry Sidgwick', *Classical Review* (Mar. 1889).

*'Some Fundamental Ethical Controversies', *Mind*, 14/56 (1889), 473–87. (Ch. 6 this vol.)

'Shakespeare's Methods, with special reference to *Julius Caesar* and *Coriolanus*', 1889, in *MEA*.[3]

'Shakespeare and the Romantic Drama, with special reference to *Macbeth*', 1889, in *MEA*.

1890　'A Lecture Against Lecturing', *New Review* (May 1890); repr. *MEA*.

'The Census of Hallucinations', Address to the SPR, *Proceedings, SPR*, 6, part XVII (July 1890), 429.

'Second ad interim Report on the Census', *Proceedings, SPR*, 6, part XVII (1890).

'The Morality of Strife', *IJE*, 1 (1890), 1; repr. *PE*.

1892　*'The Feeling-Tone of Desire and Aversion', *Mind*, NS, 1/1 (1892), 94–101. (Ch. 12 this vol.)

*Critical Notice: Herbert Spencer's *Justice*, in *Mind*, NS, 1/1 (1892), 107–18. (Ch. 30 this vol.)

'Aristotle's Classification of Forms of Government', *Classical Review* (Apr. 1892).

*'Is the Distinction between "Is" and "Ought" Ultimate and Irreducible?', *Proceedings of the Aristotelian Society*, NS, 2/1, part II (1892), 88–92. (Ch. 8 this vol.)[4]

1893　*'Unreasonable Action', *Mind*, NS, 2/6 (Apr. 1893), 174–87; repr. *PE*. (Ch. 13 this vol.)

'My Station and its Duties', *IJE*, 4 (1893), 1; repr. *PE*, under the title 'The Aims and Methods of an Ethical Society'.

1894　Note to the Report of the Gresham University Commission (Jan. 1894), p. lix.

'Luxury', *IJE*, 5 (1894), 1; repr. *PE*.

'A Dialogue on Time and Common Sense', *Mind*, 3/12 (1894), 441; repr. *LPK*. (*Cf*. Ch. 16 this vol.)

'Political Prophecy and Sociology', *The National Review* (Dec. 1894), 563–76; repr. *MEA*.

'The Trial Scene in the Iliad', *Classical Review* (Feb. 1894).

'Note on the Term *hektemoroi* or *hektemorioi*', *Classical Review* (July 1894).

'Conjectures on the Constitutional History of Athens', *Classical Review* (Oct. 1894).

---

[3] I follow Schneewind, *Sidgwick's Ethics* (p. 439) both in listing this and the following item and dating them as 1889, even though they were not published separately and were compiled by the editors of *MEA* from lectures Sidgwick gave at Newnham College 'at different times from 1889 to 1898'; see editors' note in *MEA*, 91.

[4] This and the preceding item are unaccountably missing from the bibliography in *Mem.*; both are listed in Schneewind, *Sidgwick's Ethics*.

Article: 'Economic Science and Economics', *Dictionary of Political Economy*, i, ed. Palgrave (1894).

'Report on the Census of Hallucinations', with Alice Johnson, F. W. H. Myers, Frank Podmore, and Eleanor Mildred Sidgwick, *Proceedings, SPR*, 10, part XXVI (1894).

'Disinterested Deception', *Journal of the Society for Psychical Research*, 6 (1894).

1895 *'The Philosophy of Common Sense', *Mind*, 4/14 (1895), 145–58; repr. *LPK*. (Ch. 16 this vol.)

'Theory and Practice', *Mind*, 4/15 (1895), 370–5.

Critical Notice: D. G. Ritchie's *Natural Rights*, *Mind*, 4/15 (1895), 384.

'The Economic Lessons of Socialism', *Economic Journal* (Sept. 1895); repr. *MEA*.

Note on the Memorandum of Sir R. Giffen to the Royal Commission on the Financial Relations of Great Britain and Ireland, *Report of the Commission*, vol. ii of Minutes of Evidence (1895), 180.

Memorandum in Answer to Questions from the Royal Commission on Secondary Education, *Report of the Commission*, vol. v (1895), 243.[5]

Prefatory Note to V. Solovev's *A Modern Priestess of Isis*, abridged and trans. Walter Leaf, London 1895.

1896 Review: Prof. Gidding's *Principles of Sociology*, *Economic Journal* (Sept. 1896).

'The Ethics of Religious Conformity', *IJE*, 6 (Apr. 1896); repr. *PE*. (Cf. Rashdall 1897, Sect. IV, *inf*.)

Preface to J. R. Seeley, *Introduction to Political Science*, ed. by Henry Sidgwick (London: Macmillan, 1896), pp. v–xi.

1897 'The Pursuit of Culture as an Ideal', part of a lecture delivered to the students of the University College of Wales, Aberystwith in 1897; pub., but only in part, in *MEA*; see eds'. note *MEA*, 352.

'The Pursuit of Culture', *PE*, 205–34 (113–28 in Oxford edn.).

'Involuntary Whispering considered in Relation to Experiments in Thought Transference', *Proceedings, SPR*, 12, part XXI (1897).

'Public Morality', read to the Eranus Society, Cambridge, on 26 Jan. 1897; pub. in *PE*.

'Clerical Veracity', *PE*, 142–77 (79–97 in Oxford University Press reprint, with an error in the editorial note on p. 79; this address was *not* published in the *International Journal of Ethics*, in 1896 or any other year). (A reply to Rashdall 1897, part IV *below*.)

'Comments on Tennyson', in H. Tennyson, *Alfred, Lord Tennyson, A Memoir*, 2 vols., vol. i: 300–4; repr. *Mem.*, 538–42.

1898 'Concessions and Questions for the Synthetic Society', 1898, in Maisie Ward, *The Wilfred Wards and the Transition* (London, 1934,[6] Appendix B).

'On the Nature of the Evidence for Theism', read to the Synthetic Society (25 Feb. 1898); in *Mem.*, app. I: 600–8.

1899 Review: Prof. Gidding's *Elements of Sociology*, *Economic Journal*, 9 (Sept. 1899).

'Authority, Scientific and Theological', read to the Synthetic Society (24 Feb. 1899); in *Mem.*, app. I: 608–15.

---

[5] Schneewind, *Sidgwick's Ethics*, lists this as vol. vi; it is listed as vol. v in *Mem.*

[6] This is the date supplied by Schneewind (*Sidgwick's Ethics*).

*'The Relation of Ethics to Sociology', *IJE*, 10/1 (Oct. 1899), 1–21; repr. *MEA*. (Ch. 9 this vol.)

Memorandum to the Royal Commission on Local Taxation, in Reply to Questions on the Classification and Incidence of Taxation, *Report of the Commission*, volume of Memoranda (1899), 99.

Article: 'Political Economy, its Scope', *Dictionary of Political Economy*, iii, ed. R. H. Inglis Palgrave (London: Macmillan, 1899).

Article: 'Political Economy, its Method', *Dictionary of Political Economy*, iii, ed. R. H. Inglis Palgrave (London: Macmillan, 1899).

Article: 'Political Economy and Ethics', *Dictionary of Political Economy*, iii, ed. R. H. Inglis Palgrave (London: Macmillan, 1899).

Autobiographical Note, in *Life of E. W. Benson*, by A. C. Benson (1899), i: 145–51; ii: 249–55.[7]

1900   *'Criteria of Truth and Error', *Mind*, 10/33 (Jan. 1900), 8–25; repr. *LPK*. (Ch. 17 this vol.)

1901   'The Philosophy of T. H. Green' (an address delivered to the Oxford Philosophical Society in May 1900—Sidgwick's last public appearance), *Mind*, 10/37 (Jan. 1901), 18–29; repr. *LPK*, 257–66, with first six paragraphs omitted.

'Prof. Sidgwick's Ethical View: An Auto-Historical Fragment', *Mind*, 10/38 (Apr. 1901); repr. in preface to 6th edn. of *ME*.

III. Biographical Notices of Henry Sidgwick[8]

James Bryce, 'Henry Sidgwick', in *Studies in Contemporary Biography* (Macmillan, 1903); repr. from *The Nation* (17 Sept. 1900). (See n. 9.)

Frederick Pollock, 'Henry Sidgwick', *The Pilot*, 2 (15 Sept. 1900).

J. Peile, 'Reminiscences of Henry Sidgwick', *Cambridge University Journal* (25 Oct. 1900).

—— An Address on Henry Sidgwick, given as president of Newnham College at the Annual General Meeting on 3 Nov. 1900, *Newnham College Report*.

Anon., in the *Charity Organisation Review*, NS, 8 (Oct. 1900).

G. F. G. Masterman, 'Henry Sidgwick', *The Commonwealth* (Oct. 1900). Repr. in Masterman's *In Peril of Change: Essays Written in Time of Tranquillity* (London: Fisher Unwin, 1905).

E. E. C. J. [Constance Jones], 'Professor Henry Sidgwick', *Journal of Education* (Oct. 1900).

Alice Gardner, 'The Late Professor Sidgwick', *Secondary Education* (15 Nov. 1900).

---

[7] I take this reference from Schneewind, *Sidgwick's Ethics*, 432. E. W. Benson (Archbishop) was the husband of Sidgwick's sister Mary. Schneewind reports this item reprinted 'In part in *Mem.*', but I have not been able to locate it there, though there is a brief reference on p. 580 to this biography of Benson.

[8] Reprinted here almost exactly as it appears in *Mem.*, 623, where it does not appear in any obvious ordering relation, with a few additions of my own, where I had information to add. Some of these items, which I regard as having special philosophical significance, are listed later in Sect. IV. But I have not been able to examine each and every one of these items, so I cannot say that there are no other items listed here with special philosophical significance.

F. W. H. Myers, 'In Memory of Henry Sidgwick', *Proceedings of the Society for Psychical Research*, 15 (Dec. 1900), 452–62. repr. in F. H. W. Myers, *Fragments of Prose and Poetry*, ed. Eveleen Myers (London: Longmans, 1904).

Sir Oliver Lodge, 'In Memory of Henry Sidgwick', *Proceedings, SPR*, 15: 463.

'Report of the Proceedings for Promoting a Memorial of the Late Henry Sidgwick', *Cambridge University Reporter* (7 Dec. 1900).

F. W. C., 'The Sidgwick Memorial Meeting', *The Pilot* (22 Dec. 1900).

J. N. Keynes, 'Obituary: Henry Sidgwick', *Economic Journal* (Dec. 1900).

W. R. Sorley, 'Henry Sidgwick', *International Journal of Ethics* (Jan. 1901).

Anon., 'Professor Sidgwick', *Cambridge Letter* for 1900 (privately printed for the Newnham College Club).

Leslie Stephen, 'Henry Sidgwick', *Mind*, 10 (Jan. 1901).

—— 'Henry Sidgwick', *Dictionary of National Biography*, xxii, suppl. (London: Oxford University Press, 1901), 1214–17; provides some personal and bibliographical information not readily available elsewhere.

J. Bryce, 'Obituary Notice: Henry Sidgwick', *Proceedings of the British Academy* (1903–4).[9]

IV. Secondary Works

The writings about Sidgwick referred to in the introduction and also many of the works discussed by Sidgwick in this collection are listed here, along with some other items referred to above. Also listed are some other writings that may be of special interest for students of Sidgwick or anyone interested in pursuing the subject further.

Albee, Ernest, *A History of English Utilitarianism* (London: George Allen & Unwin, 1901).

Annan, Noel Gilroy, *Leslie Stephen: His Thought and Character in Relation to His Time* (Cambridge, Mass.: Harvard University Press, 1952).

Audi, Robert, ed., *The Cambridge Dictionary of Philosophy* (Cambridge: University Press, 1995; 2nd edn., 1999). [Contains an interesting article on Alexander Bain (by Thomas H. Leahey), as well as one on Sidgwick (by J. B. Schneewind), along with nice brief articles on some other writers referred to in this book.]

Bain, Alexander, 'Mr Sidgwick's Methods of Ethics', *Mind*, OS, 1/2 (Apr. 1876), 179–97.

Barker, Ernest, 'Sidgwick, Henry', in *Encyclopedia of the Social Sciences* (cited *inf.*), 14: 48. [Interesting on Sidgwick's career at Cambridge, but on the philosophy now pretty much outmoded.]

Barratt, Alfred, 'The "Suppression" of Egoism', *Mind*, OS, 2/6 (1877), 167–86. [The opening paragraph of this paper runs this way: 'As Mr Sidgwick's book on *The Methods of Ethics* seems thought to have cast some discredit on the system which he calls "Egoistic Hedonism," and which indeed he himself distinctly claims to have "suppressed," I propose in this paper to consider his treatment and non-treatment of that system.']

---

[9] James Bryce (1838–1922), author of the famous *The American Commonwealth*, 2 vols. (London and New York: Macmillan, 1888; 2nd edn., 1893–5; 3rd edn., 1910), and *Studies in History and Jurisprudence* (1901), as well as *Studies in Contemporary Biography*, along with numerous other works. In the preface to the first edition of *The American Commonwealth* Bryce thanks, among others, his 'friend Mr Henry Sidgwick, who has read most of the proofs with great care and made valuable suggestions upon them . . .'.

—— 'Ethics and Politics', *Mind*, OS, 2/8 (Oct. 1877), 453–76. [Another essay by the author of 'The "Suppression" of Egoism', containing *inter alia* a critique of utilitarianism and a response to Ch. 4 this vol.]

Becker, Lawrence C., and Becker, Charlotte B., eds., *Encyclopedia of Ethics*, 2 vols. (New York and London: Garland Publishing, 1992); (2nd edn., rev. and expanded, forthcoming).

Benson, Arthur Christopher, 'Henry Sidgwick', *The Leaves of the Tree: Studies in Biography* (London: Smith, Elder & Co., 1911), 49–77.

Blanshard, Brand, *Reason and Goodness* (London: George Allen & Unwin, 1961).

—— 'Sidgwick the Man', *The Monist*, 58/3 (July 1974), 349–70.

—— *Four Reasonable Men: Marcus Aurelius, John Stuart Mill, Ernest Renan, Henry Sidgwick* (Middletown, Conn.: Wesleyan University Press, 1984).

Bosanquet, Bernard, Critical Notice of Sidgwick's *Green, Spencer, and Martineau, Mind*, 12 (1903), 381.

Bradley, F. H., *Ethical Studies* (Oxford: Clarendon Press, 1876).

*—— 'Mr Sidgwick on *Ethical Studies*', *Mind*, OS, 2/7 (1877), 122–5 (Ch. 23A this vol.)

—— 'Mr Sidgwick's Hedonism: An Examination of the Main Argument of the *Methods of Ethics*' (1877), repr. in Bradley's *Collected Essays* (Oxford: Clarendon Press, 1935), i: 71–128. (Cf. Edgeworth, *inf.*)

Brink, David O., 'Sidgwick's Dualism of Practical Reason', *Australasian Journal of Philosophy*, 66 (1988), 291–307.

—— 'Sidgwick and the Rationale for Rational Egoism', in Schultz, ed., *Essays on Sidgwick*, 199–240.

Broad, C. D., *Five Types of Ethical Theory* (London: Routledge and Kegan Paul, 1930). [The five types discussed are those of Spinoza, Butler, Hume, Kant, and Sidgwick.]

—— 'Henry Sidgwick' (1938), in *Ethics and the History of Philosophy* (London: Routledge & Kegan Paul, 1952), 49–69.

Bryce, James, 'The Late Mr Henry Sidgwick', *Nation*, 62/1839 (27 Sept. 1900), 244–6. Reprinted as 'Henry Sidgwick', in J. B. Bryce, *Studies in Contemporary Biography* (London: Macmillan, 1903), 327–42.[10] *(BN)*

Calderwood, Henry, 'Mr Sidgwick on Intuitionalism', *Mind*, OS, 1/2 (Apr. 1876), 197–206.

Darwall, Stephen L., 'Pleasure as Ultimate Good in Sidgwick's Ethics', *The Monist*, 58 (July 1974), 475–89. [Argues, *inter alia*, that 'in large measure Sidgwick's position is the analogue in practical philosophy of an empiricist epistemology' (p. 475), roughly the contrary of what was maintained in the introd., above.]

Daurio, Janice, 'Sidgwick on Moral Theories and Common Sense Morality', *History of Philosophy Quarterly*, 14 (1997), 425–45. [Especially penetrating and original, particularly on Sidgwick's distinction between method and principle; argues for the 'essential unity' of *The Methods*, that the work advances one 'single moral theory . . . the one implicit in common sense morality'.] Repr. in *The Philosopher's Annual*, xx, ed. P. Grim, K. Baynes, and G. Mar (1997), 49–67.

Deane, Phyllis, 'Sidgwick, Henry (1838–1900)', in *The New Palgrave* (cited *infra*), iv: 328–9. [Although the article has a certain interest, it commits an astonishing error in claiming

---

[10] Also listed in Sect. III of this bibliography, 'Biographical Notices of Henry Sidgwick'. Pieces double listed in this way are noticed henceforth by the symbol '*BN*'.

that Sidgwick modified 'the greatest happiness formula so as to include equal distribution of happiness as a requirement ranking with its maximization' (p. 329). Sidgwick's actual view (whether we like it or not) is quite the opposite, and is set forth in unmistakable terms in Ch. 1 of this volume and in *The Methods of Ethics*, bk. IV, ch. i, pp. 415–16.]

Donagan, Alan, 'Sidgwick and Whewellian Intuitionism: Some Enigmas', *Canadian Journal of Philosophy*, 7/3 (Sept. 1977), 447–65; repr. in Schultz's *Essays on Sidgwick*.

—— 'A New Sidgwick?' *Ethics*, 90 (Jan. 1980), 282–95. [A very good discussion of Schneewind's *Sidgwick's Ethics*.]

Edgeworth, F. Y., *New and Old Methods of Ethics, or 'Physical Ethics' and 'Methods of Ethics'* (Oxford and London: Parker & Co., 1877). [Discounting Bradley's 1877 attempt at demolition, this is probably the first commentary on *ME*. (Cf. Hayward, *The Ethical Philosophy of Sidgwick*, 1901) Contains a critique of Barratt, cited *sup*.]

Edwards, Paul, ed., *The Encyclopedia of Philosophy*, 8 vols. (New York and London: The Macmillan Company and The Free Press, 1967).

Edwards, Rem B., *Pleasures and Pains: A Theory of Qualitative Hedonism* (Ithaca, NY and London: Cornell University Press, 1979). [The opening statement reads 'So far as I know, this book is the only sustained attempt to make sense out of John Stuart Mill's claim that pleasures and pains differ qualitatively as well as quantitatively . . .'. This the book does, and does very well, and so far as I (MGS) know it is still the only such sustained attempt. Edwards provides references to other writers who attempt a similar defence (p. 154, n. 14).]

Fowler, Thomas, *Progressive Morality: An Exercise in Ethics* (London: Macmillan, 1884). [Discussed in Ch. 28 this vol.]

—— 'Professor Sidgwick on "Progressive Morality" ', *Mind*, OS, 10 (1885), 481–6.

—— 'Some Fundamental Ethical Controversies', *Mind*, OS, 15 (1890), 89–93. [A discussion of Ch. 6 this vol. Cf. Selby-Bigge, 'Some Fundamental Ethical Controversies'.]

Frankena, William K., 'Sidgwick, Henry', in *An Encyclopedia of Morals*, ed. Vergilius Ferm (New York: Philosophical Library, 1956), 539–44. [An acute and excellent article, which deserves to be better known.]

—— 'Sidgwick and the Dualism of Practical Reason', *The Monist*, 58 (July 1974), 449–67.

—— 'Sidgwick and the History of Ethical Dualism', in Schultz, *Essays on Sidgwick*, 175–98.

Garcia, J. L. A., 'Why Sidgwick's Project had to Fail', *History of Philosophy Quarterly*, 4/1 (Jan. 1987), 79–91.

Gibbins, John R., 'John Grote and Modern Cambridge Philosophy', *Philosophy*, 73/285 (1998), 453–77.

Green, Thomas Hill, *Prolegomena to Ethics*, ed. A. C. Bradley (Oxford: Clarendon Press, 1883). [Discussed by Sidgwick in Ch. 27. Cf. Thomas, *The Moral Philosophy of T. H. Green*.]

Griffin, James, *Well-Being* (Oxford: Clarendon Press, 1986). [An important work, revising, *inter alia*, the utilitarian tradition. See index for Sidgwick refs.]

Grote, John, *An Examination of the Utilitarian Philosophy*, ed. J. B. Mayor (Cambridge: Deighton, Bell, and Co., 1870). [Discussed by Sidgwick in Chs. 19 and 20.]

—— *A Treatise on the Moral Ideals*, ed. J. B. Mayor (Cambridge: Deighton, Bell, and Co., 1876).

Halévy, Elie, *The Growth of Philosophic Radicalism* (trans. from the French by Mary Morris) (London: Faber & Faber Ltd., 1928). Originally pub., in French, in 1901–4. See Vergara, 'A Critique of Elie Halévy'.

Harrison, Ross, 'Henry Sidgwick', *Philosophy*, 71 (1996), 423–38. [Very interesting, thorough.]

—— Review of Schultz's *Essays on Sidgwick*. *British Journal for the History of Philosophy*, 4 (1996), 203–6.

Harrod, Roy F., *The Life of John Maynard Keynes* (London: Macmillan & Co., 1951).

Havard, William C., *Henry Sidgwick & Later Utilitarian Political Philosophy* (Gainesville, Fla.: University of Florida Press, 1959).

Hayward, F. H., 'The True Significance of Sidgwick's "Ethics"', *International Journal of Ethics*, 11 (1900–1), 175–87. (Cf. E. E. C. Jones, 'Mr Hayward's Evaluation of Professor Sidgwick's Ethics'.)

—— *The Ethical Philosophy of Sidgwick* (London: Swan Sonnenschein & Co., 1901). [Among other virtues, contains 'Some Hints to the Student Commencing *The Methods of Ethics*', pp. v–xvi. (Cf. Edgeworth, *New and Old Methods of Ethics*.) Excluding Ch. 6 this vol., the second commentary on *The Methods*.]

Huxley, Thomas Henry, 'Administrative Nihilism' (1871), repr. in *Method and Results*, vol. i of the *Collected Essays* of T. H. Huxley (London: Macmillan and Co., 1893), 251–89.

James, D. G., *Henry Sidgwick: Science and Faith in Victorian England* (London: Oxford University Press, 1970). [An interesting but curious work (unfortunately left unfinished by the death of the author), which claims that Sidgwick 'remained John Stuart Mill's disciple' to the end (p. 32) and speaks, rather disparagingly, of 'Sidgwick's exclusive preoccupation, to the exclusion of other branches of philosophy, with ethics' (p. 33). The first opinion is refuted by Chs. 14 and 19–21 of this vol.; the second by the essays in Parts II and III of this volume, as well as by the contents of *LPK* and *MEA* and many of the other essays listed in Sect. II of this bibliography. Besides, the author of the *Politics*, the *Political Economy*, and the *Development of European Polity* can hardly be said to be 'exclusively preoccupied with ethics', unless the term 'ethics' is being used in some very extended sense. Gwilym James's assertion that Bradley in his 1877 pamphlet 'blew Sidgwick's position . . . to pieces' may be in no better case than these other assertions.]

James, Henry, ed., *The Letters of William James*, 2 vols. (Boston: Atlantic Monthly Press, 1930).

Jones, E. E. Constance, 'Mr Hayward's Evaluation of Professor Sidgwick's Ethics', *International Journal of Ethics*, 11 (1900–1), 354–60.

Jones, Hardy, 'Are Fundamental Moral Principles Incapable of Proof?' *Metaphilosophy*, 10/2 (Apr. 1979), 153–60; see esp. 159–60.

Lacey, A. R., 'Sidgwick's Ethical Maxims', *Philosophy*, 34/130 (July 1959), 217–28. [A very penetrating account.]

MacIntyre, Alasdaire, *A Short History of Ethics* (New York: Macmillan, 1966).

Mackie, J. L., 'Sidgwick's Pessimism', in Schultz, *Essays on Sidgwick*, 163–74; repr. from *The Philosophical Quarterly*, 26 (1976), 317–27. [A brilliant paper on Sidgwick's Dualism, which cannot be ignored by anyone interested in the topic.]

Marshall, Henry Rutgers, 'The Physical Basis of Pleasure and Pain', Parts I and II, *Mind*, OS, 16/63 (1892), 327–54, 470–97. [The latter part is the article to which Sidgwick replied in Ch. 12.]

Marshall, Henry Rutgers, 'The Definition of Desire', *Mind*, NS, 1/3 (July 1892), 400–3. [A reply to Sidgwick's Ch. 12.]

—— 'Unreasonable Action', *Mind*, NS, 3/9 (Jan. 1894), 105–8. [A sympathetic response to Ch. 13.]

Martineau, James, *Types of Ethical Theory* (1st edn., 1885; Oxford: Clarendon Press, 2nd edn., 1886; 3rd edn., 1891), 2 vols. [Discussed by Sidgwick in Ch. 29. See index for refs. to Sidgwick (several)].

—— 'Professor Sidgwick on "Types of Ethical Theory" ', *Mind*, 10/40 (1885), 628–39.

—— Rejoinder to Sidgwick's 'Dr. Martineau's Defence of "Types of Ethical Theory" ', *Mind*, 11 (1886), 145–6.

The Monist, 58/3 (July 1974). [A special issue celebrating the centennial of the publication of *The Methods*; contains the essays by Blanshard, Frankena, and Schneewind, along with some others listed here, as well as essays by Stephen Darwall, Gertrude Ezorsky, D. D. Raphael, and Peter Singer.]

Montague, William Pepperell, *The Ways of Knowing, or The Methods of Philosophy* (London: George Allen & Unwin, 1925).

Moore, G. E., *Principia Ethica* (Cambridge: University Press, 1903). [Cf. Regan, *Bloomsbury's Prophet*.]

—— 'Autobiography', in *The Philosophy of G. E. Moore*, ed. P. A. Schilpp (Evanston, Ill.: Northwestern University, 1942), 16.

—— *The Early Essays*, ed. Tom Regan (Philadelphia: Temple University Press, 1986); ed.'s introd., 3–15.

—— *The Elements of Ethics*, ed. Tom Regan (Philadelphia: Temple University Press, 1991); ed.'s introd., pp. xiii–xxxviii.

Myers, F. W. H., 'Henry Sidgwick', *Proceedings of the Society for Psychical Research*, 15 (Dec. 1900), 95–114. (*BN*)

Parfit, Derek, *Reasons and Persons* (Oxford: Clarendon Press, 1984). [An independent and closely argued treatise; check the index for Sidgwick entries.]

Passmore, John, *A Hundred Years of Philosophy* (London: Gerald Duckworth & Co., 1957).

Phillips, David, 'Sidgwick, Dualism, and Indeterminacy in Practical Reasoning', *History of Philosophy Quarterly*, 15 (Jan. 1998).

Pollock, Frederick, 'Evolution and Ethics', *Mind*, OS, 1/3 (1876), 334–45. [A reply to Ch. 2 this vol.]

Pringle-Pattison, A. S., Critical Notice of Sidgwick's *Philosophy, Its Scope and Relations*, *Mind*, 12 (1903), 83.

Pritchard, Michael, 'Sidgwick's *Practical Ethics*: From Practice to Theory', *International Journal of Applied Philosophy*, 12/2 (fall 1998), 147–51. [Part of a symposium on Sidgwick's *Practical Ethics*, stimulated by its recent reprinting by Oxford University Press; the other two papers are by Karen Hanson and Michael Davis.]

Quinton, Anthony, *Utilitarian Ethics* (New York: St Martin's Press, 1973). [Contains sections on Grote, pp. 83–7, and Sidgwick, pp. 87–92.]

Rashdall, Hastings, 'Professor Sidgwick's Utilitarianism', *Mind*, OS, 10 (Apr. 1885), 200–26.

—— 'Professor Sidgwick on the Ethics of Religious Conformity: A Reply', *International Journal of Ethics*, 7 (1897), 137. [Replied to in turn by Sidgwick in 'Clerical Veracity' (1897), *PE*.]

—— *The Theory of Good and Evil* (London: Oxford University Press, 1907).

Rawls, John, *A Theory of Justice* (Cambridge, Mass.: Harvard University Press, 1971).

—— 'The Independence of Moral Theory', *Proceedings and Addresses of the American Philosophical Association*, 48 (1975), 5–22. Repr. in Rawls, *Collected Papers*, ed. by Samuel Freeman (Cambridge: Harvard University Press, 1999), 286–302.

—— 'Kantian Constructivism in Moral Theory', *The Journal of Philosophy*, 77 (1980), 515–72. Repr. in Rawls, *Collected Papers*, 303–58.

Rayleigh, Lord, 'Some Recollections of Henry Sidgwick', *Proceedings of the Society for Psychical Research*, 45 (1938–9), 162–73.

Regan, Tom, *Bloomsbury's Prophet: G. E. Moore and the Development of his Moral Philosophy* (Philadelphia: Temple University Press, 1986).

Ritchie, D. G., Critical Notice of Sidgwick's *Practical Ethics*, *Mind*, 7 (1898), 535.

Rogers, Arthur Kenyon, *Morals in Review* (New York: The Macmillan Co., 1927), 336–41. [An interesting brief account; curiously enough, it quotes from the 3rd edn., hardly a definitive edition.]

Rogers, Reginald A. P., *A Short History of Ethics* (London: Macmillan, 1952), 242–56.

Schilpp, Paul Arthur, ed., *The Philosophy of G. E. Moore* (Evanston, Ill: Northwestern University, 1942).

Schneewind, J. B., 'First Principles and Common Sense Morality in Sidgwick's Ethics', *Archiv für Geschichte der Philosophie*, 45/2 (1963), 137–56. [A predecessor of Schneewind's great commentary; some points are put more perspicuously here.]

—— 'John Grote', in *The Encyclopedia of Philosophy*, iii, ed. Paul Edwards (New York: The Macmillan Co., 1967), 342–3.

—— 'Sidgwick, Henry', *The Encyclopedia of Philosophy*, vii, ed. Paul Edwards (New York & London: The Macmillan Co., 1967), 434–7.

—— 'Sidgwick and the Cambridge Moralists', *The Monist* (July 1974), 371–404; repr. in Schultz, *Essays*.

—— *Sidgwick's Ethics and Victorian Moral Philosophy* (Oxford: Oxford University Press, 1977). [The standard work on Sidgwick and the moral philosophy of the period, and a great piece of philosophical writing.]

—— and Schultz, Bart, 'Henry Sidgwick, 1838–1900', in *The Cambridge Bibliography of English Literature*, 3rd edn. (Cambridge: Cambridge University Press, 1999). [An extensive bibliography; unfortunately some important items omitted.]

Schultz, Bart, ed., *Essays on Henry Sidgwick* (Cambridge: Cambridge University Press, 1992). [The ed.'s introd., 'Henry Sidgwick Today', pp. 1–61, is a substantial essay, possibly the best short account of Sidgwick's moral and political philosophy to be found. In addition to the essays listed separately here (by Brink, Donagan, Frankena, Mackie, and Schneewind), contains essays by Russell Hardin, John Deigh, Thomas Christiano, T. H. Irwin, Nicholas White, Stefan Collini, James T. Kloppenberg, and the editor of the present work.]

—— 'Sidgwick, Henry', *The Encyclopedia of Philosophy, Supplement*, ed. Donald M. Borchert (New York & London etc.: Simon & Schuster and Macmillan, 1996), 537–9.

—— Review of Sidgwick's *Practical Ethics* (repr. 1998), and introd. by Sissela Bok, *Ethics*, 109 (Apr. 1999), 678–84.

Selby-Bigge, L. A., 'Some Fundamental Ethical Controversies', *Mind*, OS, 15 (1890), 93–99. [A discussion of Ch. 6 this vol. Cf. Fowler, 'Some Fundamental Ethical Controversies'.]

Seth, James, 'The Ethical System of Henry Sidgwick', *Mind*, NS, 10 (1901).

Shaver, Robert, 'Sidgwick's False Friends', *Ethics*, 107 (1997), 314–20. [A brief account of a rather obscure point in Sidgwick, with useful references to other discussions. But mainly for scholars.]

Sidgwick, Arthur, and Sidgwick, Eleanor Mildred, *Henry Sidgwick: A Memoir* (London: Macmillan, 1906). [See full listing above, in Sect. I, *Books by Sidgwick*.]

Singer, Marcus G., 'The Many Methods of Sidgwick's Ethics', *The Monist*, 58/3 (July 1974), 420–48.

—— 'Schneewind's Sidgwick', *Nous*, 16 (1982), 339–50.

—— 'Common Sense and Paradox in Sidgwick's Ethics', *History of Philosophy Quarterly*, 3/1 (Jan. 1986), 65–78.

—— 'Sidgwick, Henry', in *Encyclopedia of Ethics*, ed. Lawrence and Charlotte Becker (New York and London: Garland Publishing, Inc., 1992), ii: 1149–52. (2nd edn., rev. forthcoming.)

—— Review of Schultz. *Philosophy and Phenomenological Research*, 59 (1999), 533–7.

—— 'Mill's Stoic Conception of Happiness and Pragmatic Conception of Utility', *Philosophy*, 75 (Jan. 2000), 25–47. [An account congruent with that of Rem Edwards, *Pleasures and Pains*.]

Singer, Peter, Review of Schultz. *Ethics*, 104 (1994), 631–3.

Skorupski, John, 'Critical Study: Sidgwick's Ethics', *Philosophical Quarterly*, 29/115 (Apr. 1979), 158–69. [An especially penetrating study of both Schneewind and Sidgwick. Strongly recommended.]

—— 'Clearly Undecided.' [Review of Schultz]. *Times Literary Supplement* (10 July 1992), 24–5.

Slater, John, 'The Importance of Henry Sidgwick', introd. to the Thoemmes Press edn. of *The Complete Works of Henry Sidgwick* (1996), in vol. i, a repr. of the 1st edn. (1874) of *The Methods*, pp. v–liv. [An important essay, very thorough and thoroughly interesting.]

Sorley, W. R., 'Henry Sidgwick', *International Journal of Ethics*, 11 (1900–1), 168–74. (BN) [I quote the last sentence of this philosophical eulogy: 'Life will be a poorer thing to very many; and there are not a few who feel that the wisest and the justest man they have ever known has passed away.']

—— *A History of English Philosophy* (Cambridge: Cambridge University Press, 1937).

Spencer, Herbert, *The Data of Ethics*, part I of *Principles of Ethics* (London, 1879). [Discussed in Ch. 25.]

—— *Justice*, part IV of *Principles of Ethics* (London, 1891). [Discussed in Ch. 30.]

—— *The Principles of Ethics* (New York and London: D. Appleton and Company, 1893), 2 vols. Contains part I, *The Data of Ethics*, in vol. i, and part IV, *Justice*, in vol. ii. [See vol. ii, appendix E, 'Replies to Criticisms' (originally published in *Mind*, Jan. 1883), 461–71, for replies to Sidgwick.]

Sprigge, T. L. S., 'Utilitarianism', in *An Encyclopedia of Philosophy*, ed. G. H. R. Parkinson (London: Routledge, 1988), 590–612; see pp. 600–4 for specific discussion of Sidgwick. [Published in the United States under the title *The Handbook of Western Philosophy* (New York: Macmillan, 1988), under which title it will be referred to henceforth.]

Stephen, Leslie, *The Science of Ethics* (New York: G. P. Putnam's Sons, 1882). [Discussed by Sidgwick in Ch. 26; and still of interest despite the harsh remarks on it by N. G. Annan.]

Strachey, Lytton, *Characters and Commentaries* (London: Chatto & Windus, 1933). [In addition to the passage quoted above (Introd. n. 18), contains Strachey's essay on Matthew Arnold, 'A Victorian Critic' (1914), 187–94. Compare with Sidgwick's 1867 essay, 'The Prophet of Culture' (listed *sup.*). Strachey, with his animus against all things and persons Victorian, is more sarcastic and sardonic—scathing even—and writes more brilliantly; Sidgwick is, as might be expected, more philosophically intelligent and penetrating. (Cited again in Sect. V.)]

Sverdlik, Steven, 'Sidgwick's Methodology', *Journal of the History of Philosophy*, 58 (1985), 537–53.

Thomas, Geoffrey, *The Moral Philosophy of T. H. Green* (Oxford: Clarendon Press, 1987). [An invaluable work, long overdue. For discussions of Sidgwick's discussions of Green, consult index; e.g. p. 244: 'Some of Sidgwick's limitations as a commentator have been noticed already . . .' or p. 312: 'Sidgwick, transparently honest intellectually but ever inclined to read differences of view in slight variations of language, was the last person to do proper justice to Green.']

Thomson, J. J., *Recollections and Reflections* (New York: The Macmillan Co., 1937), 293–300.

Trollope, Anthony, *An Autobiography* (1883), Ch. 19 (London: Oxford University Press, World's Classics edn., 1958), 299–300. [Listed here for the benefit of those who want the context of the sentence quoted in n. 17 of the Introd.: after referring to his books on 'the American States', the West Indies, and Australia, Trollope says: 'But the West Indian volume was readable. I am not sure that either of the other works are so, in the proper sense of that word. When I go back to them I find that the pages drag with me;—and if so with me, how must it be with others who have none of that love which a father feels even for his ill-favoured offspring. Of all the needs a book has the chief need is that it be readable.']

Tsanoff, Radoslav A., *The Moral Ideals of Our Civilization* (New York: E. P. Dutton & Co., 1942), 497–502. ['To have given adequate recognition to Self-Realization in his treatise would have required a radical change in his entire procedure. Sidgwick's very classification of the fundamental Methods of Ethics indicates his unresponsiveness to Perfection as an ethical alternative. . . .' (p. 502).]

Vergara, Francisco, 'A Critique of Elie Halévy', *Philosophy*, 73/283 (Jan. 1998), 97–111. [Not really about Sidgwick, though Sidgwick is quoted a couple of times, but a telling critique of a work that has been taken by a number of well-known writers (writers who should have known better) to be a 'virtually definitive analysis of utilitarianism'. Vergara argues, very convincingly, that Halévy's 'book has probably done more to distort the western world's understanding of utilitarianism than any similar work. Halévy has . . . invented nothing; he has simply embroidered all the popular gossip and hearsay on utilitarianism and economics into a neat and easy system that has captivated many scholars' (p. 111).]

Wallace, William, Critical Notice of Sidgwick's *Outlines of the History of Ethics for English Readers*, *Mind*, OS, 11 (1886), 570–7.

Ward, Wilfrid, 'Some Characteristics of Henry Sidgwick', *Ten Personal Studies* (London: Longmans, Green, and Co., 1908), 78–96. [Basically a study of the *Mem.* However, though interesting on Sidgwick as a person, whom Ward knew personally, quite mistaken on Sidgwick as a philosopher. Seems to think of Sidgwick as a sort of Humeian or sophistical skeptic, a constant 'nay-sayer'. Thus, Ward describes Sidgwick as 'a man who . . . can accept no statement as satisfactory, who finds a flaw in every theory, who bores fatal holes in every intellectual structure, theological or philosophical, which has stimulated the enthusiasm of men in the past,—and . . . after so much destruction cannot even then offer any decided alternative, whether by way of affirmation or of negation, for the systems he has killed or mutilated . . .', as a 'relentless critic . . . and concrete embodiment of intellectual indecision' (pp. 78, 79). That is not the Sidgwick of this book, of The Methods of Ethics, or of any of the works listed above in Parts I and II of this bibliography. It is evident that, although Ward knew Sidgwick as a person, he had either not read or not understood Sidgwick's writings. Yet he claims (p. 83) to have read The Methods. The conclusion is obvious.]

Williams, Bernard, 'The Point of View of the Universe: Sidgwick and the Ambitions of Ethics', *Cambridge Review* (7 May 1982), 183–91. [Sharply critical.]

—— *Ethics and the Limits of Philosophy* (London: Fontana Press/Collins, 1985), 105–10. [Likewise.]

For further information on and discussion of Martineau, see Schneewind's excellent article in the Edwards *Encyclopedia of Philosophy* (1967), v: 169–70; Schneewind's *Sidgwick's Ethics*, Ch. 8; and a very brief but quite acute piece by Michael Slote on Martineau in *The Oxford Companion to Philosophy*, ed. Ted Honderich (Oxford: Oxford University Press, 1995), 523; as Slote observes, 'Martineau's theory is perhaps the purest example of agent-basing in the . . . history of philosophy'. On Green, there is an excellent book by Geoffrey Thomas, *The Moral Philosophy of T. H. Green* (1987), listed above; an earlier discussion by W. D. Lamont, *Introduction to Green's Moral Philosophy* (London: Allen & Unwin, 1934), which tries to present Green's view by means of rephrasing and paraphrasing, is quite useful; see also the article on Green by W. H. Walsh in *The Encyclopedia of Philosophy* (1967), iii: 386–8. On Bradley, Richard Wollheim, *F. H. Bradley* (Harmondsworth: Penguin, 1959) can be recommended (Ch. 6 is on Bradley's ethics), along with the articles on Bradley by H. B. Acton in *The Encyclopedia of Philosophy* (1967), i: 359–63, and by John Atwell in the *Encyclopedia of Ethics*, ed. Lawrence and Charlotte Becker (New York and London: Garland Publishing, 1992), i: 94–6; Wollheim's *F. H. Bradley* is intriguingly reviewed by Arthur E. Murphy, in *The Philosophical Review*, 70 (1961), 254–7. There is a useful article on Spencer, by Eric Mack, in Becker and Becker, *Encyclopedia of Ethics*, ii: 1199–1200. The Edwards *Encyclopedia* also contains useful articles on Herbert Spencer—by Jack Kaminsky, vol. vii: 523–7—and on Leslie Stephen, by J. B. Schneewind, vol. viii: 14–15.

V. Tertiary Works

Nearly all of the works or writers referred to by Sidgwick or discussed by him in a more ancillary way in this collection are listed here, along with some other works or writers that I judged important or relevant for one reason or another, including some writers, especially but not solely moralists or moral philosophers, discussed in some of his other works. There are entries here on some British moral philosophers who influenced or stimulated Sidgwick, such as Cumberland, Clarke, Butler, Hutcheson, Price, and Henry More, though this listing is certainly not complete. The distinction between Sections IV and V is somewhat vague; that is unimportant. This section also lists some fairly recent discussions about these writers or their work—though I have not striven to be to-the-minute up-to-date—and provides information on years of birth and death for many of the figures. Since on a number of the writers listed the literature is practically inexhaustible, in several instances I have referred to relevant articles in the *Encyclopedia of Ethics*, *The Encyclopedia of Philosophy*, *The Handbook of Western Philosophy*, *Dictionary of the History of Ideas*, *Encyclopedia of the Social Sciences*, *Encyclopedia Britannica*, *The Cambridge Dictionary of Philosophy*, *The Oxford Companion to Philosophy*, *The Oxford Companion to English Literature*, or *The New Palgrave: A Dictionary of Economics*, the reference works listed just below. I have also listed works and guides to information about earlier writers on political economy, which at one time was a branch of moral philosophy (utility theory in economics developed out of and grew up alongside utilitarian moral, political, and economic theory), such as Mandeville, Adam Smith, Malthus, Ricardo, Bagehot, Bentham, Jevons, James Mill, J. E. Cairnes, and J. S. Mill, all of whom Sidgwick discussed, or at least cited, in the *Politics* or his *Principles of Political Economy*. And, given that Sidgwick wrote not just on ethics and on economics (then called political economy), but also on political science, then identified with political philosophy (as in his *Elements of Politics*, his *Development of European Polity*, and his editing of Seeley's *Introduction to Political Science*, 1896), psychology (as in Part II of this volume and an essay of 1880),[11] positivism (cf. Chs. 19–21 this vol.), and sociology (*e.g.*, Ch. 9 this vol., and other essays published in 1894, 1896, 1899)—all now branches of the social sciences though in Sidgwick's time and before they were branches of philosophy, I have included references to some good brief articles, not too far removed in time from Sidgwick's period, on these topics. Although I have deliberately made no attempt to cite the latest works on any given figure or subject, there are a few exceptions to that policy: I saw no need to follow what would have been, in the context, 'a foolish consistency'. What is 'the latest' this year may well be superseded by a later work coming out next year or later. Anyone interested in finding the most recent works on any of the topics or persons covered herein should be able to do so by other means, and may be aided in doing so by the information contained herein. And selections from many of the moralists—moral philosophers—cited as well as uncited can be found in the invaluable collections edited by Raphael, Schneewind (which includes commentary), and Selby-Bigge, listed below. The present section also contains further commentary on some writers or works listed earlier. This is not entirely undeliberate.

The following reference works, marked with an asterisk, are referred to several times in this section.[12]

[11] It is worth noting that Sidgwick attended the first International Congress of Experimental Psychologists, in Paris, in 1889; the Second in 1892; and The Third International Congress of Psychology, in Munich, in 1896 (*Memoir*, 501, 523, 546).

[12] Some other reference works that the reader might find useful, though I have not had occasion to cite any of them here, are: *A Companion to Ethics*, ed. Peter Singer (Oxford and Cambridge, Mass.: Basil Blackwell, 1991); and the *Routledge Encyclopedia of Philosophy*, general ed. Edward Craig, 10 vols., (London and New York: Routledge, 1998). *The Dictionary of Philosophy*, ed. Dagobert D. Runes (4th edn; New York: Philosophical Library, 1942) is also useful on some topics and writers, even though it has been to some extent controversial. However, there was a time when it had the field practically to itself, with no competitors in sight, and it contains some articles that are still valuable. *The Concise Encyclopedia of Western Philosophy and Philosophers*, ed. J. O. Urmson (New York: Hawthorn, 1960) can be useful on a number of topics and writers. It contains an article on Sidgwick on pp. 362–3, from which the adept reader of this volume is unlikely to learn anything new.

*The Cambridge Dictionary of Philosophy, ed. Robert Audi (Cambridge: Cambridge University Press, 1995; 2nd edn., 1999). [Contains an interesting article on Alexander Bain by Thomas H. Leahey as well as one on Sidgwick, by J. B. Schneewind, along with useful brief articles on some other writers referred to in this book, either in the body of this work or in this bibliography. The second edition, considerably expanded over the first, is the one referred to in every instance.]

*Dictionary of the History of Ideas, ed.-in-chief, Philip P. Wiener (New York: Charles Scribner's Sons, 1973). [The articles listed contain useful bibliographies.]

*Encyclopedia Britannica, 14th edn., 24 vols. (London and New York: Encyclopedia Britannica Company, 1929).

*Encyclopedia of Ethics, ed. Lawrence C. & Charlotte B. Becker, 2 vols. (New York and London: Garland Publishing, 1992).

*The Encyclopedia of Philosophy, ed. Paul Edwards, 8 vols. (New York and London: Macmillan and Free Press, 1967).

*Encyclopedia of the Social Sciences, ed.-in-chief, Edwin R. A. Seligman, Alvin Johnson, assoc. ed., 15 vols. (New York: The Macmillan Co., 1930–4).

*The Handbook of Western Philosophy (New York: Macmillan, 1988) (under which title it will be referred to henceforth), pub. in Britain under the title An Encyclopedia of Philosophy, general ed., G. H. R. Parkinson (assoc. eds. T. E. Burke, J. G. Cottingham, M. A. Proudfoot, J. E. Tiles) (London: Routledge, 1988).

*The New Palgrave: A Dictionary of Economics, ed. John Eatwell, Murray Milgate, and Peter Newman, 4 vols. (London: Macmillan, 1987).

*The Oxford Companion to English Literature, compiled and ed. by Sir Paul Harvey (Oxford: Clarendon Press, 1932; 2nd edn., 1937; 3rd edn., 1946).

*The Oxford Companion to Philosophy, ed. Ted Honderich (Oxford and New York: Oxford University Press, 1995).

Abrams, M. H., The Mirror and the Lamp (London, Oxford, and New York: Oxford University Press, 1953). See Carlyle, cited inf.

Arnold, Matthew (1822–88), Culture and Anarchy: An Essay in Political and Social Criticism (London: Smith, Elder & Co., 1869; John Murray, 1954). [Not, of course, directly relevant to Sidgwick, but listed here to provide a context for Sidgwick's 1867 essay on Arnold, 'The Prophet of Culture', and the essays by Lytton Strachey, Lionel Trilling, and others listed below. There is an excellent article on Arnold by Robert Morss Lovett in Encyclopedia of the Social Sciences, 2: 219–20, and a philosophical discussion of Arnold by Raymond Williams in The Encyclopedia of Philosophy, 1: 167–8. There is also an article (unsigned) in The Encyclopedia Britannica, 14th edn., ii: 423–5. See also the essay 'Matthew Arnold' in Arthur Benson's Leaves of the Tree (1911).]

Austin, John (1790–1859), Lectures on Jurisprudence, or The Philosophy of Positive Law, 2 vols. (London, 1863); 5th edn., ed. John Campbell, based in part on Stuart Mill's lecture notes (London: John Murray, 1885).

—— The Province of Jurisprudence Determined (London, 1832). [Actually the first part of the Lectures, but published much earlier. On Austin see the book by Morison, cited inf. Sidgwick has some discussion of Austin in the Politics. See the article on Austin by Herbert Morris in The Encyclopedia of Philosophy, 1: 209–11. In addition one might want to see the brief article by John Finnis in The Oxford Companion to Philosophy, 67, or the nearly as brief article by Edmund M. Pincoffs in *The Cambridge Dictionary of Philosophy*, 61.]

Bagehot, Walter (1826–77), *The Postulates of English Political Economy* (New York and London: G. P. Putnam's Sons, 1885). [See the article in *The New Palgrave*, i: 172–3, by Asa Briggs, and the excellent article by Max Lerner in the *Encyclopedia of the Social Sciences*, ii: 384–5. Bagehot also wrote *The English Constitution* (1867; 2nd edn., 1872), and *Physics and Politics* (1876). His *Economic Studies* were collected and edited by R. H. Hutton (London, 1880), who also edited his *Literary Studies* (1879): available in Everyman's Library, 2 vols. (London: J. M. Dent; New York: E. P. Dutton, 1911), with an illuminating introduction by George Sampson; of special relevance to this volume is the essay in vol. ii on Bishop Butler (1854); also, to a lesser extent, the essay on Macaulay (1856). Sidgwick discussed Bagehot in *PPE*.]

Bain, Alexander (1818–1903), *The Senses and the Intellect* (London, 1855), and *The Emotions and the Will* (London, 1859). [Bain was the founder of *Mind*, in 1876. See the article on Bain by George E. Davie in *The Encyclopedia of Philosophy*, i: 243–4; also the article by Harold C. Warren in *Encyclopedia of the Social Sciences*, ii: 390–1; and the very brief article by Vincent Hope in *The Oxford Companion to Philosophy*, 76, as well as the article by Thomas H. Leahey in *The Cambridge Dictionary of Philosophy*, 70; in addition there is an interesting article on Bain in *The Oxford Companion to English Literature*, 57. Some of Bain's other works are: *On the Study of Character* (1861); *Manual of Rhetoric* (London, 1864); *Logic, Deductive and Inductive* (London, 1870); *Autobiography* (London, 1904). Sidgwick only very briefly discusses Bain in the *History*, 252–3. Bain also published *The Moral Philosophy of Paley, with Additional Dissertations and Notes* (London and Edinburgh: William and Robert Chambers, n.d., prob. 1852); Bain's introduction, pp. 1–24, is quite interesting. Cf. Whately, *Paley's Moral Philosophy, with Annotations*, and Whewell, *On the Foundations of Morals*.]

—— *Dissertations on Leading Philosophical Topics* ('Mainly Reprints from *Mind*') (London: Longmans, Green, and Co., 1903). [Of greatest relevance to the present work are the articles 'On Moral Causation' (from *Mind*, i: 393), 9–19; 'On Some Points in Ethics' (*Mind*, viii: 46), 58–83; and 'Pleasure and Pain' (*Mind*, NS, i: 161), 189–222.]

Baumgardt, David, *Bentham and the Ethics of Today, with Bentham Manuscripts Previously Unpublished* (Princeton: Princeton University Press, 1952).

Bellamy, Edward (1850–98), *Looking Backward, 2000–1887* (1888); [Bellamy's prophecy of perfect equality by the year 2000 has not, it would appear, been realized. This, however, does not diminish the interest of the book. Bellamy is referred to by Sidgwick in Ch. 30 this volume.]

—— *Equality* (New York: D. Appleton and Company, 1897), the sequel to *Looking Backward*. [From the preface: 'I have taken the date of *Looking Backward*, the year 2000, as that of *Equality*, and have utilized the framework of the former story as a starting point for this which I now offer.' There is a brief biography of Bellamy in *Webster's American Biographies*, ed. Charles Van Doren (Springfield, Mass.: G. & C. Merriam Co., 1979), 89. There is another brief though somewhat fuller account in *A College Book of American Literature*, ed. Milton Ellis, Louise Pound, and George Weida Spohn (New York: American Book Company, 1940), ii: 542–3. There is a *philosophical* discussion of Bellamy's ideas in Herbert Schneider's *History of American Philosophy*, ch. 16, esp.

181–6, and an account of the literature on Bellamy on p. 547. See also the article by J. O. Hertzler in *Encyclopedia of the Social Sciences*, ii: p. 504.]

Benson, Arthur Christopher (1862–1925), *The Leaves of the Tree: Studies in Biography* (London: Smith, Elder & Co., 1911). [Contains the essay on Sidgwick cited *sup.* and also an essay on Matthew Arnold, pp. 284–309.]

Bentham, George, *Outline of a New System of Logic, with a Critical Examination of Dr. Whately's 'Elements of Logic'* (London: Hunt and Clarke, 1827). [George Bentham was Jeremy Bentham's nephew, and this work is based largely on 'a mass of manuscripts which my uncle, Mr Jeremy Bentham, had put into my hands' (p. v), which 'were written chiefly in the year 1811', though 'some . . . bear a date as old as 1795' (p. ix). George Bentham says that 'It is to myself . . . that the reader must attribute any errors he may observe in the details of my system; of which, however, the leading principles must be considered as founded on those of Mr [Jeremy] Bentham' (p. x).]

Bentham, Jeremy (1748–1832), *A Fragment on Government* (London, 1776). [This is a dissection of Blackstone's *Commentaries*, as was *A Comment on the Commentaries* (prepared 1775, but not pub. until 1811, in Paris). On Bentham, see the article by D. H. Monro in *The Encyclopedia of Philosophy*, i: 280–5; the article by Gerald J. Postema in *Encyclopedia of Ethics*, i: 85–9, which contains a useful bibliography; the article by Ross Harrison in *The Oxford Companion to Philosophy*, 85–8; the article by Graham Wallas in the *Encyclopedia of the Social Sciences*, ii: 104; the articles by J. S. Mill mentioned below; and Ch. 24 this vol. To be sure, the literature on Bentham is inexhaustible, and Bentham was a very prolific writer, though not a prolific publisher of his writings.]

—— *An Introduction to the Principles of Morals and Legislation* (1780; Oxford, 1789; 2nd edn., 1823). [Discussed by Sidgwick in the *History*, 240–5.]

—— *Deontology; or, The Science of Morality*, 2 vols., ed. John Bowring (London: Longmans, 1834).

Some other works by Bentham: *Defence of Usury* (1787); *Constitutional Code* (vol. i, 1830); *Chrestomathia* (1815); *Anarchical Fallacies* (Paris, 1816); *Panopticon, or the Inspection House* (1791); *A Manual of Political Economy* (written 1793–5, 1st pub. in vol. iii of Bowring (1843) [see below], 31–84);[13] *Panopticon versus New South Wales* (1812); *Rationale of Judicial Evidence*, ed. J. S. Mill, 5 vols. (London, 1827); *Rationale of Punishment* (London, 1817); *Principles of the Civil Code* and *Principles of the Penal Code* (pub. Dumont, in French, 1802), contained in *The Theory of Legislation*, ed. C. K. Ogden (London: Routledge & Kegan Paul, 1931); *The Theory of Fictions*: see *Bentham's Theory of Fictions*, ed. and introd. by

---

[13] Bentham's *Manual of Political Economy* is also available, but in a better edited and more critical edition, commissioned in 1941 by the Council of the Royal Economic Society, in *Jeremy Bentham's Economic Writings* (subtitled 'Critical Edition Based on His Printed Works and Unprinted Manuscripts'), edited by W. Stark, 3 vols. (1949; London: George Allen & Unwin, 1954; New York: Burt Franklin, 1952), vol. i: 221–73. Note Bentham's remark on p. 272: 'Nothing ought to be done for the particular purpose of promoting population. Most of the measures that have been or would be pursued in this view are necessarily inefficacious, or otherwise needless. All of them are inexpedient as being coercive.' Cf. Ch. 1 this vol. and bk. IV, ch. 1: 415–16 of *The Methods of Ethics*. See, on the *Manual of Political Economy*, Stark's introd., vol. i: 49–58. The whole introduction may be read with profit by those interested in Bentham's economic writings, and in fact Stark has interesting introductions in each of the three volumes. It is perhaps needless to say, but it may need emphasis, that none of this material was available to Sidgwick, who had to consult Bentham's *Manual* in the Bowring edition.

C. K. Ogden (London: Routledge & Kegan Paul, 1932); *The Book of Political Fallacies*, ed. P. Bingham (London, 1824), ed. Harold A. Larrabee (Baltimore: The Johns Hopkins Press, 1952). *The Works of Jeremy Bentham*, ed. J. Bowring, 11 vols. (Edinburgh: William Tait; London: Simpkin, Marshall & Co., 1838–43), contains most of these works as well as others, though it is not complete. At any rate, these are the works that were available to Sidgwick.[14]

Berkeley, George (1685–1753), *Principles of Human Knowledge* (1710).

—— *Three Dialogues Between Hylas and Philonous* (1713). [See the article on Berkeley by H. B. Acton in *The Encyclopedia of Philosophy*, i: 295–304, and the article by Geoffrey Warnock in *The Oxford Companion to Philosophy*, 89–92.]

Blackstone, William (1723–80), *Commentaries on the Laws of England*, 4 vols. (London, 1765–69; 14th edn., ed. Edward Christian, London, 1803). [See the interesting and informative article on Blackstone by H. D. Hazeltine in *Encyclopedia of the Social Sciences*, ii: 580–1; also Hanbury, cited *inf*. Cf. Bentham, *A Fragment on Government*, cited *sup*. and *A Comment on the Commentaries*. Blackstone is discussed very briefly by Sidgwick in the *Politics*.]

Bosanquet, Bernard, ed., *Lotze's System of Philosophy* (Oxford, 1884).

Brown, Alan Willard, *The Metaphysical Society: Victorian Minds in Crisis 1869–1880* (New York, 1947). [Contains the minutes of the founding meeting, pp. 25–7, a list of the papers read to the Society, pp. 314–19, and a list of members, pp. 307–12; a welcome corrective to the animadversions of Lytton Strachey (cited *inf*.).]

Buckle, Henry Thomas (1821–62), *The History of Civilization in England*, 2 vols. (London, 1857–71). [See the article on Buckle by Patrick Gardiner in *The Encyclopedia of Philosophy*, i: 413–15, which observes that 'as Sidgwick pointed out', what Buckle wrote 'represents . . . the first major attempt on the part of a thinker versed in the tradition of British empiricism and inductivism to enter the treacherous field of historical speculation, and to offer a comprehensive and detailed theory of historical development of the type that previously only Continental philosophers had ventured to provide' (pp. 413–14). Cf. *Memoir*: 'Buckle . . . is the first Englishman who has attempted to write scientific history, and I for one paid a tribute to that attempt in the intense interest with which I read it' (pp. 68–9, letter of 1861). Cf. also Sidgwick's *Development of European Polity*.]

Buckley, Jerome Hamilton, *The Victorian Temper: A Study in Literary Culture* (Cambridge, Mass.: Harvard University Press, 1951). [On the literary rather than the philosophical side. But a nice counterweight to Strachey's *Eminent Victorians*, even though nowhere near as famous. The opening sentences of its preface are striking: ' "Taste," said John Ruskin, "is not only a part and an index of morality;—it is the *only* morality.[15] The first, and last, and closest trial question to any living creature is, "What do you like?" Tell me what you like, and I'll tell you what you are." Now, however a post-Victorian world

---

[14] There is a more complete and almost certainly definitive edition of Bentham's numerous works under way, superseding the Bowring edition: *The Collected Works of Jeremy Bentham*, general eds., J. H. Burns, J. R. Dinwiddy, and F. Rosen (London: Athlone Press, 1968–81; Oxford: Clarendon Press, 1981–). I mention this here for the benefit of the interested reader who might otherwise not be aware of it; obviously it was not available to Sidgwick, and contains works of Bentham's published for the first time well after Sidgwick's death, and of course well after he wrote Ch. 24 this vol. (1877).

[15] If this is really Ruskin's conception of morality (he is not altogether consistent on these matters), then he is, clearly, confusing morality with values.

may have chosen to regard other Ruskinian dogmas, many a "moral" indictment against the Victorian character has rested squarely upon some generalized impression of Victorian taste. Such generalizations are . . . seldom quite accurate or especially useful.' Buckley goes on to say that 'Victorian taste is intelligible only in a context of thought and feeling which defies easy definition'. An interesting if dry book on the period. See index for the several references to Frederic Harrison (cited *inf.*). Cf. Clark, and Strachey, *inf.*; also *Ideas and Beliefs of the Victorians, inf.* Buckley discusses Ruskin (cited *inf.*) further, esp. 148–60.]

Burke, Edmund (1729–97), *Reflections on the Revolution in France* (1790; 2nd edn., 1793). [See the article on Burke by Michael Freeman in *Encyclopedia of Ethics*, i: 109–11; also the article by Maurice Cranston in *The Encyclopedia of Philosophy*, i: 429–31; and the article by R. S. Downie in *The Oxford Companion to Philosophy*, 110–11.]

—— *Thoughts on the Causes of the Present Discontents* (1770).

Butler, Joseph (1692–1752), *Sermons Upon Human Nature* (1726).

—— *The Analogy of Religion* (1736), including the Dissertation 'Of the Nature of Virtue', an essential supplement to the *Sermons*. [See the article on Butler by Terence Penelhum in *Encyclopedia of Ethics*, i: 115–17, and the article by Elmer Sprague in *The Encyclopedia of Philosophy*, i: 432–4; the article by T. L. S. Sprigge in *The Oxford Companion to Philosophy*, 112, and the somewhat more substantial article on Butler by Stephen Darwall in *The Cambridge Dictionary of Philosophy*, 109–10. See also *Butler's Moral Philosophy*, by Austin Duncan-Jones (Harmondsworth: Penguin Books, 1952). Sidgwick discusses Butler in several places in the *History*, most particularly on pp. 191–200. See also Broad's *Five Types of Ethical Theory* (cited *sup.*).]

Cairnes, John Elliott (1823–75), *The Character and Logical Method of Political Economy* (London: Macmillan, 1875; 2nd edn., 1888); *Some Leading Principles of Political Economy, Newly Expounded* (London: Macmillan, 1874). [See the article on Cairnes in *The Encyclopedia Britannica*, 14th edn., vol. iv: 535, which characterizes him as a 'British political economist of the classical school'. Sidgwick discusses Cairnes's *Leading Principles* in several places in PPE, describes Cairnes, favorably, as 'a disciple of Mill' (p. 5).]

Carlyle, Thomas (1793–1881), *Reminiscences*, ed. J. A. Froude (London: Longmans, 1881); 'new and complete edition', ed. K. J. Fielding and Ian Campbell, who claim that Carlyle was 'the most influential of Victorian cultural leaders' (Oxford and New York: Oxford University Press, 1997). [Even if this claim is only plausible, it entitles Carlyle to a place in this bibliography. Listing only works of his that have the most philosophical relevance, Carlyle was the author of *Sartor Resartus* (serialized first in *Fraser's Magazine*, 1833–4; Boston, 1836); *Chartism* (1840); *On Heroes, Hero-Worship, and the Heroic in History* (1840), which presents a philosophy of history; *Past and Present* (1843); and *Latter-Day Pamphlets* (1850). Although Sidgwick did not refer to Carlyle often, when he did it was not in complimentary terms, yet there is no doubt that Sidgwick read Carlyle. That Carlyle read Sidgwick is very unlikely. See, in addition to the illuminating introduction and other editorial apparatus by Fielding and Campbell, the article on Carlyle by Noël Carroll in the second edition of *The Cambridge Dictionary of Philosophy*, 118; the article about Carlyle by Leslie Stephen and D. A. Wilson in *The Encyclopedia Britannica* (14th edn.; New York and London: Encyclopedia Britannica Co., 1929), vol. iv: 880–5; the article on Carlyle by Crane Brinton in *Encyclopedia of the Social Sciences*, iii: 229–30; and the article on Carlyle in *The Oxford Companion to English Literature*, 139–40. There are also some illuminating remarks about Carlyle in *The Mirror and the Lamp*, by M. H. Abrams (cited *sup.*), to be found by consulting the index, as well as in Schneewind's *Sidgwick's Ethics*, esp. 166–8. See also, for some refreshing writing, Strachey's essay on Carlyle in *The Shorter Strachey*, 99–105.]

Chesterton, G. K. (1874–1936), *The Victorian Age in Literature* (Home University Library; London: Williams and Norgate, 1913). [Contains a discussion of Carlyle on pp. 49–62, of Matthew Arnold on pp. 73–9, and a rather amateurish comment on J. S. Mill on pp. 36–8. For example: 'Now for the great part of the Victorian era the utilitarian tradition which reached its highest in Mill held the centre of the field; it was the philosophy in office, so to speak. It sustained its march of codification and inquiry until it had made possible the great victories of Darwin and Huxley and Wallace' (pp. 38–9). Again, we have the following marvellous example of philosophical perspicacity and penetration, in his saying of Carlyle: 'His great and real work was the attack on Utilitarianism: which did real good, though there was much that was muddled and dangerous in the historical philosophy which he preached as an alternative' (pp. 54–5). Altogether, amusing and sometimes enlightening reading.]

Clark, G. Kitson, *The Making of Victorian England* (Cambridge, Mass.: Harvard University Press, 1962; repr. New York: Atheneum, 1966—the edition quoted below in the Strachey entry. Cf. Buckley, *sup.*, and *Ideas and Beliefs of the Victorians*, *inf.*

Clarke, Samuel (1675–1729), *A Discourse Concerning the Unchangeable Obligations of Natural Religion* (1706; 7th edn., 1728, often called The Boyle Lectures; 2nd ser., delivered in 1705). [The best source for this is either vol. ii of Selby-Bigge's *British Moralists*, 3–56, or vol. i of D. D. Raphael's *British Moralists 1650–1800*, 190–225. Sidgwick discusses Clarke on pp. 179–84 of the *History*. There is an article on Clarke by Elmer Sprague in *The Encyclopedia of Philosophy*, ii: 118–20, and one relating more specifically to ethics by William L. Rowe in *Encyclopedia of Ethics*, i: 171.]

Collini, Stefan, *Public Moralists: Political Thought and Intellectual Life in Britain 1850–1930* (Oxford: Clarendon Press, 1991). [Contains some interesting observations on Sidgwick, as well as on Spencer, Leslie and Fitzjames Stephens, J. S. Mill, and others; also on the Metaphysical Society. Consult index.]

Comte, Auguste (1798–1857), founder of positivism and the founder, along with Spencer and Lester Ward, of sociology. Author of *Course of Positive Philosophy*, 6 vols. (1830–42). [See the article on Comte by René Hubert, in the *Encyclopedia of the Social Sciences*, iv: 151–3; also the article by Bruce Mazlish in *The Encyclopedia of Philosophy*, ii: 173–7; the article by Michael Ruse in *The Oxford Companion to Philosophy*, 145; and Mill, *August Comte and Positivism*. Also Timasheff, cited *inf.* Discussed by Sidgwick in the *History*, 268–70, and alluded to in Ch. 21 this vol.]

Cudworth, Ralph (1617–88), *A Treatise Concerning Eternal and Immutable Morality* (1731). [Discussed by Sidgwick in the *History*, 170–1. See the article on Cudworth by Stephen Darwall in *Encyclopedia of Ethics*, i: 232–3; also the article by John Passmore in *The Encyclopedia of Philosophy*, ii: 270–3.]

Cumberland, Richard (1632–1718), *De Legibus Naturae* (London, 1672).

—— *A Treatise of the Laws of Nature* (trans. into English by John Maxwell, London, 1727). [See the article on Cumberland by Knud Haakonssen in *Encyclopedia of Ethics*, i: 233–4;

also the article by John Passmore in *The Encyclopedia of Philosophy*, ii: 277–8. Discussed by Sidgwick in the *History*, 173–5, where Sidgwick says of Cumberland that 'he is noteworthy as having been the first to lay down that "the common good of all" is the supreme end and standard, in subordination to which all other rules and virtues are to be determined. So far he may fairly be called the precursor of the later utilitarianism' (p. 174). Cf. Hutcheson, *inf.*]

Darwin, Charles (1809–82), *The Origin of Species by Means of Natural Selection* (1859; 6th edn., 1872).

—— *The Descent of Man and Selection in Relation to Sex* (1871). Cf. Alfred Russel Wallace (cited *inf.*). [Darwin, and 'Evolutional Ethics', are discussed by Sidgwick in his *History of Ethics*, ch. 4, sect. 17, pp. 253–8, and, of course, in Ch. 2 this vol. The literature on Darwin and Darwinism is immense. But, for brief accounts, see the article on Darwin by T. A. Goudge in *The Encyclopedia of Philosophy*, ii: 294–5; and the article on 'Darwinism', by Morton O. Beckner, in ibid. 296–306. One statement in this latter article of 1967 is now outdated, falsified by recent developments, namely: 'Today, Darwinism no longer provides the focus of philosophical investigation, largely because so much of it forms an unquestioned background to contemporary thought' (p. 296).]

—— *Autobiography* (1st pub. 1887; corrected and restored edn., ed. Nora Barlow (London, 1958).

Descartes, René (1596–1650), *Meditations on the First Philosophy* (1641).

—— *A Discourse on Method* (1637).

—— *Objections* [to the *Meditations*] *and Replies* (1641).

—— *The Principles of Philosophy* (1644). [On Descartes, see the article by Bernard Williams in *The Encyclopedia of Philosophy*, ii: 344–54, the article by John Cottingham in *The Cambridge Dictionary of Philosophy*, 2nd edn., 223–7, or the article by the same writer in *The Oxford Companion to Philosophy*, 188–92.]

Donagan, Alan, 'Whewell's Elements of Morality', *Journal of Philosophy*, 71 (7 Nov. 1974), 724–36. See Schneewind, *inf.*

'Economics', *Encyclopedia of the Social Sciences*, iii: 344–95. [This is a very long article, in eleven sections, with nearly as many authors, which I will not list in detail here, except to say that the author of the first section (pp. 344–6), was Edwin R. A. Seligman, the editor-in-chief of the *Encyclopedia*.]

Edel, Abraham, 'Happiness and Pleasure', *Dictionary of the History of Ideas*, ii: 374–87.

—— 'Right and Good', *Dictionary of the History of Ideas*, iv: 173–87, esp. 177–81.

Eliot, George (1819–80), *Middlemarch, A Study of Provincial Life* (1871–2). [Sidgwick and George Eliot were friends, and he occasionally read and commented on her novels—especially *Middlemarch*—in manuscript. See the index to the *Memoir*. Although George Eliot was not a philosopher, she was a philosophical novelist and essayist, as well as a moralist in the ordinary sense of the term. See the article on George Eliot by J. B. Schneewind in *The Encyclopedia of Philosophy*, ii, cited *inf.*; the article (unsigned) in *Encyclopedia Britannica*, viii: 358–9; and the article in *The Oxford Companion to English Literature*, 256. See also Leslie Stephen, *George Eliot*, cited *inf.*]

Ensor, George, *An Inquiry concerning the Population of Nations*, 'Containing a Refutation of Mr Malthus's *Essay on Population*' (London: Effingham Wilson, 1818). [Given

Sidgwick's interest in the population problem, this work has a certain relevance, if only a tangential one.]

'Ethics', *Encyclopedia of the Social Sciences*, v: 602–7, by T. V. Smith.

Fifoot, C. H. S., *Frederic William Maitland: A Life* (Cambridge, Mass.: Harvard University Press, 1971). [Maitland, the great historian of English law, was a student of Sidgwick's, then a friend, and there are some interesting sidelights on Sidgwick to be found in this book, mainly in relation to Maitland. Consult the index.]

Flew, A., *Evolutionary Ethics* (New York: St Martin's Press, 1973).

Fowler, Thomas, *The Principles of Morals*, ii (Oxford: Clarendon Press, 1887). (Vol. i was written jointly by Fowler and his late colleague John Wilson; vol. i is solely historical, and vol. ii is solely by Fowler.)

George, Henry (1839–97), *A Perplexed Philosopher: Being an Examination of Mr Herbert Spencer's Various Utterances on the Land Question, with some Incidental Reference to his Synthetic Philosophy* (New York: Doubleday Page & Co., 1892). By the author of the famous *Progress and Poverty* (New York: D. Appleton & Co., 1879; rev. edn., 1897; New York: The Modern Library, 1929); see note referring to Spencer's books *Social Statics* and *Justice* in bk. VII, ch. 3—p. 364 of Modern Library edn. For a *philosophical* discussion of George's ideas see Schneider's *History of American Philosophy*, ch. 16, esp. 177–81, and 547.

Ginzberg, Eli, *The House of Adam Smith* (New York: Columbia University Press, 1934). See Adam Smith, listed *inf*.

Godwin, William (1756–1836), *Enquiry Concerning Political Justice* (1793; 2nd edn., 1796; 3rd edn., 1798). [See the article by D. H. Monro in *The Encyclopedia of Philosophy*, iii: 358–62, and Monro's book, *Godwin's Moral Philosophy*; also the book by Don Locke, listed *inf.*, as well as the book by Kegan Paul, listed *inf.* Sidgwick has two brief references to Godwin in the *History*, 267 and 272.]

Goudge, Thomas A., 'Evolutionism', *Dictionary of the History of Ideas*, ii: 174–89, esp. 179–82.

Green, Thomas Hill (1836–82), *Lectures on the Principles of Political Obligation*, ed. R. L. Nettleship (London, 1886); delivered in 1879. [See *Memoir of Thomas Hill Green*, by R. L. Nettleship (listed *inf.*); also the article on Green in *Encyclopedia of Ethics*, by John Howes, vol. i: 418–20, and the article on Green by Stephen Priest in *The Oxford Companion to Philosophy*, 327. In addition to his discussion of Green in Ch. 27 this vol., Sidgwick has a brief discussion of Green in the *History*, 259–60.]

—— 'Introductions to Hume's *Treatise of Human Nature*' (1874), in *Works of Thomas Hill Green*, ed. R. L. Nettleship (3 vols.), vol. i (London: Longmans, Green, 1885), 1–371. [See part II, sect. 6: 'The term "happiness" is the familiar cover for confusion between the animal imagination of pleasure and the conception of personal well-being' (p. 306); and part II, sect. 7: 'Happiness "in its fullest extent," as "the utmost pleasure we are capable of," is an unreal abstraction if there ever was one' (p. 307).]

Hanbury, H. G., *The Vinerian Chair and Legal Education* (Oxford: Basil Blackwell, 1958). Chs. 2–4 are on Blackstone; ch. 3, in particular, on the *Commentaries*.

Harrison, Frederic (1831–1923), *Order and Progress* (1875).

—— *Introduction to Comte's Positive Philosophy* (1896). [Harrison was 'from 1880 to 1905 president of the English Positivist Committee, formed to represent in this country the philosophic doctrines of Auguste Comte'. [Quotation taken from *The Oxford Companion to English Literature*, 335.] Referred to by Sidgwick in Ch. 21 this volume. See Buckley, cited *sup*.]

Hartmann, Eduard von (1842–1906), 'German pessimistic philosopher', *Die Philosophie des Unbewussten* (Berlin, 1869); 9th edn. trans. W. C. Coupland as *The Philosophy of the Unconscious*, 3 vols. (London, 1884). [See the article on von Hartmann, by L. E. Loemker, in *The Encyclopedia of Philosophy*, iii: 419–21 (from which the above quotation is taken); also the article by M. J. Inwood in *The Oxford Companion to Philosophy*, 334–5.]

Helvétius, Claude-Adrien (1715–71), *De l'esprit; or, Essays on the Mind and its Special Faculties* (London, 1759); and *A Treatise on Man and his Education*, trans. William Hooper (London, 1777). [See the article by Aram Vartanian in *The Encyclopedia of Philosophy*, iii: 471–3; also the brief article by Thomas Pink in *The Oxford Companion to Philosophy*, 351. Helvétius is briefly discussed by Sidgwick in the *History*, 267–8.]

Hobbes, Thomas (1588–1679), *De Cive (The Citizen)* (Paris, 1642; London, 1651); *Leviathan* (1651). [Again, there is an immense literature. However, see the article on Hobbes by Jean Hampton in *Encyclopedia of Ethics*, i: 543–9, the article on Hobbes by R. S. Peters in *The Encyclopedia of Philosophy*, iv: 30–46, and the article by Bernard Gert in *The Oxford Companion to Philosophy*, 367–70. Also *Thomas Hobbes*, by A. E. Taylor (London: Archibald Constable, 1908), and cf. Leslie Stephen, *inf*. Discussed by Sidgwick in the *History*, 163–70.]

Howe, Mark DeWolfe, ed., *Holmes–Pollock Letters: The Correspondence of Mr Justice Holmes and Sir Frederick Pollock, 1874–1932*, 2 vols. (Cambridge, Mass.: Harvard University Press, 1941).

Hudson, W. D., *Reason and Right: A Critical Examination of Richard Price's Moral Philosophy* (San Francisco, Cal.: Freeman, Cooper & Company, 1970). [See pp. 125 and 132 for some interesting observations on Sidgwick's ethics. In particular: 'Sidgwick found, by a "profound and discriminating examination of our common moral thought", that there are three "real ethical axioms", namely justice or equity, rational self-love or prudence, and benevolence. Add to these another principle: that the sole ultimate good is pleasure or happiness, and according to Sidgwick, you have utilitarianism. But he does not establish any logical connection between this theory of ultimate good and his three axioms' (p. 125).]

Hudson, William Henry, *An Introduction to the Philosophy of Herbert Spencer* (1904).

—— *Herbert Spencer* (New York: Dodge Publishing Company, n.d.—probably in the period 1904–6).

Hume, David (1711–76), *A Treatise of Human Nature* (1739, 1740); ed. L. A. Selby-Bigge (Oxford: Clarendon Press, 1888).

—— *An Enquiry Concerning Human Understanding* (1748).

—— *An Enquiry Concerning the Principles of Morals* (1751). A convenient and valuable edition of the two *Enquiries* is the one edited by L. A. Selby-Bigge (Oxford: Clarendon Press, 1893). [The literature on Hume is inexhaustible. However, I can recommend Annette C. Baier's article on Hume in *Encyclopedia of Ethics*, i: 565–77; also the long and thorough article on Hume by D. G. C. MacNabb in *The Encyclopedia of Philosophy*, iv: 74–90. See also the article by Justin Broackes in *The Oxford Companion to Philosophy*, 377–81. And Hume's ethics is discussed by Sidgwick in the *History*, 204–12.]

Hutcheson, Francis (1694–1747), *An Inquiry into the Original of our Ideas of Beauty and Virtue* (London, 1725).

—— *An Essay on the Nature and Conduct of the Passions and Affections, with Illustrations on the Moral Sense* (London, 1728).

—— *A System of Moral Philosophy*, 2 vols. (London, 1755). [Stephen Darwall has an informative article on Hutcheson in *Encyclopedia of Ethics*, i: 580–2, as does Elmer Sprague in *The Encyclopedia of Philosophy*, iv: 99–101. Sidgwick says of Hutcheson that 'As regards . . . goodness of actions, he adopts explicitly and unreservedly the formula afterwards taken as fundamental by Bentham: holding that "that action is best which procures the greatest happiness for the greatest numbers, and worst which in a like manner occasions misery" ' (*History*, 203). Cf. Cumberland, *sup.*]

Huxley, T. H. (1825–95), *Evolution and Ethics and Other Essays* (London: Macmillan, 1894); see, in particular, the title essay (1893) and the 'Prolegomena' (1894). ['Ethical nature, while born of cosmic nature, is necessarily at war with its parent . . . this seeming paradox is a truth . . . the recognition of which is essential for the ethical philosopher (preface, p. viii). Heretical doctrine for an evolutionist. See the article on Huxley by T. A. Goudge in *The Encyclopedia of Philosophy*, iv: 100–3. Sidgwick has some occasional remarks about Huxley in the *Memoir*.]

Ideas and Beliefs of the Victorians: An Historic Revaluation of the Victorian Age (1949; New York: E. P. Dutton & Co., Inc., 1966). Many and various authors. [A series of talks given on the British Broadcasting Corporation. From the Foreword by Harman Grisewood, 'Those who undertook the preparation of these talks hoped that they might prove to be of some enduring value as a contribution to the study of the Victorian Age. The fulfilment of these hopes is greatly helped by the appearance of the series in book form . . . The series went on for four months . . .' Sidgwick was undoubtedly a Victorian, in the sense that he lived his whole life during the reign of Queen Victoria. I have included this item, and one or two others on the period, for those who think that a philosopher's ideas can be understood only against the background of his age or period or milieu. See also Buckley, Chesterton, and Clark, *sup.*, and Strachey, cited *inf.*]

Ingram, John Kells, *A History of Political Economy* (1883; new and enlarged edn., New York: Augustus M. Kelley, 1969, with an introd. by Richard T. Ely, 1915). [Discusses Sidgwick's ideas on pp. 133, 143, 216, 220–1, though only incidentally, and devotes much more space, no doubt fittingly so, to J. S. Mill and others, such as J. E. Cairnes; consult index.]

Jastrow, Joseph, 'Psychology', *Encyclopedia of the Social Sciences*, xii: 588–96.

Jevons, William Stanley (1835–82), *Theory of Political Economy* (London, 1871; 2nd edn., 1879), a work characterized by Sidgwick in *PPE* (3rd edn.) as 'the most important contribution to economic theory that had been made in England for a generation' (p. 9). Author also of *The Principles of Science* (London: Macmillan, 1874; 2nd edn., 1877), and of *Money and the Mechanism of Exchange* (London, 1875), the latter discussed by Sidgwick on pp. 224–5 and elsewhere in *PPE*. Author of many other works, primarily in logic, political economy, and philosophy of science. See the article on Jevons by P. L. Heath in *The Encyclopedia of Philosophy*, iv: 260–1; the article by Robert E. Butts in *The Cambridge Dictionary of Philosophy*, 451; the article by Andrew Belsey in *The Oxford Companion to Philosophy*, 425; and the article (unsigned) in *The Encyclopedia Britannica*, 14th edn., vol. xiii: 30–1.

'Jurisprudence', *Encyclopedia of the Social Sciences*, viii: 477–92, by Roscoe Pound.

Kant, Immanuel (1724–1804), *Critique of Pure Reason* (1781; 2nd edn., much rev., 1787).

—— *Prolegomena to any Future Metaphysics Which Will be able to present itself as a Science* (1783).

—— *The Groundwork* (or *Fundamental Principles*) *of the Metaphysic of Morals* (1785; 2nd edn., 1786).

—— *Critique of Practical Reason* (1788).

—— *The Metaphysics of Morals*, containing the *Rechtslehre*, *The Metaphysical Elements of Justice*, and the *Tugendlehre*, or *The Metaphysical Principles of Virtue* (1797). See the article on Kant by W. H. Walsh in *The Encyclopedia of Philosophy*, iv: 305–24; also the article by Christine M. Korsgaard in *Encyclopedia of Ethics*, i: 664–74, and the article 'Kantian Ethics' by John Marshall, ibid. 674–7; also the article by Henry Allison in *The Oxford Companion to Philosophy*, 435–8. Sidgwick discusses Kant in the *History*, 271–8.

Kegan Paul, C., *William Godwin: His Friends and Contemporaries*, 2 vols. (London, 1876).

Keynes, John Neville (1852–1949), *The Scope and Method of Economic Science* (1891). [Neville Keynes was a friend of Sidgwick's, was known as one of the Cambridge economists at the time, edited and brought to publication the 3rd edn. of Sidgwick's *Principles of Political Economy*. Author also of *Studies and Exercises in Formal Logic* (London: Macmillan, 1884; 2nd edn., 1887; 3rd edn., 1894). Article on Neville Keynes by Phyllis Deane in *The New Palgrave*, iii: 42.]

Lively, Jack, and Rees, John, eds., *Utilitarian Logic and Politics: James Mill's 'Essay on Government', Macaulay's Critique and the Ensuing Debate* (Clarendon Press: Oxford, 1978). [Contains the original essays in the famous debate that went on in the pages of the *Edinburgh Review* and the *Westminster Review* between Macaulay and anonymous writers in the *Westminster* (Mar. 1829–Jan. 1830) stimulated by James Mill's 'Essay on Government'. The editors observe: 'The general contemporary verdict on the debate, even amongst Benthamites themselves, was that the Utilitarian cause suffered great damage. What was thought to have been damaged was both a philosophic and a political position, both the general Utilitarian approach to social theorizing and Utilitarian arguments for Radical reform' (p. 5).]

Locke, Don, *A Fantasy of Reason: The Life and Thought of William Godwin* (London: Routledge & Kegan Paul, 1980).

Locke, John (1632–1704), *An Essay Concerning Human Understanding* (London, 1690; 2nd edn., 1694; 3rd edn., 1695; 4th edn., 1700; 5th edn., 1706).

—— *Two Treatises of Government* (London, 1690; 2nd edn., 1694). [On Locke, see the article by James Gordon Clapp in *The Encyclopedia of Philosophy*, iv: 487–503, and the article by Roger Woolhouse in *The Oxford Companion to Philosophy*, 493–6. Sidgwick discusses Locke in the *History*, 175–8.]

Lotze, Rudolf Hermann (1817–81), *Metaphysics* (Leipzig, 1841).

—— *Logic* (Leipzig, 1843). See the article on Lotze by Rubin Gotesky in *The Encyclopedia of Philosophy*, v: 87–9; also the brief article by M. J. Inwood in *The Oxford Companion to Philosophy*, 513.

—— *System of Philosophy*, trans. and ed. Bernard Bosanquet (Oxford, 1884). Cf. Bosanquet, cited *sup*.

Lyons, David, *In the Interest of the Governed: A Study in Bentham's Philosophy of Utility and Law* (Oxford: Clarendon Press, 1973; rev. edn., 1991). [An interesting discussion of Bentham, providing a distinctly different interpretation of Bentham's principle of utility. For a striking comment on Sidgwick on Bentham see p. 80.]

Macaulay, Thomas Babington, 'Mill's Essay on Government', *The Edinburgh Review*, 97 (Mar. 1829); reprinted in *The Complete Works of Thomas Babington Macaulay, Critical and Historical Essays*, i (New York: Sully and Kleinteich, 1900: 381–422 (q.v. Lively and Rees). [Its first appearance in book form was in Macaulay's *Critical and Historical Essays, contributed to the Edinburgh Review*, 3 vols. (London: Longmans, 1843).]

—— 'Westminster Reviewer's Defence of Mill', *The Edinburgh Review*, 98 (June 1829); ibid., *i.e., The Complete Works*, 423–59. [Of special interest in this essay is Macaulay's argument that: 'The principle of Mr Bentham . . . is this, that mankind ought so to act as to produce their greatest happiness. The word *ought*, he tells us, has no meaning, unless it be used with reference to some interest. But the interest of a man is synonymous with his greatest happiness:—and therefore to say that a man ought to do a thing is to say that it is for his greatest happiness to do it. And to say that mankind *ought* to act so as to produce their greatest happiness is to say that the greatest happiness is the greatest happiness—and this is all!' (pp. 450–1). I know of no prior occurrence of this line of argument, which anticipates Sidgwick and Moore (though it has been argued that a similar line of argument appears in Price).]

—— 'Utilitarian Theory of Government', *The Edinburgh Review*, 99 (Oct. 1829); ibid. 460–95.

Mace, C. A. See Peters and Mace, *inf.*

MacIntyre, Alasdair, 'Histories of Moral Philosophy', in *The Oxford Companion to Philosophy*, 357–60. [An excellent account of a subject very rarely written about, with some interesting observations on Sidgwick and also on Schneewind's *Sidgwick's Ethics*.]

MacIver, R. M., 'Sociology', *Encyclopedia of the Social Sciences*, 14: 232–47.

Maine, Henry J. S. (1822–88), *Ancient Law: Its Connection with the Early History of Society and its Relation to Modern Ideas* (London, 1861; 10th edn., 1884); Cf. Pollock, 'Notes on Maine's *Ancient Law*', cited *inf.*

—— *Lectures on the Early History of Institutions* (1874). A Sequel to *Ancient Law*. [Sidgwick has some discussion of Maine in the *Politics*.]

Maitland, F. W., *The Life and Letters of Leslie Stephen* (London, 1906).

Malebranche, Nicolas (1638–1715), *The Search After Truth*, 2 vols. (1674, 1675). See the article on Malebranche by Willis Doney in *The Encyclopedia of Philosophy*, v: 140–4; also the article by John Cottingham in *The Oxford Companion to Philosophy*, 518–19.

—— *Dialogues on Metaphysics* (1688).

Malthus, Thomas Robert (1766–1834), *An Essay on the Principle of Population* (London: 1798). Discussed by Sidgwick in *PPE*.

—— *Principles of Political Economy considered with a view to their Practical Application* (1820; 2nd edn., 1836). There is an article on Malthus by Antony Flew in *The Encyclopedia of Philosophy*, v: 145–7.

Mandeville, Bernard de (*c.*1670–1733), *The Fable of the Bees: or Private Vices, Public Benefits* (1714; 2nd edn., 1739). [Discussed very briefly, and negatively, by Sidgwick in the

History. See the article on Mandeville by Elmer Sprague in *The Encyclopedia of Philosophy*, v: 147–9; also the article by R. G. Frey in *Encyclopedia of Ethics*, ii: 761–2.]

Marshall, Alfred, *Principles of Economics* (London, 1890; 8th edn., London: Macmillan, 1920). [Marshall had been a pupil, and then a colleague and occasionally a sharp critic, of Sidgwick's. Marshall's work *The Pure Theory of Foreign Trade: The Pure Theory of Domestic Values* was in 1879 privately printed—not published—by Henry Sidgwick. See the article on Marshall by J. K. Whitaker in *The New Palgrave*, iii: 350–63, at 351.]

Maudsley, Henry, Dr (1835–1918), *Physiology and Pathology of Mind* (London, 1867); enlarged and published separately as *Physiology of Mind* (London, 1876) and *Pathology of Mind* (new edn., London, 1895). [Sidgwick refers to Maudsley in Chs. 14 and 15 this vol.]

—— *Body and Mind* (London, 1870; rev. edn., 1873). There is an interesting article on Maudsley, by William Healy, in the *Encyclopedia of the Social Sciences*, 10: 231.

Mill, James (1773–1836), 'An Essay on Government', suppl. to the *Encyclopedia Britannica*, 1820; (London, 1828) (cf. Lively and Rees, *sup.*) Pub. in *Essays on Government, Jurisprudence, Liberty of the Press, and Law of Nations* (London: J. Innes, 1825).

—— *Analysis of the Phenomena of the Human Mind*, 2 vols. (1st edn., 1829; 2nd edn. ed. with additional notes by John Stuart Mill, London: Longmans, Green, 1869). [There is an interesting article on James Mill by Susan M. Purviance in *Encyclopedia of Ethics*, ii: 809–11.]

—— *Elements of Political Economy* (3rd edn.; London: Henry G. Bohn, 1844).

Mill, John Stuart (1806–73), *Utilitarianism* (1863; first appeared in *Fraser's Magazine*, 1861). [Discussed by Sidgwick in the *History*, 245–52. See also the article by Henry West in *Encyclopedia of Ethics*, ii: 811–16, and the article by John Skorupski in *The Oxford Companion to Philosophy*, 566–9.]

—— *Dissertations and Discussions* (1st edn., 2 vols., London, 1859; New York: Henry Holt and Co., 1874, 4 vols.) [Contains, in addition to Mill's essay on Bentham, 'Dr. Whewell on Moral Philosophy' (vol. iii), and 'Bain's Psychology' (vol. iv).]

—— 'Remarks on Bentham's Philosophy' (prob. 1833), in Schneewind, *Mill's Ethical Writings* (listed *inf.*), pp. 45–61. [Not identical with next item, though both may be compared with Sidgwick's 'Bentham and Benthamism', Ch. 24 this vol.]

—— 'Bentham', *London and Westminster Review* (Aug. 1838); included in *Dissertations and Discussions*, i.

—— *On Liberty* (London, 1859). [Discussed in part in Ch. 21 this vol.]

—— *The Subjection of Women* (London, 1869; written in 1861).

—— *Considerations on Representative Government* (London, 1861). [Discussed by Sidgwick in the *Politics*. These last three works are available in a convenient edition in The World's Classics (London: Oxford University Press, 1912).]

—— *Essays on some Unsettled Questions of Political Economy* (London: John W. Parker, 1844).

—— *Principles of Political Economy*, 2 vols. (London: Parker & Co., 1848; 7th edn., London: Longmans, Green, and Co., 1871). [Discussed extensively by Sidgwick in his *PPE*.]

—— *A System of Logic*, 2 vols. (London, 1843; 8th edn., Longmans, Green and Co., 1872).

—— *An Examination of Sir William Hamilton's Philosophy* (London, 1865).

—— *August Comte and Positivism* (London, 1865).

—— *Autobiography*, ed. Helen Taylor (1873); definitive version, ed. John Jacob Coss (New York: Columbia University Press, 1924). [Cf. *The Early Draft of John Stuart Mill's Autobiography*, ed. Jack Stillinger (Urbana, Ill.: University of Illinois Press, 1961), which provides an account of the various changes and permutations that went into the preparation and publication of Mill's *Autobiography*.]

Monro, D. H., *Godwin's Moral Philosophy* (London: Oxford University Press, 1953).

—— 'Utilitarianism', *Dictionary of the History of Ideas*, iv: 444–9.

More, Henry (1614–87), *Enchiridion Ethicum* (1666), trans. into English by Edward Southwell under the title *An Account of Virtue*: or, *Dr. Henry More's Abridgment of Morals* (London: Benj. Tooke, 1690, 1701). [Discussed by Sidgwick very briefly in the *History*, 171–2. See the article on Henry More by John Passmore in *The Encyclopedia of Philosophy*, v: 387–9; and there is an article on More by Alan Gabbey in *The Cambridge Dictionary of Philosophy*, 590–1.]

Morison, W. L., *John Austin* (Stanford, Calif.: Stanford University Press, 1982).

Morrell, Jack, and Thackray, Arnold, *Gentlemen of Science; Early Years of the British Association for the Advancement of Science* (Oxford: Clarendon Press, 1981). [There is an instructive passage on page 96: 'The term "scientist" was coined in 1833. The word "science" took on new and narrower meanings in the 1830s and 1840s. It ceased to be a synonym for all knowledge and became the party label of a particular mode of understanding, possessed—so it was said—of superior power. Science in this new sense became a familiar, ubiquitous element in early Victorian culture. The change was intimately connected with the burgeoning of the British Association for the Advancement of Science. In a direct and literal sense, the British Association made science visible. Its annual meetings dominated the daily and periodical press for weeks, and occupied the energies of hosting cities for months and even years. A Meeting was a great event, attended by thousands and heard of by the tens of thousands. Science became news . . . But science became more than news . . . Thanks to the events, the ideas, the personalities, and the achievements blazoned forth at every Meeting, science became a cultural resource. . . .'[16] Page 20 informs us that Whewell 'coined the word "scientist".' See S. Ross, 'Scientist: the story of a word', *Annals of Science*, xviii (1962): 65–85. Sidgwick was a member of the British Association, in particular of Section F, Economics and Statistics, refers to it in several places in the *Memoir*.]

Nettleship, R. L., *Memoir of Thomas Hill Green* (London: Longmans, Green, 1906). [Also included in Nettleship's edition of the *Works of T. H. Green*.]

Packe, Michael St John, *The Life of John Stuart Mill* (London: Secker and Warburg, 1954). [Contains a considerable bibliography.]

Paine, Thomas (1737–1809), *The Rights of Man* (part I, 1791; part II, 1792). See the article on Paine by Hugo Adam Bedau in *The Oxford Companion to Philosophy*, 641.

Paley, William (1743–1805), *The Principles of Moral and Political Philosophy*, 2 vols. (London, 1785; 7th edn., London: R. Faulder, 1790). [The main text of theological utilitarianism, and a required text at Cambridge and at most American colleges for many years in the nineteenth century. It is certainly one of the clearest and best-written textbooks ever to appear. Cf. Bain, cited *sup*, and Whately, cited *inf.*; also Whewell's *On the Foundations of Morals* (cited *inf.*); and see the article on Paley by Charlotte Brown in *Encyclopedia of Ethics*, ii: 931–2. Sidgwick discusses Paley only very briefly in the *History*, 238–9, also very briefly in the *Politics*.]

---

[16] But apparently not something that reached either the ears or the eyes or the sensibility of Mr Lytton Strachey. See note 19 *infra*.

Pattison, Mark (1813–84), *Memoirs* (1885). [See *Memoir* (p. 404): 'Have just finished Pattison's *Memoir*; curious as an unconscious confession of sordid egotism, mingling with a genuine ardour for an academic ideal of life. Very odd that a man of so much intellectual calibre appears never to have turned on his own character the cold and bitter criticism that he applies to others. In spite of my sympathy with his views, I cannot but admit that his life is a moral fiasco, which the orthodox have a right to point to as a warning against infidelity.' See the article on Pattison in the *Oxford Companion to English Literature* (1946), 598; also Whewell, *Lectures on the History of Moral Philosophy* (cited *inf*.).]

Peters, R. S. and Mace, C. A., 'Psychology', *The Encyclopedia of Philosophy*, 7: 1–27.

'Political Science', *Encyclopedia of the Social Sciences*, 12: 207–25, by Hermann Haller.

Pollock, Frederick (1845–1937), *Introduction and Notes to Sir Henry Maine's 'Ancient Law'* (London: John Murray, 1906).

—— *Spinoza, His Life and Philosophy* (London: C. Kegan Paul, 1880).

—— and Maitland, Frederic William, *The History of English Law, Before the Time of Edward I*, 2 vols. (Cambridge: University Press, 1895; 2nd edn., 1898). [Although Pollock's name appears first, the bulk of the writing and of the phenomenal research that went into this classic work was carried on by Maitland. See Fifoot, *Maitland: A Life* (listed *sup*.), 135–40.]

'Positivism', see Ruggiero; also Comte, and Mill on Comte.

Price, Richard (1723–91), *A Review of the Principal Questions and Difficulties in Morals* (London: T. Cadell, 1758; 2nd edn., 1769; 3rd edn., 1787). [Discussed by Sidgwick in the *History*, 224–6. There is a good modern edition, which must be accounted definitive (of Price's 3rd edn., which omitted the words 'and Difficulties'), carefully edited with an illuminating introd. by D. Daiches Raphael (Oxford: Clarendon Press, 1948). See the article on Price by Elmer Sprague in *The Encyclopedia of Philosophy*, vi: 449–51; also the article by Christine Korsgaard in *Encyclopedia of Ethics*, ii: 1010–12 and W. D. Hudson, *Reason and Right*.]

'Psychology', see Jastrow, and the long, thorough article by R. S. Peters and C. A. Mace.

Raphael, D. D., ed., *British Moralists 1650–1800* (Oxford: Oxford University Press, 1969; repr. Indianapolis: Hackett Publishing Co., 1991). [Contains, on the model of Selby-Bigge's *British Moralists*, a very useful 'Bibliographical Note of Some British Writers', ii: 347–59.]

Rashdall, Hastings (1856–1924), *Ethics* (London: T. C. & E. C. Clark and New York: Dodge Publishing Co., n.d. [but published not many years after Rashdall, *The Theory of Good and Evil*, 1907). On Rashdall, see the article by A. K. Stout in *The Encyclopedia of Philosophy*, vii: 68, and the article by R. S. Downie in *The Oxford Companion to Philosophy*, 741.]

Reid, Thomas (1710–96), *An Inquiry into the Human Mind on the Principles of Common Sense* (1764).

—— *Essays on the Intellectual Powers of Man* (Edinburgh, 1785).

—— *Essays on the Active Powers of Man* (Edinburgh, 1788). On Reid, see the article by S. A. Grave in *The Encyclopedia of Philosophy*, vii: 118–21; the article by William L. Rowe in *Encyclopedia of Ethics*, ii: 1978–80; or the article by Vincent Hope in *The Oxford Companion to Philosophy*, 754–5. Cf. Ch. 16 this vol. [Reid is discussed further by Sidgwick in the *History*, 226–31 and 262–4.]

Ricardo, David (1772–1823), *The Principles of Political Economy and Taxation* (1817; 2nd edn., 1819; 3rd edn., 1821). [Discussed by Sidgwick in *PPE*.]

Ritchie, D. G., *Natural Rights* (London: George Allen & Unwin Ltd, 1895). [A critique of the idea of natural rights and of Spencer's Law of Equal Freedom (discussed by Sidgwick in Ch. 30 this vol.).]

Ruggiero, Guido de, 'Positivism', *Encyclopedia of the Social Sciences*, xii: 260–6.

Ruskin, John (1819–1900), who has certain affinities with Carlyle, may seem an odd choice for an appearance in this listing, since there is no obvious Sidgwick relevance. But he is a prime example of an English writer of the Victorian period who developed a social theory and a theory of political economy—both of them revolutionary for his time, certainly counter to the tradition—out of an aesthetic theory. *Sesame and Lilies* (1865), *The Crown of Wild Olive* (1866), *Time and Tide* (1867), *Lectures on Art* (1870), and *Art and Socialism* (1884) may be taken as representative of his work along these lines. Was he a philosopher? Well, in one of Bradley's favorite phrases, 'in a sense, but not as such'. Jerome Buckley, in *The Victorian Temper* (cited *sup.*), says of Ruskin (whom he refers to with some frequency), 'He expressed an impetuous contempt for the measured logic and the abstract theorizing of all formal philosophy . . .' (p. 142). Yet there is an article about Ruskin, by Raymond Williams, in *The Encyclopedia of Philosophy*, vii: 234–5, and if Paul Edwards deemed Ruskin important enough, as a philosopher, to have an article about him in *The Encyclopedia of Philosophy*, then, in the immortal words of The Cookie Monster, 'That's good enough for me'. Williams says, 'Ruskin's social and ethical teaching . . . followed from his understanding of the nature of art. The artist's function is to reveal aspects of the universal truth, which is also beauty. . . . Ruskin's opposition to individualism as a social principle and to competition as a method of political economy was based on his idea of function, the fulfillment of each man's part in the general design of creation. This required a social order based on intrinsic human values. . . .' And Williams concludes that 'The most remarkable aspect of Ruskin's work . . . is the development of a philosophy of art into a moral critique of industrial capitalism'. Thus Ruskin can be taken as a counter to the standard tradition of political economy, in which Sidgwick, with his opposition to socialism, has a place. For more on Ruskin, see the article by Frederic Harrison in *The Encyclopedia Britannica*, x: 674–7; also the article in *The Oxford Companion to English Literature*, 686. For somewhat more technical discussion, see E. F. Carritt, *The Theory of Beauty* (London: Methuen and Co., 1914), esp. p. 64, and Buckley, *The Victorian Temper*, 148–60.

Schneewind, J. B., ed., *Mill's Ethical Writings* (New York: Collier Books, 1965). [Contains an excellent bibliography, as well as an excellent introduction. Also contains, *inter alia*, the text of Mill's 'Remarks on Bentham's Philosophy' (cited *sup.*), and also Mill's essay, 'Dr. Whewell on Moral Philosophy' (1852). Sidgwick's comments on Whewell, brief as they are, are contained in the *History*.]

—— 'George Eliot', in *The Encyclopedia of Philosophy*, ii: 471–2.

—— 'Whewell's Ethics', *Studies in Moral Philosophy*, American Philosophical Quarterly Monograph Series, no. 1 (Oxford: Basil Blackwell, 1968), 108–41. Cf. Donagan, *sup.*

—— ed., *Mill: A Collection of Critical Essays* (Notre Dame: University of Notre Dame Press, 1969). [The essays contained are predominantly on J. S. Mill's moral and political philosophy; one or two of note are not available elsewhere.]

Schneewind, J. B., *Backgrounds of English Victorian Literature* (New York: Random House, 1970). [A well-named book that is extraordinarily informative on the period. Ch. 3, 'Morality', is especially valuable.]

—— ed., *Moral Philosophy from Montaigne to Kant: An Anthology*, 2 vols. (Cambridge: University Press, 1990). [An excellent work, both for the selections it contains and its historical, critical, and informative introductions. See the review by the present writer, cited *inf*.]

—— 'Seventeenth and Eighteenth Century Ethics', in *A History of Western Ethics*, ed. by Lawrence C. and Charlotte B. Becker (New York and London: Garland, 1992), 80–95; also in *Encyclopedia of Ethics*, i: 500–9.

Schneider, Herbert W., *A History of American Philosophy* (2nd edn.; New York & London: Columbia University Press, 1963). [Thorough and comprehensive, so much so that it discusses the ideas of Edward Bellamy and Henry George (cited *sup.*).]

Selby-Bigge, L. A., ed., *British Moralists, being Selections from Writers principally of the Eighteenth Century* (Oxford: Clarendon Press, 1897; reprinted New York: Dover Publications, n.d.). Contains, *inter alia*, a valuable 'Bibliographical Note of some British Writers', vol. ii: 385–92, as does Raphael's similar work, cited *sup.*

Seligman, Edwin R. A., 'What are the Social Sciences?' *Encyclopedia of the Social Sciences*, i: 3–7.

Shaftesbury, Third Earl of [Anthony Ashley Cooper] (1671–1713), *Inquiry Concerning Virtue and Merit* (1699) (one part of the *Characteristics of Men, Manners, Opinions, and Times*, 3 vols., 1711). [Discussed by Sidgwick in the *History*, 184–90; Sidgwick claimed that 'The appearance of Shaftesbury's *Characteristics* marks a turning point in the history of English ethical thought' (p. 190). See the article by Stephen Darwall in *Encyclopedia of Ethics*, ii: 1147–9, and the article by Elmer Sprague in *The Encyclopedia of Philosophy*, vii: 428–30.]

Singer, Marcus G., 'Morality and Universal Law', in *The Handbook of Western Philosophy*, 568–89; Sidgwick is discussed briefly on pp. 581–2.

—— 'Nineteenth-Century British Ethics', in *A History of Western Ethics*, ed. L. C. and C. B. Becker (New York and London: Garland, 1992), 96–105; also in *Encyclopedia of Ethics*, i: 510–15. [Some of the annotations used here appear also in the revised and expanded version of the article in the forthcoming second edition of the *Encyclopedia of Ethics*.]

—— Review of Schneewind's *Moral Philosophy from Montaigne to Kant*, in *Ethics*, 104/1 (Oct. 1993), 169–73.

Smith, Adam (1723–90), *The Theory of Moral Sentiments* (1759; 2nd edn., 1761; 6th edn., 1790), ed. D. D. Raphael and A. L. Macfie (Oxford: Clarendon Press, 1976). Discussed by Sidgwick in the *History*, 213–18. See the article on Smith by Elmer Sprague in *The Encyclopedia of Philosophy*, vii: 461–3, the article by J. Ralph Lindgren in *Encyclopedia of Ethics*, ii: 1160–3, and the article by Vincent Hope in *The Oxford Companion to Philosophy*, 829.

—— *An Inquiry into the Nature and Causes of The Wealth of Nations* (1776). Discussed by Sidgwick in *PPE*. See Ginzberg, *The House of Adam Smith*, cited *sup.*

Smith, T. V., 'Ethics', *Encyclopedia of the Social Sciences*, v: 602–7.

'Sociology', see MacIver.

Spencer, Herbert (1820–1903), *Social Statics: The Conditions Essential to Human Happiness Specified* (London: John Chapman, 1851; 2nd edn., 1892).

—— *First Principles*, vol. i of *A System of Synthetic Philosophy* (London, 1862; 6th edn.; New York & London: D. Appleton & Co., 1900). On Spencer, see George and Hudson, *sup.*, and Timasheff, *inf.*

—— *The Synthetic Philosophy*, 10 vols., consisting of *The Principles of Biology*, 2 vols. (1866, 1867; rev. edn., 1898, 1899); *The Principles of Psychology*, 2 vols. (1855; 3rd edn., 1890, 1892; *The Principles of Sociology*, 3 vols. (1876; 2nd edn., 1886; 3rd edn., 1896; *The Principles of Ethics*, 2 vols. (1879, 1893). (London and New York: D. Appleton & Co., 1892–1896).[17] In the preface to vol. i of *The Principles of Ethics*, Spencer says: 'The ethical doctrine set forth is fundamentally a corrected and elaborated version of the doctrine set forth in *Social Statics*, issued at the end of 1850.' Sidgwick discusses Spencer in Chs. 25 and 30 this vol., and in his *Lectures on the Ethics of Green, Spencer, and Martineau*, but only sporadically in the *History*.

—— *The Study of Sociology* (New York & London: D. Appleton & Co., 1873).[18]

—— *The Man Versus the State* (Contemporary Review, Feb., Apr., May, June, July 1884; London, 1884).

—— *An Autobiography*, 2 vols. (London, 1904).

Spinoza, Benedict (Baruch) (1632–77), *Ethics, demonstrated in Geometrical Order* (1677, pub. posthumously); *Tractatus Theologico-Politicus* (1670); *Political Treatise* (1677); *On the Improvement of the Human Mind* (1677). See the article on Spinoza by Alasdair MacIntyre in *The Encyclopedia of Philosophy*, vii: 530–41; the article by Alan Donagan in *Encyclopedia of Ethics*, ii: 1200–4; and the article by T. L. S. Sprigge in *The Oxford Companion to Philosophy*, 845–8; also Pollock's book *Spinoza*, cited *sup*. Spinoza was not discussed by Sidgwick, but was discussed by Broad in *Five Types of Ethical Theory* (cited *sup*).

Stephen, Sir James (1829–94), *A History of the Criminal Law of England*, 3 vols. (London, 1883). See the article on Sir James Fitzjames Stephen, by K. Smellie, in *Encyclopedia of the Social Sciences*, xiv: 385.

Stephen, Leslie (1832–1904), *The English Utilitarians*, 3 vols. (London: Duckworth and Co., 1900). Vol. i is on Jeremy Bentham; vol. ii on James Mill; vol. iii on John Stuart Mill. Cf. Maitland, *sup*.

—— *The History of English Thought in the Eighteenth Century*, 2 vols. (London, 1876; 3rd edn., 1902).

—— *The Life of Sir James Fitzjames Stephen* (London, 1895).

—— *George Eliot* (1902).

—— *Hobbes* (London, 1904).

---

[17] This last work is also listed in Sect. IV, under the title *The Principles of Ethics*. When he first set out his prospectus for this series of volumes, in *First Principles*, Spencer entitled this last part *The Principles of Morality*. Whether this shift in title is significant is not a question I attempt to answer here.

[18] I cannot vouch with certainty for the accuracy of any of these publication dates; let us take them as approximate, since Spencer's *System of Synthetic Philosophy* was first issued in parts, to subscribers, and he revised most portions of it several times. In any event, these works, at least in their first editions, were available to Sidgwick when he prepared his *Lectures on the Ethics of Green, Spencer, and Martineau*, and his *LPK*, which contains lectures on the philosophy of Spencer and, of course, also his essays on Spencer (Chs. 25 and 30 this vol.).

Strachey, [Giles] Lytton (1880–1932), *Eminent Victorians* (London, 1918; repr. New York: The Modern Library, 1999). [Although Strachey never refers to Sidgwick, he does say a few things, uncomplimentary things naturally, about 'that distinguished body, the Metaphysical Society, which met once a month during the palmy years of the Seventies to discuss, in strict privacy, the fundamental problems of the destiny of man. After a comfortable dinner at the Grosvenor Hotel, the Society, which included Professor Huxley and Professor Tyndall, Mr John Morley and Sir James Stephen, the Duke of Argyll, Lord Tennyson, and Dean Church, would gather round to hear and discuss a paper read by one of the members upon such questions as "What is death?" "Is God unknowable?" or "The Nature of the Moral Principle." . . . Unfortunately, however, the answers given to these questions by the Metaphysical Society have not been recorded for the instruction of mankind.' (The passage in question appears near the end of the very long chapter on Cardinal Manning, quoted here from pp. 85–6 of the Modern Library edition.) We know that Strachey's last assertion is false, from *e.g.* Ch. 1 of this volume. Privately printed yet recorded and discoverable papers that Sidgwick read to the Metaphysical Society are listed in Sect. III of this bibliography, under dates of 1870, 1873, 1875, 1879, and 1880. Strachey had obviously neither talent nor taste for philosophy, and his research was evidently not as extensive as he led his early readers, and especially his admirers in the Bloomsbury Group, to believe. G. Kitson Clark, in *The Making of Victorian England*, cited *sup.*, speaks of 'Lytton Strachey's elegant libels' (ch. 2, para. 3; p. 29 of the Atheneum edn.). Mr Clark's elegant rebuttals of Strachey, and others, are as elegant, and as interesting to read, as Strachey's 'elegant libels' themselves. As mentioned above (sect. IV), Strachey's acid essay 'A Victorian Critic' (in *Characters and Commentaries*) is about—searingly and sneeringly about—Matthew Arnold (cited *sup.*).[19] See the article on Strachey in the *Oxford Companion to English Literature*, 753, which observes that 'The preface to "Eminent Victorians" expounded Strachey's method, avoiding "scrupulous narration" and "attacking his subject in unexpected places", shooting "a sudden revealing searchlight into obscure recesses, hitherto undivined".' There is another side to Strachey, not encompassed solely in the fact of his brilliant writing: his essay on 'Froude', the historian, is curiously sympathetic—at least in part (*The Shorter Strachey*, 106–11).]

Strachey, Lytton, *The Shorter Strachey*, ed. Michael Holroyd and Paul Levy (London: Oxford University Press, 1980; The Hogarth Press, 1989), cited here in the latter edition. [A useful collection, containing, in addition to numerous other choice pieces, the essay 'A Victorian Critic' and the essay on Froude, which is in a section entitled 'Six English

---

[19] To get the flavor of Strachey's writing, and his attitude, that of a supercilious aesthete, note the following from the first paragraph of 'A Victorian Critic': 'Reputations, in the case of ages no less than of individuals, depend, in the long run, upon the judgments of artists; and artists will never be fair to the Victorian Age. To them its incoherence, its pretentiousness, and its incurable lack of detachment will always outweigh its genuine qualities of solidity and force. They will laugh and they will shudder, and the world will follow suit. The Age of Victoria was, somehow or other, unaesthetic to its marrow-bones; and so we may be sure it will never loom through history with the glamour that hangs about the Age of Pericles or the brilliance that sparkles round the eighteenth century. But if men of science and men of action were not inarticulate, we should hear a different story' (*Characters and Commentaries*, 187; *The Shorter Strachey*, 177). Curious: Darwin was a 'man of science' and was not inarticulate; so was Huxley, and so on.

Historians', the other historians being Hume, Gibbon, Macaulay, Carlyle, and Creighton; the editors provide a useful bibliographical note, p. 268.]

Tennyson, Alfred (first Baron Tennyson) (1809–92), *In Memoriam* (1850). [Tennyson was Sidgwick's favorite poet, and *In Memoriam* was probably his favorite poem; he knew practically the whole poem by heart. In the *Memoir* there appears (pp. 538–42) a long letter Sidgwick wrote to Tennyson's son about *In Memoriam*, which was 'published in the latter's life of his father' (*Alfred, Lord Tennyson, A Memoir*, by Lord Hallam Tennyson, vol. i: 560 [1897]), which expressed Sidgwick's deep feelings about the poet and the poem. There are several other references to Tennyson in the *Memoir* (consult index). Sidgwick's feelings for poetry were deep and profound. When Tennyson died in October 1892, Sidgwick wrote to Tennyson's son: 'It is like the end of a reign—only that there is no concluding "vive le roi!" And, indeed, whatever the future may have in store for English poetry, it is impossible that any one should ever hold the sway he held over the minds of men of my generation; it is impossible that any one's thoughts and words should be so entwined with the best moments of the spring and summer of our lives: "To us he seemed the last" ' (*Mem.*, 524–5). *In Memoriam A. H. H.* may be found, along with 'The Voyage', another favorite of Sidgwick's (see *Mem.*, 119–20), in *Poems of Tennyson 1830–1870*, with an introd. by T. Herbert Warren (London: Oxford University Press, 1912), 358–448; 788–91. An abbreviated version of *In Memoriam* is contained in *The Oxford Book of English Verse*, ed. Arthur Quiller-Couch (Oxford: Clarendon Press, 1925), 836–44. See the article on Tennyson by Edmund Gosse in *Encyclopedia Britannica*, xxi: 938–42; and also the brief paragraph on Tennyson in vol. viii: 595; and the article on Tennyson in *The Oxford Companion to English Literature*, 775, as well as the article on the poem *In Memoriam A. H. H.*, ibid., 397–8.]

Timasheff, Nicholas S., *Sociological Theory: Its Nature and Growth* (New York: Random House, 1955; 2nd edn., 1957; 3rd edn., 1967). [Chs. 2 and 3 are devoted to Comte and Spencer, and, though Sidgwick is not mentioned at all, there is interesting information about some of the other writers listed here, such as Walter Bagehot, as well as about the development of sociology.]

Trilling, Lionel, *Matthew Arnold* (1st edn., 1939; rev. edn., New York: Meridian Books, 1955). [A balanced, thorough, and sympathetic view of Arnold; cf. with the essays by Strachey (1914) and Sidgwick (1867) listed above. Fairly typically, although Strachey is mentioned, Sidgwick is ignored. For another view of Arnold, very favorable, see C. E. Montague's essay 'Matthew Arnold', in Montague's *A Writer's Notes on his Trade* (1930; Penguin Books, 1949), 116–26.]

von Hartmann, Eduard: see Hartmann, *sup.*

Wallace, Alfred Russel (1823–1913), 'coformulater with Charles Darwin of the theory of natural selection', though he is nowhere near as celebrated. Author of *Contributions to the Theory of Natural Selection* (New York, 1871). There is a very informative article about Alfred Russel Wallace, by T. A. Goudge, in *The Encyclopedia of Philosophy*, viii: 276–7 (from which the above quotation is taken).

Ward, James (1843–1925) had been a pupil and later was a colleague and friend of Sidgwick's, and edited two of Sidgwick's posthumous works—*Philosophy* and *LPK*. Ward was one of the founders of scientific psychology in Britain. Author of *Naturalism and Agnosticism* (Cambridge: Cambridge University Press, 1899); *The Realm of Ends, or*

Pluralism and Theism (Cambridge: Cambridge University Press, 1911), and *Psychological Principles* (Cambridge: Cambridge University Press, 1918). See *Biographical Dictionary of Twentieth Century Philosophers* (London: Routledge, 1996), 821–2, and the interesting article on Ward by C. A. Mace in *The Encyclopedia of Philosophy*, viii: 277–8.

'What are the Social Sciences?' *Encyclopedia of the Social Sciences*, i: 3–7, by Edwin R. A. Seligman. [Brings together under the social sciences, as they were understood in 1930— the various disciplines, such as economics (political economy), sociology, psychology, political science (political theory)—which in Sidgwick's time were part of philosophy, and just beginning to break away as separate disciplines.]

Whately, Richard (1787–1863), *Introductory Lessons on Morals* (Cambridge, Mass.: John Bartlett, 1857). [Whately was a moral sense theorist, one of uncommonly good sense.]

—— *Paley's Moral Philosophy, with Annotations* (London: John W. Parker & Son, 1859). [The annotations are superb. Although Sidgwick discussed Paley in the *History* (238–9), for some unfathomable reason he never mentions Whately. And I am both shocked and surprised to discover that there is no article on Whately in the *Encyclopedia of Ethics*. There is one in *The New Palgrave*, iv: 899, by R. D. Collinson Black, but its main focus is Whately's work on political economy: *Introductory Lectures on Political Economy* (London: John W. Parker and Son, 1831; 4th edn., enlarged, 1855). Sidgwick refers to Whately just once in *PPE*. (Whately was a mentor and supporter of Cairnes, cited *sup*.) There is an article on Whately in *The Encyclopedia of Philosophy*, viii: 287–8, by Mary Prior, but it is devoted solely to discussing Whately's *Elements of Logic* (London, 1826) and his *Elements of Rhetoric* (London, 1828), says nothing about his work in ethics. So I am outnumbered, but that does not prove wrong my contention that Whately was a significant and intelligent moral philosopher, if only for his sagacious comments on Paley. Cf. Bain, *The Moral Philosophy of Paley, with Additional Dissertations and Discussions*; also Whewell, *On the Foundations of Morals*.]

Whewell, William (1794–1866), *On the Foundations of Morals, Four Sermons Preached before The University of Cambridge, November 1837* (Cambridge: Cambridge University Press, and London: John W. Parker, n.d., prob. 1837): 'In the following Discourses, disapprobation is expressed of a work now in use in the Examinations of the University of Cambridge,—Paley's Moral Philosophy. . . . [T]he evils which arise from the countenance thus afforded to the principles of Paley's system are so great, as to make it desirable to withdraw our sanction from his doctrines without further delay . . .' (p. v). There is a very brief—too brief—essay about Whewell by Alan Donagan in *Encyclopedia of Ethics*, ii: 1314–15, and another very brief article, by L. Jonathan Cohen, in *The Oxford Companion to Philosophy*, 909. However, see the essays by Donagan and Schneewind listed *sup*.; also the article in *The New Palgrave*, iv: 900–1, by G. Campanelli, and the article by Robert Blanché in *The Encyclopedia of Philosophy*, viii: 288–9.

—— *Elements of Morality, Including Polity*, 2 vols. (London, 1845; 2nd edn., 1848; 3rd edn., 1854). [Discussed overtly, but only briefly, by Sidgwick in the *History*, 233–4; in *The Methods* Sidgwick refers to Whewell in only the most cursory way (*e.g.* p. 58), even though it is evident that in large portions of his discussion of intuitionism it is Whewell's view that he has in mind and is reacting to. See J. S. Mill's essay on Whewell, listed *sup*. in Schneewind's *Mill's Ethical Writings*, and in Mill's *Dissertations and Discussions*, iii.]

—— *Lectures on Systematic Morality* (London: John W. Parker, 1846). [Actually necessary for understanding the *Elements of Morality*; as Whewell says in his preface, 'they contain a kind of commentary on some parts of the two volumes on *The Elements of Morality* . . .']

—— *Lectures on the History of Moral Philosophy* (Cambridge: Deighton, Bell and Co., 1852; 2nd edn., enlarged, 1862). See pp. vi–x of the preface to the 2nd edn. for a retort to Mr Pattison (cited *sup.*). The following sentence conveys some of the flavor of Whewell's writing: 'If Mr Pattison had done me the honour to attend to the Lectures which he has quoted, he would hardly have expected that this argument would appear to me of any force.'

—— *Six Lectures on Political Economy* (Cambridge: Cambridge University Press, 1862).

Whittaker, Edmund, *A History of Economic Ideas* (New York and London: Longmans, Green and Co., 1940). [Discusses Sidgwick's ideas on pp. 162–3, 226–7, 312, 348–50, 397, 559. In particular, pp. 349–50 discuss Sidgwick's utilitarian theory of population as stated in *The Methods* (and in Ch. 1 this vol.).]

Wollaston, William (1660–1724), *The Religion of Nature Delineated* (1722). Discussed, very briefly, by Sidgwick in the *History*, 198. See the articles by Ernest Campbell Mossner in *The Encyclopedia of Philosophy*, viii: 344–5, by Charlotte Brown in *Encyclopedia of Ethics*, ii: 1327–8, and by Elizabeth Radcliffe in *The Cambridge Dictionary of Philosophy*, 981.

Index

References to Sidgwick are occasionally abbreviated by 'S', *The Methods of Ethics* by 'ME'; 'Mill', when used without initials, always refers to J. S.